COMMON CORE BRIEF REVIEW 2015

Geometry

William Caroscio / Irene "Sam" Jovell

PEARSON

Order Information
Send orders to:
PEARSON CUSTOMER SERVICE
P.O. BOX 2500 LEBANON, IN 46052-3009
or CALL TOLL FREE 1-800-848-9500
(8:00 A.M.–6:00 P.M. EST)
• Orders can be placed via phone
Order online at k12oasis.pearson.com

Authors

William Caroscio taught mathematics for 33 years. This experience included junior high school, high school, undergraduate, and graduate college teaching experience. After retirement from the classroom Bill has worked for 10 years as a mathematics consultant providing training focused on integrating the use of technology in mathematics instruction. Bill is Past President of the Association of Mathematics Teachers of New York State and Past President of New York State Association of Mathematics Supervisors. He is a national contract instructor for the T3 (Teachers Teaching with Technology) program. Bill conducts sessions and workshops at the local, state, and national levels. During his career he has served as an item writer for the New York State Education Department assessment committees, as a member of the Commissioner's Committee on the New Mathematics Standards, and the Geometry Committee writing sample tasks for the new state standards. Bill is a member of NCTM, AMTNYS, NYSAMS, MAA, and NYSMATYC. He was inducted into the NYS Mathematics Educators Hall of Fame in 2014.

Irene "Sam" Jovell is presently a Senior Mathematics Specialist for the Questar III BOCES in Albany NY. She provides professional development for teachers and administrators, K–12, with emphasis on mathematical literacy, curriculum design, assessment development, and effective teaching practices. She previously taught at Niskayuna High School, Union University, and has served the New York State Education Department by participating on new standards and assessment development committees. Sam is a past president of both the Association of Math Teacher of NYS and the New York State Mathematics Supervisors. She has been a speaker at the local, state, and national levels and has authored texts on Algebra and Pre-Calculus. Sam was inducted into the NYS Mathematics Educators Hall of Fame in 2012.

Reviewers

Ronald Armontrout

Mathematics & Technology Teacher 9-12
The Hotchkiss School–Retired
Oxford, Maine

Michael Green

Mathematics Editor, Writer, and Reviewer
Chicago, Illinois

ISBN-13:   978-0-13-331780-0
ISBN-10:   0-13-331780-3

TABLE OF CONTENTS

Chapter 1 — Basic Geometry in the Plane

			Common Core State Standards	MP
1.1	Points, Lines, Planes, and Segments	2	G.CO.1	MP4
1.2	Rays and Angles	7	G.CO.1	
1.3	Intersecting, Perpendicular, and Parallel Lines	11	G.CO.9	MP7 MP8
1.4	Geometric Constructions	17	G.CO.12 G.CO.13	MP4 MP5
1.5	Constructing Perpendicular and Parallel Lines	22	G.CO.12	MP4

Chapter 2 — Triangles and their Properties

			Common Core State Standards	MP
2.1	Classifying Triangles and Angles of a Triangle	32	C.CO.10	MP1 MP2 MP3 MP4 MP5
2.2	Inequalities in Triangles	39	G.CO.9 G.CO.10	MP2 MP4 MP7 MP8
2.3	Special Segments, Lines, and Points.	42	C.CO.10	MP2 MP3 MP4

Chapter 3   Proof and Triangle Congruence

Chapter 4 Transformations and Congruence

Chapter 5 Transformation and Similarity

Chapter 9 Solid Geometry and Its Applications

Chapter 10 Probability

	Common Core State Standards	MP

This book has been written for you, a high school student enrolled in a Common Core Geometry mathematics course. You can use it as a tool for understanding the process and the content of the Common Core Geometry Curriculum.

The Common Core standards identify the mathematical knowledge, skills, and behaviors that students should acquire during high school, so when they graduate they will be mathematically ready to enter college or a career. The knowledge and skills for each course are defined in the **Standards for Mathematical Content,** while the **Standards for Mathematical Practice** describe the processes and behaviors that lead a student toward well-developed problem-solving skills and mathematical proficiency.

The **Standards for Mathematical Practice** can be found in their entirety at:

http://www.corestandards.org/Math/Practice

An overview of each of the eight Mathematical Practices is below.

1. Make sense of problems and persevere in solving them.
2. Reason abstractly and quantitatively.
3. Construct viable arguments and critique the reasoning of others.
4. Model with mathematics.
5. Use appropriate tools strategically.
6. Attend to precision.
7. Look for and make use of structure.
8. Look for and express regularity in repeated reasoning.

Throughout the Brief Review, look for the (MP) symbol to show that you should apply the indicated Practice(s) to the problem situation.

The **Standards for Mathematical Content** for Geometry are presented in the Brief Review first as a "snap-shot" at the start of each chapter's section, but again in the back of the book. There the content standard is stated completely and tracked to its chapter and section location in the Brief Review.

Structure of the Brief Review

Included in the front of the book are brief diagnostic tests for each chapter. These tests will allow you to measure your level of understanding of the content and concentrate on the specific concepts according to your needs.

Each lesson in this book
- addresses specific content standards of the Geometry Curriculum.
- includes definitions, formulas, and examples with complete explanations.
- provides practice exercises at the end of every lesson to check for understanding.

At the end of each chapter, review exercises entitled *Preparing for the Assessment* address the entire content of the chapter and include both short and extended response questions.

INTRODUCTION

Calculator Solutions

Graphing calculator solutions are offered throughout the text as an alternative problem-solving method.

Glossary

A complete glossary of terms is included in the back of this book. It offers a complete definition of the term, with examples as appropriate.

Problem Solving Strategies

The Brief Review models lots of problems that might appear on an Geometry assessment. These problems are either short-response questions, usually graded at 1 or 2 points with no partial credit, or an extended response question, graded with a rubric, which would assign points based on the quality of the work shown.

Based on the **Standards of Mathematical Practice,** here are problem-solving strategies that should be used throughout the Brief Review.

Problem Solving Strategies

Strategies for Short-Response Questions

- Carefully read each question before answering to be sure that you know what is being asked. MP 1

- Think about the concept of the problem and what you have been taught. MP 7

- Immediately cross out choices that you know cannot be correct. MP 2

- Work backwards from the choices. MP 2

- Use guess-and-check or trial-and-error. MP 5

- Try to estimate the answer when appropriate. This may help you eliminate some choices. MP 2

- Draw a diagram, table, or picture, or write an equation. MP 4

- Look for patterns. MP 8

- Use your calculator for square roots, decimals, percents, and fractions. MP 5

- Before choosing a final answer make sure it is labeled with correct units. MP 6

- Before choosing a final answer, check to see that it is reasonable. MP 2

- Check each choice against the wording of the question, just as you would check the solution in the problem. MP 1

- Don't give up, THINK! MP 1

While many short-response questions are multiple choice with one correct choice, other common short-response questions may be fill-in-the-blank or multiple choice with many correct choices. In the three short-response questions that follow, examine how the problem solving strategies have been used.

PROBLEM SOLVING STRATEGIES

Short Response Questions

A forest ranger spots a fire from a 21-foot tower. The angle of depression from the tower to the fire is 30°.

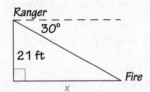

Find, *to the nearest foot*, the distance, *x*, of the fire from the foot of the tower.

(1) $7\sqrt{3}$ ft   **(2)** $21\sqrt{3}$ ft   **(3)** 36 ft   **(4)** 42 ft

Strategies: Study the diagram and look for patterns.
Use your calculator and attend to precision.

You know by studying the diagram that the triangle is a 30°-60°-90° right triangle. The choices **(1)** and **(2)** can be eliminated as they are exact values.

Now you complete the work.

The correct choice is _____.

Given: $\overleftrightarrow{AB}$ is the perpendicular bisector of $\overline{IK}$.

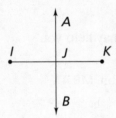

Which statement(s) are true from the given information?

(1) *J* is the midpoint of $\overleftrightarrow{AB}$.
(2) $IJ = JK$
(3) $\angle AJK$ is a right angle.
(4) $\angle AIJ$ is a right angle.

Strategies: Draw a labeled diagram; use known definitions;
eliminate choices; check all choices.

Since a perpendicular bisector is a line, segment, or ray that intersects a segment at it midpoint and forms right angles, then choice **(3)** is a correct, **but there is another correct choice as well.**

Now you finish the analysis.

The correct choices are _____ and _____.

Given: $\triangle ABC$ with $A(3, 6)$, $B(5, 6)$, $C(6, 4)$ and
$\triangle XYZ$ with $X(1, 2)$, $Y(7, 2)$, $Z(10, -4)$.

Use the choices labeled $A - H$ to complete the statement about $\triangle ABC$ and $\triangle XYZ$.

A. $(0, 0)$	**B.** $(1, 2)$	**C.** $(4, 8)$	**D.** $(6, 4)$
E. 2	**F.** 3	**G.** $\dfrac{1}{2}$	**H.** $\dfrac{1}{3}$

The triangles are similar because $\triangle ABC$ is the image of $\triangle XYZ$ under a dilation with center at _____ and scale factor of _____.

Strategies: Draw a labeled diagram; use construction tools; look for patterns.

Since you noticed that the y-coordinates of points A and B are equal, then $\overline{AB}$ is horizontal with length of 2, similarly $\overline{XY}$ is horizontal and $XY = 6$. $\overline{AB}$ and $\overline{XY}$ are corresponding sides so the scale factor is $\frac{1}{3}$ or choice H.

Now you sketch the triangles to determine the center of dilation.

The center is at _____ and the scale factor is _____.

PROBLEM SOLVING STRATEGIES

Strategies for Extended-Response Questions

You will find many of the same strategies used for short-response questions, but these extended-response strategies also stress good communication skills, as your work will be graded by others who have to understand what you have written.

- Carefully read each question before answering to be sure that you know what is being asked. MP 1

- Think about the concept of the problem and what you have been taught. MP 7

- Represent your variables at the start of each solution, so relationships are clearly understood. MP 4

- Draw a diagram, table, or picture, or write an equation. MP 4

- When asked to justify, make sure your evidence is both verbal and numerical, and clearly supports your conclusions. MP 4

- You need to show work. No work…No credit! MP 1

- If a solution includes measurements, label your answer with the proper unit of measure, such as inches, centimeters, hours, or miles per hour. MP 6

- If you are using a calculator, estimate your answers to make sure your calculator answer is reasonable. Be sure to explain your work in detail, including those steps you performed on the calculator. MP 2

- If a question has multiple parts, do all parts. Even if you can not do the first part, you can still get partial credit for any appropriate work shown in the other parts. MP 1

- Use guess-and-check or trial-and-error. Show trials both right and wrong. MP 5

- Use your calculator for square roots, decimals, percents, and fractions. MP 5

- Don't give up, THINK! MP 1

Extended-response questions are graded with a rubric. The rubric awards credit based on the correctness of the work shown. For the practice problems that follow, you will award credit to two students' solutions using the accompanying rubric.

Model Rubric

Credit	The Work Shown ...
No	is blank; is totally incorrect; lacks understanding of the problem's concept.
Little	is incomplete; has multiple calculation errors; indicates some understanding of the problem's concept.
Most	is conceptually complete but not correct; contains calculation errors; lacks unit or labels; has a weak justification.
Full	is conceptually complete and correct; includes representing variables; has all required labels; has viable justifications.

Put the rubic to work to show model solutions at each credit level.

A circle is represented by the equation: $x^2 + y^2 + 10x - 8y + 5 = 0$.
Show your work to find the center and radius of this circle.

Credit	Work shown to solve the Circle Problem...	Why the Credit?
No	Center is $(10, -8)$ and radius $= 5$	No understanding of concept.
Little	Center is $(5, -4)$ and radius $= 5$	Some understanding of concept
Most	Center is $(5, -4)$ and radius $= 6$	Conceptually correct, but not correct
Full	Center is $(-5, 4)$ and radius $= 6$	Complete and correct

The next four problems show two student solutions, but no scores are given.
At the end of each problem, you will be asked to score each student's solution
using the Model Rubric.

PROBLEM SOLVING STRATEGIES

Extended Response Questions

Circle P has radius of 2 units. The table below shows the arc length of four sectors of circle P. Complete the table to show degree measure of each sector's central angle.

Central Angle°	Sector's Arc length
	$\frac{3\pi}{2}$
	π
	$\frac{2\pi}{3}$
	2π

Imagine that you are to score two student's work. Study the scoring rubric, award appropriate credits, and give reasons for the score you gave.

Student 1's solution

Central Angle°	Sector's Arc length
270°	$\frac{3\pi}{2}$
180°	π
120°	$\frac{2\pi}{3}$
360°	2π

My score for student 1 _____
My reason(s) _____
_____

Student 2's solution

Central Angle°	Sector's Arc length
135°	$\frac{3\pi}{2}$
90°	π
60°	$\frac{2\pi}{3}$
180°	2π

My score for student 2 _____
My reason(s) _____
_____

Try this problem next with more student work for you to score.

Extended Response Questions

● $\overline{TQ}$ is defined by $T(6, 5)$ and $Q(-3, -7)$. Find the coordinates of two points on $\overline{TQ}$ that divide $\overline{TQ}$ into three equal segments. Show work or a model.

Student 1's solution

$$x_1 = 6 + \tfrac{1}{3}(-9) = 3$$
$$y_1 = 5 + \tfrac{1}{3}(-12) = 1 \therefore (3, 1)$$
and
$$x_2 = -3 + \tfrac{1}{3}(9) = 0$$
$$y_2 = -7 + \tfrac{1}{3}(12) = -3 \therefore (0, -3)$$

My score for student 1 _____
My reason(s) _____
_____

Student 2's solution

$$d = \sqrt{(x_2 - x_1)^2 + (y_2 - y_1)^2}$$
$$TQ = 81\sqrt{2}$$

$$\tfrac{1}{3} \cdot TQ = 27\sqrt{2}$$

My score for student 2 _____
My reason(s) _____
_____

● Verify that quadrilateral $ABCD$ with vertices $A(-5, -1)$, $B(-9, 6)$, $C(-1, 5)$, and $D(3, -2)$ is a rhombus.

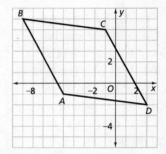

Student 1's solution

slopes:
$$\overline{AB} = -\tfrac{7}{4} \quad \overline{CD} = -\tfrac{7}{4}$$
$$\overline{BC} = -\tfrac{1}{8} \quad \overline{AD} = -\tfrac{1}{8}$$
$$\overline{AC} = \tfrac{3}{2} \quad \overline{BD} = -\tfrac{2}{3}$$
$$\therefore \text{rhombus}$$

My score for student 1 _____
My reason(s) _____
_____

Student 2's solution

slopes:
$$\overline{AB} = -\tfrac{7}{4} \quad \overline{CD} = -\tfrac{7}{4} \therefore \overline{AB} \parallel \overline{CD}$$
$$\overline{BC} = -\tfrac{1}{8} \quad \overline{AD} = -\tfrac{1}{8} \therefore \overline{BC} \parallel \overline{AD}$$
$$\therefore ABCD \text{ is parallelogram}$$
$$\overline{AC} = \tfrac{3}{2} \quad \overline{BD} = -\tfrac{2}{3} \therefore \overline{AC} \perp \overline{BD}$$
$$\therefore ABCD \text{ is parallelogram with}$$
$$\text{perpendicular diagonals}$$
$$\therefore \text{rhombus}$$

My score for student 2 _____
My reason(s) _____
_____

PROBLEM SOLVING STRATEGIES

Try this proof with student work for you to score.

Write a proof given the information below.

Given: $\overline{BC} \cong \overline{DA}$; $\overline{CF} \cong \overline{AF}$; $\angle 1 \cong \angle 2$

Prove: $\triangle CEF \cong \triangle AEF$

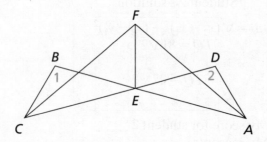

Student 1's solution

$\triangle CEF \cong \triangle AEF$ by AAS using $\overline{CF} \cong \overline{AF}$ from the Givens; $\angle CEF \cong \angle AEF$ since if 2 sides of a triangle are congruent, then angles opposite are congruent; $\angle BEC \cong \angle DEA$ are vertical angles

Student 2's solution

Statements	Reasons
1. $\overline{BC} \cong \overline{DA}$	1. Given
2. $\angle 1 \cong \angle 2$	2. Given
3. $\angle BEC \cong \angle DEA$	3. Vertical angles are congruent.
4. $\triangle BEC \cong \triangle DEA$	4. AAS $\rightarrow \triangle \cong$
5. $\overline{CE} \cong \overline{AE}$	5. $\triangle \cong \rightarrow$ CPCTC
6. $\overline{CF} \cong \overline{AF}$	6. Given
7. $\overline{EF} \cong \overline{EF}$	7. Reflexive Property
8. $\triangle CEF \cong \triangle AEF$	8. SSS $\rightarrow \triangle \cong$

My score for student 1 _____   My score for student 2 _____
My reason(s) _____   My reason(s) _____
_____   _____

081

Technology Tools and Their Potential

The CCSS - Standards for Practice call for using appropriate tools strategically. Specifically mentioned among the list of tools is dynamic geometry software. The graphing calculator and other interactive software programs are great tools for solving problems and for investigating and learning mathematics. This section gives you a concise overview of some of the ways technology can be used to solve problems and investigate mathematical concepts.

Because of the great variety in available technology—graphing calculators, computer programs, Web resources—the discussion and sample activities that follow do not show specific commands. If you need help, consult your user's manual, in which the steps are shown in detail. What is important is that you get to know what interactive geometry software can do to help you explore geometry more easily.

Geometry Enhanced with Technology

Geometry is unlike any other course you have studied in high school. It offers you the opportunity to experience what it is like to work as a mathematician. The use of technology helps make the most of this opportunity. Mathematicians combine their observations with theories and guesses before attempting to carry out a proof. As the mathematician George Polya states in <u>Mathematics and Plausible Reasoning</u>, "Yet mathematics in the making resembles any other human knowledge in the making. You have to guess a mathematical theorem before you prove it; you have to guess the idea of the proof before you carry through the details. You have to combine observations and follow analogies; **you have to try and try again.**"

Using effective geometry tools greatly strengthens the experience of studying geometry. Exciting new possibilities exist for exploring geometric concepts. Graphing calculators or computer software are great tools for learning and solving problems. The use of interactive computer software helps you follow a set of procedures while at the same time discover theorems by investigating geometric constructions.

For example, you can construct a triangle using a graphing calculator or interactive geometry software. You can then measure each angle and determine their sum. Then the triangle can be changed by dragging one of the vertices. You can make a conjecture about the sum of the angles. You can then try and prove your conjecture. When you make a discovery like this yourself, you "own" the theorem more than if a teacher simply presented you with it.

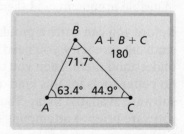

USING TECHNOLOGY TOOLS

Visual Effect

In geometry, figures are often worth a thousand words. Drawings are essential for descriptions and proofs. An interactive geometry environment allows you to conduct your own investigations and leads you to ask questions about geometric relationships. Your answers to these questions may lead you to important conjectures, properties, and theorems.

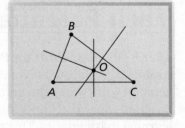

For example, consider the concurrency of the perpendicular bisectors of the sides of a triangle. When constructed within an interactive geometry environment, you can see the common point of intersection. You can manipulate the figure to verify that the concurrency is invariant. As you manipulate the figure, you may ask yourself, "When is the point of concurrency inside, outside, or on the triangle?" You can use interactive geometry software to come up with possible answers to this question.

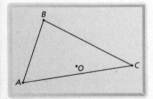 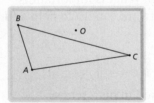 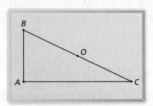

This process of drawing, manipulating, and asking can help you discover important relationships.

By using inductive reasoning you can decide whether an observed pattern is worth proving. **Inductive reasoning** is drawing a logical conclusion based on a set of specific observations. In other words, you can use interactive geometry software to generate a set of examples. If the same properties seem to be true for each of the examples, you can then decide if you want to write a formal proof.

Formal Proof

A formal proof is a cornerstone of the study of geometry. The role of proof in geometry should not merely be to verify the truth of theorems. Rather, proofs are a vehicle to gaining a better understanding of the material. Investigations add excitement and insight into the learning experiences. The geometry course should reflect a flow of observation, conjecture, validation, plausible argument, and then formal proof.

Before you can write a proof, however, you must first guess and verify. When studying geometry, you need to first discover and examine relationships to understand them. Then you can formulate a plan to write the proof. There are no better tools for this kind of conjecturing and guessing than the geometry software available today. You are encouraged to use interactive geometry software prior to attempting the proof of a theorem. Investigating the situation completely can provide the necessary insights required to complete a successful proof. Further, there are several formats you can use to write a formal proof. Using interactive geometry software can help you decide which format you should use to write your proof.

Proof Enhanced by Technology

Proving the concurrency of the altitudes of a triangle can be accomplished by different approaches. One approach could be the use of coordinate geometry. However, much is lost in all the symbol manipulation. One of the most understandable approaches for many students is through the use of construction with interactive geometry tools.

Consider $\triangle ABC$ and its altitudes.

Prove the altitudes are concurrent.

Draw a line that is parallel to side $\overline{AC}$ of the triangle and passes through the vertex opposite $\overline{AC}$. Repeat this construction for the remaining two sides of the triangle. These lines intersect at the points R, S, and T. $\overline{TB} \parallel \overline{AC}$ and $\overline{TA} \parallel \overline{BC}$. The quadrilateral $TBCA$ is a parallelogram. Similarly, the quadrilateral $ABRC$ is a parallelogram. Because opposite sides of a parallelogram are congruent, $TB = AC$ and $BR = AC$. By substitution, $TB = BR$.

By the definition of midpoint, B is the midpoint of $\overline{TR}$. $\overline{BD} \perp \overline{TR}$ because a line perpendicular to one parallel line is perpendicular to the other. So $\overline{BD}$ is the perpendicular bisector of $\overline{TR}$. Likewise, $\overline{FC}$ is the perpendicular bisector of $\overline{RS}$, and $\overline{AE}$ is the perpendicular bisector of $\overline{TS}$. Therefore, the **altitudes of $\triangle ABC$ are the perpendicular bisectors of the sides of $\triangle TRS$**, which we know are concurrent.

The more students use interactive geometry software tools for investigating mathematics the more likely they are to use methods as described above in their investigation of new and different situations.

Caution Required

When using figures as part of a proof, you must make sure that the figures are accurate. For example, suppose you were asked to prove that all triangles are isosceles.

Let ABC be a triangle with l the angle bisector of $\angle A$, m the perpendicular bisector of $\overline{BC}$ cutting $\overline{BC}$ at midpoint E, and D the intersection of l and m. Draw perpendicular line segments from D to $\overline{AB}$ and $\overline{AC}$, cutting them at F and G, respectively. Finally, draw $\overline{DB}$ and $\overline{DC}$.

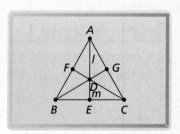

Now, consider the following argument:

Statements	Reasons
1. $\triangle ADF \cong \triangle ADG$	1. AAS
2. $\overline{AF} \cong \overline{AG}, \overline{DF} \cong \overline{DG}$	2. CPCTC
3. $\triangle BDE \cong \triangle CDE$	3. SAS
4. $\overline{BD} \cong \overline{CD}$	4. CPCTC
5. $\triangle BDF \cong \triangle CDG$	5. HL
6. $\overline{FB} \cong \overline{GC}$	6. CPCTC
7. $AB = AF + FB = AG + GC = AC$	7. Definition of midpoint and substitution
8. $\triangle ABC$ is isosceles.	8. Definition of isosceles triangle

What could be wrong? Are all triangles really isosceles? There is nothing wrong with the sequence of steps and the reasoning in this proof. The conclusion follows logically from what was given and the figure that was drawn.

This type of erroneous proof illustrates how poorly drawn and inaccurate figures can lead you to a false argument. This example offers a persuasive argument for the need to use accurately constructed diagrams, especially when they are part of a proof. This example shows how easily a logical argument can be swayed by what the eye sees in a figure, emphasizing the importance of drawing a figure correctly and accurately. The relation of points is often critical to the proof.

The following sample activities illustrate how to use interactive geometry software to help you make conjectures.

Sample Activity 1

1. Construct a triangle with an angle bisector and the perpendicular bisector of the opposite side. Use the space below to outline your steps.

2. What do you notice as you manipulate the drawing? You should notice that the angle bisector and the perpendicular bisector intersect. However, it appears that this point of intersection is not interior to the triangle. The error in the original sketch is readily observed. This construction is a great example of what Walter Whiteley, as quoted in King of Infinite Space, meant when he said, "The mathematician no longer spends any time going down the wrong track because the computer makes it obvious when reasoning in the diagram is wrong."

Sample Activity 2

1. Construct a triangle containing the circumcenter, *O*; incenter, *I*; centroid, *G*; and orthocenter, *H*, as shown in the accompanying figure. Use the space below to outline your steps.

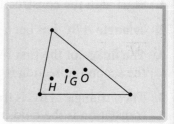

2. Consider the following questions and write your conjectures:

   a. When will all the centers be inside the triangle?

   b. Which ones leave the triangle and when?

   c. Are any of these centers ever on the triangle? When?

   d. Measure the distances between the centers and determine any relationships that exist between the measures.

Sample Activity 3

1. Start with a construction of a parallelogram as shown in the accompanying figure.

2. List five properties of the parallelogram.

3. Measure quantities in the figure and make conjectures about the relationships you observe. Use the space below to make your conjectures.

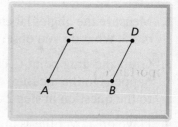

4. The accompanying figures show possible stages of exploration.

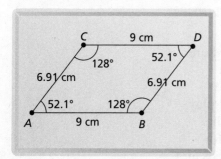

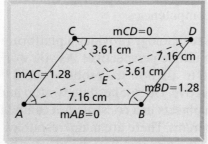

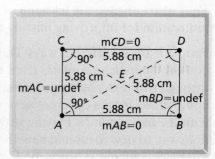

USING TECHNOLOGY TOOLS

Sample Activity 4

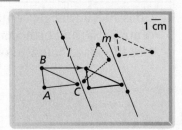

1 cm

1. Start with the construction as shown in the accompanying diagram.

2. Triangle *ABC* has been reflected over line *l* and then over line *m*.

3. The image of the first reflection is the dotted triangle and the image of the second reflection is the dashed triangle.

4. Then triangle *ABC* is translated by the vector shown. The image of the translation is the bold triangle.

5. Grab the endpoint of the vector and determine the translation vector such that the image under the translation is the same as the image under the double reflection.

6. Describe your results in complete sentences. Use the space below to describe your observations.

Sample Activity 5

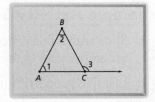

1. Start with the construction of the triangle shown in the diagram to the right.

2. Measure the angles labeled 1, 2, and 3, and compare $m\angle 1 + m\angle 2$ with $m\angle 3$. What do you observe?

3. Grab and drag point *C*, changing the shape of the triangle. What happens to the measure of each of the angles? How does your answer to the question in step 2 change?

4. Develop a hypothesis that explains your observations and write a proof that proves or disproves your hypothesis.

Use the space below to describe your observations.

Let the Fun Begin

Current technology tools can enable mathematical investigation and trialing. They also enhance the learning of algebraic concepts. This can often provide motivation for improving missing competencies.

People learn in different ways. This technology provides a platform where you can approach problems from multiple perspectives. As you work through this text, challenge yourself to ask how the problem could be approached from a different perspective. Do not hesitate to stop and play with the mathematics. Playing with objects in a construction can be the doorway to new ideas and new theorems. There are many resources for interactive geometry software. Find the tool that best meets your needs and have fun!

A major, yet often unspoken, goal of mathematics instruction is to help students become problem solvers. We want students to be able to solve not only the problems posed in class and on the test but also the problems they run into in everyday life. Throughout the problem solving episode, the problem solver may continually change his or her point of view. One may have to shift one's approach again and again, and try and try again. The perception of the problem will be less complete at the outset and may well be different once some progress has been made. It might again be different when the solution is near at hand.

Providing students with a guide to approach the problem solving experience will assist them in becoming improved problem solvers. Having a guide to follow will help students avoid the situation that is often verbalized with "I don't know what to do."

One of the best heuristics was developed and presented many years ago, in 1945, by the mathematician George Pólya. His method has four steps.

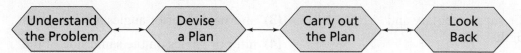

The impact of Pólya's method can be seen in many heuristics presented since that time. Below is the model included in the NYS P-12 Common Core Learning Standards for Mathematics document.

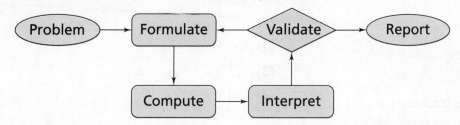

What is important here is that students are empowered to develop a problem solving method that they can successfully implement when presented with a novel problem solving situation.

Diagnostic Test: Geometry

Name _____ Date _____

Diagnostic Test 1: Chapter 1

Basic Geometry in the Plane

Choose the numeral preceding the word or expression that best completes the statement or answers the question.

1 Which best describes skew lines?

(1) Lines that never meet.

(2) Lines that do not lie in the same plane.

(3) Lines that are coplanar.

(4) Lines that are parallel.

2 If two angles are supplementary and congruent, then they are

(1) acute angles.

(2) obtuse angles.

(3) right angles.

(4) complementary.

3 If two lines cut by a transversal are parallel, what is true of the corresponding angles?

(1) The angles are supplementary.

(2) The angles are complementary.

(3) The angles are right angles.

(4) The angles are congruent.

4 If two planes intersect, the intersection is a

(1) point.

(2) line.

(3) plane.

(4) triangle.

5 What are 3 sets of minimum conditions that determine a unique plane?

(1) 3 non-collinear points

(2) any 3 points

(3) a line and a point not on the line

(4) two intersecting lines

6 Two lines are intersected by a transversal. Which statement must be true for the lines to be parallel?

(1) vertical angles are congruent

(2) alternate interior angles are supplementary

(3) alternate exterior angles are congruent

(4) interior angles on the same side of the transversal are complementary

7 Find the measure of an angle that is 21° more than twice the measure of its supplement.

(1) 67°

(2) 100.5°

(3) 127°

(4) 190.5°

Questions 8–10 will be graded using the model rubric from Problem Solving Strategies. Points for your solution are based on the amount of credit awarded your work:

NO = 0; LITTLE = 1; MOST = 2; FULL = 3

8 If two lines, m and n are both perpendicular to line z, then it is possible for m and n to be either parallel, skew or intersecting. Explain how each case is possible.

9 B is the midpoint of $\overline{AD}$ and C is a point between B and D. If $AD = 8$ and CD is 2 units greater than BC, find AC.

10 $\overleftrightarrow{AB}$ intersects $\overleftrightarrow{CD}$ at T. Find the $m\angle BTD$ if $m\angle CTA = 25x - 14$ and $m\angle ATD = 5x + 44$.

Name _____   Date _____

Diagnostic Test 2: Chapter 2

Triangles and their Properties

Choose the numeral preceding the word or expression that best completes the statement or answers the question.

1 The measure of two angles of a triangle are 50° and 20°. This triangle must be

  (1) right.

  (2) isosceles.

  (3) acute.

  (4) obtuse.

2 What is the measure of $\angle A$ in the accompanying figure?

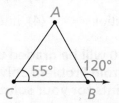

  (1) 55°   **(3)** 65°

  (2) 60°   **(4)** 120°

3 A triangle with two complementary angles is classified as which kind of triangle?

  (1) obtuse   **(3)** complementary

  (2) acute   **(4)** right

4 Which is a possible length for the third side of a triangle whose other two sides are 10 and 18?

  (1) 8   **(3)** 12

  (2) 28   **(4)** 35

5 What is the $m\angle C$ in isosceles $\triangle ABC$, with $\overline{AC} \cong \overline{BC}$ and $m\angle A = 42°$.

  (1) 48°

  (2) 69°

  (3) 96°

  (4) 159°

6 Which point can be a midpoint of a side of a triangle?

  (1) circumcenter

  (2) orthocenter

  (3) centroid

  (4) incenter

7 In right $\triangle PQR$ with right angle at Q, if $m\angle P = 35°$, then which statement is true?

  (1) $\tan 35° = \dfrac{PQ}{QR}$

  (2) $\tan 55° = \dfrac{PQ}{QR}$

  (3) $\sin 35° = \dfrac{PQ}{PR}$

  (4) $\cos 55° = \dfrac{PQ}{PR}$

Questions 8–10 will be graded using the model rubric from Problem Solving Strategies. Points for your solution are based on the amount of credit awarded your work;

NO = 0; LITTLE = 1; MOST = 2; FULL = 3

8 The shadow of the top of a flagpole is 6 feet from the pole's base. From that point, the angle of elevation of the top of the pole is 75°. How tall is pole to the nearest foot?

9 Find the area of a triangle with sides of 10 cm and 16 cm and an included angle measuring 45°.

10 In right $\triangle ABC$ with right $\angle B$, altitude $\overline{BD}$ is drawn. If $AB = 5$ cm and $BC = 12$ cm, find BD.

Diagnostic Test: Geometry

Name _____ Date _____

Diagnostic Test 3: Chapter 3

Proof and Triangle Congruence

Choose the numeral preceding the word or expression that best completes the statement or answers the question.

1 What is any statement written in "If, Then" form called in geometry?

(1) disjunction   **(3)** bi-conditional

(2) conjunction   **(4)** conditional

2 What is the statement called when two simple statements are joined with the word *and*?

(1) disjunction   **(3)** biconditional

(2) negation   **(4)** conjunction

3 A disjunction is false when which condition holds?

(1) Both disjuncts are true.

(2) Both disjuncts are false.

(3) The first disjunct is true and the second false.

(4) The first disjunct is false and the second true.

4 What must be true before using CPCTC in proving triangle congruent?

(1) Two triangles are similar.

(2) Two triangles are congruent.

(3) SAS must be used in the proof.

(4) AA must be used in the proof.

5 Which of the following is not a postulate or theorem of congruence for triangles?

(1) If $ASA \cong ASA$, then $\triangle s \cong$.

(2) If $SAS \cong SAS$, then $\triangle s \cong$.

(3) If $AAS \cong AAS$, then $\triangle s \cong$.

(4) If $SSA \cong SSA$, then $\triangle s \cong$.

6 $\triangle ABC \cong \triangle PQR$ and $\triangle PQR \cong \triangle LJK$. If $m\angle B = 65°$ and $m\angle R = 45°$, what is the $m\angle L$?

(1) 45°   **(3)** 70°

(2) 65°   **(4)** 110°

7 Given two sets of points, what is the set operation that names the points common to both sets?

(1) addition   **(3)** union

(2) subtraction   **(4)** intersection

Questions 8–10 will be graded using the model rubric from Problem Solving Strategies. Points for your solution are based on the amount of credit awarded your work;

NO = 0; LITTLE = 1; MOST = 2; FULL = 3

8 Median $\overline{BD}$ is drawn in $\triangle ABC$ where $\overline{AB} \cong \overline{BC}$. Justify why and how $\triangle ABD \cong \triangle CBD$.

9 Use the diagram of collinear points A, B, C, and D.

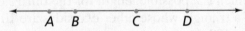

Find $\overrightarrow{AC} \cap (\overrightarrow{BD} \cup \overrightarrow{CA})$

10 Given: $\overline{AR} \perp \overline{BC}$
$\overline{CP} \perp \overline{AB}$
$\angle CAQ \cong \angle ACQ$
    Prove: $\angle PAQ \cong \angle RCQ$

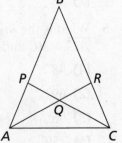

Name _____ Date _____

Diagnostic Test 4: Chapter 4

Transformations and Congruence

For 1–7 choose the numeral preceding the word or expression that best completes the statement or answers the question.

1 The image of the point $P(x, y)$ under a reflection in the x-axis is.

(1) (y, x) **(3)** $(x, -y)$

(2) $(-x, y)$ **(4)** $(-x, -y)$

2 The regular octagon shown in the accompanying diagram is rotated about its center. What is the minimum number of degrees it must be rotated to carry the octagon onto itself?

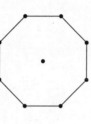

(1) $45°$ **(3)** $90°$

(2) $60°$ **(4)** $180°$

3 Which of the following transformations has/have an opposite orientation with its preimage?

(1) Rotation   **(3)** Translation

(2) Reflection   **(4)** Dilation

4 If a transformation is an isometry then which of the following are true?

(1) Angle measure is preserved.

(2) Parallelism is preserved.

(3) There are no fixed points.

(4) An image is congruent to its pre-image.

5 In the accompanying figure $\triangle AB'C'$ is the image of $\triangle ABC$. Which transformation best describes this result?

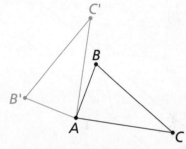

(1) A reflection over $\overleftrightarrow{AB}$

(2) A translation by vector AB'

(3) A rotation about point A of $90°$

(4) A rotation about point A of $180°$

6 Which of the following characters are their own image under a half-turn?

(1) A

(2) H

(3) K

(4) B

7 If the point $D(3, 4)$ is reflected over the line $y = x$ its image will be which of the following?

(1) $(-3, -4)$ **(3)** $(3, 4)$

(2) $(-4, -3)$ **(4)** $(4, 3)$

8 Describe the transformation defined as $R_{A,60°} \circ R_m$.

Diagnostic Test: Geometry

Name _____ Date _____

9 The accompanying figure shows the results of a number of transformations. Which triangle best represents the image of $\triangle ABC$ under the transformation $R_l \circ R_m$ given $l \parallel m$. Explain your answer.

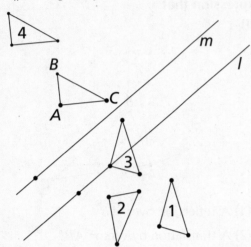

10 Sketch the image of $\triangle JKL$ under a reflection in line h.

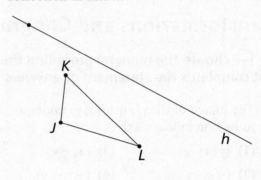

Name _____ Date _____

Diagnostic Test 5: Chapter 5

Transformations and Similarity

For 1–7 choose the numeral preceding the word or expression that best completes the statement or answers the question.

1 In which transformation is side length not necessarily preserved?

(1) Reflection   **(3)** Rotation

(2) Translation   **(4)** Dilation

2 If the scale factor of a dilation is 2, the area of an image triangle will be how many times the area of the pre-image triangle?

(1) $\dfrac{1}{2}$ **(3)** 2

(2) 1   **(4)** 4

3 Which of the following is not true about a dilation?

(1) Is an isometry

(2) Preserves angle measure

(3) Preserves collinearity

(4) Images are parallel to pre-images

4 If the image of point P under a dilation about the origin with a scale factor of 3 is $P'(6, 12)$ what are the coordinates of P?

(1) $(18, 36)$ **(3)** $(3, 4)$

(2) $(12, 24)$ **(4)** $(1, 2)$

5 In the accompanying figure the small triangle is the image of the larger triangle under a dilation about the origin. What is the scale factor of this dilation?

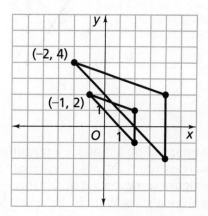

(1) 2   **(3)** 0.5

(2) -2 **(4)** -0.5

6 If you look at an ant through a magnifying glass the image is 8 times as large as the actual ant. If the ant's image is 1.6 cm. what is the actual size of the ant?

(1) 0.2 cm

(2) 0.8 cm

(3) 1.6 cm

(4) 8 cm

7 The image of the point $(4, -3)$ under the composite transformation $D_{0,2} \circ D_{0,4}$ would be

(1) $(16, -12)$ **(3)** $(8, -6)$

(2) $(32, -24)$ **(4)** $(24, -18)$

Diagnostic Test: Geometry

Name _____ Date _____

8 Sketch the image of $\overline{AB}$ under a dilation about P with a scale factor of $-\dfrac{1}{2}$.

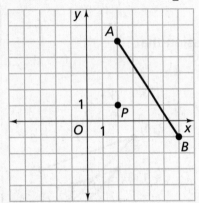

9 The image of an ant under a magnifying glass is six times the object's actual length. The figure shows an ant under this magnifying glass. What is the actual length of the ant?

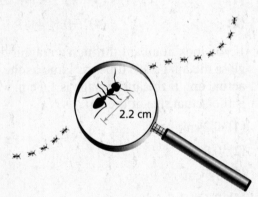

2.2 cm

10 In the accompanying figure $\triangle A'B'C'$ is the image of $\triangle ABC$ under a dilation. Determine the center of the dilation.

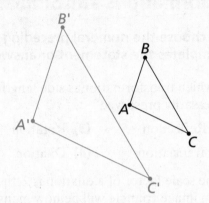

Name _____ Date _____

Diagnostic Test 6: Chapter 6

Quadrilaterals and Other Polygons

For 1–7 choose the numeral preceding the word or expression that best completes the statement or answers the question.

1 Which of the following is/are not a trapezoid?

(1) Parallelogram (3) Rectangle

(2) Kite (4) Square

2 The measure of each interior angle of a regular octagon is

(1) 80° (3) 135°

(2) 90° (4) 180°

3 Opposite angles of a kite are

(1) Congruent (3) Complementary

(2) Supplementary (4) Acute

4 A quadrilateral has perpendicular diagonals. This polygon could be

(1) A rectangle

(2) A parallelogram

(3) A kite

(4) A square

5 The sum of the interior and exterior angles of a polygon are equal. This polygon could be

(1) A square (3) An octagon

(2) A triangle (4) A trapezoid

6 If a polygon is broken up into non-overlapping triangles by drawing diagonals, the number of triangles is always

(1) Equal to the number of sides

(2) One less than the number of sides

(3) Two less than the number of sides

(4) Two more than the number of sides

7 Which of the following is/are not true?

(1) Every square is a rectangle.

(2) Every parallelogram is a trapezoid.

(3) Every rectangle is a parallelogram

(4) Every square is a parallelogram

8 The expandable lift shown in the accompanying figure is known as a pantograph. As the lift expands and contract the region within the braces forms a parallelogram as indicated by $DEFG$ in the figure. When $m\angle D = 35°$ what is the measure of the external angle at G?

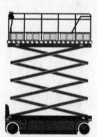

9 For what values of x and y must $ABCD$ be a parallelogram?

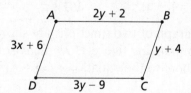

10 The design shown in the figure is part of a tile pattern on the floor. It is made up of a regular pentagon and five isosceles triangles. Determine the $m\angle 1$.

Name _____ Date _____

Diagnostic Test 7: Chapter 7

Coordinate Geometry

For 1–7 choose the numeral preceding the word or expression that best completes the statement or answers the question.

1 Point F divides the directed line segment EG in the ratio of 3:1. What are the coordinates of F when $E(-3, 4)$ and $G(5, -4)$?

(1) $(-2, 3)$ **(3)** $(3, -2)$

(2) $(-1, 2)$ **(4)** $(2, -1)$

2 What is true about the slope of two parallel lines?

(1) The slopes are reciprocals.

(2) The slopes have a product of -1.

(3) The slopes are opposite in sign.

(4) The slopes are equal.

3 The slope of a line is $\frac{2}{5}$. A line perpendicular to this line will have a slope of

(1) $-\frac{2}{5}$ **(3)** $\frac{2}{5}$

(2) $-\frac{5}{2}$ **(4)** -1

4 What is the midpoint of the segment joining the points $A(-3, 6)$ and $B(5, -3)$?

(1) $(1, 1.5)$ **(3)** $(2, 3)$

(2) $(-4, 4.5)$ **(4)** $\left(\frac{2}{2}, \frac{3}{2}\right)$

5 The graph of two functions are shown in the accompanying figure. How many solutions are there to the equation $f_1(x) = f_2(x)$.

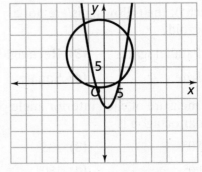

(1) One   **(3)** Three

(2) Two   **(4)** Four

6 Which pair of points has the point $(2, 1)$ as a midpoint?

(1) $(1, 2)$ and $(5, 4)$

(2) $(-1, -2)$ and $(5, 4)$

(3) $(-1, -2)$ and $(-5, -4)$

(4) $(-3, -1)$ and $(5, 5)$

7 When proving the triangle in the figure shown is isosceles, which of the following formulas would be most useful?

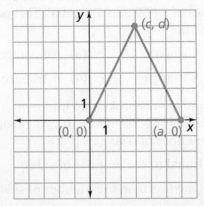

(1) Area   **(3)** Midpoint

(2) Circumference   **(4)** Distance

Name _____ Date _____

8 A figure has vertices at $(m, 0)$, $(-m, 0)$, $(0, m)$, and $(0, -m)$. Prove that this quadrilateral is a square.

9 Write the equation of the circle passing through the point $(8, 6)$ with a center at the origin.

10 Write the equation of the perpendicular bisector of the segment joining the points $(-4, -2)$ and $(6, 3)$.

Diagnostic Test: Geometry

Name _____   Date _____

Diagnostic Test 8: Chapter 8

Circles

Choose the numeral preceding the word or expression that best completes the statement or answers the question. Use the information in the figure to answer questions 1–7.

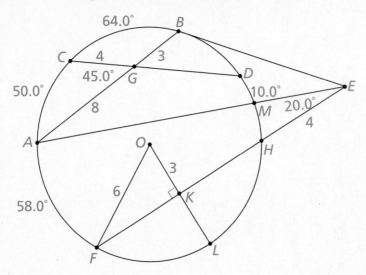

1 Determine the length of $\overline{KL}$.

(1) 6   (3) 3

(2) 8   (4) 12

2 Determine the $m\widehat{BD}$.

(1) 50°   (3) 45°

(2) 40°   (4) 90°

3 $GD = ?$

(1) 6   (3) 8

(2) 12   (4) 24

4 $m\angle FOL = ?$

(1) 20°   (3) 45°

(2) 50°   (4) 60°

5 Determine the length of $\overline{KH}$.

(1) 6   (3) $3\sqrt{3}$

(2) $3\sqrt{2}$ (4) $3\sqrt{6}$

6 Determine the length of the tangent segment BE (to the nearest integer).

(1) 5   (3) 7

(2) 6   (4) 8

7 Determine the $m\angle BEA$.

(1) 32°   (3) 64°

(2) 57°   (4) 114°

Name _____ Date _____

Questions 8–10 will be graded using the model rubric from Problem Solving Strategies. Points for your solution are based on the amount of credit awarded your work;

NO = 0; LITTLE = 1; MOST = 2; FULL = 3

For Exercises 8–10 use the following diagram.

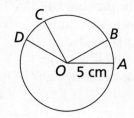

8 Radius $\overline{OA}$ is 5 cm in length and the length of $\overarc{AC}$ is 10 cm. Find the radian measure of $\angle AOC$.

9 $m\angle AOD = 144°$. What is the area, in terms of π, of sector AOD?

10 $m\angle AOB = 36°$. Find the length of $\overarc{AB}$ to the nearest centimeter.

Diagnostic Test: Geometry

Name _____ Date _____

Diagnostic Test 9: Chapter 9

Solid Geometry and Its Applications

For 1–7 choose the numeral preceding the word or expression that best completes the statement or answers the question.

1 A watermelon is approximately the shape of a prolate spheroid. That is a solid formed by rotating an ellipse about it major axis. If the watermelon is sliced perpendicular to its major axis, what is the shape of the cross section?

(1) Sphere

(3) Circle

(2) Parabola

(4) Ellipse

2 What would be true about the volume of the stacks of coins shown in the accompanying figure?

(1) They are equal.

(2) The stack on the left has a greater volume.

(3) The stack on the right has a greater volume.

(4) The volume of the stack on the right cannot be determined.

3 A paper filter is to be designed for the conical funnel shown. How much filter paper is needed to line the funnel if it is 6 in. in diameter and 5 in. high?

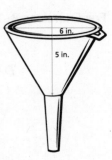

(1) 30 in.^{2}

(3) 55 in.^{2}

(2) 30π in.^{2}

(4) 165 in.^{2}

4 A backpack is shaped like a rectangular prism with half a cylinder on top. If the prism has dimensions of $w = 12$ in., $h = 12$ in., $d = 4$ in. and the total height of the backpack is 16 in. determine the volume of the backpack to the nearest cubic in.

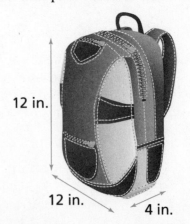

12 in.

12 in.

4 in.

(1) 576 in.^{2}

(3) 768 in.^{2}

(2) 677 in.^{2}

(4) 9216 in.^{2}

Name _____ Date _____

5 A log is cut as shown in the figure. What is the area for the face of the cut?

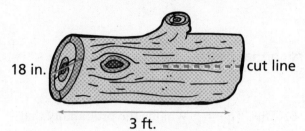

18 in.

cut line

3 ft.

   (1) 18 in^2 **(3)** 36 in^2

   (2) 27 in^2 **(4)** 54 in^2

6 A pyramid has a volume of 108 m^3. A similar pyramid has base edges and height that are one-third those of the original pyramid. What is the volume of the second pyramid?

   (1) 3 m^3 **(3)** 12 m^3

   (2) 4 m^3 **(4)** 36 m^3

7 The circle whose equation is $x^2 + y^2 = 16$ is rotated about the x-axis. What is the volume of the resulting sphere?

   (1) 268 units^3 **(3)** 2145 units^3

   (2) 201 units^3 **(4)** 804 units^3

8 The two containers shown in the accompanying figure have the same volume. What is different about the two containers and why might these different shapes be used?

9 A ball fits into a box such that it just touches each side and the top and bottom of the box. What is the ratio of the volume of the box to the volume of the ball?

10 A cone has a radius of 5 in. and a height of 12 in. Your friend calculates the lateral area of the cone to be: $L.A. = \pi r l$
$$= \pi(5)(12)$$
$$= 60\pi.$$
What is your friend's error?

Name _____ Date _____

Diagnostic Test 10: Chapter 10

Probability

Choose the numeral preceding the word or expression that best completes the statement or answers the question.

1 What is the probability that the spinner shown will land on an even number?

    (1) $\dfrac{2}{5}$ **(3)** $\dfrac{1}{2}$

    (2) $\dfrac{1}{5}$ **(4)** $\dfrac{3}{5}$

2 A die is rolled. Which choice has the same probability as $P(\text{prime})$?

    (1) $P(\text{greater than 4})$

    (2) $P(\text{1 or 6})$

    (3) $P(\text{odd})$

    (4) $P(\text{multiple of 3})$

3 $_5P_3 = ?$

    (1) 10   **(3)** 60

    (2) 1   **(4)** 20

4 A bag contains 3 red and 5 blue marbles. What is the probability that if two marbles are selected *without replacement* they will both be blue?

    (1) $\dfrac{5}{8} + \dfrac{4}{8}$ **(3)** $\dfrac{5}{8} + \dfrac{4}{7}$

    (2) $\dfrac{5}{8} \cdot \dfrac{4}{8}$ **(4)** $\dfrac{5}{8} \cdot \dfrac{4}{7}$

5 How many six letter "words" can be made by using the letters in *butter*?

    (1) 360   **(3)** 720

    (2) 120   **(4)** 36

6 The $P(E) = \dfrac{5}{8}$. What is the probability that event E does not occur?

    (1) $\dfrac{5}{8}$ **(3)** $\dfrac{8}{8}$

    (2) $\dfrac{3}{8}$ **(4)** $\dfrac{0}{8}$

7 If A and B are independent, then

    (1) $P(A \text{ and } B) = P(A) + P(B)$.

    (2) $P(A \text{ and } B) = P(A) + P(B) - P(A \text{ or } B)$.

    (3) $P(A \text{ and } B) = P(A) - P(B)$.

    (4) $P(A \text{ and } B) = P(A) \cdot P(B)$.

Questions 8–10 will be graded using the model rubric from Problem Solving Strategies. Points for your solution are based on the amount of credit awarded your work;

NO = 0; LITTLE = 1; MOST = 2; FULL = 3

8 A group of 6 men and 4 women are chosen at random to form a committee of 5 people. Show all work to find the probability that the committee consists of 2 men and 3 women.

9 Explain the relationship of event A and event B if you know $P(A \text{ and } B) = 0$. Give an example of A and B.

10 A trio is being formed from a group of 5 girls including Sue. If Sue must be in the trio, in how many ways can the trio be formed? Show work.

1 Basic Geometry in the Plane

Geometry and Abraham Lincoln

"He [Lincoln] studied and nearly mastered the Six-books of Euclid (geometry) since he was a member of Congress. He began a course of rigid mental discipline with the intent to improve his faculties, especially his powers of logic and language. Hence his fondness for Euclid, which he carried with him on the circuit till he could demonstrate with ease all the propositions in the six books; often studying far into the night, with a candle near his pillow, while his fellow-lawyers, half a dozen in a room, filled the air with interminable snoring."

–Abraham Lincoln, *Short Autobiography of 1860*

The foundation of geometry begins with three undefined terms: **point**, **line**, and **plane**. All other terms can be defined by using these terms.

Undefined Terms

A **point** can be described as a location in space. It has no length, width, or height. All geometric figures consist of points. **Space** consists of the infinite set of points. The physical representation of a point is a **dot**. A capital letter next to the dot is used to name the point.

A **line** is a set of points extending in opposite directions without end. A line indicates direction and has one dimension, length. A line is named by any two points on the line, in any order, or by a single lowercase letter.

A **plane** is a flat surface of points extending in every direction without end. It has two dimensions, length and width. A single letter or at least three points in the plane can name a plane.

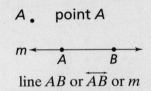

line AB or $\overrightarrow{AB}$ or m

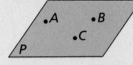

plane P or plane ABC

Collinear points are points that lie on the same line. Points that do not lie on the same line are **noncollinear**.

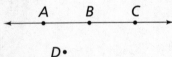

A, B, and C are collinear points. A, B, and D are non-collinear points.

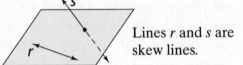

Lines m and n are intersecting lines.

Points and lines that lie in the same plane are **coplanar**. If two lines intersect, then they are coplanar. Lines that do not lie in the same plane are **skew** lines.

Lines r and s are skew lines.

Assumptions that are accepted as true without proof are called **postulates** or **axioms**. However, while we do not prove postulates, it is important to note that no example of these postulates has ever been found that is false.

Here are four basic **postulates** about points, lines, and planes.

- Through any two points, there is exactly one line. (Any two points determine a line.)

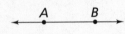

- If two distinct lines intersect, they intersect in exactly one point.

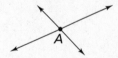

- If two distinct planes intersect, they intersect in exactly one line.

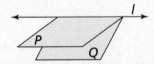

- Through any three non-collinear points, there is exactly one plane.

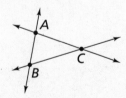

Using the basic postulates for points, lines, and planes

1 Name three labeled points that determine plane *R*.

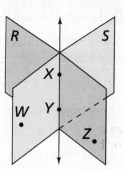

■ **SOLUTION**

Because three noncollinear points determine a plane, three points that determine plane *R* are **points** *X*, *Y*, and *Z*.

2 Name the intersection of plane *R* and plane *S*.

■ **SOLUTION**

The intersection of two planes is a line. The intersection of plane *R* and plane *S* is $\overleftrightarrow{XY}$.

Recall that a number line is a line whose points have been placed in one-to-one correspondence with the set of real numbers. This pairing between the points of a line and the real numbers is a fundamental postulate of geometry.

Ruler Postulate

The points of a line can be paired with the real numbers one-to-one so that any two points on the line can be paired with 0 and 1. The real number that corresponds to a point is called the **coordinate** of that point. The **distance** between two points of the line is equal to the absolute value of the difference of their coordinates.

The distance between point *A* and point *B* is denoted *AB* or *BA*.

EXAMPLE 3 **Using the Ruler Postulate**

3 Find *AB* on the number line at the right.

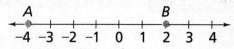

■ **SOLUTION**

The coordinate of *A* is −4. The coordinate of *B* is 2. Subtract the coordinates in either order, and then find the absolute value of the difference.

$$AB = |-4 - 2| = |-6| = 6 \quad \text{or} \quad BA = |2 - (-4)| = |6| = 6$$

3

The Ruler Postulate provides a basis for the following definitions.

Definitions Related to Segments

A **line segment,** or **segment,** is a part, or a subset, of a line. The points are called the **endpoints of the segment.** You name a segment by its endpoints.

J •————• K   segment JK ($\overline{JK}$)

The **length of a segment,** JK, is the distance between its endpoints.

Segments that are equal in length are called **congruent segments.** You indicate congruent segments by marking them with an equal number of tick marks. The symbol for congruence is $\cong$.

C •———————• D
  E •———• F $\overline{CD} \cong \overline{EF}$

The **midpoint** of a segment is the point on the line between the endpoints that divides the segment into two congruent segments.

P •———|———•———|———• Q   If M is the midpoint of $\overline{PQ}$, then
         M $\overline{PMQ}$ and $\overline{PM} \cong \overline{MQ}$.

On a number line, a point C is **between** point A and point B if the coordinate of point C is between the coordinates of points A and B. This leads to an important postulate concerning segments.

Segment Addition Postulate

If point C is between point A and point B, then A, B, and C are collinear and $AC + CB = AB$.

EXAMPLE 4   **Using the Segment Addition Postulate**

 In the figure at the right, point U is between point V and point W, and $VW = 31$. Find UW.

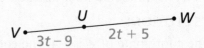

■ SOLUTION

$VU \ + \ UW \ = VW$ ← **Apply the Segment Addition Postulate.**
$3t - 9 + 2t + 5 = 31$ ← **Substitute.**
$5t - 4 = 31$ ← **Combine like terms.**
$5t = 35$ ← **Solve.**
$t = 7$

Therefore: $UW = 2t + 5 \rightarrow 2(7) + 5 = 19$.

If the endpoints of a segment on a number line have coordinates A and B, you can find the coordinate of the midpoint by simplifying the expression $\frac{A + B}{2}$.

EXAMPLE 5 **Finding the midpoint of a segment on a number line**

5 Find the coordinate of the midpoint of $\overline{AB}$.

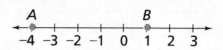

■ **SOLUTION**

The coordinate of A is -4. The coordinate of B is 1.

The coordinate of the midpoint is $\frac{-4 + 1}{2} = \frac{-3}{2} = -1\frac{1}{2}$.

EXAMPLE 6 **Finding a proportional point of a segment on a number line**

6 On a number line, the coordinates of P and Q are -3 and 12, respectively. Find the coordinate of R if $\overline{PRQ}$ and $PR:RQ = 3:2$.

■ **SOLUTION**

$PQ = |12 - (-3)| = 15$ units. If $PR:RQ = 3:2$, then $PR = \frac{3}{5}PQ = \frac{3}{5}(15) = 9$ units.

The 9 units are measured from P at -3, so the coordinate of $R = -3 + 9 = 6$.

Practice

Choose the numeral preceding the word or expression that best completes the statement or answers the question.

1 Three noncollinear points determine a

  (1) plane.

  (2) line.

  (3) segment.

  (4) midpoint.

2 Which of the following statements is true?

  (1) Any three points determine a line.

  (2) Collinear points are always coplanar.

  (3) Skew lines lie in the same plane.

  (4) Any two lines determine a plane.

3 On a number line, the coordinate of point A is m and the coordinate of point B is n. Which expression represents the length of $\overline{AB}$?

  (1) $n - m$ **(3)** $m + n$

  (2) $|m - n|$ **(4)** $\frac{m + n}{2}$

4 Given that point R is the midpoint of $\overline{PQ}$, which statement is false?

  (1) $PR = QR$ **(3)** $PR = 2PQ$

  (2) $QR = \frac{1}{2}PQ$ **(4)** $PR + RQ = PQ$

5 On a number line, the coordinates of X and Y are "m" and "n", respectively, where $n > m$. Which expression represents the coordinate of Z, $\overline{XZY}$, and $XZ = \frac{2}{3}XY$.

  (1) $\frac{2}{3}(m - n)$ **(3)** $\frac{2}{3}(m + n)$

  (2) $m + \frac{2}{3}|m - n|$ **(4)** $n + \frac{2}{3}|m + n|$

In Exercises 6–15, refer to the figure below.

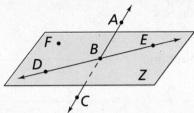

Are the points collinear? Write *Yes* or *No*.

6 B, E, A   7 D, B, E

8 A, B, D   9 A, C, B

Are the points coplanar? Write *Yes* or *No*.

10 C, B, A, E   11 E, F, B, D

12 D, B, F, A   13 D, B, F, C

14 Use the labeled points to name plane Z in three different ways.

15 Name the intersection of $\overleftrightarrow{AC}$ and $\overleftrightarrow{ED}$.

In Exercises 16–21, refer to the figure below. Use the labeled points to answer each question.

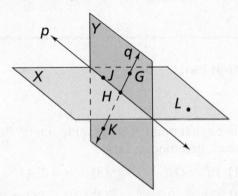

16 Name two points that determine line p.

17 Name three points that determine plane X.

18 Name the intersection of line p and line q.

19 Name line q in three different ways.

20 Name the intersection of planes X and Y.

21 Name the intersection of line q and plane X.

In Exercises 22–25, refer to the number line below. Find each length.

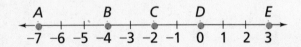

22 AC   23 BD   24 CB   25 AE

In Exercises 26–29, refer to the number line below.

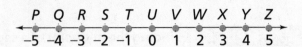

Give the letter that names the midpoint of each segment.

26 $\overline{QS}$ 27 $\overline{SW}$ 28 $\overline{VZ}$ 29 $\overline{RZ}$

In Exercises 30–31, use the figure below. Point M is the midpoint of $\overline{JK}$.

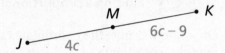

30 Find c.

31 Find JM and JK.

In Exercises 32–34, draw a labeled diagram to show these geometric relations.

32 XZ = ZY and Z is NOT the midpoint of $\overline{XY}$.

33 Plane P contains $\overleftrightarrow{AB}$. M is non-coplanar to P. N is collinear to $\overleftrightarrow{AB}$. $\overline{MN}$ is drawn.

34 The towns of Ames, Bradley, and Carlton lie along the same straight road. Ames is 45 miles due east of Bradley, and Carlton is 10 miles due west of Ames.

For Exercises 35–38, A, B, and C are points on a number line with B between A and C. Find the coordinate of B.

35 Coordinates of A and C are 0 and −10, respectively. AB : BC = 1 : 4.

36 Coordinates of A and C are 1 and 13, respectively. AB : AC = 3 : 4.

37 Coordinates of A and C are −3 and 27 respectively. AC : BC = 10 : 2.

38 Coordinates of A and C are 5 and −10, respectively. AC : AB = 3 : 2.

Another set of definitions and postulates is associated with the concept of a ray.

Definitions Related to Rays

A **ray** is part of a line that begins at one point and extends without end in one direction. The point is called the **endpoint of the ray.** You name a ray by its endpoint and one other point on it.

On a line, if point B is between point A and point C, then $\overrightarrow{BA}$ and $\overrightarrow{BC}$ are **opposite rays.**

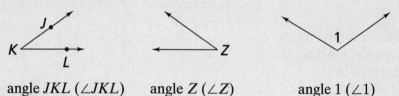

An **angle** (or **plane angle**) is the figure formed by two rays with a common endpoint. Each ray is a **side** of the angle, and the endpoint is the **vertex** of the angle. The symbol for angle is $\angle$. There are several ways to name an angle.

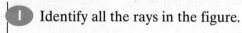

angle JKL ($\angle JKL$)   angle Z ($\angle Z$)   angle 1 ($\angle 1$)

EXAMPLE 1   **Identifying rays**

1 Identify all the rays in the figure.

■ **SOLUTION**
$\overrightarrow{CA}, \overrightarrow{CD}, \overrightarrow{CB}, \overrightarrow{BD}, \overrightarrow{DB}$

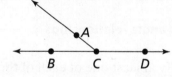

Angles are classified according to their degree measure.

Definitions Related to Angle Measure

An **acute angle** is an angle whose measure is greater than 0° and less than 90°.

An **obtuse angle** is an angle whose measure is greater than 90° and less than 180°.

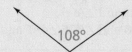

A **right angle** is an angle whose measure is equal to 90°.

A **straight angle** is an angle whose measure is equal to 180°.

This symbol indicates a right angle.

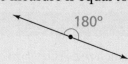

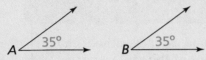

Definitions Relating to Angle Relationships

Congruent angles are two angles that have the same degree measure.

If $m\angle A = m\angle B$, then $\angle A \cong \angle B$.

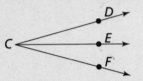

An **angle bisector** is a ray in the plane of the angle that divides an angle into two congruent angles. If $\overrightarrow{CE}$ bisects $\angle DCF$, then $\angle DCE \cong \angle ECF$.

Adjacent angles are two coplanar angles that share a common side and the same vertex but no common interior points.

In the diagram on the left, $\angle DCE \cong \angle FCE$ and $\angle DCE$ is also adjacent to $\angle FCE$.

Complementary angles are two angles whose measures add up to 90°. In the diagram at the right, $\angle 1$ and $\angle 2$ are complementary.

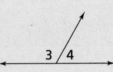

Supplementary angles are two angles whose measures add up to 180°. A **linear pair** of angles is two adjacent angles whose sides form opposite rays. In the diagram at the right, $\angle 3$ and $\angle 4$ are a linear pair. If two angles form a linear pair, then they are supplementary. $\angle 3$ and $\angle 4$ are supplementary.

Note

The statement $m\angle A = m\angle B$ is read "The measure of angle A equals the measure of angle B."

The statement $\angle A \cong \angle B$ is read "Angle A is congruent to angle B."

You can use the statements interchangeably.

You can use these definitions to identify the angle relationships in a given figure.

EXAMPLE 2   **Identifying angle relationships**

2 Use the figure to identify at least one of each of the following:

Angle bisector   Congruent angles
Adjacent angles   Complementary angles
Linear pair   Supplementary angles

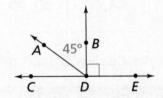

■ **SOLUTION**

Angle bisector: $\overrightarrow{DA}$ bisects $\angle CDB$ and $\overrightarrow{DB}$ bisects $\angle CDE$.
Adjacent angles: $\angle CDA$ and $\angle ADB$ or $\angle ADB$ and $\angle BDE$
Linear pair: $\angle CDA$ and $\angle ADE$ or $\angle CDB$ and $\angle BDE$
Congruent angles: $\angle CDA \cong \angle ADB$ or $\angle CDB \cong \angle BDE$
Complementary angles: $\angle CDA$ and $\angle ADB$
Supplementary angles: $\angle CDB$ and $\angle BDE$, $\angle CAD$ and $\angle ADE$

An angle separates a plane into three sets of points: the angle itself, the points in the *interior* of the angle, and the points in the *exterior* of the angle.

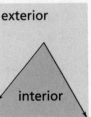

Angle Addition Postulate

If point B is in the interior of $\angle AOC$, then $m\angle AOB + m\angle BOC = m\angle AOC$.

3 In the figure, $m\angle AOB = 74°$ and $m\angle AOC = 106°$. Find $m\angle BOC$.

■ SOLUTION

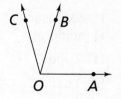

$m\angle AOB + m\angle BOC = m\angle AOC$ ← Apply the Angle Addition Postulate.
   $74° + m\angle BOC = 106°$ ← Substitute.
      $m\angle BOC = 32°$ ← Solve.

4 Use the figure to find $m\angle GDE$ if $\overrightarrow{DG}$ bisects $\angle BDE$ and $m\angle CDB = 2m\angle BDE$.

■ SOLUTION

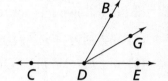

$\angle CDB$ and $\angle BDE$ are a linear pair.
$\angle CDB$ and $\angle BDE$ are supplementary.
$m\angle CDB + m\angle BDE = 180°$
$2m\angle BDE + m\angle BDE = 180°$ ← Substitution
$3m\angle BDE = 180°$ ← Simplify
$m\angle BDE = 60°$ ← Solve
Since $\overrightarrow{DG}$ bisects $\angle BDE$, $m\angle BDG = m\angle GDE$, so $m\angle GDE = 30°$.

Practice

Choose the numeral preceding the word or expression that best completes the statement or answers the question.

1 The measure of a straight angle is

   (1) less than 90°.   **(3)** exactly 90°.

   (2) less than 180°.   **(4)** exactly 180°.

2 The supplement of an acute angle is

   (1) an acute angle.

   (2) an obtuse angle.

   (3) a right angle.

   (4) a straight angle.

3 Which is the most reasonable estimate of the measure of $\angle QRS$?

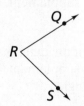

   (1) about 115°   **(3)** about 75°

   (2) about 95°   **(4)** about 15°

4 In the figure below, $\overrightarrow{AX}$ and $\overrightarrow{AZ}$ are opposite rays, and $\angle XAY$ is a right angle. Which statement is false?

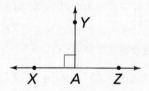

   (1) $\angle YAZ$ is the complement of $\angle XAY$.

   (2) $\angle YAZ$ is adjacent to $\angle XAY$.

   (3) $\angle YAZ$ is congruent to $\angle XAY$.

   (4) $\angle XAY$ and $\angle YAZ$ are a linear pair.

5 If $\angle 1$ is supplementary to $\angle 2$ and $\angle 2$ is supplementary to $\angle 3$, which statement is always true?

   (1) $\angle 1$ is supplementary to $\angle 3$.

   (2) $\angle 1$ is complementary to $\angle 3$.

   (3) $\angle 1$ is congruent to $\angle 3$.

   (4) $\angle 1$ is adjacent to $\angle 3$.

6 Two acute angles can be which of the following?

    I. congruent   III. complementary
    II. adjacent   IV. supplementary

    (1) I and II   **(3)** I, II, and III

    (2) I and III   **(4)** I, II, and IV

7 $\overrightarrow{OF}$ bisects $\angle EOG$. Which of the following is not true?

    (1) $m\angle EOF = m\angle FOG$

    (2) $m\angle FOG = m\angle EOG - m\angle EOF$

    (3) $m\angle EOF = m\angle EOG$

    (4) $m\angle FOG = \frac{1}{2}m\angle EOG$

8 $\angle YXZ$ and $\angle ZXW$ are adjacent and supplementary angles. If $m\angle YXZ = 37°$, what is $m\angle ZXW$?

    (1) 143°   **(3)** 37°

    (2) 53°   **(4)** unknown

9 What is the measure of the angle formed by opposite rays?

    (1) 90°   **(3)** 360°

    (2) 180°   **(4)** unknown

10 $\angle AZB$ and $\angle CZB$ are supplementary. The $m\angle AZB = 2x - 4$ and $m\angle CZB = 8x + 4$. What is the measure of each angle?

    (1) $m\angle AZB = 32°$ and $m\angle CZB = 148°$

    (2) $m\angle AZB = 12°$ and $m\angle CZB = 76°$

    (3) $m\angle AZB = 43°$ and $m\angle CZB = 22°$

    (4) $m\angle AZB = 68°$ and $m\angle CZB = 292°$

In Exercises 11–13, state the measure of the complement of an angle of the given measure.

11 56°   **12** 12.5°   **13** $x°$

In Exercises 14–16, state the measure of the supplement of an angle of the given measure.

14 113°   **15** 41.5°   **16** $y°$

In Exercises 17–18, $\overrightarrow{OA}$ and $\overrightarrow{OB}$ are opposite rays. Find $m\angle AOC$.

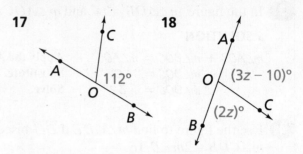

In Exercises 19–20, $m\angle PZR$ is a right angle. Find $m\angle PZQ$.

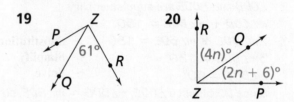

All the statements in Exercises 21–24 are *sometimes* true. Explain why.

21 Complementary angle are always adjacent.

22 Supplementary angles always form a linear pair.

23 If $\overrightarrow{PQ}$ and $\overrightarrow{PR}$ are names for the same ray, then Q and R must be names for the same point.

24 If the union of two rays is a line, then the rays are opposite rays.

In Exercises 25–28, solve the problem.

25 The measure of an angle is equal to the measure of its complement. Find the measure of each angle.

26 The measure of an angle is equal to the measure of its supplement. Find the measure of each angle.

27 The measure of an angle is twice the measure of its supplement. Find the measure of the larger angle.

28 The measure of an angle is fourteen degrees less than the measure of its complement. Find the measure of the smaller angle.

1.3 Intersecting, Perpendicular, and Parallel Lines

G.CO.9

The figure at the right shows intersecting lines ℓ and *m*. The lines form the following four pairs of adjacent angles, and each is a linear pair.

∠1 and ∠2   ∠2 and ∠3   ∠3 and ∠4   ∠4 and ∠1

The figure also contains two pairs of *vertical* angles.

∠1 and ∠3   ∠2 and ∠4

Vertical angles are two angles whose sides form two pairs of opposite rays. There is a special relationship between vertical angles, stated as follows.

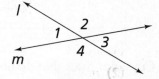

Vertical Angles Theorem

If two angles are vertical angles, then they are congruent.

Note

You can prove the Vertical Angles Theorem algebraically.

Notice that the above statement is called a *theorem*. A **theorem** is a statement that can be proved true.

EXAMPLE 1   **Using the Vertical Angles Theorem**

1. In the figure at the right, lines *s* and *t* intersect at point *P*, $m\angle 1 = (3n - 14)°$, and $m\angle 3 = (2n + 17)°$. Find $m\angle 2$.

   ■ **SOLUTION**

   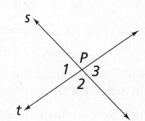

   $m\angle 1 = m\angle 3$ ← **Apply the Vertical Angles Theorem.**
   $3n - 14 = 2n + 17$ ← **Substitute.**
   $n - 14 = 17$ ← **Solve.**
   $n = 31$

   Therefore: $m\angle 1 = (3n - 14)° \rightarrow (3[31] - 14)° = 79°$
   Because ∠1 and ∠2 are a linear pair, $m\angle 2 = 180° - m\angle 1 = 180° - 79° = 101°$.

Perpendicular lines are two lines that intersect to form right angles. The symbol for perpendicular is ⊥.

$\overleftrightarrow{EF}$ is perpendicular to $\overleftrightarrow{GH}$, denoted $\overleftrightarrow{EF} \perp \overleftrightarrow{GH}$.

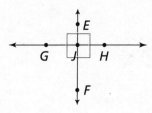

If $\overleftrightarrow{EF} \perp \overleftrightarrow{GH}$, then ∠EJG, ∠GJF, ∠EJH, and ∠HJF are right angles and each measures 90°.

Note

A small square at the intersection of two lines denotes a right angle.

EXAMPLE 2   **Working with perpendicular lines**

2   In the figure, $\overleftrightarrow{AB} \perp \overleftrightarrow{CD}$ and $m\angle EZD = 53°$. Find $m\angle AZE$.

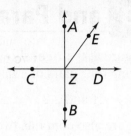

■ **SOLUTION**

Because $\overleftrightarrow{AB} \perp \overleftrightarrow{CD}$, $\angle AZD$ is a right angle and $m\angle AZD = 90°$.

$m\angle AZE + m\angle EZD = m\angle AZD$	←	**Apply the Angle Addition Postulate.**
$m\angle AZE + \quad 53° \;= 90°$	←	**Substitute.**
$m\angle AZE = 37°$	←	**Solve.**

Coplanar lines that do not intersect are called **parallel lines.** In the diagram at the right, lines p and q are parallel, denoted $p \parallel q$.

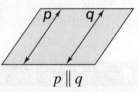

$p \parallel q$

Parallel Postulate

Through a point not on a line, there is exactly one line parallel to the given line.

Distance between two points has been previously defined as the length of the line segment between the two endpoints of the segment.

Given: *A*   *B.* The distance between A and B is length AB.

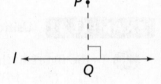

We need now to defined **distance between a line and a point not on that line.**

Given point P not on line l, the distance from P to l is the shortest distance which is the length of the perpendicular from P to l.

Parallel lines are equidistant; that is, they are the same distance apart at every point. The **distance between two parallel lines** is the perpendicular distance between any point on one of them and the other line.

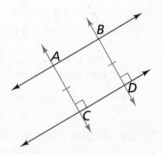

$\overleftrightarrow{AB} \parallel \overleftrightarrow{CD}$ is illustrated by the diagram at the right.

The lines are parallel if they are the same distance apart at every point. The distance between $\overleftrightarrow{AB}$ and $\overleftrightarrow{CD}$ is the length of $\overline{AC}$ or $\overline{BD}$. If $\overleftrightarrow{AC} \perp \overleftrightarrow{CD}$, $\overline{BD} \perp \overleftrightarrow{CD}$, and $\overline{AC} \cong \overline{BD}$, then $\overleftrightarrow{AB} \parallel \overleftrightarrow{CD}$.

EXAMPLE 3   **Working with parallel lines**

3   If $\overline{ZW} \perp \overline{WX}$, then how many lines containing Z are parallel to $\overleftrightarrow{WX}$ and what is the distance between them?

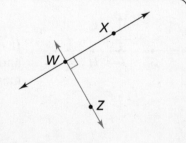

■ **SOLUTION**

Using the Parallel Postulate, there is exactly one line parallel to $\overleftrightarrow{WX}$ that goes through Z. The distance between them is equal to the length of segment WZ.

A line that intersects two or more coplanar lines at different points is called a **transversal.** The diagram shows *l* and *m* intersected by transversal *t* at points *P* and *Q*.

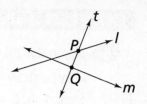

The following postulate and theorems apply to the angles formed when a transversal intersects two **parallel** lines.

Angles Formed by a Transversal

In the figure at the right, lines *a* and *b* are intersected by transversal *t*. **(MP)**

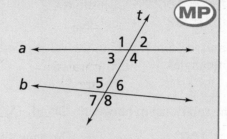

The **interior angles** are:
∠3, ∠4, ∠5, and ∠6

The **exterior angles** are:
∠1, ∠2, ∠7, and ∠8

Corresponding angles are a pair of nonadjacent angles, one interior and one exterior, that are both on the same side of the transversal. In the figure above, these are the pairs of corresponding angles.

∠1 and ∠5   ∠2 and ∠6   ∠3 and ∠7   ∠4 and ∠8

Alternate interior angles are a pair of nonadjacent interior angles on opposite sides of the transversal. The alternate interior angles are:

∠3 and ∠6   ∠4 and ∠5

Alternate exterior angles are a pair of nonadjacent exterior angles on opposite sides of the transversal. The alternate exterior angles are:

∠1 and ∠8   ∠2 and ∠7

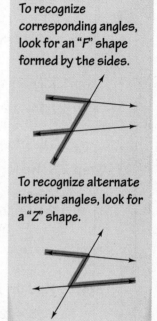

Note

To recognize corresponding angles, look for an "F" shape formed by the sides.

To recognize alternate interior angles, look for a "Z" shape.

When a transversal intersects parallel lines, the pairs of angles have special relationships. These are summarized by the following postulate and theorems.

Angle Relationships when Lines are Parallel

Corresponding Angles Postulate If two parallel lines are cut by a transversal, then corresponding angles are congruent.

Alternate Interior Angles Theorem If two parallel lines are cut by a transversal, then alternate interior angles are congruent.

Alternate Exterior Angles Theorem If two parallel lines are cut by a transversal, then alternate exterior angles are congruent.

Same-Side Interior Angles Theorem If two parallel lines are cut by a transversal, then interior angles on the same side of the transversal are supplementary.

4 $p \| q$ and $m\angle 1 = 118°$. Find $m\angle 7$.

■ SOLUTION

Step 1 $m\angle 8 = m\angle 1$ ← Use Alternate Exterior Angles Theorem.
$m\angle 8 = 118°$ ← Substitute.

Step 2 $m\angle 7 + m\angle 8 = 180°$ ← Apply definition of linear pair.
$m\angle 7 + 118° = 180°$ ← Substitute.
$m\angle 7 = 62°$ ← Solve.

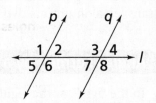

5 $m\angle 3 = 24(n + 1)$ and $m\angle 5 = 15n$. Find the value of n and the measure of both angles.

■ SOLUTION

Step 1 Identify the relationship between $\angle 3$ and $\angle 5$.

$\angle 3 + \angle 2 = 180°$ ← Use Same-Side Interior Angle Theorem.
$\angle 2 \cong \angle 5$ ← Use Vertical Angle Theorem.
Therefore, $\angle 3 + \angle 5 = 180°$.   ← Substitute. Therefore they are supplementary.

Step 2 Solve for n.

$24(n + 1) + 15n = 180°$ ← Substitute.
$24n + 24 + 15n = 180°$ ← Use Distributive Property.
$39n + 24 = 180°$ ← Solve.
$39n = 156°$
$n = 4°$

Step 3 Find the measure of both angles.

$m\angle 3 = 24(n + 1)$ and $m\angle 5 = 15n$ ← Given.
$m\angle 3 = 24(4 + 1)$ $m\angle 5 = 15(4)$ ← Substitute.
$m\angle 3 = 120°$ $m\angle 5 = 60°$ ← Solve.

Therefore, the value of $n = 4$, $m\angle 3 = 120°$, and $m\angle 5 = 60°$.

Perpendicular to Parallels Theorem

If a line is perpendicular to one of two parallel lines, then it is perpendicular to the other parallel line.

EXAMPLE 6   **Applying the Perpendicular to Parallels Theorem**

6 In the figure at the right, $a \perp c$, $c \| d$, $m\angle 1 = (7x - 8)°$, and $m\angle 2 = (4x)°$. Find $m\angle 2$.

■ SOLUTION

Because $a \perp c$ and $c \| d$, it follows that $a \perp d$. So $\angle 1$ is a right angle.

Step 1 $m\angle 1 = (7x - 8)° = 90°$ ← Apply definition of right angle.
$7x - 8 = 90$ ← Solve.
$x = 14$

Step 2 $m\angle 2 = (4x)°$ ← Substitute.
$m\angle 2 = (4[14])°$ ← Simplify.
$m\angle 2 = 56°$

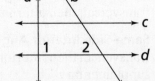

You can use the following postulate and theorems to show that two lines are parallel.

Using Angle Relationships to Show Lines Parallel

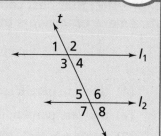

Corresponding Angles Postulate If two lines are cut by a transversal so that a pair of corresponding angles are congruent, then the lines are parallel.

If $\angle 1 \cong \angle 5$, then $l_1 \parallel l_2$.

Alternate Interior Angles Theorem If two lines are cut by a transversal so that a pair of alternate interior angles are congruent, then the lines are parallel.

If $\angle 4 \cong \angle 5$, then $l_1 \parallel l_2$.

Alternate Exterior Angles Theorem If two lines are cut by a transversal so that a pair of alternate exterior angles are congruent, then the lines are parallel.

If $\angle 1 \cong \angle 8$, then $l_1 \parallel l_2$.

Same-Side Interior Angles Theorem If two lines are cut by a transversal so that a pair of same-side interior angles are supplementary, then the lines are parallel.

If $\angle 3$ and $\angle 5$ are supplementary, then $l_1 \parallel l_2$.

EXAMPLES 7 and 8   Justifying a statement that lines are parallel

7 Given the figure at the right, state the postulate or theorem that justifies the conclusion $\overline{AB} \parallel \overline{CD}$.

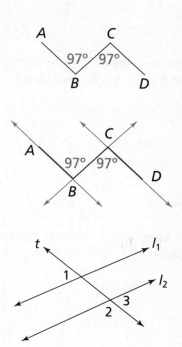

- **SOLUTION**

The segments $\overline{AB}$ and $\overline{CD}$ are parts of two lines, $\overleftrightarrow{AB}$ and $\overleftrightarrow{CD}$, that are cut by transversal $\overleftrightarrow{BC}$. You may find it helpful to copy the figure and extend the lines as shown at the right.

The labeled angles, $\angle ABC$ and $\angle DCB$, are a pair of alternate interior angles. Because these angles are congruent, $\overline{AB} \parallel \overline{CD}$.

Justification: If Alternate Interior angles are congruent, then lines are parallel.

8 Given the figure at the right, state the postulate or theorem that justifies the conclusion that $l_1 \parallel l_2$, given that $m\angle 1 = 35°$ and $m\angle 2 = 145°$.

- **SOLUTION**

Lines l_1 and l_2 are cut by the transversal t. Therefore, $\angle 2$ and $\angle 3$ are supplementary and $m\angle 3 = 180 - 145 = 35°$. Therefore, $\angle 1 \cong \angle 3$ and $l_1 \parallel l_2$.

Justification: If Alternate Exterior angles are congruent, then lines are parallel.

Choose the numeral preceding the word or expression that best completes the statement or answers the question.

1 If two lines are each parallel to a third line, then

    (1) they are parallel to each other.

    (2) they are perpendicular to each other.

    (3) they are a pair of skew lines.

    (4) their relationship cannot be determined.

2 Given the figure below, which statement is true?

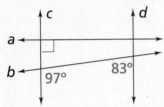

    (1) $a \parallel b$ **(3)** $a \perp d$

    (2) $c \parallel b$ **(4)** $b \perp d$

3 If two lines are coplanar, then they cannot be

    (1) intersecting.   **(3)** perpendicular.

    (2) parallel.   **(4)** skew.

In Exercises 4–6, refer to the figure below. Find each angle measure.

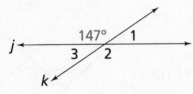

4 $m\angle 1$ **5** $m\angle 2$ **6** $m\angle 3$

In Exercises 7–12, refer to the figure below. Given $r \parallel s$, find each angle measure.

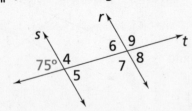

7 $m\angle 4$ **8** $m\angle 5$ **9** $m\angle 6$

10 $m\angle 7$ **11** $m\angle 8$ **12** $m\angle 9$

In Exercises 13–18, refer to the figure below. Given $\overleftrightarrow{BE} \perp \overleftrightarrow{FC}$, find each angle measure.

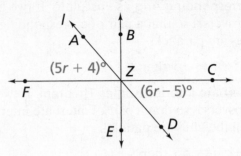

13 $m\angle CZD$ **14** $m\angle AZB$ **15** $m\angle BZC$

16 $m\angle DZE$ **17** $m\angle AZC$ **18** $m\angle AZE$

In Exercises 19–24, refer to the figure below. Given $l \parallel m$, find each angle measure.

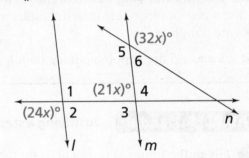

19 $m\angle 1$ **20** $m\angle 2$ **21** $m\angle 3$

22 $m\angle 4$ **23** $m\angle 5$ **24** $m\angle 6$

In Exercises 25–26, state the postulate or theorem that justifies the conclusion $\overline{AB} \parallel \overline{DC}$.

25

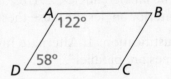

26

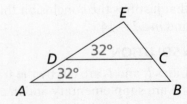

1.4 Geometric Constructions

A **geometric construction** is an accurate drawing that produces a required geometric shape. The construction can be called a **locus** (plural **loci**) which locates a set of points that satisfies a given set of conditions needed to draw that shape. Constructions are traditionally done using a compass and a straightedge (ruler), but also can be done using string, MIRAs™, paper folding, or dynamic geometric software.

One locus is basic to all constructions.

Circle Locus

The locus of all points at a fixed distance from a given point is a circle.

The given point is the center of the circle and the fixed distance is the circle's radius.
The circle is the construction or new shape.

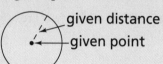

The **compass** is the tool that all constructions use to model the circle locus. The point end of the compass locates the given point and the compass opening is the fixed distance. Usually only an **arc** of the circle is drawn to mark the distance.

EXAMPLE 1   Copying a segment   (MP)

1   Make a copy of $\overline{AB}$ shown at the right.

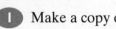

■ **SOLUTION**

Step 1 Draw a line n and place point C on it.

Step 2 Set your compass point on A and use it to measure the radius AB. Draw the locus of points a distance AB from given point C.

Step 3 The arc of circle C with radius AB will intersect line n. Label this point of intersection D. As a result, $\overline{CD} \cong \overline{AB}$.

You can add two line segments together using basic constructions. To do this, copy the two segments so that they are placed end-to-end. The length of the final construction is the sum of the length of the two segments.

EXAMPLE 2   Constructing a segment from two specified segments

2   Given $\overline{KL}$ and $\overline{XY}$, construct $\overline{EG}$ so that $EG = KL + XY$.

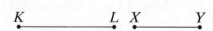

■ **SOLUTION**

Step 1 Draw a line n and place point E on it.

Step 2 Construct $\overline{EF} \cong \overline{KL}$ on n.

Step 3 Construct $\overline{FG} \cong \overline{XY}$ on n with F between E and G. As a result, $EG = KL + XY$.

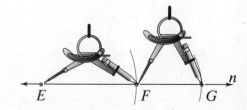

17

Just like segments, you can also use a straightedge and a compass to make copies of angles and to construct the sum of two angles.

By definition, an equilateral triangle has three congruent sides. You can construct the triangle by constructing the three congruent segments.

EXAMPLE 3 Constructing an equilateral triangle

3 Construct equilateral $\triangle CDE$ given $\overline{CD}$

SOLUTION

Step 1 Draw a line n and place point C on it.

Step 2 Copy $\overline{CD}$ to n.

Step 3 Draw the locus of points CD from C and the locus of points CD from D.

Step 4 Label the intersection of the two arcs point E. Draw $\overline{CE}$ and $\overline{DE}$.

Since $\overline{CD} \cong \overline{CE} \cong \overline{DE}$, $\triangle CED$ is an equilateral triangle.

You can construct other types of triangles. For example, you can construct an isosceles triangle by copying two congruent segments and placing them onto a common base.

Example 4 shows the construction of an angle congruent to a given angle.

EXAMPLE 4 Copying an angle

4 $\angle PQR$ is shown at right and also below in Step 1. Make a copy of $\angle PQR$.

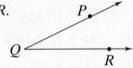

SOLUTION

Step 1 On $\overrightarrow{QP}$ draw an arc to represent the locus of points QR from Q. Label the point of intersection of the arc and $\overrightarrow{QP}$ as Z.

Step 2 Draw a new ray, $\overrightarrow{YS}$. Using QR as the radius of an arc, draw a long arc to represent the locus of points QR from Y. Label the point of intersection of the long arc and $\overrightarrow{YS}$ as X.

Step 3 Reset your compass to draw the locus of points ZR from X. Place the compass point on R and spread it to point Z. The arc from step 2 and this locus will intersect. Label the point of intersection T.

Step 4 Use a straightedge to construct $\overrightarrow{YT}$.

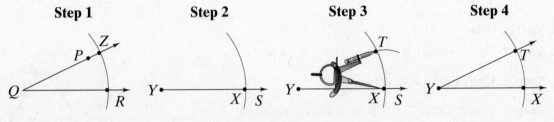

As a result of this construction, $\angle TYX \cong \angle PQR$.

EXAMPLE 5 **Constructing an angle whose measure is a specified sum**

5 Given ∠A and ∠B, construct ∠C such that $m\angle C = m\angle A + m\angle B$.

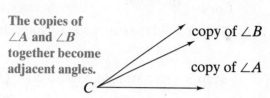

■ **SOLUTION**

Step 1 Copy ∠A. Call the vertex of the copy point C.

Step 2 Copy ∠B so that point C is the vertex of the copy of ∠B, the copy shares a side with one side of the copy of ∠A, and the copy of ∠B does not lie inside the copy of ∠A.

The copies of ∠A and ∠B together become adjacent angles.

As a result of this construction, $m\angle C = m\angle A + m\angle B$.

Many constructions will define the center of the circle locus but leave the radius undefined. When this happens, choose **any** compass opening for the radius making sure it is large enough for required arc intersections to occur.

EXAMPLE 6 **Constructing the angle bisector of a given angle**

6 Construct the angle bisector of ∠P.

■ **SOLUTION**

Step 1 Construct an arc centered at P and intersecting both sides of ∠P. Label the points of intersection A and B.

Step 2 Construct arcs with the same radius centered at A and at B. Make sure the arcs intersect in a point. Label the point of intersection X.

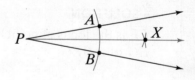

Step 3 Draw $\overrightarrow{PX}$.

This ray is the angle bisector of ∠APB. As a result ∠APX ≅ ∠XPB.

The construction of an angle bisector can also be done using paper folding. Tracing paper or patty paper is used so points, lines, and rays can be seen through the paper. When the paper is folded, the fold or crease represents the construction.

EXAMPLE 7   **Folding to find the Angle Bisector of a given angle**

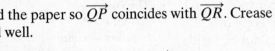

7 Fold the angle bisector of ∠PQR.

■ **SOLUTION**

Step 1 Place a square of patty paper over ∠PQR and trace this angle.

Step 2 Fold the paper so $\overrightarrow{QP}$ coincides with $\overrightarrow{QR}$. Crease the fold well.

Step 3 Use a straight edge to draw $\overrightarrow{QT}$ over the crease.

Step 1	**Step 2**	**Step 3**

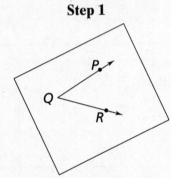
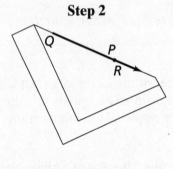
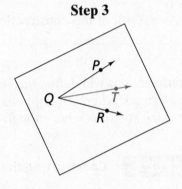

$\overrightarrow{QT}$ is the angle bisector of ∠PQR. As a result ∠PQT ≅ ∠TQR.

EXAMPLE 8   **Using a locus to describe a figure**

 Given ∠DEF ≅ ∠FEG, describe $\overrightarrow{EF}$ as a locus of points.

■ **SOLUTION**

$\overrightarrow{EF}$ is the locus of points equidistant from sides $\overrightarrow{ED}$ and $\overrightarrow{EG}$ of ∠DEG.

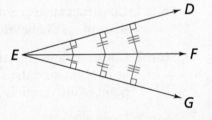

Choose the numeral preceding the word or expression that best completes the statement or answers the question.

1 Use a compass to determine which of the following statements about $\overline{AB}$ and $\overline{CD}$ is true.

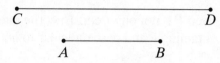

   (1) $AB = CD$ **(3)** $CD = 0.5(AB)$

   (2) $2(AB) = CD$ **(4)** $5CD = 2(AB)$

2 Which of the following statements about $m\angle A$ and $m\angle B$ is not true?

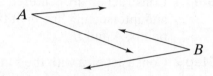

   (1) $m\angle A = m\angle B$

   (2) $m\angle A + m\angle B = 2(m\angle A)$

   (3) $m\angle A + m\angle B = 2(m\angle B)$

   (4) $m\angle A = 0.5(m\angle B)$

3 Use a compass to decide which of the following statements is false.

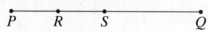

   (1) $PQ = 2(PS)$

   (2) $PQ = 4(PR)$

   (3) $PQ = PS + SQ$

   (4) $PS = SQ + 2(PR)$

In Exercises 4–8, use the segments below. Use a compass and straightedge for each construction.

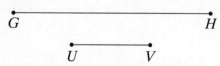

4 $\overline{AB}$, whose length is $2(UV)$

5 $\overline{AB}$, whose length is $GH - 2(UV)$

6 $\overline{AB}$, whose length is $3(UV)$

7 $\overline{AB}$, whose length is $UV + GH$

8 $\overline{AB}$, whose length is $GH - UV$

In Exercises 9–11, use the angles below. Use a compass and straightedge for each construction.

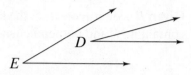

9 $\angle A$, whose measure is $2(m\angle D)$

10 $\angle A$, whose measure is $m\angle E + m\angle D$

11 $\angle A$, whose measure is $m\angle E - m\angle D$

12 Construct the angle bisector of $\angle Z$.

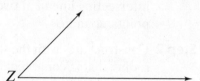

13 Construct the bisector of $\angle PTA$.

14 Construct an isosceles triangle using the segments below. (There are two constructions possible.)

15 Construct an equilateral triangle using the segment below.

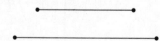

16 Construct a triangle from the segments below.

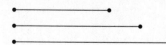

17 Construct $\overline{AB}$, whose length is $2(FD) - NY$.

21

1.5 Constructing Perpendicular and Parallel Lines

 G.CO.12

In plane Q, given any line m and any point P, there is exactly one line in the plane that contains P and that is perpendicular to m.

EXAMPLES 1 and 2 — **Constructing a line perpendicular to a given line**

① Given P is on m, construct the line containing P and perpendicular to line m.

② Given P is not on m, construct the line containing P and perpendicular to line m.

■ SOLUTION

Step 1 Construct arcs with the same radius centered at P and intersecting line m at two points, A and B.

Step 2 Construct arcs with the same radius, that is, congruent arcs centered at A and the other centered at B. The radius must be greater than half the distance between A and B. Label the intersections X and Y.

Step 3 Draw line n through X and Y.

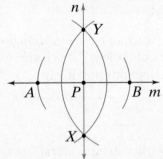

■ SOLUTION

Step 1 Construct an arc centered at P and intersecting line m at two points, A and B.

Step 2 Construct arcs with the same radius centered at A and B, with the radius being greater than half the distance between A and B. Label the intersections X and Y.

Step 3 Draw line n through X and Y.

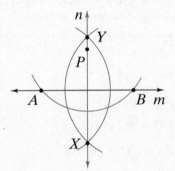

In each construction, line n contains P and is perpendicular to line m.

A **perpendicular bisector** of a segment is a line, ray, or segment that is perpendicular to the segment at its midpoint. The construction of the perpendicular at a point, shown in Example 1, can help you construct the perpendicular bisector.

In Step 1 of Example 1, you drew arcs that made $\overline{AP}$ and $\overline{BP}$ congruent. That means P is the midpoint of $\overline{AB}$. By construction, line n is perpendicular to $\overline{AB}$ and passes through P. This makes n the perpendicular bisector of $\overline{AB}$.

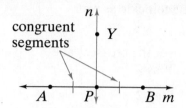

EXAMPLE 3   Constructing the perpendicular bisector of a given segment

3. Construct the perpendicular bisector of $\overline{CD}$ shown here.

- **SOLUTION**

Step 1 Using a compass, construct arcs centered at C and at D and having the same radius. Be sure that the two arcs intersect at two points X and Y. (Make sure the radius used for both arcs is more than half the distance between C and D.)

Step 2 Draw line n through points X and Y. Line n is the perpendicular bisector of $\overline{CD}$.

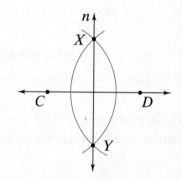

EXAMPLE 4   Using a locus to describe a figure.

4. Given $\overline{XZ} \cong \overline{ZY}$, describe m, the perpendicular bisector of $\overline{XY}$, as a locus of points.

- **SOLUTION**

m, the perpendicular bisector of $\overline{XY}$, is the locus of points equidistant from X and Y, the endpoints of $\overline{XY}$. Since points A and B are on m, then $AX = AY$ and $BX = BY$.

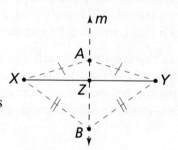

EXAMPLE 5 **Folding to find the perpendicular bisector of a segment**

5   Fold the perpendicular bisector of $\overline{XY}$.   

■ SOLUTION

Step 1   Place a square of patty paper over $\overline{XY}$ and trace this segment.

Step 2   Fold the paper so point Y coincides with point X and all the remaining points of the segment coincide as well. Crease the fold well.

Step 3   Use a straight edge to draw line m over the crease. Label the point of intersection of m and $\overline{XY}$ as Z.

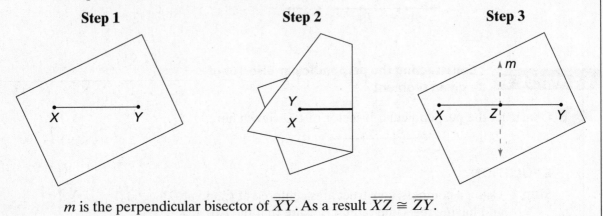

| Step 1 | Step 2 | Step 3 |

m is the perpendicular bisector of $\overline{XY}$. As a result $\overline{XZ} \cong \overline{ZY}$.

Recall that if lines m and n in the figure below are parallel, then corresponding angles $\angle 1$ and $\angle 2$ are congruent. That is, $\angle 2$ is a copy of $\angle 1$.

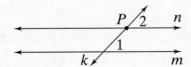

So, to construct a line through a given point P parallel to a given line m, you can draw a transversal line through P and intersecting line m. Then construct a line such that corresponding angles $\angle 1$ and $\angle 2$ are congruent.

How does this construction tell you that line n is parallel to line m? By copying $\angle 2$, you created an angle that is congruent to $\angle 1$, as shown in the diagram below. Because the corresponding angles 1 and 2 are congruent, you know that lines m and n are parallel.

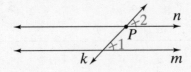

EXAMPLE 6   **Constructing a parallel line**

6 Through a point P not on given line m, construct the line through P parallel to line m.

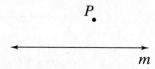

■ SOLUTION

Step 1 Draw any line k through P and intersecting line m. Label the intersection Q. Locate and mark another point R on line m.

Step 2 Copy $\angle PQR$ in such a way that the vertex of the copy is at P and one side of the copy of $\angle PQR$ lies along line k as shown.

Step 1   **Step 2**

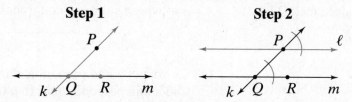

The side of the angle constructed in the second step not lying along line k lies along the line through P parallel to line m.

Once you know how to construct a line parallel to another line, you can use this construction along with others to construct the following:

    parallelogram   rhombus   rectangle   square   trapezoid

Practice

Choose the numeral preceding the word or expression that best completes the statement or answers the question.

1 Centered at points B and C on $\overline{BC}$, arcs are made with the same compass setting and the arcs intersect in two points X and Y. Which statement is not always true?

(1) $\overline{BX} \cong \overline{CX}$

(2) $\overline{BY} \cong \overline{CY}$

(3) $\overline{BX} \cong \overline{XY}$

(4) $\overline{XY}$ contains the midpoint of $\overline{BC}$.

2 Plane R contains line n and T a point on n. How many lines exist that are perpendicular to n and pass through T?

(1) 0   **(3)** two

(2) exactly one   **(4)** infinitely many

Use the following construction for Exercises 3 and 4.

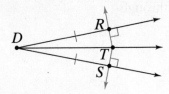

3 Which conclusion is false?

(1) $\angle RDT \cong \angle TDS$

(2) $\overline{TR} \cong \overline{ST}$

(3) $m\angle RDT = 0.5(m\angle RDS)$

(4) $\overline{RD} \cong \overline{TD} \cong \overline{SD}$

4 Which of the following best describes $\overrightarrow{DT}$?

(1) $\overrightarrow{DT}$ is perpendicular to $\overrightarrow{RT}$.

(2) $\overrightarrow{DT}$ is parallel to $\overrightarrow{DR}$.

(3) $\overrightarrow{DT}$ bisects $\angle RDS$.

(4) $\overrightarrow{DT}$ bisects $\overrightarrow{DS}$.

 In Exercises 5–14, copy the given figure, then carry out the specified construction.

5 Construct the locus of points equidistant from points M and N.

$\overset{\bullet}{M}$ $\qquad$ $\overset{\bullet}{N}$

6 Construct the line containing A and perpendicular to the line containing $\overline{BC}$.

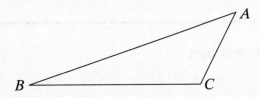

7 Construct the line through G perpendicular to $\overline{ST}$.

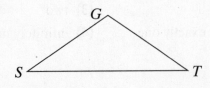

8 Construct the line containing B and parallel to $\overline{EF}$.

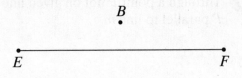

9 Construct the line containing U and perpendicular to $\overline{AW}$.

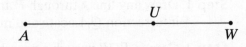

10 Construct a rhombus that is not a square and whose sides are congruent to $\overline{XY}$.

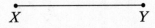

11 Construct a line perpendicular to line p at V and a line perpendicular to p through K.

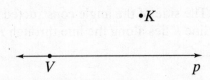

12 Construct the line parallel to $\overline{BZ}$ that contains the midpoint of $\overline{PW}$.

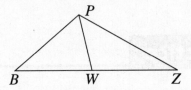

13 Construct the parallelogram whose adjacent sides are $\overline{AB}$ and $\overline{BC}$.

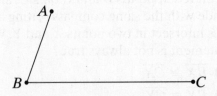

14 Construct the parallelogram whose adjacent sides are $\overline{CZ}$ and $\overline{CD}$, where S and T are the midpoints of $\overline{CZ}$ and $\overline{CD}$, respectively.

Answer all questions in this part. For each question, select the numeral preceding the word or expression that best completes the statement or answers the question.

1 If two planes intersect, then they intersect in exactly

   (1) one line   **(3)** one point

   (2) one plane   **(4)** two points

2 Which three points determine plane B in the diagram below?

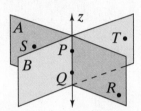

   (1) $P, Q,$ and R **(3)** $R, S,$ and T

   (2) $P, Q,$ and T **(4)** $Q, R,$ and S

3 Which is a possible relationship between two acute angles?
   I vertical   III complementary
   II adjacent   IV supplementary

   (1) I and II only   **(3)** I, II, and III only

   (2) I and III only   **(4)** I, II, III, and IV

4 Given that $\overrightarrow{KM}$ bisects $\angle JKL$ and $m\angle JKM = 74°$, then $m\angle JKL =$

   (1) 26°.   **(3)** 106°.

   (2) 37°.   **(4)** 148°.

5 In the figure below, $\ell \parallel m$ and $m\angle 1 = 48°$. Which other numbered angles have a measure of 48°?

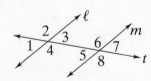

   (1) $\angle 2, \angle 4,$ and $\angle 8$
   (2) $\angle 2, \angle 4, \angle 6,$ and $\angle 8$
   (3) $\angle 3, \angle 5,$ and $\angle 7$
   (4) $\angle 3, \angle 4, \angle 5,$ and $\angle 6$

6 Which of the following statements must be true in order for p to be parallel to q in the diagram below?

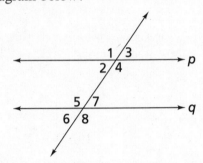

   (1) $m\angle 1 = m\angle 2$ **(3)** $m\angle 1 = m\angle 6$

   (2) $m\angle 1 = m\angle 5$ **(4)** $m\angle 1 = m\angle 7$

7 In the figure below, x is parallel to y. If the $m\angle 1 = 111°$, find $m\angle 6$.

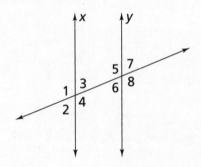

   (1) 69°   **(3)** 111°

   (2) 90°   **(4)** 180°

8 Use a compass to determine which of the following figures shows a line segment whose length is $PQ + XY$.

   (1) $\overset{A}{\bullet}\underline{\hspace{3cm}}\overset{B}{\bullet}$

   (2) $\overset{A}{\bullet}\underline{\hspace{3cm}}\overset{B}{\bullet}$

   (3) $\overset{A}{\bullet}\underline{\hspace{3cm}}\overset{B}{\bullet}\underline{\hspace{1cm}}\overset{C}{\bullet}$

   (4) $\overset{A}{\bullet}\underline{\hspace{3cm}}\overset{B}{\bullet}\underline{\hspace{2cm}}\overset{C}{\bullet}$

9 In the figure below, lines k and l intersect at the point A. What is $m\angle 3$ when $m\angle 1 = 3n + 21$ and $m\angle 2 = 36n + 3$?

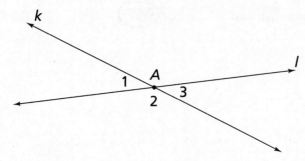

(1) 4   **(3)** 57

(2) 33   **(4)** 147

10 Use a compass to determine which of the following statements about $m\angle A$ and $m\angle B$ is true.

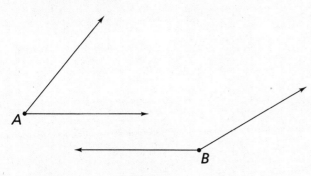

(1) $m\angle A = 2(m\angle B)$

(2) $m\angle B = 2(m\angle A)$

(3) $m\angle A = 3(m\angle B)$

(4) $m\angle B = 3(m\angle A)$

11 Which conclusion can you draw from the construction below?

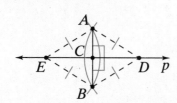

(1) $\overline{AE} \cong \overline{AB}$ **(3)** $\overline{AE} \perp \overline{AD}$

(2) $\overline{AE} \cong \overline{EB}$ **(4)** $\overline{AE} \perp \overline{EB}$

12 Which conclusion about the following construction is true?

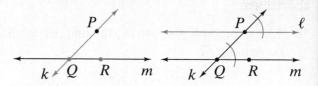

(1) l bisects $\angle PQR$ **(3)** $k \perp m$

(2) $\overline{QR} \cong \overline{QP}$ **(4)** $l \parallel m$

13 In a plane, two lines m and n are perpendicular to the same line at points A and B. Which conclusion is always correct about lines m and n.

(1) $m \perp n$

(2) $m \parallel n$

(3) m and n are skew lines

(4) A and B are midpoints

14 In the diagram, lines l and m are parallel. $\overline{PQ} \perp m$ and $\overline{PR}$ is drawn. What is the distance between l and m.

(1) $\overline{PR}$

(2) $\overline{QR}$

(3) $\overline{PQ}$

(4) none of these segments

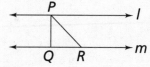

15 $\overrightarrow{QT}$ is the angle bisector of $\angle PQR$. As a result $\angle PQT \cong \angle TQR$. Which conclusion is not always true.

(1) $\angle PQT \cong \angle TQR$

(2) $\overrightarrow{QT}$ is the locus of points equidistant from $\overrightarrow{QP}$ and $\overrightarrow{QR}$.

(3) $\overline{QP} \cong \overline{QR}$

(4) Segments from T to the angle's sides are congruent.

Answer all questions in this part. Clearly indicate the necessary steps, including appropriate formula substitutions, diagrams, graphs, charts, etc.

16 Use a compass to construct the line perpendicular to $\overleftrightarrow{SA}$ and containing R.

R•

17 Use a compass to construct the locus of points equidistant from parallel lines m and n.

The constructions in Exercises 18–19 use $\overline{CD}$ shown below.

C ———— D

18 Construct a square with sides of CD.

19 Construct an isosceles trapezoid with congruent sides of CD.

2 Triangles and Their Properties

A Minimum Distance Problem

A solid waste center is to serve three different municipalities. They wish to locate the new center in a place that minimizes the total distances to the three cities. Your team has been hired to determine the best location for the center. You can assume that all land is available as a site for the center and that there are no obstacles to the building of the solid waste center. The figures below represent two different locations for point S. The task is to locate S such that the sum of the distances from S to P, Q, and R is a minimum.

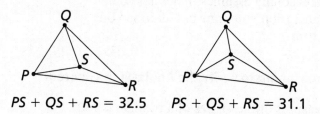

$$PS + QS + RS = 32.5 \qquad PS + QS + RS = 31.1$$

Using an interactive geometry environment to investigate this problem situation can assist in determining a general solution. After formulating a conjecture for the solution research the Fermat-Torricelli Point.

2.1 Classifying Triangles and Angles of a Triangle

In the study of Geometry, the triangle plays a very important role. Many times, the study of other geometric figures is done by decomposing them into triangles and then using the properties of triangles to investigate the more complex figures.

A triangle is a polygon with three sides. We name a triangle by its three vertices, and name its sides by the endpoints of the segments.

In the accompanying figure $\triangle ABC$ has sides $\overline{AB}$, $\overline{AC}$, and $\overline{BC}$.

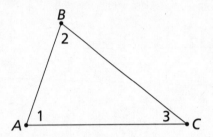

The three angles are the **interior angles** and can be named in the following ways:

$$\angle A \text{ or } \angle BAC \text{ or } \angle CAB \text{ or } \angle 1$$
$$\angle B \text{ or } \angle ABC \text{ or } \angle CBA \text{ or } \angle 2$$
$$\angle C \text{ or } \angle BCA \text{ or } \angle ACB \text{ or } \angle 3$$

Angle-Sum Theorem for Triangles

The sum of the measures of the angles of a triangle is 180°.

In our triangle this means $m\angle 1 + m\angle 2 + m\angle 3 = 180°$.

In example 1 as you justify a conclusion based upon observation, you are using **inductive reasoning.** Inductive reasoning assumes that what you observe will continue to occur. The conclusion you draw based upon your inductive reasoning is called a **conjecture.**

EXAMPLE 1   **Using inductive reasoning to verify the Angle-Sum Theorem**   **MP**

1   Verify that the sum of the measures of the angles of a triangle is 180°.

■ **SOLUTION**

To verify the **Angle-Sum Theorem,** draw a triangle on a piece of paper, number each angle, and then tear off each angle. Now arrange the angles adjacent to each other and observe that they form a straight angle, 180°.

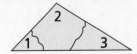 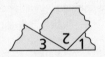

To **prove** a statement means that you justify its truth for **all** cases. When you prove a conclusion from a true statement using known facts, you are using **deductive reasoning.** The conclusion you draw based upon your deductive reasoning is called a **theorem.**

Proof is thought of as a logical argument and this argument can be presented in many forms; an explanation in paragraph form, a flowchart, transformations, or a two-column format.

The truth of the Angle-Sum Theorem can be established more formally by the following two-column proof.

To understand the deductive reasoning, read the proof by first reading a **Statement** (known truth), then the corresponding **Reason** justifying that truth.

EXAMPLE 2   **Proving the Angle-Sum Theorem** ────────────────── (MP)

    Given: $\triangle ABC$
Prove: $m\angle 1 + m\angle 2 + m\angle 3 = 180°$

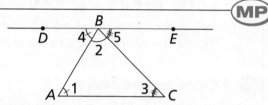

- **SOLUTION**

Statements	Reasons
1. Construct $\overline{DE}$ parallel to $\overline{AC}$ through B.	1. If a point is not on a line, then one and only one line can be constructed parallel to the given line through that point.
2. $\angle DBC$ and $\angle 5$ are supplementary.	2. If 2 angles form a linear pair, then the angles are supplementary.
3. $m\angle DBC + m\angle 5 = 180°$	3. If supplementary, then sum of measures equals 180°.
4. $m\angle DBC = m\angle 4 + m\angle 2$	4. Angle addition (part-part-whole).
5. $m\angle 4 + m\angle 2 + m\angle 5 = 180°$	5. Substitution.
6. $m\angle 4 = m\angle 1; m\angle 5 = m\angle 3$	6. If parallel lines are cut by a transversal, the alternate interior angles are congruent.
7. $m\angle 1 + m\angle 2 + m\angle 3 = 180°$	7. Substitution.

You can use the Angle-Sum Theorem to find the measure of angles in a triangle.

EXAMPLES 3 through 5   **Finding the measures of interior angles** ──────

Find the measures of the interior angles.

  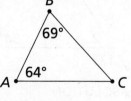

- **SOLUTION**

$m\angle C + 69° + 64° = 180°$
$m\angle C + 133° = 180°$
$m\angle C = 47°$

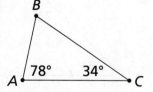

- **SOLUTION**

$m\angle B + 78° + 34° = 180°$
$m\angle B + 112° = 180°$
$m\angle B = 68°$

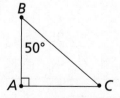

- **SOLUTION**

$m\angle C + 50° + 90° = 180°$
$m\angle C + 140° = 180°$
$m\angle C = 40°$

Notice that many of the Reasons in the two-column proof are written as **If...then** sentences. These If...then sentences are called **Conditional** statements and are often used in a proof. The If-clause represents a known truth **(hypothesis)**, while the Then-clause is the **conclusion** that can be drawn when the hypothesis is met.

| EXAMPLES 6 and 7 | Writing conditionals and identifying the hypothesis and conclusion |

Write each statement as a conditional in *if . . . then* form and identify the hypothesis and conclusion.

6 You can go to the movies if you finish your homework.

■ **SOLUTION**

If you finish your homework, then you can go to the movies.

Hypothesis: you finish your homework
Conclusion: you can go to the movies

7 All triangles have 3 sides.

■ **SOLUTION**

If it is a triangle, then it has 3 sides.

Hypothesis: it is a triangle
Conclusion: it has 3 sides

Note

A conditional statement is false only when the hypothesis is true and the conclusion is false.

When a side of a triangle is extended, the angle formed outside the triangle is called an **exterior angle**.

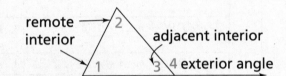

Exterior Angle Theorem

The **remote interior angles** are the nonadjacent angles to the exterior angle. If an angle is an exterior angle, then its measure is equal to the sum of its remote interior angles.

| EXAMPLES 8 through 10 | Finding the measures of exterior angles |

Find the measures of the numbered angles.

8

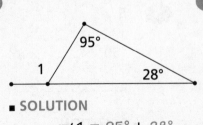

■ SOLUTION

$m\angle 1 = 95° + 28°$
$m\angle 1 = 123°$

9

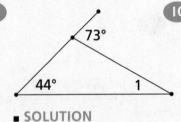

■ SOLUTION

$73° = 44° + m\angle 1$
$29° = m\angle 1$

10

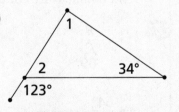

■ SOLUTION

$123° = m\angle 1 + 34°$
$89° = m\angle 1$

$123° + m\angle 2 = 180°$
$m\angle 2 = 57°$

Triangles can be classified by their sides and their angles.

Classification by Sides		
Triangle	Description of Sides	Angle Properties
Equilateral Triangle	All three sides are congruent.	All three angles are congruent and measure 60°.
Isosceles Triangle	Two sides are congruent.	The angles opposite the congruent sides are congruent.
Scalene Triangle	No sides are congruent.	No angles are congruent.

Classification by Angles	
Triangle	Description of Angles
Acute Triangle	All angles are acute.
Right Triangle	One angle is a right angle and the other two are acute.
Obtuse Triangle	One angle is obtuse and the other two are acute.

EXAMPLE 11   **Classifying a triangle**

11 Classify the accompanying triangle by using its sides and angles.

■ SOLUTION

Two sides of this triangle are equal and one angle is obtuse.
This is an **obtuse isosceles triangle**.

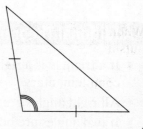

When the If and Then clauses of a conditional are switched, the new conditional is called the **Converse** of the original conditional statement.

Note

A converse statement **sometimes** has the same truth value as its original conditional.

Isosceles Triangle Theorem and Its Converse

If two sides of a triangle are congruent, then the angles opposite those sides are congruent.

The converse is also true:

If two angles of a triangle are congruent, then the sides opposite the angles are also congruent.

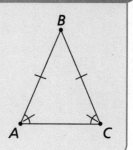

EXAMPLE 12   **Verifying the Isosceles Triangle Theorem**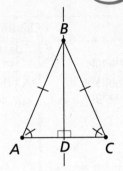

MP

12 On a piece of patty paper, construct any isosceles triangle and use it to verify the Isosceles Triangle theorem.

▪ **SOLUTION**

After the isosceles triangle is constructed, construct the perpendicular bisector of the base. The perpendicular bisector should pass through the vertex of the triangle. Fold the paper on the perpendicular bisector. $\angle A$ coincides with $\angle C$ and so $\angle A \cong \angle C$. So, if two sides of a triangle are congruent, then the angles opposite those congruent sides are congruent.

Equilateral Triangle Corollaries

If a triangle is equilateral, then it is equiangular.

   If $AB = BC = AC$, then $m\angle A = m\angle B = m\angle C$.

If a triangle is equiangular, then it is equilateral.

   If $m\angle A = m\angle B = m\angle C$, then $AB = BC = AC$.

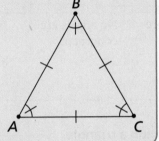

Note

A **corollary** is a theorem that follows directly from a previously proved theorem.

Additional Theorems About Angles

- If a triangle is a right triangle, then the acute angles are complementary.
- All right angles are congruent.
- If two angles are both congruent and supplementary, then they are right angles.
- If two angles of one triangle are congruent to two angles of another, the third angles are congruent.

36

Practice

Choose the numeral preceding the word or expression that best completes the statement or answers the question.

1 If two angles of a triangle measure 55° and 25°, then the triangle is

    (1) right.   **(3)** obtuse.

    (2) acute.   **(4)** isosceles.

2 The triangle in the accompanying figure can best be described as

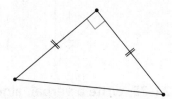

    (1) acute, scalene.

    (2) right, isosceles.

    (3) right, scalene.

    (4) acute, isosceles.

3 The exterior angle of a triangle is represented by $5x - 15$, and the two remote interior angles are represented by $2x$ and $x + 5$, respectively. What are the measures of the interior angles of this triangle?

    (1) 10°, 15°, 20°

    (2) 15°, 25°, 35°

    (3) 10°, 35°, 145°

    (4) 15°, 20°, 145°

4 Which of the following types of triangles **cannot** be a right triangle?

    (1) equilateral

    (2) scalene

    (3) isosceles

    (4) all of the above

5 Which term best describes the acute angles of a right triangle?

    (1) equal

    (2) supplementary

    (3) complementary

    (4) obtuse

6 If an exterior angle of a right triangle is 160°, then the measure of the remote interior angle is

    (1) 20°.   **(3)** 90°.

    (2) 70°.   **(4)** 110°.

7 In triangle CAT the measure of $\angle A$ is 50° and the measure of $\angle T$ is 30°. Classify triangle CAT by both its sides and its angles.

8 $\triangle MNO$ is isosceles with $\overline{MO} \cong \overline{NO}$. If MO is represented by $3x + 11$, NO is represented by $5x - 9$, and MN is represented by $7x + 3$, determine the perimeter of $\triangle MNO$.

In Exercises 9–11, write the given statement as a conditional, then form its converse. Determine if each is True or False.

9 All right angles are congruent.

10 Parallel lines form congruent alternate interior angles.

11 A midpoint forms two congruent segments.

Use the accompanying figure to answer Exercises 12–15.

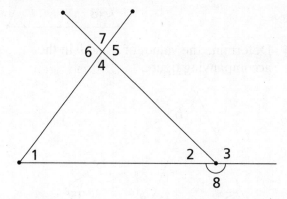

12 Name the remote interior angles for angle 5.

13 How are angles 4 and 7 related?

14 $m\angle 1 + m\angle 4 = m\angle ?$

15 Name the exterior angles at the vertex of angle 4.

Use the following figure to answer Exercises 16–17.

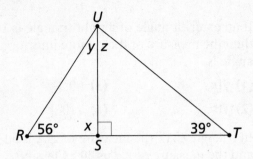

16 Determine the values of x, y, and z. Classify triangle RTU.

17 If $\overrightarrow{TR}$ is extended through R to a point V, what is the measure of exterior angle URV?

18 For any triangle, draw all six exterior angles. Label them 1–6.

19 The angles of a triangle are in the ratio of 3:4:5. Determine the measure of each angle.

20 Determine the value of s in the accompanying figure.

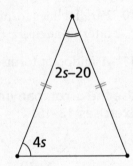

21 Determine the values of a and b in the accompanying figure.

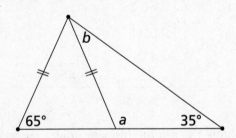

In Exercises 22–23, determine the value of x.

22

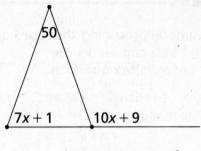

23

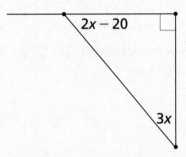

In Exercises 24–25, write a verbal, algebraic, or two-column argument to prove the following theorems. (MP)

24 If a triangle is a right triangle, then the acute angles are complementary.

25 If two angles are both congruent and supplementary, then they are both right angles.

26 Match the **Reasons** labeled A–E, to the **Statements** below to prove the Exterior Angle Theorem.

A. If linear pair, then angles supplementary

B. Subtraction property of =.

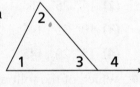

C. If triangle, then sum of the angles is 180°

D. Substitution

E. If supplementary, then sum of the angles is 180°

Statements

1. $m\angle 1 + m\angle 2 + m\angle 3 = 180°$

2. $\angle 3$ and $\angle 4$ are supplementary.

3. $m\angle 3 + m\angle 4 = 180°$

4. $m\angle 1 + m\angle 2 + m\angle 3 = m\angle 3 + m\angle 4$

5. $m\angle 1 + m\angle 2 = m\angle 4$

2.2 Inequalities in Triangles

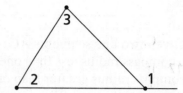

Using inductive reasoning, you will investigate some inequality relationships in triangles.

In any part-part-whole relationship, the key concept is that the whole is equal to the sum of its parts.

So, if $10 = 7 + 3$, then $10 > 7$ and $10 > 3$.

Whole:	10	
Parts:	7	3

In the drawing to the right, we will apply this concept to the Exterior Angle Theorem. You know $m\angle 1 = m\angle 2 + m\angle 3$ so then $m\angle 1 > m\angle 2$ and $m\angle 1 > m\angle 3$.

By this reasoning, you have justified the inequality relationship of a triangle's exterior angle.

Exterior Angle Corollary

The measure of an exterior angle of a triangle is greater than the measure of each of its remote interior angles.

$$m\angle 1 > m\angle 2 \text{ and } m\angle 1 > m\angle 3$$

EXAMPLE 1   Using the Exterior Angle Corollary   MP

 In the accompanying figure $QT = ST$.
Explain why $m\angle 1 > m\angle 3$.

SOLUTION

$m\angle 1 = m\angle 2$ by the Isosceles Triangle Theorem, and $m\angle 2 > m\angle 3$ by the Exterior Angle Corollary. By substituting $m\angle 1$ for $m\angle 2$, you get $m\angle 1 > m\angle 3$.

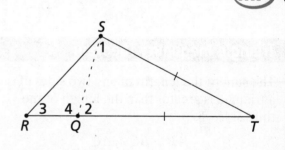

Use two pencils and make an angle. Stretch an elastic band near the ends of the pencils. What happens to the size of the elastic band as you make the pencil angle larger? Apply this reasoning to the angles of a triangle and the length of the sides opposite those angles.

Larger Side Theorem and Its Converse

Larger Side Theorem If one side of a triangle is larger than another, then the angle opposite the larger side is the larger angle.

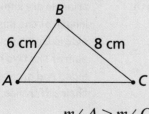

$$m\angle A > m\angle C$$

Converse of the Larger Side Theorem
If one angle of a triangle is larger than another, then the side opposite the larger angle is the larger side.

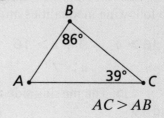

$$AC > AB$$

EXAMPLE 2   Ordering the parts of a triangle

2 Order the measurements of the parts of the accompanying triangle from least to greatest.

- **SOLUTION**

$m\angle B = 34°$, therefore $m\angle B < m\angle A < m\angle C$ and $AC < BC < AB$.

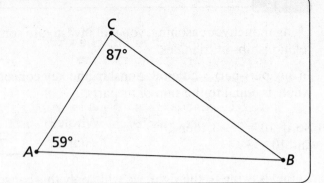

Given two line segments $\overline{AC}$ and $\overline{DF}$, try to construct isosceles $\triangle ABC$ using a compass radius less than one-half of AC. Construct isosceles $\triangle DEF$ using a compass radius greater than one-half of DF. Do your constructions look like the figures below? Think how these constructions help justify the triangle inequality theorem.

(MP)

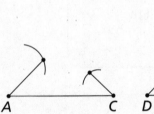 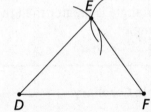

Triangle Inequality Theorem

The sum of the lengths of any two sides of a triangle is greater than the length of the third side.

$$AB + BC > AC$$
$$AC + BC > AB$$
$$AB + AC > BC$$

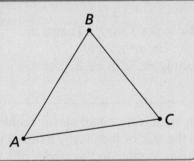

EXAMPLE 3   Determining possible lengths for the side of a triangle

3 A triangle has sides of length 9 and 16. What are possible lengths for the missing side?

- **SOLUTION**

Call the missing side n. Using the Triangle Inequality Theorem, you know that the following inequalities must be true:

$9 + 16 > n$	$9 + n > 16$	$16 + n > 9$
$15 > n$	$n > 7$	True for any value of n

Therefore $7 < n < 15$. The missing side must have a length between 7 and 15.

Note

When two sides of a triangle are known, the length of the missing side is less than the sum of the two known sides and greater than their difference.

40

Practice

Choose the numeral preceding the word or expression that best completes the statement or answers the question.

1 If the sides of a triangle are 8 and 14, which of the following is *not* the length of the third side?

(1) 17.5   **(2)** 12   **(3)** 10.5   **(4)** 6

2 Which of the following are *not* sides of a triangle?

(1) 11 cm, 12 cm, 15 cm

(2) 1 cm, 15 cm, 15 cm

(3) 2 in., 3 in., 6 in.

(4) 2 yd, 9 yd, 10 yd

3 In $\triangle ABC, m\angle A = 35°, m\angle B = 75°,$ $m\angle C = 70°$. Which is the longest side?

(1) $\overline{AB}$

(2) $\overline{AC}$

(3) $\overline{BC}$

(4) cannot be determined

4 Which statement is true about the accompanying figure?

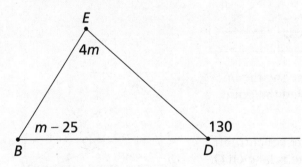

(1) $ED > EB$

(2) $ED > BD$

(3) $\overline{BE}$ is the shortest side.

(4) $\overline{BD}$ is the longest side.

Use the figure below to answer Exercises 5–6.

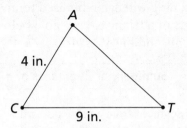

5 What are the possible integer values for the length of side AT?

6 Which angle has the smallest measure?

7 Can you construct the triangle sketched below? Explain why or why not. **MP**

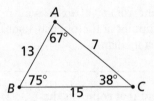

8 Fill in the reasons for each step of the following argument, which proves the following theorem: *If two sides of a triangle are not congruent, then the larger angle lies opposite the larger side.*

Given: $\triangle TOP, PO > PT$
Prove: $m\angle OTP > m\angle 3$

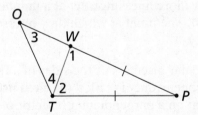

Statements	Reasons
1. Construct $\overline{TW}$ such that $TP = WP$.	
2. $\triangle TPW$ is isosceles.	
3. $m\angle 1 = m\angle 2$	
4. $m\angle OTP = m\angle 4 + m\angle 2$	
5. $m\angle OTP > m\angle 2$	
6. $m\angle OTP > m\angle 1$	
7. $m\angle 1 > m\angle 3$	
8. $m\angle OTP > m\angle 3$	

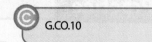
Inductive reasoning will again be used to investigate important segments, lines, and points of a triangle. The table below is a summary of important triangle segments and lines.

Summary of Segments of a Triangle		
Altitude	Segment from a vertex drawn perpendicular to the opposite side. $\overline{AB}$ is an altitude.	
Angle bisector	Segment part of a ray which divides an angle into 2 congruent angles. $\overline{CD}$ is an angle bisector.	
Median	Segment from a vertex drawn to the midpoint of the opposite side. $\overline{MN}$ is a median.	
Midsegment	Segment that connects the midpoints of two sides of a triangle. $\overline{PQ}$ is a midsegment.	
Perpendicular Bisector	A line perpendicular to a side at its midpoint. $\overleftrightarrow{XY}$ is a perpendicular bisector.	

When three or more lines intersect at a unique point, we say the lines are **concurrent**. The point at which they intersect is called the **point of concurrency**.

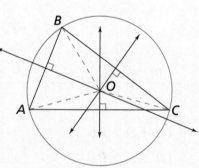

The perpendicular bisectors of the sides of a triangle are concurrent. The point of concurrency is called the **circumcenter,** and is labeled **O**. Since any point on a perpendicular bisector of a segment is equidistant to the segment's endpoints, the circumcenter is equidistant to all three vertices of the triangle, $OA = OB = OC$. The **circumscribed circle,** constructed with center at O and radius OA, will pass through all vertices of the triangle.

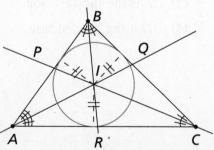

The three angle bisectors of a triangle are also concurrent. Their point of concurrency is called the **incenter** of the triangle, and is labeled I. Since any point on an angle bisector is equidistant to the angle's sides, the incenter is equidistant to all three sides of the triangle. That distance is the length of the perpendicular from I to any side, $IP = IQ = IR$. The **inscribed circle,** constructed with center I and radius IP, will touch each side of the triangle at exactly one point.

The point of concurrency for all the medians in a triangle is called the **centroid,** or **center of gravity.** The centroid is labeled *G*.

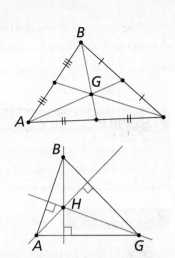

The three altitudes of a triangle are concurrent. This point of concurrency is called the **orthocenter** and labeled *H*.

Summary of the Centers of a Triangle

Circumcenter (O)	Center of the circumscribed circle	Point of concurrency of the perpendicular bisectors of the sides of a triangle
Incenter (I)	Center of the inscribed circle	Point of concurrency of the angle bisectors of the triangle
Centroid (G)	Center of gravity or balancing point	Point of concurrency of the medians of the triangle
Orthocenter (H)		Point of concurrency of the altitudes of the triangle

If you construct the four centers of a triangle, you should make some interesting observations.

EXAMPLE 1   **Finding points of concurrency** ———————————— (MP)

1   Have students work in groups. Each group needs patty paper, or compass and straightedge, or access to interactive geometry software. Each group will be given a triangle type to investigate. Triangle types include acute, equilateral, isosceles, obtuse, and right triangles.

Task: Construct all four points of concurrency for your assigned triangle type. Discuss your findings.

■ SOLUTION

Acute Triangle	**Obtuse Triangle**	**Right Triangle**
All interior centers	two interior, two exterior centers	two interior centers, two on the triangle

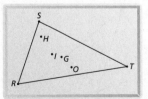

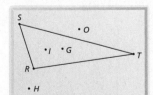

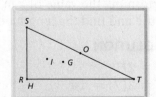

Isosceles Triangle: All centers are collinear.

Equilateral Triangle: All centers are the same point.

The line passing through the orthocenter, the centroid, and the circumcenter is called the **Euler line** because Euler first discovered the colinearality in 1765.

The midsegment and proportional reasoning is used in an important theorem about the centroid.

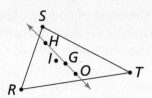

The Median Measure Theorem

The centroid is located $\frac{2}{3}$ of the distance from the vertex to the opposite side and divides the median into segments whose lengths are in the ratio of 2:1.

EXAMPLE 2 **Verifying the Median Measure Theorem** —————————————— MP

2   Using $\triangle ABC$ with its medians $\overline{AM}$ and $\overline{BN}$, justify that $\dfrac{\overline{BG}}{\overline{GN}} = \dfrac{2}{1}$.

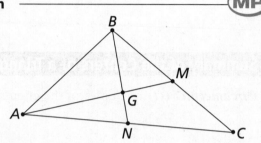

■ SOLUTION

Using interactive geometry software draw $\triangle ABC$. Using the construction tools of the software construct the midpoints N and M of sides $\overline{AC}$ and $\overline{BC}$ respectively. Draw $\overline{AM}$ and $\overline{BN}$ and label their point of intersection G. Using the measuring tool measure $\overline{BG}$ and $\overline{GN}$. Make sure to drag the vertices of $\triangle ABC$ to verify that the relationship holds for many cases. See several examples below. Note in each case the calculated value of the ration remains invariant.

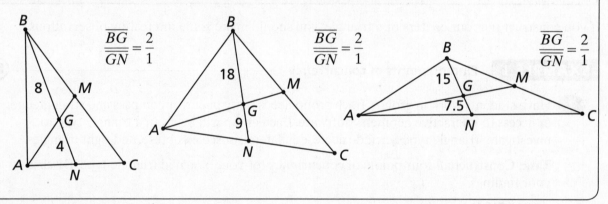

You can apply the Median Measure Theorem to find missing lengths of triangles.

EXAMPLE 3 **Finding the length of a side** —————————

3   Determine the value of x in the accompanying figure and find the length of BD.

■ SOLUTION

$BF = 2FD$

$BF = 2(7) = 14$

$BD = 14 + 7 = 21$

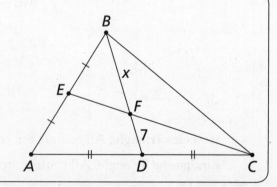

Choose the numeral preceding the word or expression that best completes the statement or answers the question.

1 Which triangle center is *never* outside the triangle?

(1) orthocenter only

(2) incenter only

(3) both orthocenter and circumcenter

(4) both incenter and centroid

2 In a right triangle, which center is the midpoint of the hypotenuse?

(1) orthocenter   **(3)** incenter

(2) circumcenter   **(4)** centroid

3 In the accompanying diagram $\overline{RN}$ and $\overline{TM}$ are medians of $\triangle RST$. If $TM = 12z^2 - 9k$, which expression represents TW?

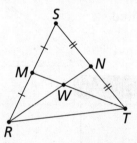

(1) $4z^2 - 3k$ **(3)** $6z^2 - 3k$

(2) $4z^2 - 9k$ **(4)** $8z^2 - 6k$

4 $\overline{AK}$ is a median of a triangle. The length of $\overline{AK}$ is 15. What is the distance from the vertex A to the centroid?

(1) 5   **(2)** 10   **(3)** 15   **(4)** 30

5 In $\triangle ABC$, $\overline{AM}$, $\overline{BN}$, and $\overline{CW}$ are medians with a point of intersection P. If $AM = 12$, what is the length of PM?

(1) 4   **(2)** 8   **(3)** 12   **(4)** 16

6 What is the segment drawn from a vertex to the midpoint of the opposite side is called?

(1) altitude

(2) median

(3) angle bisector

(4) perpendicular bisector

7 In an obtuse triangle, which of the segments will be drawn to the triangle's exterior?

(1) altitude

(2) median

(3) angle bisector

(4) perpendicular bisector

8 In an isosceles triangle, which of the segments, if drawn from the vertex angle to the triangle's base, will coincide?

(1) altitude and median

(2) angle bisector and perpendicular bisector

(3) angle bisector and median

(4) all the above

9 In a scalene triangle, which of the segments has a length that represents the distance from a vertex to its opposite side?

(1) altitude

(2) angle bisector

(3) median

(4) perpendicular bisector

In Exercises 10–11, copy $\triangle ABC$, then construct the required circle.

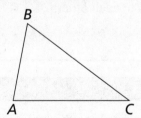

10 Circumscribed circle

11 Inscribed circle

12 Draw a triangle on a piece of paper. Construct an equilateral triangle on each side of the triangle. Connect each vertex of the original triangle to the vertex of the equilateral triangle constructed on the opposite side with a segment. What do you notice about these three segments?

2.4 A Special Right Triangle Relationship

G-SRT.6

The figure shown is a right triangle with sides a, b, and c. The side opposite the right angle, called the **hypotenuse,** is the longest side. Each of the sides, a and b, that form the right angle is called a **leg** of the right triangle.

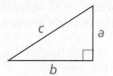

For two positive numbers a and b, the number x such that $\frac{a}{x} = \frac{x}{b}$ is called the **geometric mean** of a and b. Solving this proportion leads to $x = \sqrt{ab}$. x is also referred to as the **mean proportional** between a and b.

EXAMPLE 1   **Solving for the geometric mean**

   What is the geometric mean (mean proportional) of 2 and 8?

■ **SOLUTION**

$$\frac{2}{x} = \frac{x}{8} \qquad x = -\sqrt{16}$$
$$x^2 = 16 \quad \text{or} \quad x = -4 \; \text{reject}$$
$$x = \sqrt{16}$$
$$x = 4$$

> **Note**
>
> Only the positive square root is used since in geometry both length and angle measure are represented as 0 or a positive value.

Consider the accompanying figure in which right triangle ABC has an altitude drawn from the right angle to the hypotenuse ($\overline{BD}$). This altitude divides the triangle into two right triangles, $\triangle ADB$ and $\triangle BDC$.

Altitude Drawn to Hypotenuse Theorem

The altitude drawn to the hypotenuse of a right triangle divides the triangle into two triangles that are similar to the original and to each other.

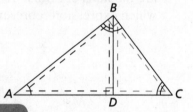

Corollary 1

The altitude drawn to the hypotenuse of a right triangle is the mean proportional between the segments of the hypotenuse.

That is, $\frac{AD}{BD} = \frac{BD}{DC}$.

 MP

Corollary 2

When the altitude is drawn to the hypotenuse of a right triangle, each leg of the triangle is the geometric mean between the whole hypotenuse and the segment of the hypotenuse attached to the leg.

That is, $\frac{AC}{AB} = \frac{AB}{AD}$ and $\frac{AC}{BC} = \frac{BC}{DC}$.

> **Note**
>
> Altitude • Hypotenuse
> = Leg 1 • Leg 2

EXAMPLE 2   **Verifying the Altitude Drawn to Hypotenuse Theorem**

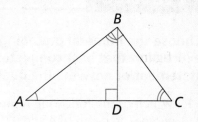

2 Verify that $\triangle ABC \sim \triangle ADB \sim \triangle BDC$.

■ **SOLUTION**

$\triangle ABC \sim \triangle ADB$ because $\angle A$ is in both triangles and both contain a right angle. Therefore, the triangles are similar by the AA Theorem. Likewise, $\triangle ABC \sim \triangle BDC$ because $\angle C$ is in both triangles and both contain a right angle. Again, the AA Theorem applies. By the transitive property, $\triangle ABC \sim \triangle ADB \sim \triangle BDC$.

You can use the geometric mean and the Altitude Drawn to Hypotenuse Theorem to solve a variety of real-world problems.

EXAMPLES 3 and 4   **Applying proportions**

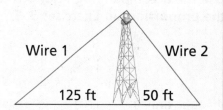

3 A radio tower has two guy wires attached at the top forming a right angle. One is located 50 ft from the base of the tower and the other is 125 ft from the base of the tower. Find the height of the tower, rounded to the nearest foot.

■ **SOLUTION**

Let h represent the height of the tower. The tower is the altitude to the hypotenuse of a right triangle, which establishes the following proportion.

$$\frac{125}{h} = \frac{h}{50} \Rightarrow h^2 = 6250$$
$$h = \sqrt{6250} = 25\sqrt{10} \approx 79 \, ft$$

4 At Panguitch Lake, the first-aid station is located directly across the lake from the lodge. The beach is 200 yards directly east of the first-aid station. The paths from the lodge to the beach and from the lodge to the campground form a right angle. If the distance from the lodge to the beach is 450 yards, what is the distance from the beach to the campground?

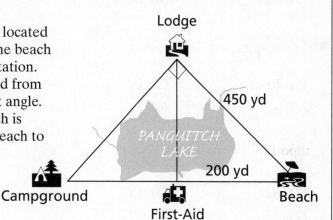

■ **SOLUTION**

Let x = the distance from the beach to the campground.

$$\frac{x}{450} = \frac{450}{200}$$
$$200x = 202{,}500$$
$$x = \frac{202{,}500}{200} = 1012.5 \, yd$$

Choose the numeral preceding the word or expression that best completes the statement or answers the question.

1 Which of the following represents the geometric mean of 4 and 9?

   (1) 6   **(3)** 18

   (2) 6.5   **(4)** 36

2 8 is the geometric mean between 4 and which of the following values?

   (1) 64   **(3)** 16

   (2) 24   **(4)** 4

Use the accompanying figure to complete the proportions in Exercises 3–5.

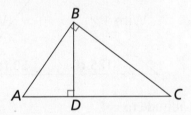

3 $\dfrac{AC}{?} = \dfrac{?}{AD}$

   (1) BD **(3)** DC

   (2) AB **(4)** BC

4 $\dfrac{DC}{?} = \dfrac{?}{AD}$

   (1) BD **(3)** DC

   (2) AB **(4)** BC

5 $\dfrac{AC}{BC} = \dfrac{BC}{?}$

   (1) BD **(3)** DC

   (2) AB **(4)** BC

In Exercises 6–10, determine the value of the variables.

6

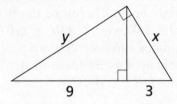

7

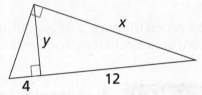

8

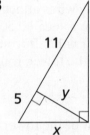

9

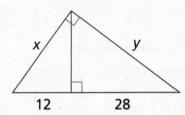

10

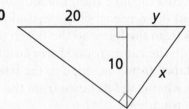

Pythagorean Theorem
2.5 and Its Converse

You can use the Pythagorean Theorem to find an unknown side length of a right triangle.

The Pythagorean Theorem

In any right triangle, the sum of the squares of the lengths of the legs is equal to the square of the length of the hypotenuse. That is,
$leg^2 + leg^2 = hypotenuse^2$.

EXAMPLE 1   Justifying the Pythagorean Theorem

MP

1. Use the accompanying figure to algebraically justify the Pythagorean Theorem.

   ■ **SOLUTION**

   The area of the large square is $(a + b)^2 = a^2 + 2ab + b^2$.
   The parts of the large square are 4 right triangles and the dark blue square. Their combined area is
   $$4(\tfrac{1}{2}ab) + c^2 = 2ab + c^2$$
   Whole is the sum of parts, so
   $$a^2 + 2ab + b^2 = 2ab + c^2$$
   $$a^2 + b^2 = c^2$$

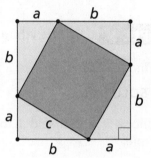

EXAMPLES 2 and 3   Finding lengths of sides in a right triangle by using the Pythagorean Theorem

2. Find n in the right triangle below.

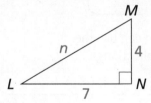

   ■ **SOLUTION**

   The unknown n is the length of the hypotenuse.
   $$n^2 = 7^2 + 4^2$$
   $$n^2 = 65$$
   $$n = \pm\sqrt{65} \approx \pm 8.06$$
   $$n = \sqrt{65} \text{ units, or about 8.06 units}$$

3. Find z in the right triangle below.

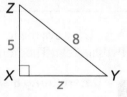

   ■ **SOLUTION**

   The unknown z is the length of a leg.
   $$8^2 = z^2 + 5^2$$
   $$39 = z^2$$
   $$z = \pm\sqrt{39} \approx \pm 6.24$$
   $$z = \sqrt{39} \text{ units, or about 6.24 units}$$

If the lengths of all three sides of a right triangle are counting numbers, they form a **Pythagorean Triple.** The following are some examples of side lengths that form Pythagorean Triples written as the lengths of leg, leg, hypotenuse.

a) 3, 4, 5   b) 5, 12, 13   c) 8, 15, 17   d) 7, 24, 25

EXAMPLE 4 **Proving Pythagorean Triples**

 Determine if 3, 4, 5 and 4, 6, 8 are sets of Pythagorean Triples.

■ **SOLUTION**

Apply the Pythagorean Theorem to each set of numbers and determine if the resulting equation is true.

$3^2 + 4^2 \stackrel{?}{=} 5^2$ $\qquad$ $4^2 + 6^2 \stackrel{?}{=} 8^2$

$9 + 16 \stackrel{?}{=} 25$ $\qquad$ $16 + 36 \stackrel{?}{=} 64$

$\qquad 25 \stackrel{?}{=} 25$ $\qquad\qquad 52 \stackrel{?}{=} 64$

True $\qquad\qquad\qquad$ **False**

3, 4, 5 is Pythagorean Triple; 4, 6, 8 is not.

Multiples of Pythagorean Triples are also Pythagorean Triples.

EXAMPLE 5 **Using Pythagorean Triples ratios**

 Find the hypotenuse of a right triangle whose legs are 45 and 108.

■ **SOLUTION**

Since $45 = 5(9)$ and $108 = 12(9)$, then THINK 5-12-13 Pythagorean triple.

Therefore, the hypotenuse $= 9(13) = 117$

The Converse of the Pythagorean Theorem

If a, b, and c are the lengths of the sides of a triangle such that $a^2 + b^2 = c^2$, then the triangle is a right triangle with hypotenuse of length c.

Since the hypotenuse is always the longest side of a right triangle, you can use the Converse of the Pythagorean Theorem to find out if a triangle is a right triangle.

EXAMPLE 6 **Determining if side lengths form a right triangle**

 Do 5, 12, and 14 determine a right triangle?

■ **SOLUTION**

Since the hypotenuse of a right triangle must be the longest side, check to see if $5^2 + 12^2$ equals 14^2.

$$5^2 + 12^2 = 169 \qquad 14^2 = 196$$

Since $169 \neq 196$, these numbers *cannot be the sides of a right triangle.*

The next example shows how you can use the Pythagorean Theorem to solve problems.

EXAMPLE 7   **Solving problems involving the Pythagorean Theorem**

7 A ladder is placed against the side of a building. To climb this kind of ladder safely, the ladder must be placed against the building at a height that is three times the distance from the foot of the ladder to the base of the building. To the nearest tenth of a foot, how far from the base of a building should the foot of a 24-foot ladder be placed to meet safety recommendations?

■ **SOLUTION**

Step 1 Draw a sketch. Let x represent the distance from the foot of the ladder to the base of the building.

Step 2 Use the Pythagorean Theorem to solve for x.

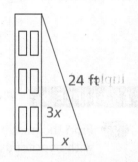

$$x^2 + (3x)^2 = 24^2$$
$$10x^2 = 576$$
$$x^2 = 57.6$$
$$x = \sqrt{57.6} \approx 7.6$$

The foot of the ladder should be placed about 7.6 feet from the base of the building.

There are 2 special right triangles that have characteristics that make it possible to apply the Pythagorean theorem knowing only the length of one side.

An isosceles right triangle with congruent sides represented as s and congruent base angles of 45° is called a 45°-45°-90° triangle.

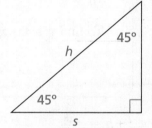

Let each leg = s.
Then $h^2 = s^2 + s^2$
      $h^2 = 2s^2$
$\sqrt{h^2} = \sqrt{2s^2}$
      $h = s\sqrt{2}$

So, in an isosceles 45°-45°-90° triangle:

hypotenuse = leg · $\sqrt{2}$ and hypotenuse ÷ $\sqrt{2}$ = leg

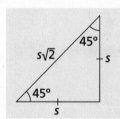

EXAMPLE 8   **Finding lengths in a 45°-45°-90° triangle**

8 Find the length of the legs of the given right triangle with hypotenuse length 20.

■ **SOLUTION**

Since hypotenuse ÷ $\sqrt{2}$ = leg, then $20 ÷ \sqrt{2} = 10\sqrt{2} \approx 14.1$

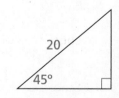

The other special right triangle is called a 30°-60°-90° triangle. To understand its special attributes, think of it as half of an equilateral triangle. The figure shows that the segment labeled a is an angle bisector forming two angles of 30°. This segment a is also a perpendicular bisector forming two segments of length x.

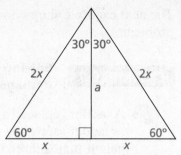

So in a 30°-60°-90° triangle:

side opposite 30° angle = x
hypotenuse = 2 · side opposite 30° angle = $2x$

using the Pythagorean theorem...

side opposite 60° angle = a = side opposite 30° angle · $\sqrt{3} = x\sqrt{3}$.

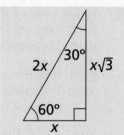

EXAMPLE 9   **Finding lengths in a 30°-60°-90° triangle**

 Find the missing lengths in the given right triangle with hypotenuse 14 units.

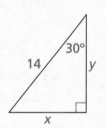

■ **SOLUTION**

To find x: hypotenuse = 2 · side opposite 30° angle

$$14 = 2x$$
$$x = 7$$

To find y: side opposite 60° angle = side opposite 30° angle · $\sqrt{3}$,

$$y = 7 \cdot \sqrt{3}$$
$$y \approx 12.1$$

Choose the numeral preceding the word or expression that best completes the statement or answers the question.

1 Which of the following is the measure of the side of a square whose diagonal is 14?

(1) 7 (2) $7\sqrt{2}$ (3) $7\sqrt{3}$ (4) 14

2 Which of the following is not a Pythagorean Triple?

(1) 15, 20, 25 (3) 5, 12, 13

(2) 7, 24, 25 (4) 12, 16, 30

3 The distance from home plate to first base on a baseball field is 90 feet. How far is it from home plate to second base?

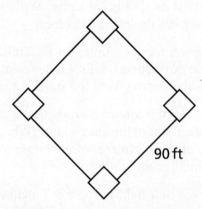

90 ft

(1) $\sqrt{90}$ ft (3) $90\sqrt{2}$ ft

(2) 90 ft (4) $90\sqrt{3}$ ft

4 The length of the hypotenuse of an isosceles right triangle is $10\sqrt{6}$ ft. What is the length of the leg?

(1) $5\sqrt{3}$ ft (3) $10\sqrt{3}$ ft

(2) $5\sqrt{6}$ ft (4) $10\sqrt{12}$ ft

5 The hypotenuse of a right triangle measures 20 in. and one of its legs measures 8 in. Determine the length of the other leg in simplest radical form.

(1) $\sqrt{336}$ in. (3) $2\sqrt{42}$ in.

(2) $\sqrt{168}$ in. (4) $4\sqrt{21}$ in.

6 Determine the area of the triangle in the accompanying figure.

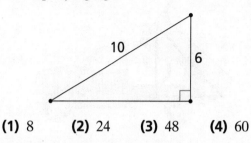

10 6

(1) 8 (2) 24 (3) 48 (4) 60

7 Determine the area of the shaded region in the accompanying figure.

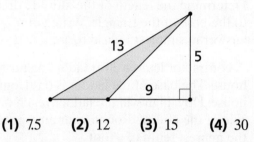

13 5 9

(1) 7.5 (2) 12 (3) 15 (4) 30

8 Determine the value of a such that a, 13, and 85 form a Pythagorean Triple.

(1) $7\sqrt{2}$

(2) 84

(3) $\sqrt{7394}$

(4) 98

9 The longer leg of a 30°-60°-90° triangle is 6. What is the length of the hypotenuse?

(1) 12

(2) $4\sqrt{3}$

(3) $3\sqrt{2}$

(4) $2\sqrt{3}$

10 The lengths of the sides of a 45°-45°-90° right triangle is 8. What is the length of the hypotenuse?

(1) 4 (3) $8\sqrt{2}$

(2) $4\sqrt{2}$ (4) 16

11 A raised truck bed is shown in the accompanying figure. The base of the right triangle shown is 6 ft and the length of the bed is 10 ft. How high does the bed rise?

12 An isosceles triangle has legs that measure 20 cm and a base that measures 16 cm. Determine the length of the altitude drawn to the base of the triangle. Write your answer in simplest radical form.

13 A contractor leans a 30-ft ladder against a house. The base of the ladder is 6 ft from the house. How high will the ladder reach on the side of the house? Round your answer to the nearest tenth of a foot.

14 A rectangular prism that measures $3 \times 4 \times 12$ has a straw placed from the corner of one face to the corner diagonally opposite on the parallel face as shown in the accompanying figure. What is the length of the straw?

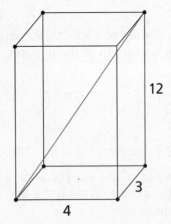

15 The length of the altitude of an equilateral triangle is 1 m. Determine the length of the side of the triangle. Write your answer in simplest radical form.

16 Determine all of the missing lengths in triangle ABC.

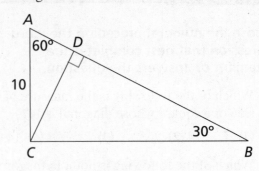

17 Determine the length of the diagonal of a cube if its side has a length of 4 units. Write your answer in simplest radical form.

18 Do the numbers 11, 20, and 23 form a Pythagorean Triple?

19 Determine the length of the diagonal of a square if its area is 256 units². Write your answer in simplest radical form.

20 A person travels 5 miles north, 2 miles east, 1 mile north, and finally 4 miles east. How far is the person from the starting point?

21 The side of a square is equal to the length of the diagonal of another square. What is the ratio of the perimeter of the larger square to the smaller square?

22 One leg of a right triangle is 7 inches longer than the other. The length of the hypotenuse is 13 inches. Find the lengths of the two legs algebraically.

23 The length of the hypotenuse of a 30°-60°-90° triangle is $4\sqrt{3}$. What is the area of this triangle?

24 The lengths of the side of a triangle are $\sqrt{50}$, 5, and 5. Classify the triangle as right, acute, or obtuse.

25 The lengths of the legs of a right triangle measure x and $(x + 2)$ in. The hypotenuse of the triangle measures $2\sqrt{5}$ in. Find x.

2.6 Right-Triangle Trigonometry

G.SRT.8

In a right triangle, the sides of the triangle have names relative to an acute angle such as $\angle A$. In the diagram below, $\overline{AC}$ is the leg adjacent to $\angle A$ and $\overline{BC}$ is the leg opposite $\angle A$. Relative to $\angle B$, $\overline{BC}$ is the leg adjacent to $\angle B$ and $\overline{AC}$ is the leg opposite $\angle B$.

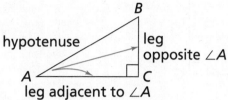

The diagram at the right shows three right triangles, $\triangle ABC$, $\triangle ADE$, and $\triangle AFG$, nesting inside one another. All three triangles are similar to one another. So, the ratios below are equal.

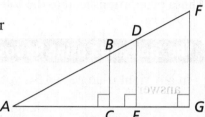

$$\frac{BC}{AC} = \frac{DE}{AE} = \frac{FG}{AG}$$

Notice each ratio represents the length of the leg opposite $\angle A$ to the length of the leg adjacent to $\angle A$ and that these ratios are equal.

The Tangent Ratio

In any right triangle $\triangle ABC$ with right angle at C, the ratio of the length of the leg opposite an acute angle such as $\angle A$ to the length of the leg adjacent to that angle is a constant called the **tangent** of $\angle A$, denoted tan A.

$$\text{tangent of } \angle A = \frac{\text{length of leg opposite } \angle A}{\text{length of leg adjacent to } \angle A}$$

You can use a calculator when working with the tangent ratio. The display at the right shows tan 75° and the measure of the angle whose tangent is 0.75. Notice that, on many calculators, when you press ｜2nd｜ then ｜TAN｜ the display shows $\tan^{-1}$ and is read "the measure of the angle whose tangent is 0.75."

```
tan(75)
          3.732050808
tan⁻¹(0.75)
          36.86989765
```

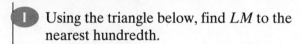

EXAMPLES 1 and 2   Using the tangent ratio

1 Using the triangle below, find LM to the nearest hundredth.

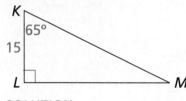

. SOLUTION

$$\tan 65° = \frac{LM}{LK}$$
$$\tan 65° = \frac{LM}{15}$$
$$15 \tan 65° = LM$$
$$32.17 \approx LM$$

2 Using the triangle below, find the measure of $\angle A$ to the nearest degree.

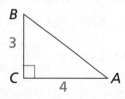

. SOLUTION

$$\tan A = \frac{3}{4}$$
$$m\angle A = \tan^{-1}\left(\frac{3}{4}\right)$$
$$m\angle A \approx 37°$$

The tangent ratio is the ratio of the lengths of the opposite leg to the adjacent leg. Other trigonometric ratios use the ratio of the length of a leg to the length of the hypotenuse. Use the same diagram from the previous page, since the triangles are similar, to set up other equal ratios.

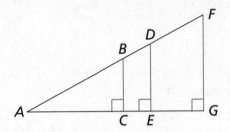

These proportions lead to the following definitions.

The Sine and Cosine Ratios

In any right triangle $\triangle ABC$ with right angle at C:

$$\text{sine of } \angle A = \frac{\text{length of leg opposite } \angle A}{\text{length of hypotenuse}}$$

$$\text{cosine of } \angle A = \frac{\text{length of leg adjacent to } \angle A}{\text{length of hypotenuse}}$$

The sine of $\angle A$ is denoted $\sin A$.
The cosine of $\angle A$ is denoted $\cos A$.

Note

An acronym for remembering the correct ratios is SOHCAHTOA. For example, the SOH would mean

$\text{Sine} = \frac{Opposite}{hypotenuse}.$

EXAMPLE 3   **Using trigonometric ratios to find angles**

3 In $\triangle ABC$, find $m\angle A$ and $m\angle B$ to the nearest degree.

■ **SOLUTION**

You can use the sine ratio to find $m\angle A$.

$$\sin \angle A = \frac{opposite}{hypotenuse}$$

$$= \frac{5}{13} = 0.384615384$$

Then $m\angle A = \sin^{-1}(0.384615384) = 22.61986495 \approx 23°$

To find $m\angle B$, use the fact that $\sin \angle A = \cos \angle B$.

Therefore, $\cos \angle B = \frac{adjacent}{hypotenuse} = \frac{5}{13} = 0.384615384$.

Then $m\angle B = \cos^{-1}(0.384615384) = 67.38013505 = 67°$.

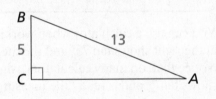

There are alternate methods for finding the measure of the second angle. Once you have found the measure of the acute angle $\angle A$, you can subtract it from its complement. Therefore, $\angle B = 90° - \angle A$, so $\angle B = 90° - 23 = 67°$. You can also use the Pythagorean Theorem to find side b (Pythagorean Triple 5, 12, 13), then use $\sin \angle B = \frac{opposite}{hypotenuse} = \frac{12}{13}$, and proceed from there.

If you use a ruler or tape measure to find the distance between two points on a flat surface, you are using **direct measurement.** If the points are far apart or you cannot easily get from one point to another, you may be able to find the distance indirectly. Trigonometric ratios may enable you to calculate distance and thereby use **indirect measurement** to find distance. Indirect measurement can also be used to find the measure of an angle.

The diagram below shows two horizontal lines cut by a transversal. If you look down from the upper line to the lower one, your sight line forms an **angle of depression.** If you sight from the lower line to the upper one, your sight line forms an **angle of elevation.** Notice that because the horizontal lines are parallel, the angles of elevation and depression are equal in measure.

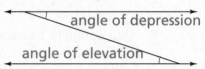

angle of depression

angle of elevation

EXAMPLES 4 and 5 — Solving problems involving angles of elevation and depression

MP

4 A steel cable extends from the top of a building to a point on level ground that is 1000 ft from the base of the building. At the point where the cable is anchored to the ground, it is determined that the measure of its angle of elevation is 42°. To the nearest foot, how tall is the building?

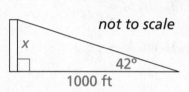

not to scale

x

42°

1000 ft

■ **SOLUTION**

This problem involves the leg adjacent to the 42° angle and the leg opposite it. Choose the tangent ratio.

$$\tan 42° = \frac{x}{1000}$$
$$x = 1000 \tan 42°$$
$$x \approx 900$$

The building is *about 900 feet* tall.

5 Rose is flying a kite and has played out 300 feet of string. The kite is 120 feet above the ground and Rose is 5 feet tall. To the nearest tenth of a degree, at what angle of elevation does she sight the kite?

■ **SOLUTION**

First sketch a diagram showing what is known and what is unknown. If Rose is 5 feet tall and the kite is 120 feet above the ground, then the height of the right triangle shown is 115 ft.

To find the angle of elevation use the sine ratio.

$$\sin x° = \frac{115}{300}$$
$$x \approx 22.5°$$

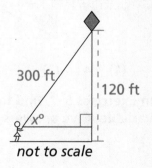

300 ft

120 ft

$x°$

not to scale

She sights the kite along a line making an angle of *about 22.5°* with the horizontal.

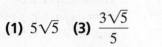
Choose the numeral preceding the word or expression that best completes the statement or answers the question.

1 What is sin *B*?

(1) $5\sqrt{5}$ (3) $\dfrac{3\sqrt{5}}{5}$

(2) 3 (4) $\dfrac{2\sqrt{5}}{5}$

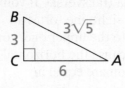

2 Which equation can be used to find the height of this building?

(1) $\sin M = \dfrac{LK}{500}$

(2) $\tan M = \dfrac{LK}{500}$

(3) $\cos M = \dfrac{500}{LM}$

(4) $\tan M = \dfrac{500}{LK}$

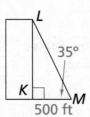

3 Which represents $m\angle X$ to the nearest whole number?

(1) 31° (3) 45°

(2) 41° (4) 59°

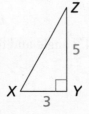

4 To the nearest tenth, which represents the length of the diagonal $\overline{AC}$ in the rectangle below?

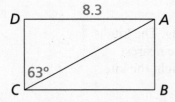

(1) 7.4 (2) 9.3 (3) 16.3 (4) 18.3

In Exercises 5–7, find the value of each variable. Give answers to the nearest tenth.

5

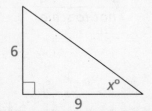

6

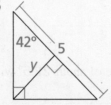

7

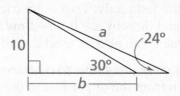

In Exercises 8–12, find the missing value to solve the problem.

8 The captain of a ship spots the top of a lighthouse at a 6° angle of elevation. The lighthouse is on the edge of the shore and is 50 ft tall. To the nearest foot, how far is the ship from shore?

9 An airplane pilot can see the top of a traffic control tower at a 20° angle of depression. The straight-line distance between the plane and the top of the tower is 5,000 feet. To the nearest foot, how far above the tower is the plane?

10 A forest ranger looking out from a ranger's station can see a forest fire at a 35° angle of depression. The ranger's position is 100 ft above the ground. To the nearest foot, how far is it from the base of the ranger's station to the fire on level ground with it?

11 To the nearest whole number, find the measures of the angles in $\triangle PQR$.

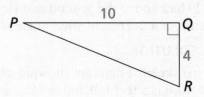

12 Find *a* to the nearest whole number.

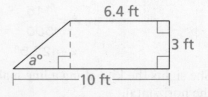

2.7 Law of Sines and Cosines

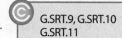
G.SRT.9, G.SRT.10
G.SRT.11

A triangle that does not contain a right angle is called an **oblique triangle**. An oblique triangle is either **acute**—all the angles measure less than 90°—or **obtuse**—one angle is obtuse and two are acute.

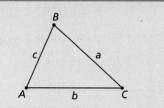

Acute Oblique Triangle	Obtuse Oblique Triangle

When you are asked to solve an oblique triangle, you must determine the measure of all the parts of the triangle. You can use the **Law of Sines** and the **Law of Cosines** to find the missing parts.

If you know the measures of two angles and any side (AAS) or two sides and the angle opposite one of them (SSA), you will have to use the **Law of Sines**.

Law of Sines

Given $\triangle ABC$ with sides a, b, and c, then
$$\frac{\sin A}{a} = \frac{\sin B}{b} = \frac{\sin C}{c}.$$

Note

Capital letters identify the vertices of a triangle, and the same letter in lower case will be used to label opposite sides.

EXAMPLE 1 — Proving the Law of Sines

1. Prove the Law of Sines.

   ■ **SOLUTION**

   Start by constructing two altitudes of the triangle.

   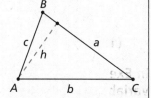

   $\sin A = \dfrac{h}{c} \qquad \sin C = \dfrac{h}{a} \qquad \sin B = \dfrac{h}{c} \qquad \sin C = \dfrac{h}{b}$

   $c \sin A = h \qquad a \sin C = h \qquad c \sin B = h \qquad b \sin C = h$

   $\therefore\ c \sin A = a \sin C \qquad\qquad \therefore\ c \sin B = b \sin C$

   $\therefore\ \dfrac{c \sin A}{ac} = \dfrac{a \sin C}{ac} \qquad\qquad \therefore\ \dfrac{c \sin B}{bc} = \dfrac{b \sin C}{bc}$

   $\therefore\ \dfrac{\sin A}{a} = \dfrac{\sin C}{c} \qquad\qquad \therefore\ \dfrac{\sin B}{b} = \dfrac{\sin C}{c}$

   Therefore, $\dfrac{\sin A}{a} = \dfrac{\sin B}{b} = \dfrac{\sin C}{c}$.

EXAMPLE 2   **Using the Law of Sines**

2   Find AB in the accompanying figure.

■ SOLUTION

This is an AAS case of the Law of Sines.

$$\frac{\sin A}{a} = \frac{\sin C}{c} \rightarrow \frac{\sin 60°}{12} = \frac{\sin 75°}{c}$$

$$c = \frac{12 \sin 75°}{\sin 60°}$$

$$c \approx 13.38$$

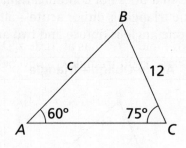

If you know the measures of two sides and the angle between them (SAS), or all three sides (SSS), you will have to use **Law of Cosines.**

Law of Cosines

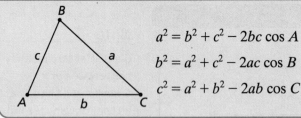

$$a^2 = b^2 + c^2 - 2bc \cos A$$

$$b^2 = a^2 + c^2 - 2ac \cos B$$

$$c^2 = a^2 + b^2 - 2ab \cos C$$

In mathematics the Pythagorean theorem is used in many different forms. To prove the Law of Cosines the **Pythagorean Identity** will be used. It states that if

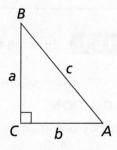

$$a^2 + b^2 = c^2 \text{ then } \frac{a^2}{c^2} + \frac{b^2}{c^2} = 1$$

In right $\triangle ABC$: $\sin^2 A = \dfrac{a^2}{c^2}$ and $\cos^2 A = \dfrac{b^2}{c^2}$,

so if $a^2 + b^2 = c^2$, then $\mathbf{\sin^2 A + \cos^2 A = 1}$.

EXAMPLE 3 — **Proving the Law of Cosines**

 Prove the Law of Cosines for an acute triangle.

■ **SOLUTION**

Triangle ABC has altitude $\overline{BD}$ drawn to $\overline{AC}$.
Using right triangle trigonometry

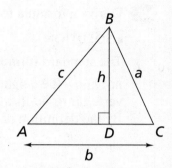

In right $\triangle ADB$: $\sin A = \dfrac{h}{c}$, then $h = c\sin A$;

In right $\triangle ADB$: $\cos A = \dfrac{\overline{AD}}{c}$, then $\overline{AD} = c\cos A$;

Since $b = \overline{AD} + \overline{CD}$, then $\overline{CD} = b - c\cos A$

Applying the Pythagorean theorem in right $\triangle CDB$:

$a^2 = h^2 + \overline{CD}^2$	Pythagorean theorem
$\quad = (c\sin A)^2 + (b - c\cos A)^2$	Substitution
$\quad = c^2 \cdot \sin^2 A + b^2 - 2bc\cos A + c^2 \cdot \cos^2 A$	Exponent and binomial multiplication
$\quad = b^2 + (c^2 \cdot \sin^2 A + c^2 \cdot \cos^2 A) - 2bc\cos A$	commutative property of addition
$\quad = b^2 + c^2(\sin^2 A + \cos^2 A) - 2bc\cos A$	factoring
$\quad = b^2 + c^2(1) - 2bc\cos A$	Pythagorean Identity
$a^2 = b^2 + c^2 - 2bc\cos A$	multiplication property of 1

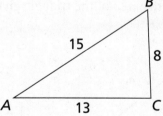 Find the measure of angle A in the accompanying diagram.

■ **SOLUTION**

$$a^2 = b^2 + c^2 - 2bc\cos A$$
$$8^2 = 13^2 + 15^2 - 2(13)(15)\cos A$$
$$390\cos A = 330$$
$$A = \cos^{-1}\left(\frac{330}{390}\right) \approx 32.2°$$

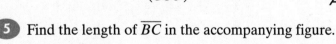

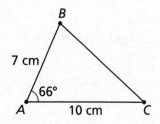 Find the length of $\overline{BC}$ in the accompanying figure.

■ **SOLUTION**

$$a^2 = b^2 + c^2 - 2bc\cos A$$
$$a^2 = 10^2 + 7^2 - 2(10)(7)\cos 66°$$
$$x^2 = 92.0569$$
$$x = \sqrt{92.0569} \approx 9.595$$

The formula for the area of a triangle can be written using the sine ratio.

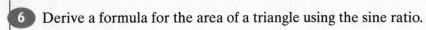

EXAMPLE 6   **Deriving the formula for the area of a triangle**

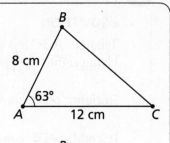

6 Derive a formula for the area of a triangle using the sine ratio.

■ **SOLUTION**

The standard formula for the area of a triangle is $A = \frac{1}{2}bh$. You do not know the height of the given triangle. Draw the altitude from vertex B to $\overline{AC}$ forming the right triangle shown to the right. By the definition of the sine ratio, you know that

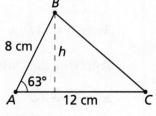

$$\sin A = \frac{h}{c}$$
$$h = c \sin A \quad \leftarrow \textbf{Multiply both sides by } c.$$

Substituting this equation into the formula $A = \frac{1}{2}bh$, you get

$$A = \frac{1}{2}bc \sin A.$$

Formula for the Area of a Triangle

The area of a triangle is equal to one-half the product of any two sides times the sine of their included angle.

So the area of the triangle can be expressed as:

$$A = \frac{1}{2}bc \sin A \text{ or } A = \frac{1}{2}ac \sin B \text{ or } A = \frac{1}{2}ab \sin C.$$

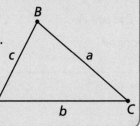

EXAMPLE 7   **Finding the area of a triangle**

7 Determine the area of the triangle given below.

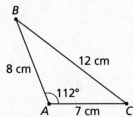

■ **SOLUTION**

$$A = \frac{1}{2}bc \sin A = \frac{1}{2}(8)(7) \sin 112°$$
$$= 25.96 \text{ cm}^2$$

You can apply the Law of Sines and Cosines and the area of triangles in many practical ways.

EXAMPLES 8 and 9 **Solving application problems**

8 The distance from home plate to the center field wall of a baseball stadium is 400 feet. The distance from home plate to third base is 90 feet. The angle at each base is a right angle. How long is a throw from the center field wall to third base?

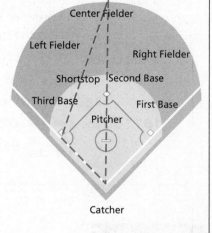

■ **SOLUTION**

The angle at home plate of the triangle in the accompanying diagram is 45°. The Law of Cosines applies.

$$x^2 = 90^2 + 400^2 - 2(90)(400)\cos 45°$$

$$x^2 = 168,100 - 72,000\left(\frac{\sqrt{2}}{2}\right) \approx 117,188.31$$

$$x = \sqrt{117,188.31} \approx 342.3 \text{ ft}$$

9 In order to approximate the surface area of a pond, a surveyor takes the measurements shown in the figure to the right. What is the estimate for the area of the pond?

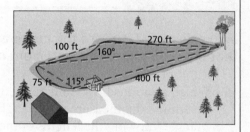

■ **SOLUTION**

$$A = \frac{1}{2}ab\sin C$$

$$A_1 = \frac{1}{2}(100)(270)\sin 160° \approx 4,600 \text{ ft}^2$$

$$A_2 = \frac{1}{2}(75)(400)\sin 115° \approx 13,600 \text{ ft}^2$$

Total area = 18,200 ft²

EXAMPLE 10 **Using the Law of Sines to solve problems**

10 The famous leaning tower in Pisa, Italy, is 184.5 feet tall. From a point 123 feet from the center of the base, an angle of elevation is measured to be 60°. At what angle is the tower leaning?

■ **SOLUTION**

First find the angle opposite the 123-foot side.

$$\frac{\sin A}{a} = \frac{\sin B}{b}$$

$$\frac{\sin 60°}{184.5} = \frac{\sin B}{123}$$

$$\frac{123 \sin 60°}{184.5} = \sin B$$

$$0.5774 = \sin B$$

$$35.3° = m\angle B$$

Now find the angle at C.
$$180° - 60° - 35.3° = 84.7°$$

So, the tower leans 5.3 degrees from the vertical.

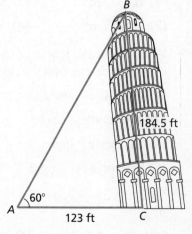

63

Using the Law of Cosines to solve a map problem

11. Buffalo, Yonkers, and Syracuse are the vertices of an oblique triangle. The distance between Buffalo and Syracuse is 150 miles. The distance between Syracuse and Yonkers is 250 miles. The distance between Buffalo and Yonkers is 375 miles. What is the measure of the angle at Yonkers?

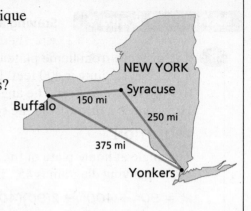

- **SOLUTION**

$$a^2 = b^2 + c^2 - 2bc \cos A$$
$$150^2 = 250^2 + 375^2 - 2(250)(375) \cos A$$
$$187{,}500 \cos A = 180{,}625$$
$$A = \cos^{-1}\left(\frac{180{,}625}{187{,}500}\right) \approx 15.56°$$

Practice

In Exercises 1–7, choose the numeral preceding the word or expression that best completes the statement or answers the question.

1 Which relationship should be used to determine the measure of the angles of a triangle knowing the lengths of the three sides?

   (1) Pythagorean Theorem

   (2) Law of Sines

   (3) Law of Cosines

   (4) Tangent Theorem

2 Determine the area of a triangle with two sides of 10 cm and 15 cm. Their included angle has measure of 63°.

   (1) 66.83 cm^2 **(3)** 13.37 cm^2

   (2) 34.05 cm^2 **(4)** 4.46 cm^2

3 If you know the length of two sides of a triangle, you can find the area if you also know

   (1) the largest angle.

   (2) the smallest angle.

   (3) the vertex angle.

   (4) the included angle.

4 In $\triangle PQR$, $p = 7$, $q = 5$, $r = 8$. What is the $m\angle P$?

   (1) 20°   **(2)** 30°   **(3)** 60°   **(4)** 120°

5 In $\triangle ABC$, $m\angle A = 45°$, $m\angle B = 60°$, $a = 2\sqrt{6}$. Determine the length of b.

   (1) 6   **(2)** $6\sqrt{2}$ **(3)** $6\sqrt{3}$ **(4)** 12

6 Two people observe a helicopter at the same time from different locations. The angle of elevation from each location is 25° and 40°. If the people are 100 feet apart, approximately how high is the helicopter?

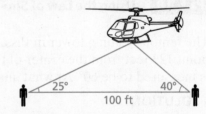

   (1) 20 feet   **(3)** 40 feet

   (2) 30 feet   **(4)** 50 feet

7 In $\triangle ABC$, which of the following completes the statement: $b = \dfrac{?}{\sin A}$?

   (1) $a \sin B$ **(3)** $\sin B$

   (2) $a \sin C$ **(4)** A

8 In $\triangle ABC$, $b = 20$, $\sin B = \dfrac{2}{3}$, and $\sin C = \dfrac{1}{2}$. What is the measure of c?

9 In $\triangle DEF$, $d = 5$, $e = 7$, and $f = 8$. What is the cosine of the largest angle?

10 Determine the area of a parallelogram with two sides of 18 cm and 21 cm. Their included angle has measure of 40°. Show your work.

11 Joe needs to determine the height of a tree. Refer to the accompanying diagram.

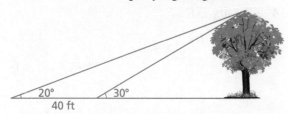

The angle of elevation to the top of the tree is 20°. From a point closer to the base of the tree, the angle of elevation is 30°. How tall is the tree?

12 Use the diagram below to determine the distance between the houses.

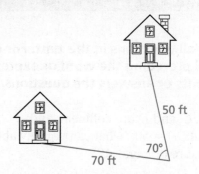

In Exercise 13, find the area of $\triangle ABC$. Round your answer to the nearest tenth.

13 $m\angle C = 68°$, $b = 12.9$, $c = 15.2$

Chapter 2 Preparing for the Assessment

Answer all questions in this part. For each question, select the numeral preceding the word or expression that best completes the statements or answers the questions.

1 If B, C, and D are collinear, and $m\angle ACD = 50°$, what can you say about the measure of angle A?

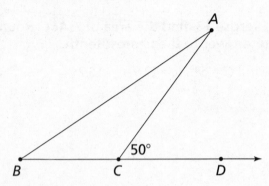

(1) $m\angle A > 50°$

(2) $m\angle A = 50°$

(3) $m\angle A < 50°$

(4) $m\angle A = 40°$

2 What is true about the sides of a scalene triangle?

(1) All sides are congruent.

(2) Two sides are congruent.

(3) All sides add up to 180°.

(4) No sides are congruent.

3 The lengths of the sides of a triangle are integers. If two of the sides measure 4 and 7, which of the following are all the possible lengths of the third side?

(1) 6, 7, 8, 9, 10, 11, 12

(2) 3, 4, 5, 6, 7, 8

(3) 5, 6, 7, 8

(4) 4, 5, 6, 7, 8, 9, 10

4 Classify $\triangle RST$.

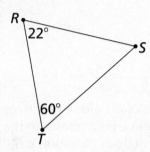

(1) isosceles **(3)** obtuse

(2) equilateral **(4)** acute

5 If the angle measures of a triangle are 60°, 60°, and 60°, what type of triangle is it?

(1) scalene **(3)** right

(2) equiangular **(4)** obtuse

6 The measures of two angles of a triangle are 60° and 10°. Classify the type of triangle.

(1) acute

(2) isosceles

(3) obtuse

(4) right

7 If the side lengths of a triangle are 6 m, 3 m, and 6 m, what type of triangle is it?

(1) equilateral

(2) isosceles

(3) right

(4) scalene

8 Which is not a possible length for the third side of a triangle whose other two sides are 12 and 20?

(1) 10 **(2)** 16 **(3)** 24 **(4)** 40

9 If the angles of a triangle are $x°$, $3x°$, and 60°, what type of triangle is it?

(1) acute **(3)** obtuse

(2) isoscele **(4)** right

10 The Pythagorean Theorem holds for which type of triangle?

(1) acute   **(3)** obtuse

(2) right   **(4)** left

11 The length of the hypotenuse of an isosceles right triangle is 12. Which of the following represents the length of the leg?

(1) $6\sqrt{2}$ **(3)** $2\sqrt{6}$

(2) $2\sqrt{3}$ **(4)** 6

12 The circumcenter is the point of concurrency of which lines or segments in a triangle?

(1) medians

(2) altitudes

(3) bisectors of the sides

(4) perpendicular bisectors of the sides

13 Which point can be a vertex of a triangle?

(1) circumcenter

(2) orthocenter

(3) centroid

(4) incenter

14 $\overline{RS}$ is the median of a triangle. The length of $\overline{RS}$ is 21. What is the distance from vertex R to the centroid of the triangle?

(1) 7   **(3)** 14

(2) 10.5   **(4)** 31.5

15 The area of a square is 49 cm². What is the length of the diagonal of the square?

(1) 7   **(2)** $2\sqrt{7}$ **(3)** $7\sqrt{2}$ **(4)** $7\sqrt{3}$

Use the following figure to answer Exercise 16.

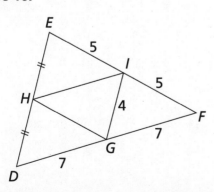

16 Determine the length of $\overline{HG}$ in the accompanying figure.

(1) 4   **(2)** 5   **(3)** 7   **(4)** 9

Use the following figure to answer Exercises 17 and 18.

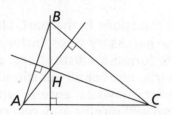

17 If H is in the interior of $\triangle ABC$, then $\triangle ABC$ must be what type of triangle?

(1) acute   **(3)** obtuse

(2) scalene   **(4)** right

18 If point H is outside $\triangle ABC$, what type of triangle is it?

(1) right   **(3)** obtuse

(2) acute   **(4)** equilateral

19 What is the height of $\triangle XYZ$?

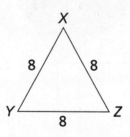

(1) 4   **(2)** $4\sqrt{3}$ **(3)** 8   **(4)** $8\sqrt{3}$

20 What is the geometric mean of 4 and 6?

(1) $3\sqrt{4}$ **(2)** $4\sqrt{3}$ **(3)** $2\sqrt{6}$ **(4)** $3\sqrt{6}$

21 What is the length of the hypotenuse of a right triangle with leg lengths of 9 in. and 12 in.?

(1) 10   **(2)** 15   **(3)** 21   **(4)** 25

22 The centroid is the point of concurrency of which lines and segments?

(1) altitudes

(2) medians

(3) bisectors of the sides

(4) perpendicular bisectors of the sides

Answer all questions in this part. Clearly indicate the necessary steps, including appropriate formula substitutions, diagrams, graphs, charts, etc. For all questions in this part, a correct numerical answer with no work shown will receive only one credit.

23 In the accompanying figure, squares have been constructed on the sides of a right triangle. How do the areas of the squares relate to each other? Would this relationship be true for any other shapes constructed on the sides of the right triangle?

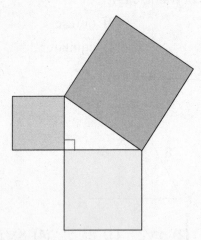

24 Determine the area and perimeter of *ABCD*.

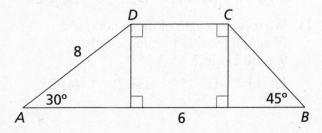

25 Which represents $m\angle A$ to the nearest whole degree?

(1) 38°

(2) 55°

(3) 66°

(4) 99°

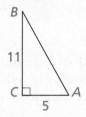

In Exercise 26, find the missing values to solve the problem.

26 Two trees are 100 ft apart on level ground. The height of the taller tree is 75 ft. The angle of depression from the top of the taller tree to the top of the shorter tree is 15°. Find the height of the shorter tree to the nearest tenth of a foot.

27 $\triangle ABC$ is an isosceles triangle whose vertex angle is $\angle B$. If the exterior angle at $\angle A$ measures 148°, find the $m\angle B$.

28 A handsome young man is locked in (**MP**) a tower 50' tall. From the top of the tower he spies, at an angle of depression of 26° a fair damsel. He calls to her and she runs toward the tower. At a point near the tower base and at an angle of elevation of 75° to the squire, she finds the tower key. If the damsel's line of sight is 6' from ground level, how far, to the nearest foot did she run before finding the key?

3 Proof and Triangle Congruence

Purpose of Geometry

In *The Teaching of Geometry*, the Fifth Yearbook of the National Council of Teachers of Mathematics (NCTM), Professor William David Reeve writes that "the purpose of geometry is to make clear to the pupil the meaning of demonstrations, the meaning of mathematical precision, and the pleasure of discovering absolute truth. If demonstrative geometry is not taught in order to enable the pupils to have the satisfaction of proving something, to train them in deductive thinking, to give them the power to prove their own statements, then it is not worth teaching at all."

3.1 Statements

A **statement** is any mathematical sentence. A statement is called an **open statement** if it cannot be determined whether or not the statement is true or false. The equation $x + 8 = 16$ is an example of an open statement. Until we know what the value of x is, the truth value of the statement cannot be determined.

Any statement that can be classified as true or false is called a **closed statement**. *A triangle is a four-sided figure* is an example of a closed statement. Its truth value is false.

EXAMPLE 1 **Determining the type and truth value of statements**

1. Classify each of the following statements as open or closed. If the statement is closed, determine its truth value.

Statement (Sentence)	Type	Truth Value
$5 + 2 = 7$	Closed	True
$n + 4 = 12$	Open	
If point C is between A and B, then $AC + CB = AB$.	Closed	True
Measures of supplementary angles add up to 90°.	Closed	False
The complement of a 50° angle is an angle of 40°.	Closed	True
Every segment has a unique midpoint.	Closed	True
$\sqrt{3}$ is a rational number.	Closed	False
$x + y = 6$	Open	

An unproven statement concerning an observation is called a **conjecture**. Much of geometry was developed by observation and formulating conjectures. To prove that a conjecture is true, you must show it is true for **all** cases. To prove that a conjecture is false, you need to find only one case where the statement is false. This case is called a **counterexample**.

EXAMPLE 2 **Working with counterexamples**

2. Is the following statement true or false?
No square has a perimeter numerically equal to its area.

- **SOLUTION**

Side	1	3	5	4
Perimeter	$4(1) = 4$	$4(3) = 12$	$4(5) = 20$	$4(4) = 16$
Area	$1^2 = 1$	$3^2 = 9$	$5^2 = 25$	$4^2 = 16$

If a square has a side that is 4 units in length, then its perimeter and area are numerically equal. This counterexample shows that the statement is false.

EXAMPLE 3   **Working with conjectures and counterexamples**

3   What is the truth value of the following conjecture?
For a given line segment there is one and only one bisector.

■ **SOLUTION**

This conjecture is false because the example to
the right shows $\overline{AB}$ with more than one bisector.
The segment, lines, and ray shown in the figure
all pass through the midpoint of the segment
and therefore are all bisectors of the segment.
This drawing provides a **counterexample** to
the conjecture.

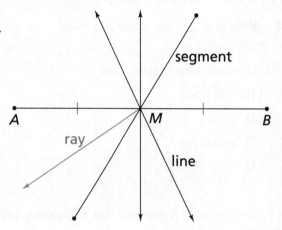

By inserting or removing the word *not* in a statement, the **negation** of the
statement is formed.

> **Note**
>
> If a statement is true,
> its negation is false. If
> a statement is false,
> its negation is true.

EXAMPLE 4   **Negations and their truth value**

4   Determine the truth value of each statement. Then write its negation
and the negation's truth value.

■ **SOLUTION**

Statement	Truth Value	Negation	Truth Value
All right angles measure 90°.	T	All right angles do not measure 90°.	F
Parallel lines intersect.	F	Parallel lines do not intersect.	T
All triangles are not right.	T	All triangles *are* right.	F

Choose the numeral preceding the word or expression that best completes the statement or answers the question.

1 What best describes the following statement?

All squares have four sides.

(1) true open

(2) open

(3) true closed

(4) false closed

2 Which of the following is the negation of the statement, *Vertical angles are congruent*?

(1) Vertical angles are congruent.

(2) Nonvertical angles are congruent.

(3) Vertical angles are not congruent.

(4) Congruent angles are vertical.

In Exercises 3–7, complete the following table.

Statement	Truth Value	Negation	Truth Value
3 Perpendicular lines meet to form right angles.			
4 The supplement of an acute angle is an obtuse angle.			
5 The bisector of an angle is unique.			
6 Three noncollinear points do not determine a plane.			
7 The complement of an acute angle is an acute angle.			

In Exercises 8–15, find a counterexample for each of the statements.

8 Two angles are never congruent and supplementary.

9 If two lines don't intersect, they are parallel.

10 A point that is equidistant from the endpoints of a segment must be the midpoint of the segment.

11 If $AM = \frac{1}{2}AB$ then M is the midpoint of $\overline{AB}$.

12 All polygons have five sides.

13 All complementary angles are congruent.

14 All right triangles are isosceles.

15 $a^2 + b^2 = c^2$ for all integers a, b, and c.

3.2 Statements and their Truth Values G.CO.1

A **compound statement** is formed by joining two statements. When the word *and* is used to join two statements, the new statement is called a **conjunction.**

 EXAMPLES 1 and 2   **Identifying conjunctions**

1 What is the truth value of the conjunction, *Acute angles measure less than 90° and supplementary angles add up to 90°*?

■ **SOLUTION**

Since the statement *acute angles measure less than 90°* is true and the statement *supplementary angles add up to 90°* is false, the conjunction is *false.*

2 What is the truth value of the conjunction, *A square has congruent angles and a square has congruent sides?*

■ **SOLUTION**

Since the statement *A square has congruent* angles is true and the statement *A square has congruent sides* is true, the conjunction is **true.**

A conjunction is true only when both statements are true. When a compound statement is formed by joining two statements with the word *or,* the new statement is known as a **disjunction. A disjunction is true if at least one of its parts is true.**

 EXAMPLES 3 and 4   **Identifying disjunctions**

3 Form a disjunction from the following statement and determine its truth value.

Statement 1: *Supplementary angles add up to 180°.*

Statement 2: *Supplementary angles add up to 90°.*

■ **SOLUTION**

Disjunction: Supplementary angles add up to 180°, or supplementary angles add up to 90°.

Since the first statement is true and the second statement is false, the disjunction is *true.*

4 Given that $m\angle A = 90°$, determine the truth value of the following statement: $\angle A$ is an acute angle or $\angle A$ is a right angle.

■ **SOLUTION**

The first statement of this disjunction is false and the second statement is true. Therefore, the disjunction is *true.*

The *TEST* feature of a graphing calculator can be used to verify the truth values of conjunctions and disjunctions. The calculator reports a 1 for a true statement and a 0 for a false statement.

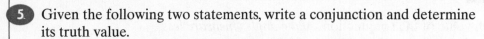

EXAMPLES 5 to 7 **Finding truth values involving conjunctions and disjunctions**

5. Given the following two statements, write a conjunction and determine its truth value.

Statement 1:   All right angles measure 90°.

Statement 2:   All squares are quadrilaterals.

■ SOLUTION

The conjunction: All right angles measure 90°, and all squares are quadrilaterals.

The conjunction is ***true*** because both statements are true.

6. Given the following two statements, write a disjunction and determine its truth value.

Statement 1:   All quadrilaterals are squares.

Statement 2:   Complementary angles add up to 180°.

■ SOLUTION

The disjunction: All quadrilaterals are squares, or complementary angles add up to 180°.

Both of the original statements are false; therefore, the disjunction is ***false.***

7. Given the following two statements, write a disjunction and determine its truth value.

Statement 1:   Parallel lines intersect.

Statement 2:   Perpendicular lines meet to form right angles.

■ SOLUTION

The disjunction: Parallel lines intersect, or perpendiculars line meet to form right angles. Statement 1 is false. Statement 2 is a true statement. This results in a ***true*** disjunction.

The elements of geometry, lines, segments, rays, and planes, are all sets of points, and so to describe their relationships, the set operations of **union** and **intersection** are often used.

The **union** of two sets A and B is the set containing elements either from A **or** B. The symbol for union is $\cup$.

The **intersection** of two sets A and B is the set containing only elements from both A **and** B. The symbol for intersection is $\cap$.

Suppose Set A contains the numbers 1, 2, and 3 and Set B contains the numbers 3 and 4.
The numbers in $A \cap B$ = common elements in A and B = number 3.
The numbers in $A \cup B$ = any elements in A or B = 1, 2, 3, 4.

EXAMPLES 8 and 9 **Geometric Union and Intersection**

Use the diagram of collinear points $A, B, C,$ and D for Examples 8 and 9.

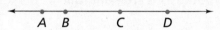

8 Set A is the set of all points on $\overline{AC}$. Set B is the set of all points on $\overline{BD}$. Find $A \cap B$.

■ **SOLUTION**

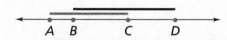

The points on $\overline{AC}$ are **blue**. The points on $\overline{BD}$ are **black**.
$A \cap B$ = common points both **blue** and **black** = $\overline{BC}$.

9 Find $\overline{AC} \cup \overline{BD}$

■ **SOLUTION**

Using the diagram above: $A \cup B$ = any points which are **blue** or **black** = $\overline{AD}$.

If you study hard, then you will earn good grades. This type of statement is called a **conditional** statement. In a conditional statement, the words *if* and *then* are used to join two mathematical statements.

Recall that the *if* part of a conditional statement is called the **hypothesis**, and the *then* part is called the **conclusion**.

EXAMPLE 10 **Writing conditionals and identifying the hypothesis and conclusion**

Note

If hypothesis, then conclusion.

Write each statement as a conditional in *if . . . then* form and identify the hypothesis and conclusion.

10 You will get an allowance if you do all your chores.

■ **SOLUTION**

If you do all your chores, then you will get an allowance

Hypothesis: you do all your chores
Conclusion: you will get an allowance

When is a conditional statement true? Consider that your parent makes this statement:

"If you pass the geometry test, then you'll get a reward!"

You pass the test and you get a reward. The conditional statement was true, but what if you pass the test and you don't get any reward? You would consider the conditional statement a lie, a false statement.

A conditional statement is false only if the hypothesis is true and the conclusion is false.

 EXAMPLE 11 **Determining the truth value of conditional statements**

11 What is the truth value of the statement *Triangles have three angles if parallel lines do not intersect*?

■ **SOLUTION**

Rewrite the statement in *if . . . then* form: *If parallel lines do not intersect, then triangles have three angles.*

Both the hypothesis and conclusion are true. Therefore, the conditional statement is true.

One way to show that a conditional statement is false is to find a counterexample.

 EXAMPLE 12 **Finding a counterexample**

12 Show that this conditional statement is false by finding a counterexample:

If a quadrilateral has two pairs of congruent sides, then the quadrilateral is a parallelogram.

■ **SOLUTION**

To show that this conditional is false, it is necessary to find a quadrilateral that makes the hypothesis true and the conclusion false.

In the kite to the right, the quadrilateral has two pairs of congruent sides. Therefore, the hypothesis is true. However, this quadrilateral is not a parallelogram. The conclusion is false. The original conditional statement is false because a counterexample has been found.

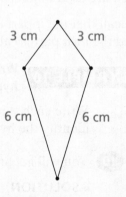

A conditional statement can sometimes be referred to as an **implication** and written using → instead of the if and then. If you pass the geometry test, then you'll get a reward!, would be written as: You pass the geometry test → you'll get a reward!

The statement is read: "You pass the geometry test **implies** you'll get a reward!"

In an earlier chapter, you learned that most theorems are expressed as conditional statements and if the hypothesis and conclusion statements are switched then the **converse** statement is formed.

Conditional: Statement A → Statement B

Converse: Statement B → Statement A

Remember that the conditional and its converse only **sometimes** have the same truth values.

EXAMPLES 13 and 14   **Writing the converse of a theorem**

Write the converse of each theorem and determine its truth value. If false, state a counterexample.

13 The true conditional: If two angles are right angles, then they are congruent.

■ **SOLUTION**

The converse is: If two angles are congruent, then they are right angles. The converse is false and the counterexample would be two angles that each measure 56°.
Since they have the same measure, the angles are congruent, but they are not right angles.

14 The true conditional: Two parallel lines are cut by a transversal → the alternate interior angles are congruent.

■ **SOLUTION**

The converse is: Two lines are cut by a transversal and the alternate interior angles are congruent → the lines are parallel. The converse is true.

Another type of compound statement is a conjunction formed with a conditional and its converse. An example of such a statement is shown below.

*If a polygon has four sides then it is a quadrilateral, and
if a polygon is a quadrilateral then it has four sides.*

A **biconditional statement** is the conjunction of a conditional statement and its converse. A biconditional can be abbreviated using the words *if and only if* or *symbolically:*

*A polygon is a quadrilateral if and only if it has four sides.
A polygon is a quadrilateral ↔ it has four sides.*

Most important: **All definitions can be written as biconditional statements.**

EXAMPLE 15 **Writing biconditionals**

15 Write the biconditional for this statement and its converse: *If you like music, then you watch music videos.*

■ **SOLUTION**

The converse of this statement is *If you watch music videos, then you like music.* The biconditional is the conjunction of the original statement and its converse: *If you like music videos, then you watch music videos* and *if you watch music videos, then you like music.* The more common and simpler form of the biconditional is *You like music if and only if you watch music videos.*

Practice

Choose the numeral preceding the word or expression that best completes the statement or answers the question.

1 To form a conjunction, two simple statements are connected with which of the following words?

  (1) and

  (2) or

  (3) not

  (4) maybe

2 Which statement about the figure below is true?

  (1) The figure is a rectangle or a square.

  (2) The figure is a rectangle and a square.

  (3) The figure is a rectangle and a trapezoid.

  (4) The figure is a square or a trapezoid.

3 A conditional statement is false when

  (1) both the hypothesis and conclusion are true.

  (2) the hypothesis is true and the conclusion is false.

  (3) the hypothesis is false and the conclusion is true.

  (4) both the hypothesis and conclusion are false.

4 Write the following statement as a conditional in *if . . . then* form and identify the hypothesis and conclusion.

A good job implies a good salary.

In Exercises 5–9, determine the truth value of the statement and justify your answer.

5 Every square has four sides, and every pentagon has five sides.

6 Triangles do not have three sides, or trapezoids are parallelograms.

7 Supplementary angles add up to 180°, and complementary angles add up to 90°.

8 Right triangles contain one right angle, and squares contain at least one right angle.

9 Justify the truth value of the biconditional formed in Example 15.

10 Write the following biconditional as a conditional and its converse: *Two angles are supplementary if and only if the sum of their measures is 180°.*

11 Given the conditional statement *If two lines in a plane intersect, then they are not parallel*, write its converse and determine its truth value.

12 Give a counterexample to show that the following statement is not always true: *If a parallelogram has four right angles, then all the sides are equal.*

13 Rewrite the true statement *Two circles have the same area if they have the same radius* in *if . . . then* form and then write its converse. If the converse is true, combine the statements to form a biconditional.

14 Suppose set *A* contains the numbers 0, 3, 6, 9, 12 and set *B* contains the numbers 0, 2, 4, 6, 8.

List the numbers in $A \cup B$.
List the numbers in $A \cap B$.

In Exercises 15–19, use the diagram of collinear points *A*, *B*, *C*, and *D*.

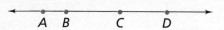

15 Find $\overline{AB} \cup \overline{BC}$

16 Find $\overline{AB} \cap \overline{CD}$

17 Find $\overrightarrow{AB} \cap \overline{CD}$

18 Find $\overrightarrow{AC} \cup \overrightarrow{CA}$

19 Find $\overrightarrow{BA} \cap \overrightarrow{BC}$

In Exercises 20–23, write the converse of each theorem and determine its truth value. If false, state a counterexample.

20 The true conditional: Two angles are vertical angles → they are congruent angles.

21 The true conditional: If a point is the midpoint of a segment, then it forms two congruent segments.

22 The true conditional: Two angles are right angles → the angles measure 90°.

23 The true conditional: In a triangle, if $a^2 + b^2 = c^2$, then the triangle is a right triangle.

In Exercises 24–26, using words or pictures, explain the meaning of the underlined word in the context of the definition or theorem.

24 An angle is the **union** of two non-collinear rays with a common endpoint.

25 If two lines intersect, then their **intersection** is one point.

26 Two angles both congruent **and** supplementary → the angles are right angles.

Thinking, Reasoning, Verifying, and Proof

G.CO.9
G.CO.10

Recall that when you reach a conclusion from a true statement justified with known facts, you are using **deductive reasoning.** Deductive reasoning is the basis for all algebraic and geometric proof.

EXAMPLE 1 **Using deductive reasoning to solve an equation**

 Given the equation $2x - 3 = 11$, solve for x. Justify each step.

■ **SOLUTION**

Step 1 $2x - 3 = 11$ Given

Step 2 $2x = 14$ **Addition property of equality**

Step 3 $x = 7$ **Division property of equality**

The solution was done in two-column form. In the left column are specific statements of fact. In the right column are the reasons you know the new facts are true. This two-column form is a traditional form for proof in geometry as well.

MP

EXAMPLE 2 **Using deductive reasoning to prove a theorem**

Prove the theorem *If two angles are supplementary to the same angle, then they are equal to each other.*

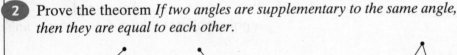

■ **SOLUTION**

Given: $\angle 1$ and $\angle 2$ are supplementary.
     $\angle 2$ and $\angle 3$ are supplementary.
Prove: $m\angle 1 = m\angle 3$

Statements	Reasons
1. $\angle 1$ and $\angle 2$ are supplementary. $\angle 2$ and $\angle 3$ are supplementary.	1. Given
2. $m\angle 1 + m\angle 2 = 180°$ $m\angle 2 + m\angle 3 = 180°$	2. If 2 $\angle$'s supplementary, then sum of measures $= 180°$
3. $m\angle 1 + m\angle 2 = m\angle 2 + m\angle 3$	3. substitution
4. $m\angle 1 = m\angle 3$	4. Subtraction prop of $=$

A two column proof follows a pattern called the **syllogism** of proof. A syllogism uses a chain of conditional statements, where each conclusion is the hypothesis for the next conditional. The proof below shows this pattern using variables to represent statements. Follow the variables to "see" the syllogism.

Given: *A*   **Prove:** *D*

Statements	Reasons
1. *A*	1. Given
2. *B*	2. If *A*, then *B*
3. *C*	3. If *B*, then *C*
4. *D*	4. If *C*, then *D*

EXAMPLE 3   **Syllogism in proof**

3 Write a two-column proof using the syllogism pattern to prove:
If a line bisects a segment, then two segments of equal length are formed.

■ **SOLUTION**

Given: *l* bisects $\overline{AB}$ at *M*.   **Prove:** $AM = MB$

Statements	Reasons
1. *l* bisects $\overline{AB}$ at *M*.	**1.** Given
2. *M* is the midpoint of $\overline{AB}$.	**2.** If bisect a segment, then midpoint formed
3. $\overline{AM} \cong \overline{MB}$	**3.** If midpoint, then 2 ≅ segments
4. $AM = MB$	**4.** If 2 ≅ segments, then = lengths.

Proof is thought of as a logical argument and this argument can be presented in many forms: two-column format, paragraph form, in a flowchart, or as a transformation. All proof uses Statements justified with known theorems, definitions, or properties as Reasons.

In Exercises 1 and 2 place the lettered reasons in the two-column format to prove the given theorem.

1 **Prove:** *If two lines intersect, then vertical angles are congruent.*

Given: *l* intersects *m*.
Prove: ∠1 ≅ ∠3

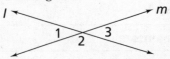

Statements	Reasons	Choose from
1. *l* intersects *m*.	1. _____	**A.** Substitution
2. ∠1 and ∠2 are supplementary. ∠2 and ∠3 are supplementary.	2. _____	**B.** Subtraction prop of =
3. $m\angle 1 + m\angle 2 = 180°$ $m\angle 2 + m\angle 3 = 180°$	3. _____	**C.** If angles of a Linear Pair, then angles are supplementary
4. $m\angle 1 + m\angle 2 = m\angle 2 + m\angle 3$	4. _____	**D.** Given
5. $m\angle 1 = m\angle 3$	5. _____	**E.** If angles = in measure, then angles ≅
6. ∠1 ≅ ∠3	6. _____	**F.** If 2 ∠s supplementary, then sum of measures = 180°

2 **Prove:** *In a plane, if two lines are perpendicular to the same line, then the lines are parallel.*

Given: $l \perp m$; $n \perp m$
Prove: $l \parallel n$

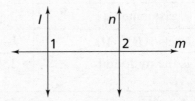

Statements	Reasons	Choose from
1. $l \perp m$; $n \perp m$	1. _____	**A.** If perpendicular, then right angles
2. ∠1 and ∠2 are right angles	2. _____	**B.** If right angles, then angles ≅
3. ∠1 ≅ ∠2	3. _____	**C.** If corresponding ∠s ≅ , then lines are parallel
4. $l \parallel n$	4. _____	**D.** Given

3.4 | Triangle Congruence

Congruent triangles are triangles that are the same size and the same shape. Congruent triangles have three pairs of **corresponding angles congruent** and three pairs of **corresponding sides congruent**.

You do not need all six pairs of congruent sides and congruent angles to prove that two triangles are congruent. There are five different ways, each using only three conditions, to prove triangles congruent.

Side-Side-Side Postulate (SSS)

If the three sides of one triangle are congruent to the three corresponding sides of another triangle, then the two triangles are congruent.

$$\triangle ABC \cong \triangle DEF$$
$$\text{SSS} \rightarrow \triangle\text{s congruent}$$

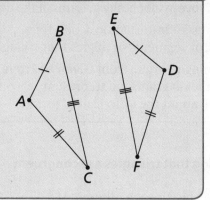

EXAMPLE I   **Matching corresponding parts**

 List the pairs of corresponding parts for the triangles shown in the postulate above.

■ **SOLUTION**

$\angle A \cong \angle D$	$\overline{AB} \cong \overline{DE}$
$\angle B \cong \angle E$	$\overline{AC} \cong \overline{DF}$
$\angle C \cong \angle F$	$\overline{BC} \cong \overline{EF}$

Note

Since $\overline{AB} \cong \overline{DE}$ if and only if $AB = DE$, and $\angle A \cong \angle D$ if and only if $m\angle A = m\angle D$, these congruence and equality statements will be used interchangeably.

Recall that postulates are statements accepted without proof. The next postulate is one of the most self-evident.

Side-Angle-Side Postulate (SAS)

If two sides and the included angle of one triangle are congruent to the corresponding two sides and the included angle of another triangle, then the triangles are congruent.

$$\triangle ABC \cong \triangle DEF$$
$$\text{SAS} \rightarrow \triangle\text{s congruent}$$

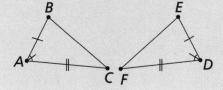

Included angles and included sides are often used when showing that triangles are congruent. An included side is the common side of two angles of a triangle. An included angle is the angle formed by two sides of the triangle.

In the accompanying figure, $\angle J$ is included between $\overline{KJ}$ and $\overline{LJ}$ and side $\overline{KL}$ is included between $\angle K$ and $\angle L$.

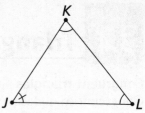

Writing a Proof

1 Draw and label a diagram that represents the geometry of the situation.

2 State the **Given** conditions symbolically in terms of the labeled diagram.

3 State what you are to **Prove** symbolically in terms of the diagram.

4 Study the diagram to "see" information. Look for vertical angles, linear pairs of angles, or segments or angles that triangles share.

5 Use deductive reasoning to argue from **Given** to **Prove**. Remember to use the visuals from the diagram, and to present reasons that justify each statement. Think about the syllogism of proof!

EXAMPLE 2   **Proving that triangles are congruent**

2   **Given:** $\overline{AB}$ and $\overline{CD}$ bisect each other at M.

   Prove: $\triangle ACM \cong \triangle BDM$

   ■ **SOLUTION**

Statements	Reasons
1. $\overline{AB}$ and $\overline{CD}$ bisect each other.	1. Given
2. M is the midpoint of $\overline{AB}$. M is the midpoint of $\overline{CD}$.	2. If bisect, then midpoint
3. $\overline{AM} \cong \overline{BM}$; $\overline{CM} \cong \overline{DM}$	3. If midpoint, then $\cong$ segments.
4. $\angle 1 \cong \angle 2$ (from diagram)	4. If two lines intersect, the vertical angles are $\cong$.
5. $\triangle ACM \cong \triangle BDM$	5. SAS → $\triangle$s congruent

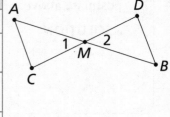

Given a correspondence of two angles and a side, you can show that triangles are congruent.

Angle-Side-Angle Postulate (ASA)

If two angles and the included side of one triangle are congruent to the corresponding parts of another triangle, the triangles are congruent.

$\triangle RST \cong \triangle GHI$

ASA → $\triangle$s congruent

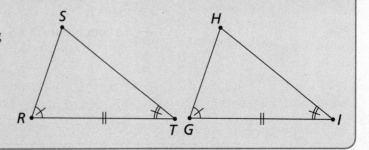

Angle-Angle-Side Theorem (AAS)

If two angles and the nonincluded side of one triangle are congruent to the corresponding parts of another triangle, the triangles are congruent.

$$\triangle DEF \cong \triangle XYZ$$
$$\text{AAS} \rightarrow \triangle \text{s congruent}$$

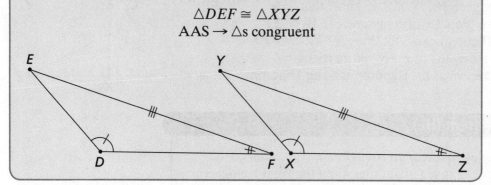

Note

AAS is a theorem and not a postulate because it can be proved from known facts.

Another type of proof known as a **flow proof** uses arrows to show the logical connection between statements. The reasons are usually written below the statements.

EXAMPLE 3   Using a flow proof to prove triangle congruence   (MP)

3 Given that $\angle E \cong \angle F$ and $\overline{DH} \cong \overline{GH}$, use a flow proof to prove that $\triangle DEG \cong \triangle GFD$.

■ **SOLUTION**

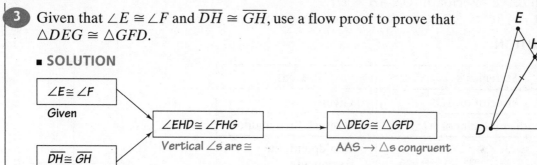

Some side-angle relationships cannot be used to show that triangles are congruent. For example, SSA cannot be used to show congruence. In the figure below, $\angle ACD$ was constructed to be congruent to the given angle and $\overline{DC} \cong b$. Notice that there are two possible triangles that can now be completed; $\triangle ADC$ and $\triangle BDC$. $\triangle ADC$ and $\triangle BDC$ are NOT congruent.

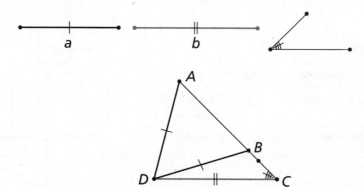

AAA cannot be used to show congruence of triangles. For example, equilateral triangles have three 60° angles, yet they are not all congruent.

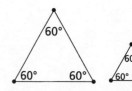

85

If $\triangle ABC$ and $\triangle XYZ$ are right triangles, with $\overline{BC} \cong \overline{YZ}$ and $\overline{BA} \cong \overline{YX}$, then $\triangle ABC \cong \triangle XYZ$. Extend $\overline{ZX}$ to a point W such that $\overline{XW} \cong \overline{AC}$. $\triangle ABC \cong \triangle YXW$ by SAS. Because these triangles are congruent, their hypotenuses are congruent. That is, $\overline{BC} \cong \overline{YW}$. Since we were given $\overline{BC} \cong \overline{YZ}$, we know that $\overline{YW} \cong \overline{YZ}$ by the transitive property of congruence. $\angle W \cong \angle Z$ by the Isosceles Triangle Theorem. So, $\triangle YXW \cong \triangle YXZ$ by AAS. Therefore, $\triangle ABC \cong \triangle XYZ$ by the transitive property of congruence. This result is known as the **Hypotenuse-Leg Theorem.**

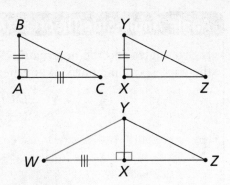

Hypotenuse-Leg Theorem (HL)

If the hypotenuse and a leg of one right triangle are congruent to the hypotenuse and corresponding leg of another, then the right triangles are congruent. HL $\rightarrow$ right $\triangle$s congruent

---

EXAMPLES 4 and 5   **Different methods of proof**

4 **Given:** $\overline{BE} \perp$ bisector of $\overline{AD}$, $\overline{AB} \cong \overline{DE}$
Prove: $\triangle ABC \cong \triangle DEC$ using a two-column proof.

■ **SOLUTION**

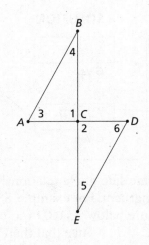

Statements	Reasons
1. $\overline{BE} \perp$ bisector of $\overline{AD}$	1. Given
2. C is the midpoint of $\overline{AD}$.	2. If bisect, then midpoint
3. $\overline{AC} \cong \overline{DC}$	3. If midpoint, the $\cong$ segments.
4. $\angle 1$ & $\angle 2$ are right $\angle$s	4. $\perp$s form right $\angle$s
5. $\triangle ABC$ and $\triangle DEC$ are right $\triangle$s	5. If rt angle, then rt $\triangle$.
6. $\overline{AB} \cong \overline{DE}$	6. Given
7. $\triangle ABC \cong \triangle DEC$	7. HL $\rightarrow$ rt $\triangle$s congruent

5 Prove the same result as Example 5, using a flow proof.

■ **SOLUTION**

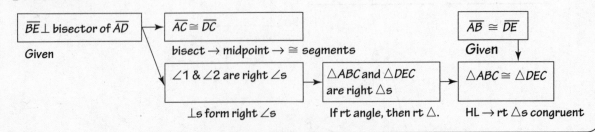

86

Showing That Triangles Are Congruent

Side-Side-Side (SSS) Congruence Postulate
If three sides of one triangle are congruent to the corresponding three sides of another triangle, then the triangles are congruent.

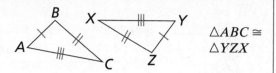

$\triangle ABC \cong \triangle YZX$

Side-Angle-Side (SAS) Congruence Postulate
If two sides and the included angle of one triangle are congruent to the corresponding two sides and the included angle of another triangle, then the triangles are congruent.

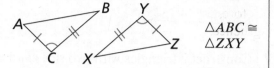

$\triangle ABC \cong \triangle ZXY$

Angle-Side-Angle (ASA) Congruence Postulate
If two angles and the included side of one triangle are congruent to the corresponding two angles and the included side of another triangle, then the triangles are congruent.

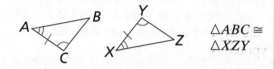

$\triangle ABC \cong \triangle XZY$

Angle-Angle-Side (AAS) Congruence Theorem
If two angles and the nonincluded side of one triangle are congruent to the corresponding two angles and the nonincluded side of another triangle, then the triangles are congruent.

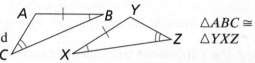

$\triangle ABC \cong \triangle YXZ$

Hypotenuse-Leg (HL) Congruence Theorem
If the hypotenuse and one leg of a right triangle are congruent to the hypotenuse and the corresponding leg of another right triangle, then the right triangles are congruent.

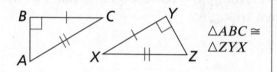

$\triangle ABC \cong \triangle ZYX$

Practice

Choose the numeral preceding the word or expression that best completes the statement or answers the question.

1 Suppose $AB = RS$ and $\angle A = \angle R$. What other information is needed to prove that $\triangle ABC \cong \triangle RST$ by ASA?

  (1) $\angle C = \angle T$ **(3)** $\angle B = \angle S$

  (2) $AC = RT$ **(4)** $\angle A = \angle B$

2 Which congruence statement can be used to prove that the two triangles in the accompanying figure are congruent?

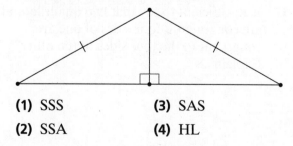

  (1) SSS   **(3)** SAS

  (2) SSA   **(4)** HL

In Exercises 3–6, determine if there is enough information to prove the triangles congruent. If so, write the statement; otherwise, write "not possible."

3

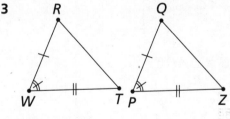

4

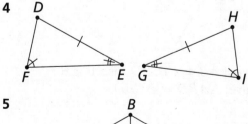

5

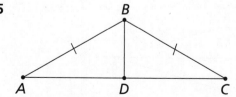

87

6

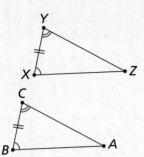

7 Construct 2 triangles with two sides and a nonincluded angle congruent. Verify that this construction demonstrates that SSA is not a valid argument for congruence.

8 Prove the AAS Theorem: *If two angles and the nonincluded side of one triangle are congruent to the corresponding parts of another triangle, the triangles are congruent.*

Given the congruent triangles in Exercises 9–11, name the corresponding parts of the two triangles.

9 $\triangle ABC \cong \triangle CDA$

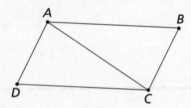

10 $\triangle ACB \cong \triangle ECD$

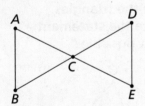

11 $\triangle ABC \cong \triangle ADC$

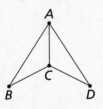

12 **Given:** $\overline{AB} \cong \overline{CB}$, $\overrightarrow{BD}$ bisects $\angle B$
   Prove: $\triangle ABD \cong \triangle CBD$

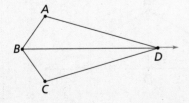

13 **Given:** $\angle ABC \cong \angle DCB$, $\angle DBC \cong \angle ACB$
   Prove: $\triangle ABC \cong \triangle DCB$

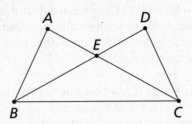

14 **Given:** $\overline{SW}$ is the $\perp$ bisector of $\overline{RT}$
   $\overline{RS} \cong \overline{TS}$.
   Prove: $\triangle RWS \cong \triangle TWS$

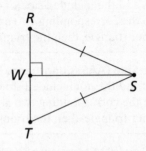

15 **Given:** $\angle G \cong \angle E$, $\angle 2 \cong \angle 3$, $\overline{AB} \cong \overline{DC}$
   Prove: $\triangle GAC \cong \triangle EDB$

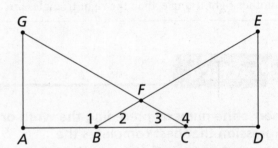

16 The diagonal legs of this chair have equal lengths and are joined at their midpoints. Is this enough information to prove that $\triangle ABE \cong \triangle DCE$? Justify your answer.

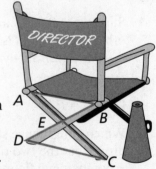

17 Is it sufficient to say that two quadrilaterals are congruent if four sides of one are congruent to the four sides of the other? Explain.

3.5 More Formal Proofs Involving Triangles

When writing a proof always think and plan before you write. If you are proving segments or angles congruent, they will be **corresponding parts** of a pair of triangles in the diagram. Look at all the triangle pairs in the diagram and how the given information best fits each pair, then pick a pair of target triangles to prove congruent. Justify the final side or angle congruence with: **If triangles are congruent, then corresponding parts of those congruent triangles are congruent.** Use the abbreviation: △s ≅ → **CPCTC**.

EXAMPLES 1 and 2 — Using corresponding parts of congruent triangles are congruent

1 Prove that in an isosceles triangle, the segment joining the vertex angle to the midpoint of the opposite side bisects the vertex angle and is perpendicular to the opposite side.

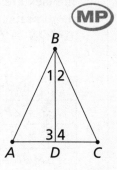

■ **SOLUTION**

Given: △ABC; $\overline{AB} \cong \overline{CB}$; D is the midpoint of $\overline{AC}$.
Prove: $\angle 1 \cong \angle 2$; $\overline{BD} \perp \overline{AC}$

Statements	Reasons
1. $\overline{AB} \cong \overline{CB}$; D is the midpoint of $\overline{AC}$.	1. Given
2. $\overline{AD} \cong \overline{CD}$	2. midpoint → congruent segs
3. $\overline{BD} \cong \overline{BD}$	3. Reflexive Property of Congruence
4. △$ABD \cong$ △CBD	4. SSS → △s congruent
5. $\angle 1 \cong \angle 2$	5. △s congruent → CPCTC
6. $\overline{BD}$ bisects $\angle ABC$.	6. congruent angles → angle bisector
7. $\angle 3 \cong \angle 4$	7. △s congruent → CPCTC
8. $\overline{BD} \perp \overline{AC}$	8. If two lines intersect to form ≅ adjacent ∠s, the lines are ⊥.

2 **Given:** $\overline{AB} \cong \overline{AC}$; $\overline{AD} \cong \overline{AE}$
Prove: $\angle 1 \cong \angle 2$

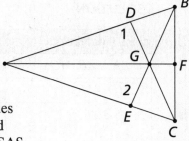

■ **SOLUTION**

Analysis: Begin by analyzing the figure to see the corresponding parts. If $\angle 1$ and $\angle 2$ are corresponding parts of △ACD and △ABE then the proof is done. $\overline{AB}$ and $\overline{AE}$ are sides of △AEB. $\overline{AC}$ and $\overline{AD}$ are sides of △ADC. $\angle DAE$ is included between both pairs of sides, so the triangles are congruent by SAS.

Statements	Reasons
1. $\overline{AB} \cong \overline{AC}$; $\overline{AD} \cong \overline{AE}$	1. Given
2. $\angle DAC \cong \angle EAB$	2. Reflexive Property
3. △$ABE \cong$ △ACD	3. SAS → △s congruent
4. $\angle 1 \cong \angle 2$	4. △s congruent → CPCTC

3 **Given:** $\angle N \cong \angle P$, $\overline{MO} \cong \overline{QO}$
Prove: $\overline{MP} \cong \overline{QN}$

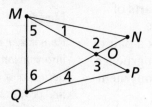

■ **SOLUTION**

Analysis: In the diagram to the right, $\triangle QNM$ in blue and $\triangle MPQ$ in black are our target triangles to prove $\overline{QN} \cong \overline{MP}$. We need more parts to prove our target triangles congruent, so first prove $\triangle MON \cong \triangle QOP$ for those needed parts.

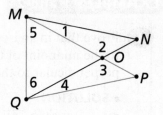

Statements	Reasons
1. $\angle N \cong \angle P$, $\overline{MO} \cong \overline{QO}$	1. Given
2. $\angle 2 \cong \angle 3$	2. Vertical angles are congruent.
3. $\triangle MON \cong \triangle QOP$	3. AAS → △s congruent
4. $\overline{MN} \cong \overline{QP}$	4. △s congruent → CPCTC
5. $\overline{MO} \cong \overline{QO}$	5. Given or CPCTC
6. $\angle 5 \cong \angle 6$	6. If two sides of a triangle are congruent, the angles opposite those sides are congruent. ($\triangle MOQ$)
7. $\triangle QNM \cong \triangle MPQ$	7. AAS → △s congruent
8. $\overline{MP} \cong \overline{QN}$	8. △s congruent → CPCTC

4 Now prove Example 3 using only ONE pair of congruent triangles.

■ **SOLUTION**

Statements	Reasons
1. $\angle N \cong \angle P$, $\overline{MO} \cong \overline{QO}$	1. Given
2. $\overline{MQ} \cong \overline{MQ}$	2. Reflexive Property
3. $\angle 5 \cong \angle 6$	3. If two sides of a triangle are congruent, the angles opposite those sides are congruent. ($\triangle MOQ$)
4. $\triangle QNM \cong \triangle MPQ$	4. AAS → △s congruent
5. $\overline{MP} \cong \overline{QN}$	5. △s congruent → CPCTC

As shown in the above examples, there is often more than one way of doing a proof. Use the type of proof that you recognize and can complete.

If a valid argument from a statement leads to a false conclusion (a contradiction), then the statement is false.

An **indirect proof** is one that involves the use of indirect reasoning. In this type of proof, a statement and its negation are often the only possibilities.

Writing an Indirect Proof

1 Assume the negation of what you want to prove.

2 Use logical reasoning to show a contradiction.

3 Conclude that your assumption must be false and that what you wanted to prove must be true.

EXAMPLES 5 through 7 **Writing indirect proofs**

5 Prove that $3(4x + 3) \neq 6(2x + 4)$.

■ **SOLUTION**

Assume that $3(4x + 3) = 6(2x + 4)$ is true.

$12x + 9 = 12x + 24$ ← **Distributive property**
$\quad\quad 9 = 24$ ← **Subtraction property of equality**

This is false. Therefore, the original statement must be false:
$3(4x + 3) \neq 6(2x + 4)$.

6 **Given:** $\triangle ABC$ with $m\angle 1 \neq m\angle 2$
Prove: $AB \neq CB$

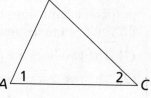

■ **SOLUTION**

Assume that $AB = CB$. If two sides of a triangle are equal, then the angles that are opposite those sides are equal. Therefore, $m\angle 1 = m\angle 2$. But this contradicts what is given, that $m\angle 1 \neq m\angle 2$. The original assumption $AB = CB$ must be false. This means its negation is true: $AB \neq CB$.

7 **Given:** $\triangle ABC$
Prove: $\triangle ABC$ has at most one right angle.

■ **SOLUTION**

Assume that $\triangle ABC$ has more than one right angle. That is, assume $\angle A$ and $\angle B$ are both right angles. Then

$m\angle A + m\angle B + m\angle C = 90° + 90° + m\angle C = 180° + m\angle C$
and m angle $C > 0$.

Since $m\angle C$ must be greater than 0, then the sum of the measures of $\triangle ABC$ is greater than 180 which contradicts a known fact. Therefore, $\triangle ABC$ has at most one right angle.

Choose the numeral preceding the word or expression that best completes the statement or answers the question.

1 Which of the following can *not* be used when writing a proof?

(1) axioms

(2) definition

(3) theorems that are yet to be proven

(4) theorems that have been proven

2 Which of the following statements contradict each other?

    I *l* and *m* are coplanar lines.
    II *l* and *m* are parallel lines.
    III *l* and *m* are intersecting lines.

(1) I and II

(2) II and III

(3) I and III

(4) None of the statements contradict each other.

3 If you wanted to prove that two lines are perpendicular using an indirect proof, what do you need to assume?

(1) The two lines are parallel.

(2) The two lines are congruent.

(3) The two lines are not perpendicular.

(4) The angle formed by the two lines is 90°.

4 If two triangles are congruent, which of the following allows you to conclude that their corresponding angles have the same measure?

(1) AAS

(2) CPCTC

(3) Reflexive Property

(4) All right angles are congruent.

For Exercises 5–10, fill in the blanks in the following flow proof.

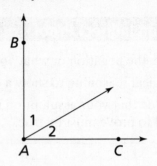

Given: ∠1 and ∠2 are complementary.
Prove: $\overrightarrow{AB} \perp \overrightarrow{AC}$

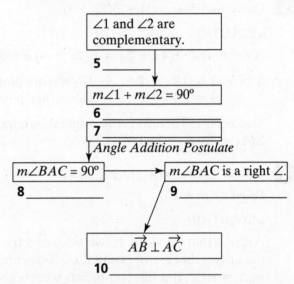

11 **Given:** $\overline{AD} \cong \overline{CE}$, ∠DAC ≅ ∠ECA
    Prove: △CED ≅ △ADE

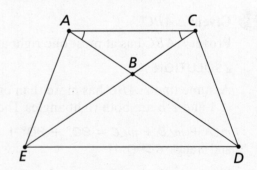

12 **Prove:** If $m\angle 1 \neq m\angle 2$, then $\angle 1$ and $\angle 2$ are not vertical angles. Hint: Use an indirect proof.

13 Complete the following proof.

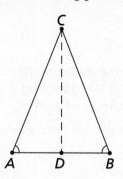

Given: $\triangle ABC$, $\angle A \cong \angle B$
Prove: $\overline{AC} \cong \overline{BC}$

Statements	Reasons
1. Construct the angle bisector of $\angle C$ and let D be the point where it intersects side $\overline{AB}$.	1.
2. $\angle ACD \cong \angle BCD$	2.
3. $\angle A \cong \angle B$	3.
4. $\overline{CD} \cong \overline{CD}$	4.
5. $\triangle ACD \cong \triangle BCD$	5.
6. $\overline{AC} \cong \overline{BC}$	6.

14 Prove that the median drawn from the vertex of an isosceles triangle bisects the vertex angle.

15 **Given:** $\overline{AD} \cong \overline{BE}$, $\angle DAB \cong \angle EBA$
Prove: $\overline{BD} \cong \overline{AE}$

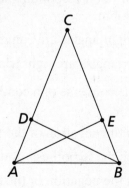

16 **Given:** $\overline{AD} \cong \overline{BE}$, $\overline{CD} \cong \overline{CE}$
Prove: $\overline{AE} \cong \overline{BD}$

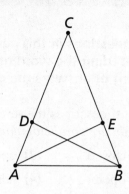

17 **Given:** $\angle 2 \cong \angle 3$, $\angle 4 \cong \angle 5$
Prove: $\overline{BA} \cong \overline{BC}$

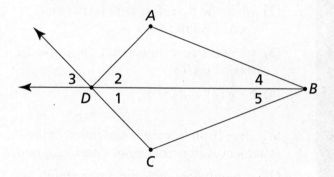

18 **Given:** $\overline{AD} \cong \overline{CD}$ and $\overline{BD}$ bisects $\angle ADC$
Prove: $\angle 2 \cong \angle 3$

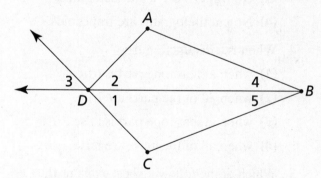

19 **Prove:** Any point on the perpendicular bisector of a line segment is equidistant from the endpoints of the segment.

20 **Prove:** The altitude drawn to the base of an isosceles triangle bisects the vertex angle.

Chapter 3 Preparing for the Assessment

Answer all questions in this part. For each question, select the numeral preceding the word or expression that best completes the statement or answers the question.

1 Which best describes the statement *All rhombi are parallelograms*?

   (1) true closed   (3) open

   (2) true open   (4) false closed

2 When is a conjunction false?

   (1) when both statements are true

   (2) when the first statement is true and the second is false

   (3) when the first statement is false and the second is true

   (4) both (2) and (3)

3 Which of the following is a negation of the statement *A trapezoid is not a parallelogram*?

   (1) A parallelogram is not a trapezoid.

   (2) A trapezoid is a parallelogram.

   (3) No trapezoid is a parallelogram.

   (4) No parallelograms are trapezoids.

4 When is a disjunction true?

   (1) when at least one part is true

   (2) when all of the parts are true

   (3) when at least one part is false

   (4) when all of the parts are false

5 Which of the following best explains the truth value of the statement *If triangles have three sides, then quadrilaterals have five sides*?

   (1) true, because the hypothesis is true and the conclusion is false

   (2) true, because both the hypothesis and conclusion are false

   (3) false, because the hypothesis is true and the conclusion is false

   (4) false, because both the hypothesis and conclusion are false

6 Which of the following statements is the converse of the statement *If you study, then you will earn good grades*?

   (1) You will earn good grades if you study.

   (2) If you earn good grades, then you studied.

   (3) If you do not earn good grades, then you did not study.

   (4) If you do not study, then you will not earn good grades.

7 Given the statement *If the measure of an angle is 125°, then the angle is obtuse*, which of the following is correct?

   (1) The statement is a conditional statement.

   (2) The statement is a biconditional statement.

   (3) The converse of the statement is true.

   (4) The original statement is false.

8 Which condition is **NOT** needed to prove triangles congruent using the Hypotenuse-Leg Theorem?

   (1) The hypotenuse are congruent.

   (2) A pair of corresponding legs are congruent.

   (3) The right angles are congruent.

   (4) The triangles are right triangles.

9 How is the converse of a conditional formed?

   (1) Form the negation of the hypothesis.

   (2) Switch the hypothesis and conclusion.

   (3) Form the negation of the conclusion.

   (4) Negate both the hypothesis and conclusion.

10 Which type of statement can always be represented as a bi conditional?

   (1) theorems

   (2) postulates

   (3) corollaries

   (4) definitions

11 What phrase represents the common elements of two sets?

   (1) the sets' intersection

   (2) the sets' union

   (3) the sets' complements

   (4) the sets' supplements

12 What is the type of reasoning used in proof?

   (1) inductive reasoning

   (2) deductive reasoning

   (3) counter examples

   (4) converse reasoning

In Exercises 13–15, use the diagram of collinear points *A*, *B*, *C*, and *D*.

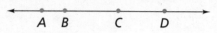

13 Find $\overrightarrow{AB} \cup \overrightarrow{DC}$

14 Find $\overline{AC} \cap \overline{DC}$

15 Find $\overrightarrow{AB} \cap \overrightarrow{CB}$

16 Place the lettered reasons in the two-column format to prove the given theorem.

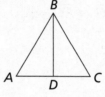

Given: $\triangle ABC$ with $\overline{AB} \cong \overline{BC}$
         $\overline{BD}$ bisects $\angle ABC$.

Prove: $\overline{AD} \cong \overline{CD}$

Statements	Reasons	Choose from
1. $\overline{AB} \cong \overline{BC}$	**1.** _____	**A.** 2 sides of a $\triangle \cong \rightarrow \angle s$ opposite $\cong$
2. $\angle BAD \cong \angle BCD$	**2.** _____	**B.** $\triangle s \cong \rightarrow$ CPCTC
3. $\overline{BD}$ bisects $\angle ABC$.	**3.** _____	**C.** ASA $\rightarrow \triangle's \cong$
4. $\angle ABD \cong \angle CBD$	**4.** _____	**D.** Given
5. $\triangle ABD \cong \triangle CBD$	**5.** _____	**E.** SAS $\rightarrow \triangle s \cong$
6. $\overline{AD} \cong \overline{CD}$	**6.** _____	**F.** $\angle$ bisector $\rightarrow 2 \angle s \cong$

Answer all questions in this part using any method of proof.

17 Given: $\overline{AB} \cong \overline{CB}, \overline{AE} \cong \overline{CD},$
$\angle AED \cong \angle CDE$

Prove: $\triangle ABE \cong \triangle CBD$

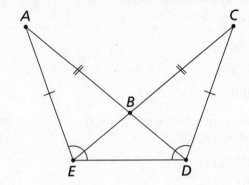

18 Given: $\overline{AF} \perp \overline{BC}; \overline{DG} \cong \overline{EG}$
$\angle ADG \cong \angle AEG$

Prove: $\overline{BF} \cong \overline{CF}$

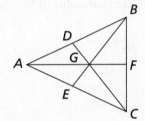

19 Given: $\triangle QTR$ with $\overline{QT} \cong \overline{TR}$
$\angle PQT \cong \angle SRT$

Prove: $\overline{PR} \cong \overline{SQ}$

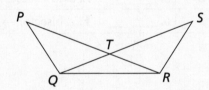

4 Transformations and Congruence

M.C. Escher

Maurits Cornelis Escher (1898-1972) is one of the world's most famous graphic artists. His art is enjoyed by millions of people all over the world, as can be seen on the many web sites on the internet. He is most famous for his so-called impossible constructions, such as *Ascending and Descending* and *Relativity,* his *Transformation Prints,* such as *Metamorphosis I, Metamorphosis II, and Metamorphosis III; Sky & Water I;* and *Reptiles.*

Source: www.mcescher.com

4.1 Transformations and Translations

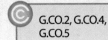
G.CO.2, G.CO.4, G.CO.5

We know from algebra that a **function** is a mapping from one set, the **domain,** to another set, the **range,** such that no domain element has more than one range element.

Definition

A **transformation of the plane** is a one to one mapping (function) that maps points in the plane, the **pre-image** or **domain,** to points in the plane, the **image** or **range.**

Often a transformation of the plane is simply referred to as transformation. Frequently a point and its image are referred to as **corresponding points**.

There are any number of ways that a figure could be transformed. For example a triangle could be "slid," "rotated," "enlarged," "shrunk," or "morphed" in some other way.

In the figure below, $\triangle ABC$ has been transformed in a number of different ways. In some cases the image appears to be comparable to the preimage. In other cases there appear to be differences. In all these cases however the original figure has been *transformed* and the operation that was applied to the figure is called a ***transformation***.

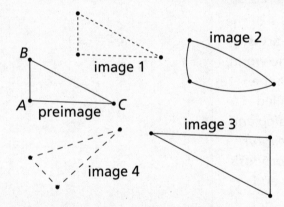

In the figure below, $\triangle ABC$ has been transformed by a **translation through vector** $\vec{v}$ into $\triangle A'B'C'$.

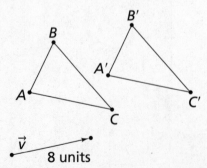

Note

A *vector* has a given length (magnitude) and a given direction.

Use a ruler and draw $\overleftrightarrow{AA'}$, $\overleftrightarrow{BB'}$, $\overleftrightarrow{CC'}$. What appears to be true?

The lines $\overleftrightarrow{AA'}$, $\overleftrightarrow{BB'}$, $\overleftrightarrow{CC'}$ appear to be parallel to each other and to the vector $\vec{v}$. Using an interactive geometry environment this transformation could be constructed and this relationship and the ones that follow could be verified for a number of different cases.

Using a ruler compare the measure of $\vec{v}$ to the measure of the lengths of $\overline{AA'}$, $\overline{BB'}$, $\overline{CC'}$. What is true about these measurements?

The measure of $\vec{v}$ and the segments $\overline{AA'}$, $\overline{BB'}$, $\overline{CC'}$ are all equal.

Definition

A translation by vector $\vec{v}$ of the pre-image point **P** in the plane results in an image point **P'** such that the vector $\overrightarrow{PP'}$ is equal in length to $\vec{v}$ and $\overrightarrow{PP'}$ is parallel to $\vec{v}$. Symbolically this is written as $T_{\vec{v}}(P) = P'$.

Now measure the angles of $\triangle ABC$ and $\triangle A'B'C'$. This can be done using a protractor or interactive geometry software. What do you observe about these measures? Corresponding angles are all the same. Therefore $\triangle ABC$ and $\triangle A'B'C'$ are the same size and shape or **congruent**.

A transformation that preserves distance is called a **rigid motion,** also known as an **isometry**.

Definition

If z is a transformation of the plane such that for any two points P and Q in the plane, $z(P) = P'$ and $z(Q) = Q'$, and $PQ = P'Q'$, then z is called an **isometry** or **rigid motion**.

This leads to a question: Is a translation an isometry?

Consider the points P and Q in the plane. $T_{\vec{v}}$ is a translation such that $T_{\vec{v}}(P) = P'$ and $T_{\vec{v}}(Q) = Q'$. What must be shown is that $PQ = P'Q'$. What is known is that $\vec{v}$, $\overrightarrow{PP'}$ and $\overrightarrow{QQ'}$ are parallel and congruent by the definition of a translation. Therefore quadrilateral $PP'Q'Q$ is a parallelogram and $\overline{PQ} \cong \overline{P'Q'}$. This implies that $PQ = P'Q'$.

A translation is an isometry.

(MP)

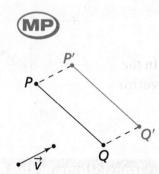

99

Translations can also be performed in the coordinate plane. In the accompanying figure △ABC is translated by the vector $\vec{v}$ to the image △A'B'C'.

EXAMPLE 1 **Determining coordinates**

Determine the coordinates of △A'B'C', the image of △ABC under this translation by vector $\vec{v}$.

■ **SOLUTION**

$A'(-1, 1), B'(1, 4), C'(6, 0)$

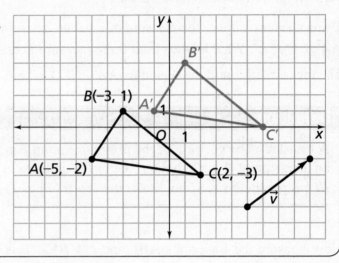

If the horizontal and vertical components of vector $\vec{v}$ are determined a relationship for finding the image coordinates can be found. In this case the horizontal component is 4 units and the vertical component is 3 units. When working in the coordinate plane a translation can be denoted as $T_{a,b}$ where a is the horizontal component of the vector and b is the vertical component.

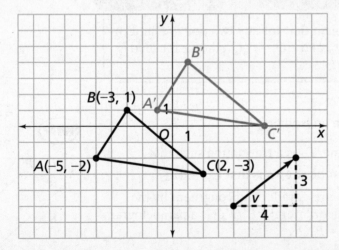

Translations in the Plane

The image of $P(x, y)$ under a translation a units horizontally and b units vertically is given by:

$$T_{a,b}(x, y) \rightarrow (x + a, y + b)$$

EXAMPLE 2 **Determining coordinates and length of a vector**

2 The figure shows $\triangle ABC$ under the translation $T_{-3,-4}$. Determine the coordinates of the vertices of the image triangle and the length of the translation vector.

■ **SOLUTION**

The image of $\triangle ABC$ under the translation $T_{-3,-4}$ will have coordinates

$A(-1, 4) \rightarrow A'(-1 + (-3),$
$4 + (-4)) = A'(-4, 0)$
$B(3, 3) \rightarrow B'(3 + (-3),$
$3 + (-4)) = B'(0, -1)$
$C(2, -1) \rightarrow C'(2 + (-3),$
$-1 + (-4)) = C'(-1, -5)$

The horizontal and vertical components of the translation form a right triangle. Using the Pythagorean Theorem the length of the vector can be determined. **Note:** We consider directed distance to help determine the direction of the vector.

$c = \sqrt{a^2 + b^2}$
$\quad = \sqrt{(-3)^2 + (-4)^2}$
$\quad = \sqrt{25} = 5$

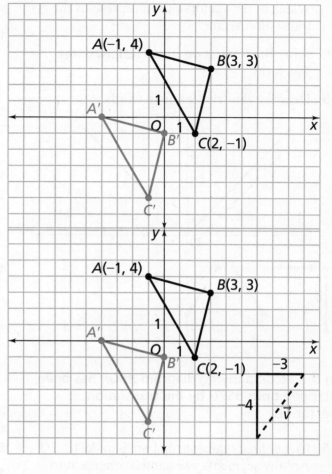

A question to consider is: Are there any points that are their own image under a translation? In other words are there any points that remain **fixed** under a translation? The answer in no, unless the magnitude of the vector is zero which wouldn't seem to make any sense. There are **no fixed points in a translation**.

Practice

1 $\triangle RST$ is the image of $\triangle JKL$ under a translation by vector k. Which of the following is always true?

(1) $\triangle RST$ is congruent to $\triangle JKL$.

(2) $\triangle RST$ coincides with $\triangle JKL$.

(3) $\triangle RST$ is smaller than $\triangle JKL$.

(4) $\triangle RST$ is larger than $\triangle JKL$.

2 Translate the figure shown by the vector shown.

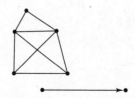

3 In the accompanying graph the dashed function is the image of the solid function. Which of the vectors shown represents the translation vector?

4 Write the translation from Exercise 3 in $T_{a,b}$ form.

5 Describe this translation in words.

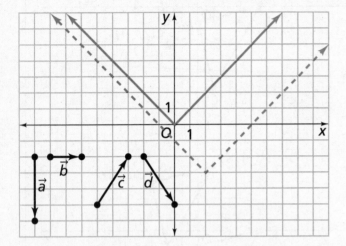

In the accompanying diagram $\triangle PQR$ has been mapped onto $\triangle STU$ by the translation vector $\overrightarrow{CD}$.

6 Name three segments that are parallel to $\overline{CD}$. Are the segments you named congruent to $\overline{CD}$?

7 What is the image of P? What is the pre-image of T?

8 What segment is parallel to and congruent to $\overline{ST}$?

9 What point corresponds to U? What segment corresponds to $\overline{QR}$?

10 Name three other vectors that would be equivalent to $\overrightarrow{CD}$.

Choose the numeral preceding the word or expression that best completes the statement or answers the question.

11 Under which transformation will $P'(2, -4)$ be the image of $P(1, 1)$?

  (1) reflection in the x-axis

  (2) translation 1 unit right and 5 units down

  (3) rotation of $180°$ about the origin

  (4) translation 1 unit right and 1 unit up

12 What are the coordinates of the image of $A(3, 5)$ under $T_{-5, -4}$?

  (1) $A'(-2, 1)$ **(3)** $A'(8, 9)$

  (2) $A'(-2, 9)$ **(4)** $A'(8, 1)$

13 Which represents the translation under which the image of $H(-3, -5)$ is $H'(7, 0)$?

  (1) 10 units right and 5 units down

  (2) 10 units right and 5 units up

  (3) 10 units left and 5 units down

  (4) 10 units left and 5 units up

In Exercises 14–15, write the coordinates of the image of the given point under the specified transformation.

14 $C(-5, 4)$; translation 2 units left and 4 units up

15 $D(-5, 4)$; translation 4 units right and 4 units down

In Exercise 16, graph the given points in the coordinate plane. In the same plane, sketch the image under the specified transformation.

16 Under a translation, the image of $A(4, -3)$ is $A'(6, -7)$. Find the image of $B(-2, 7)$ under the same translation.

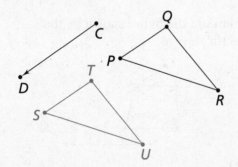

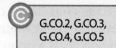
4.2 Reflections and Symmetry

When we look in a mirror we see a reflection. The accompanying figure shows a reflection in the plane. The *mirror* is a line which is known as the **line of reflection**. In this transformation the blue figure is the image of the black figure in a reflection about the given line (the mirror).

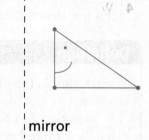

Using a ruler connect each pre-image point to its corresponding image point. What seems to be true about these segments? It appears that these segments are parallel to each other. The mirror or line of reflection appears to be the perpendicular bisector of each segment joining a pre-image point to its image point. This investigation can be enhanced if done using an interactive geometry environment or patty paper and the results verified.

mirror

EXAMPLE 1 **Using a reflection**

 Verify that the line of reflection is the perpendicular bisector of the segments joining a pre-image point to its image point in the accompanying figure.

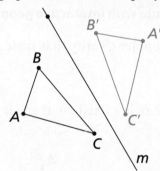

■ **SOLUTION**

Using a ruler and a protractor the measures can be found to verify that *m* is the perpendicular bisector of the segments. The protractor can be used to determine the 90° angles.

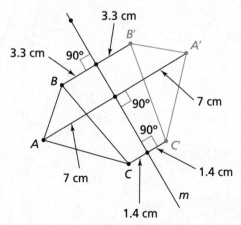

When placing your finger tip on a mirror, where is its reflection? Correct, the reflection is the point where your finger is touching the mirror. The same is true in the plane. If a point is on the line of reflection, its image is the point itself. In the accompanying figure $\triangle CAT$ is reflected over line l. Point A is on the line of reflection and is therefore its own image. Recall, a **fixed point** under a transformation is any point that is its own image.

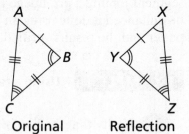

Definition

A **reflection** in the plane over a line l, notated R_l, is a transformation where $R_l(A) = A'$ such that the line l is the perpendicular bisector of $\overline{AA'}$ provided A is not on line l. If the point P is on l, the $R_l(P) = P$ and P is called a **fixed point**.

Is a reflection an isometry? Informally, if the figure were to be folded along the line of reflection the image figure will fall on top of the pre-image. Try this by drawing a figure on a piece of patty paper and folding along a line of reflection. Can you determine the image? Is distance preserved?

Original   Reflection

EXAMPLE 2   Confirming angle measure with interactive geometry tools

2 Using an interactive geometry environment, verify that angle measure is preserved when a triangle is reflected over a line.

■ SOLUTION

Note that the result is true even if there is a fixed point and if the line of refection cuts the triangle.

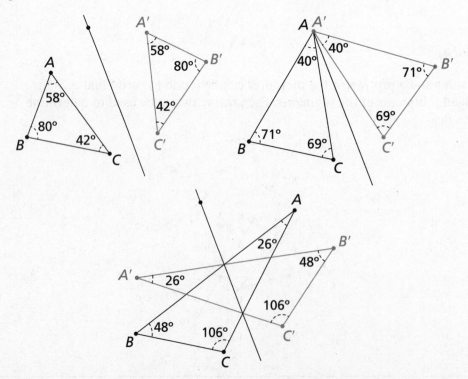

EXAMPLE 3 **Proving a reflection is an isometry**

Prove that if $\triangle B'HC'$ is a reflection of $\triangle BHC$ over line l, then $\triangle B'HC' \cong \triangle BHC$.

3 To prove that a reflection is an isometry requires looking at a number of cases. The case shown here is for a segment that is contained in the half plane determined by the line of reflection.

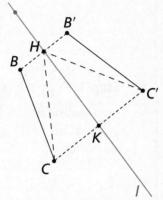

Statements	Reasons
1. l is the $\perp$ bisector of $\overline{BB'}$ and $\overline{CC'}$	1. The line of reflection is the $\perp$ bisector of the segments joining the preimage to the image.
2. $\overline{CK} \cong \overline{C'K}$	2. A bisector divides a segment into two $\cong$ segments.
3. $\angle CKH \cong \angle C'KH$	3. If two lines are $\perp$ then they form rt. $\angle$s & all rt. $\angle$s are $=$
4. $\overline{HK} \cong \overline{HK}$	4. Reflexive property
5. $\triangle CKH \cong \triangle C'KH$	5. If S.A.S of one $\triangle$ are $\cong$ to the corresponding S.A.S. of another then $\triangle$ are $\cong$
6. $\overline{CH} \cong \overline{C'H}$	6. If two $\triangle$ are $\cong$ then CPCTC.
7. $\angle BHK = \angle BHC + \angle CHK$	7. Angle addition
8. $\angle B'HK = \angle B'HC' + \angle C'HK$	8. Angle addition
9. $\angle BHC + \angle CHK = \angle B'HC' + \angle C'HK$	9. Substitution
10. $\angle CHK = \angle C'HK$	10. If two $\triangle$ are $\cong$ then CPCTC.
11. $\angle BHC = \angle B'HC'$	11. Subtraction
12. $\overline{BH} \cong \overline{B'H}$	12. A bisector divides a segment into two $\cong$ segments.
13. $\triangle BHC \cong \triangle B'HC'$	13. If S.A.S of one $\triangle$ are $\cong$ to the corresponding S.A.S. of another then $\triangle$ are $\cong$

In the following example a double reflection will be considered.

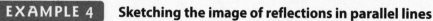

EXAMPLE 4 **Sketching the image of reflections in parallel lines**

4 Sketch the image of $\triangle ABC$ after reflections across line m and n where $m \parallel n$.

▪ **SOLUTION**

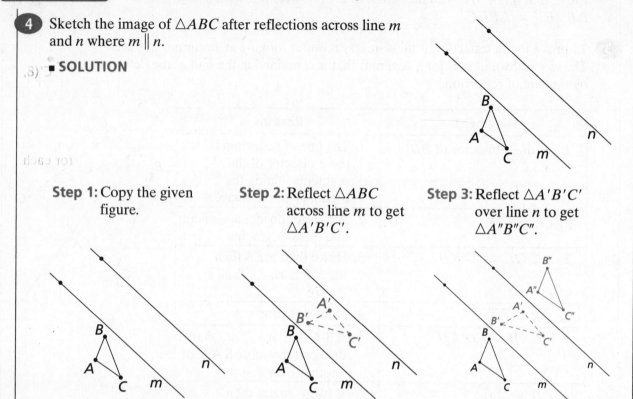

Step 1: Copy the given figure.

Step 2: Reflect $\triangle ABC$ across line m to get $\triangle A'B'C'$.

Step 3: Reflect $\triangle A'B'C'$ over line n to get $\triangle A''B''C''$.

Investigate the final drawing from Example 4 further. Can you identify a relationship between $\triangle ABC$ and $\triangle A''B''C''$?

The segments $\overline{BB''}$, $\overline{AA''}$, and $\overline{CC''}$ appear to be parallel and their measures are equal. This would indicate that $\triangle A''B''C''$ is the image of $\triangle ABC$ under a translation by a vector of magnitude equal to the measure of these segments and parallel to them.

Translations Related to Reflections

If the reflection of A in line m is A' and the refection of A' over line $n \parallel m$ is A'', then A'' is a translation of A.

A word about *orientation*. When $\triangle ABC$ is navigated so as to come upon A, B, and C, in that order, the direction navigated is said to be clockwise (or counterclockwise). If a figure and its image have the same orientation the transformation is referred to as a *direct transformation*. If the orientations are different the transformation is said to be an *opposite transformation*. In the example above $\triangle ABC$ and $\triangle A'B'C'$ have opposite orientation and $\triangle ABC$ and $\triangle A''B''C''$ direct.

From this we see that *a reflection is an opposite transformation* and *a translation is a direct transformation*.

106

Reflections in the Coordinate Plane

In the accompanying figure △ABC is reflected over the x-axis with the resulting image △A′B′C′. The image △A″B″C″ is the result of a reflection of △ABC over the y-axis. The coordinates of the vertices are shown in the table below.

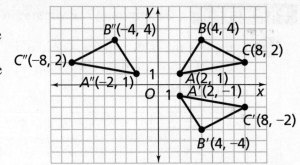

A	(2, 1)	A′	(2, −1)	A″	(−2, 1)
B	(4, 4)	B′	(4, −4)	B″	(−4, 4)
C	(8, 2)	C′	(8, −5)	C″	(−8, 2)

Make a conjecture concerning the pattern in the coordinates for each reflection.

EXAMPLES 5 and 6 Determining coordinates under a reflection

Determine the image point when the point with coordinates (3, −5) is reflected over the

5 x-axis

6 y-axis

■ SOLUTION

5 (3, 5)   **6** (−3, −5)

Consider two more reflections in the plane. The first is determining a reflection in the line y = x. In this figure △CAT has been reflected over the line y = x.

EXAMPLE 7 Determining coordinates of a reflection in y = x

7 Complete the table with the coordinates of the image of △CAT in this reflection.

■ SOLUTION

C	(4, 1)	A	(8, 3)	T	(5, −2)
C′	(1, 4)	A′	(3, 8)	T′	(−2, 5)

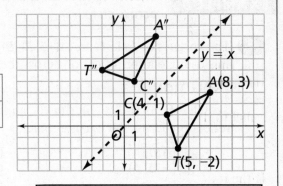

Look for a pattern in these results.

In the figure on the next page △FUN has been reflected in the line y = −x and the resulting image △F′U′N′ is shown.

EXAMPLE 8   Determining coordinates in a reflection in $y = x$

8   Complete the table with the coordinates of the image of $\triangle FUN$ in this reflection.

■ **SOLUTION**

F	$(2,5)$	U	$(7,-1)$	N	$(1,1)$
F'	$(-5,-2)$	U'	$(1,-7)$	N'	$(-1,-1)$

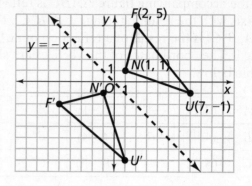

In the coordinate plane, there are three common line reflections. Reflections are isometries.

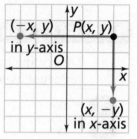

Special Reflections

The image of $P(x, y)$ under a **reflection across the x-axis** is the point $P'(x, -y)$.

$$r_{x\text{-axis}}(x, y) \qquad \rightarrow \qquad (x, -y)$$

The image of $P(x, y)$ under a **reflection across the y-axis** is the point $P'(-x, y)$.

$$r_{y\text{-axis}}(x, y) \qquad \rightarrow \qquad (-x, y)$$

The image of $P(x, y)$ under a **reflection across y = x** is the point $P'(y, x)$.

$$r_{y=x}(x, y) \qquad \rightarrow \qquad (y, x)$$

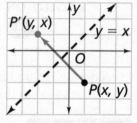

EXAMPLE 9   Sketching the image of a polygon under a reflection across an axis

9   The vertices of $\triangle ABC$ are $A(-3, 3)$, $B(6, 6)$, and $C(4, 1)$. Sketch the image of this triangle after reflection across the x-axis and across the y-axis.

■ **SOLUTION**

Sketch $A(-3, 3)$, $B(6, 6)$, $C(4, 1)$, and $\triangle ABC$. Under a reflection across the x-axis, replace y with $-y$.

$$
\begin{aligned}
r_{x\text{-axis}}(x, y) &\rightarrow (x, -y) \\
r_{x\text{-axis}}(-3, 3) &\rightarrow (-3, -3) \\
r_{x\text{-axis}}(6, 6) &\rightarrow (6, -6) \\
r_{x\text{-axis}}(4, 1) &\rightarrow (4, -1)
\end{aligned}
$$

Graph $A'(-3, -3)$, $B'(6, -6)$, and $C'(4, -1)$. Draw $\triangle A'B'C'$. The image is shown with solid blue segments.

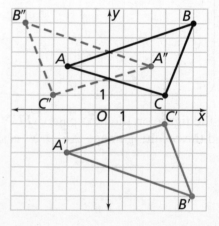

Under a reflection across the y-axis, replace x with $-x$.

$$
\begin{aligned}
r_{y\text{-axis}}(x, y) &\rightarrow (-x, y) \\
r_{y\text{-axis}}(-3, 3) &\rightarrow (3, 3) \\
r_{y\text{-axis}}(6, 6) &\rightarrow (-6, 6) \\
r_{y\text{-axis}}(4, 1) &\rightarrow (-4, 1)
\end{aligned}
$$

Graph $A''(3, 3)$, $B''(-6, 6)$, and $C''(-4, 1)$. Draw $\triangle A''B''C''$. The image is shown with dashed blue segments.

A **reflection about a point** is another type of transformation. A symbol for a reflection in point (a, b) is $r_{(a, b)}$. In the figure at the right, the image of point P is itself and the image of any other point Q is the point Q' where P is the midpoint of $\overline{QQ'}$. Point P is called the *point of reflection*. This diagram shows $\overline{QR}$ and its image $\overline{Q'R'}$ under a reflection in point P.

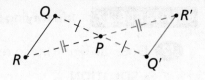

Now consider a special point of reflection in the coordinate plane. Suppose that the point of reflection is the origin. In that case, the coordinates (x, y) of any point in the preimage are reflected to $(-x, -y)$ in the image.

EXAMPLE 10 **Sketching an image under reflection about the origin**

10 The vertices of $\triangle ABC$ are $A(-3, 3)$, $B(6, 6)$, and $C(4, 1)$. Sketch the image of this triangle after reflection about the origin.

■ **SOLUTION**

Sketch $A(-3, 3)$, $B(6, 6)$, $C(4, 1)$, and $\triangle ABC$. Under a reflection about the origin, replace x with $-x$ and y with $-y$.

$$r_{(0,0)}(x, y) \rightarrow (-x, -y)$$
$$r_{(0,0)}(-3, 3) \rightarrow (3, -3)$$
$$r_{(0,0)}(6, 6) \rightarrow (-6, -6)$$
$$r_{(0,0)}(4, 1) \rightarrow (-4, -1)$$

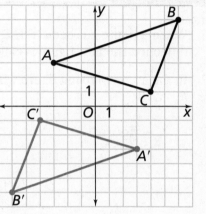

Graph $A'(3, -3)$, $B'(-6, -6)$, and $C'(-4, -1)$. Draw $\triangle A'B'C'$. The image is shown with solid blue segments.

A figure may be its own image after reflection across a line. For example, if m is a line of reflection, then the image of the regular octagon $ABCDEFGH$ after reflection across line m is the octagon $AHGFEDCB$, which is the same figure. A figure in the plane has **line symmetry** if it is its own image after reflection across some line in the plane. The line of reflection is called a **line of symmetry**.

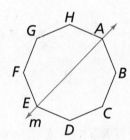

EXAMPLE 11 **Drawing lines of symmetry**

11 Sketch all lines of symmetry for a square.

■ **SOLUTION**

Sketch a square. The diagonals of the square are lines of symmetry. The lines passing through the midpoints of opposite sides are too.

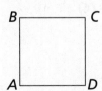 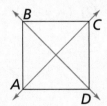 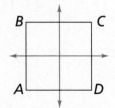

Lines of symmetry can be identified and specifically named when the figure is placed on a coordinate grid.

EXAMPLE 12   **Identifying lines of symmetry**

12 Does the figure at the right have line symmetry? Explain.

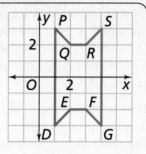

■ **SOLUTION**

The line $y = 0$ (the x-axis) and the line $x = 2.5$ are lines of symmetry. The figure is its own image after a reflection over either of those two lines.

Practice

1 When a figure has been transformed by a reflection the new figure is called the __?__.

2 In the accompanying figure which is $R_l(\triangle ABC)$?

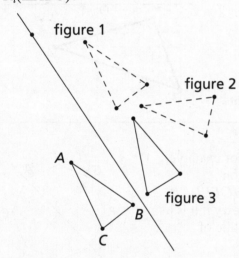

3 If $R_m(K) = K$ then which is true?

(1) K is not on line m.

(2) K is the line of reflection.

(3) K is a fixed point.

(4) K is on line m.

4 Describe how you would determine A' the image of A in a reflection about line l.

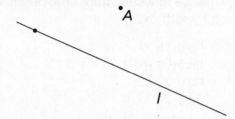

5 Is a reflection an isometry? Why?

6 Which is the image of $K(3, 1)$ after reflection in the line $y = -1$?

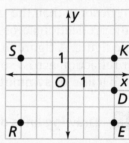

(1) D (2) E (3) R (4) S

7 Which of the following is the image of $r_{y=4}(x, y)$?

(1) $(x, 8 - y)$ (3) $(x, 4)$

(2) $(x, y + 4)$ (4) (x, y)

8 Copy this figure. Sketch all lines of symmetry.

In Exercises 9–11, write the coordinates of the image under the specified reflection.

9 $\triangle RST$ with vertices having coordinates $R(1, 1)$, $S(5, 1)$, and $T(5, 3)$; in the x-axis

10 $\triangle NBA$ with vertices having coordinates $N(1, 1)$, $B(5, 1)$, and $A(5, 3)$; in the y-axis

11 quadrilateral $EUDP$ with vertices having coordinates $E(3, 3)$, $U(5, 3)$, $D(1, -1)$, and $P(-1, -1)$; about $(2, 4)$

12 Under the reflection across line m, the image of $(0, 4)$ is $(2, 2)$. Write the equation of line m.

In Exercises 13–15, solve the problem. Clearly show all necessary work.

13 One vertex of a quadrilateral is $A(-3, -2)$. Find the coordinates of the other three vertices that complete a quadrilateral symmetric about the x-axis and the y-axis.

14 One vertex of a quadrilateral is $P(4, 2)$. Find the coordinates of the other three vertices that complete a quadrilateral symmetric about the lines $x = 1$ and $y = 1$.

15 Sketch the reflection of the parabola in the line $y = x$.

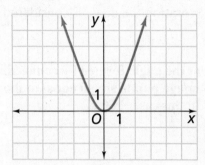

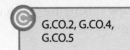
4.3 Rotations

In this figure $\triangle RST$ has been rotated about point C by an angle of 60°. Under a *rotation* in the plane a figure is "turned" using a fixed distance from a fixed point in the plane. The fixed angle is the *angle of rotation* and the fixed point is the *center of rotation*.

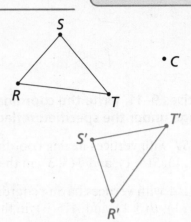

The rotation may be clockwise or counterclockwise. In this case $\triangle R'S'T'$ is the image in a rotation of 60° counterclockwise. In a counterclockwise rotation the angle is considered positive. In a clockwise rotation the angle is considered negative.

Notice that the angle formed by connecting preimage points to image points are all equal to the angle of rotation. In this case +60°.

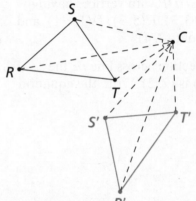

$m\angle SCS' = +60°$
$m\angle RCR' = +60°$
$m\angle TCT' = +60°$

EXAMPLE 1 **Verifying that a rotation is an isometry** ⎯⎯⎯⎯⎯⎯ **MP**

1 Using a ruler or an interactive geometry environment verify that a rotation preserves distance.

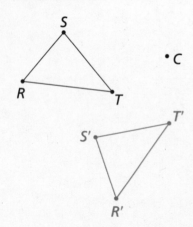

■ **SOLUTION**

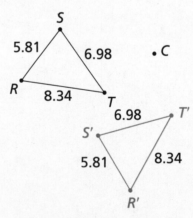

Image segments are the same length as the preimage segments.

What is the image of the center of a rotation? The center of rotation is a **fixed point** in this transformation. Notice further that the image and pre-image have the same orientation and therefore a rotation is a **direct transformation**.

EXAMPLE 2 **Sketching the image of a rotation**

2   Sketch the image of △*JKL* under a rotation of 100° counterclockwise about *J*.

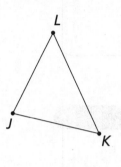

■ **SOLUTION**

Step 1 Use a protractor to measure the 100° angles to locate points *L'* and *K'*. Use a compass to draw $\overline{JL'}$ and $\overline{JK'}$ equal in length to $\overline{JL}$ and $\overline{JK}$.

Step 2 Join *J*, *L'*, and *K'* to form △*JL'K'*, the image of △*JLK*.

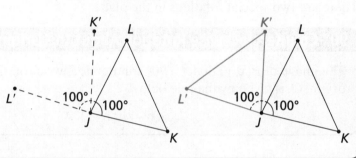

Definition

A transformation in the plane is a **rotation** if, when *P* is any point in the plane and θ is the measure of any angle, then $R_{P,\theta}(P) = P$ (*P* is the center of the rotation) and if *Q* is any other point in the plane $Q \neq P$ then $R_{P,\theta}(Q) = Q'$ and $m\angle QPQ' = \theta$.

In the accompanying figure line *m* and *n* intersect. Triangle *ABC* is reflected over *n* and the result is reflected over *m*, resulting in △*A'B'C'*. Make a conjecture about this outcome.

When an object is reflected over two intersecting lines the resulting image is the same as a rotation of the original figure.

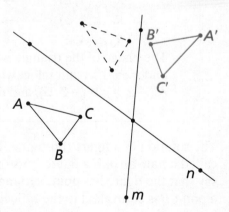

Rotations Related to Reflections

If the reflection of $\triangle ABC$ across line l_1 is $\triangle A'B'C'$, and the reflection of $\triangle A'B'C'$ across line l_2 is $\triangle A''B''C''$ then $\triangle A''B''C''$ is a rotation of $\triangle ABC$. The center of rotation is the point where lines l_1 and l_2 intersect and the angle of rotation is twice the measure of the acute angle formed by the intersecting lines.

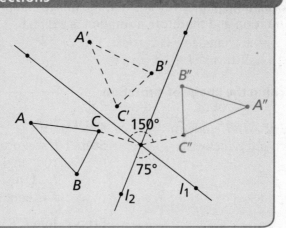

There are two special rotations in the plane.

90° Counterclockwise Rotation About the Origin

The image of $P(x, y)$ under a 90° counterclockwise rotation about the origin, O, is given by the rule below.

$$R_{O, 90°}(x, y) \rightarrow (-y, x)$$

EXAMPLE 3   **Sketching the image of a rotation in the coordinate plane**

 Sketch the image of the triangle with vertices $A(1, 2)$, $B(5, 3)$, and $C(4, 6)$ under a 90° counterclockwise rotation about the origin.

- **SOLUTION**

Apply the rule for a 90° counterclockwise rotation about the origin.

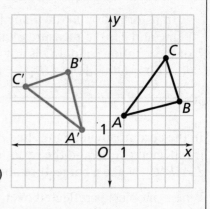

$R_{0, 90°}(1, 2)$ → $(-2, 1)$
$R_{0, 90°}(5, 3)$ → $(-3, 5)$
$R_{0, 90°}(4, 6)$ → $(-6, 4)$

The image of the triangle with vertices $A(1, 2)$, $B(5, 3)$, $C(4, 6)$ under a 90° counterclockwise rotation about the origin has $A'(-2, 1)$, $B'(-3, 5)$, and $C'(-6, 4)$ as its vertices.

The rotation of a figure through a 180° angle is a special type of rotation called a **half-turn**. If a figure is its own image under a half-turn, you can say that the figure has **point symmetry**. A rotation of a figure 180° about a point P is equivalent to the reflection about P.

180° Rotation About the Origin

The image of $P(x, y)$ under a 180° rotation about the origin, O, is given by:

$$R_{O, 180°}(x, y) \rightarrow (-x, -y)$$

114

EXAMPLE 4   **Sketching the image of a half-turn in the coordinate plane**

4 Sketch the image of the triangle with vertices $X(2, 2)$, $Y(5, 3)$, and $Z(4, 5)$ under a half-turn about the origin.

■ **SOLUTION**

Apply the rule for a 180° rotation about the origin.

$R_{O, 180°}(2, 2) \quad \rightarrow \quad (-2, -2)$

$R_{O, 180°}(5, 3) \quad \rightarrow \quad (-5, -3)$

$R_{O, 180°}(4, 5) \quad \rightarrow \quad (-4, -5)$

The coordinates of the image of $\triangle XYZ$ are $X'(-2, -2)$, $Y'(-5, -3)$, and $Z'(-4, -5)$.

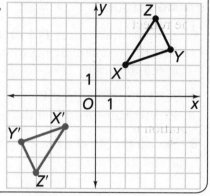

Recap of the Properties of Transformations			
Transformation	Fixed Points	Orientation	Image of segment a parallel segment
Translation	None	Direct	Yes
Reflection	Any points on line of reflection	Opposite	Sometimes (When segment is ‖ or ⊥ to line of reflection)
Rotation	One	Direct	Sometimes (Rotation of 180°)

Practice

Choose the numeral preceding the word or expression that best completes the statement or answers the question.

1 Which transformation is illustrated below?

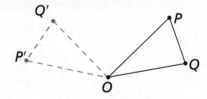

(1) rotation of $\triangle OPQ$ about O

(2) translation of $\triangle OPQ$ along $\overrightarrow{OQ}$

(3) translation of $\triangle OPQ$ along $\overrightarrow{OP}$

(4) reflection of $\triangle OPQ$ across $\overleftrightarrow{PQ}$

2 Which of the following are the coordinates of the image of $G(4, 6)$ under a $R_{O, 90°}$?

(1) $G'(4, -6)$ (3) $G'(-6, 4)$

(2) $G'(-4, 6)$ (4) $G'(-6, -4)$

3 If the length of $\overline{LM}$ is 10 units, what is the length of its image under a half-turn?

(1) 20 units   (3) 5 units

(2) 10 units   (4) −10 units

In Exercises 4 and 5, write the coordinates of the image of the given point under the specified transformation.

4 $A(4, 1)$; half-turn about the origin

5 $B(3, 4)$; 90° counterclockwise rotation about the origin

In Exercises 6–8, graph the given points in the coordinate plane. In the same plane, sketch the image under the specified transformation.

6 $\triangle PQR$ with vertices $P(3, 0)$, $Q(0, 4)$, $R(0, 0)$; 90° counterclockwise rotation about the origin

7 $\triangle XYZ$ with vertices $X(4, 0)$, $Y(0, 4)$, and $Z(0, 0)$; half-turn about the origin

8 Sketch the 90° clockwise rotation of $\triangle LTY$ about T.

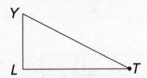

9 The sketch of a double reflection shows the preimage segment $\overline{ST}$ and its image in a double reflection segment $\overline{S''T''}$.

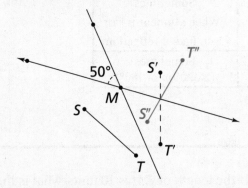

a. What is the center of the rotation that would send $\overline{ST} \rightarrow \overline{S''T''}$?

b. What is the $m\angle SMS''$?

10 Imagine that each morning you must travel from your house (M) to the river (R) to fetch a pail of water to take to Grandma's house (G). What transformation could you use to locate R to minimize the distance traveled each morning?

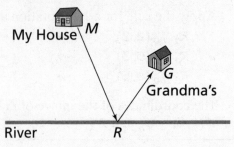

4.4 Composite Transformations

We have already seen more than one transformation applied to a figure in succession. We looked at reflecting a figure over parallel lines and reflecting a figure over intersecting lines. When more than one transformation is applied to a figure in succession it is called a ***composition*** of transformations.

The notation for such a combination of transformations—in this case, "a translation of $\triangle ABC$ to $\triangle A'B'C'$ and then a reflection of $\triangle A'B'C'$ over line m"—is $r_m \circ T_{a,b}$, where r_m denotes the reflection over line m, and $T_{a,b}$ denotes the translation of a units on the x-axis and b units on the y-axis. The notation that denotes a 90° rotation about point N is $R_{N,90°}$.

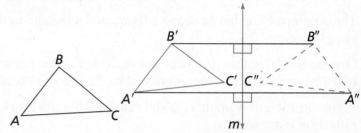

Notice that the translation listed last in the notation is performed first, followed by the reflection. The notation for composite transformations lists the first transformation to be performed last. For example, the notation $T_{a,b} \circ R_{Q,90°} \circ r_n$ denotes that first the object is to be reflected over line n, then rotated 90° about point Q, and finally translated a units on the x-axis and b units on the y-axis.

> **Note**
>
> When working with compositions, work right to left.

You can use transformation notation to determine which tranformations to perfom and in what order.

EXAMPLE **Performing composite transformations**

Perform the composite transformation $r_m \circ R_{P,90°}$ on $\triangle ABC$.

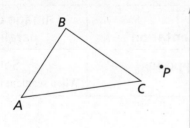

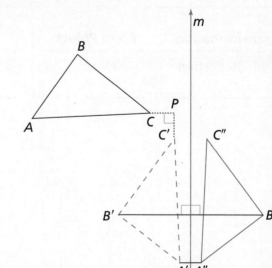

■ **SOLUTION**

Remember that the transformations are performed right to left. Therefore, the rotation is performed first, resulting in the dashed $\triangle A'B'C'$. Then the reflection over line m is performed, resulting in the image of this composite transformation, $\triangle A''B''C''$.

A special composite transformation made up of a reflection and a translation is called a **glide reflection**.

Definition of a Glide Reflection

A **glide reflection** is the composition of a line reflection and a translation in the direction parallel to the line of reflection.

The accompanying figure shows a figure and its image under a glide reflection.

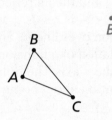

One composition that produces this result is a reflection and a translation (glide) by a vector parallel to the line of reflection.

A composition of isometries is an isometry. Therefore a glide reflection is an isometry.

The sequence of steps is shown below.

First reflect over line *m*.   Determine vector *v*.   Translate by vector *v*.

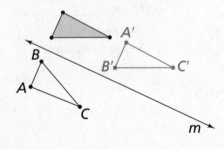   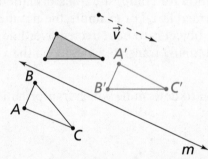   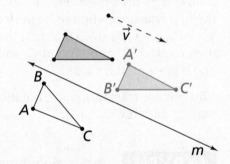

Properties of Glide Reflection			
Transformation	Fixed Points	Orientation	Image of segment a parallel segment
Glide Reflection	None	Opposite	Sometimes (When segment is ∥ to line of reflection)

Choose the numeral preceding the word or expression that best completes the statement or answers the question.

1 Which of the following accurately denotes the composition transformation of pentagon $ABCDE$ to pentagon $A''B''C''D''E''$ shown below?

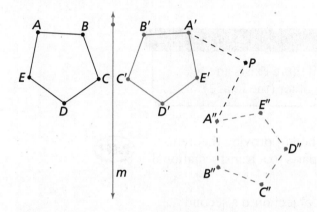

(1) $r_m \circ R_{P,90°}$　　**(3)** $T_{a,b} \circ r_m$

(2) $T_{a,b} \circ R_{P,90°}$　　**(4)** $R_{P,90°} \circ r_m$

2 What composite transformation is shown below?

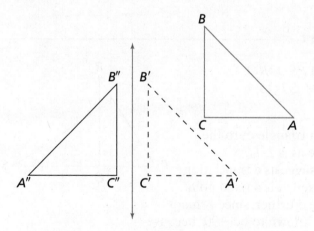

(1) a reflection followed by a translation

(2) a translation followed by a rotation

(3) a dilation followed by a reflection

(4) a translation followed by a reflection

3 Which composition is not an isometry?

(1) $r_{y\text{-axis}} \circ r_{(0,0)}$

(2) $T_{3,1} \circ R_{0,90°}$

(3) $D_{0.5} \circ r_{y=x}$

(4) $T_{3,8} \circ r_{(3,1)}$

In Exercises 4–5, use the following diagram.

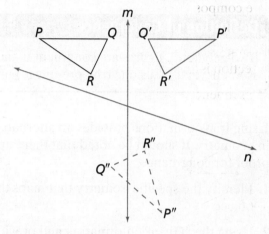

4 Which transformation is performed last in the composition?

(1) the reflection of $\triangle PQR$ over line m

(2) the reflection of $\triangle PQR$ over line n

(3) the reflection of $\triangle P'Q'R'$ over line m

(4) the reflection of $\triangle P'Q'R'$ over line n

5 Which denotes the composite transformation shown?

(1) $r_m \circ r_n$

(2) $r_m \circ R_{n,180°}$

(3) $r_n \circ r_m$

(4) $R_{n,180°} \circ r_m$

6 Find the image of $A(6, -2)$ under $r_{y=x} \circ T_{1, 4}$.

7 Find the image of $B(-4, -3)$ under $T_{3, -2} \circ R_{(0,0), 90°}$.

8 Explain why a composition of isometries is an isometry.

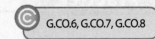

4.5 Congruence Proofs Using Transformations

The use of transformations dates at least as far back as Euclid's <u>Elements</u>. As Euclid stated in his Common Notion number 4: "Things which coincide with one another are equal to one another." It seems clear that the Common Notion, as here formulated, is intended to assert that superposition is a legitimate way of proving the equality of two figures which have the necessary parts respectively equal, or, in other words, to serve as an *axiom of congruence*.

Definition of Congruence

Two geometric figures are congruent if and only if there exists an isometry that maps one (the pre-image) onto the other (the image).

Using transformations provides an alternative method of proving theorems in geometry. It should be noted that there are two parts to a transformational proof for congruence.

1. Identify the specific isometry that maps the first object onto a second object.

2. Using the "Given" information and previous results show that the isometry you selected achieves the desired result. For example, to prove two triangle are congruent, it is necessary to show that the chosen isometry maps all three vertices of one triangle onto the vertices of a second triangle.

EXAMPLE I   Proving two triangles congruent

 In the accompanying figure, T is on $\overline{RQ}$ and $\overline{PS} \perp \overline{RQ}$. If $\overline{PQ} \cong \overline{TQ}$ and $\overline{RQ} \cong \overline{QS}$, prove $\triangle PQR \cong \triangle TQS$.

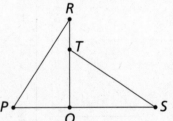

■ SOLUTION

First identify an isometry that maps the first triangle onto the second. $\triangle PQR$ is oriented counterclockwise as is $\triangle TQS$ therefore the transformation is direct. This suggests a translation or a rotation. Since Q is being mapped to itself, it is a fixed point. Therefore the translation must be a rotation. Further, since R maps to S the angle of rotation is $\angle RQS$ which is known to be $-90°$ because it is a clockwise rotation. Consider $R_{Q,-90°}$. Second, show that $R_{Q,-90°}(\triangle PQR) = \triangle TQS$. By definition the center of rotation is a fixed point, $R_{Q,-90°}(Q) = Q$. Now $R_{Q,-90°}(R) = K$. K must be on $\overleftrightarrow{PS}$ because the angle of rotation is $-90°$. It was given that $\overline{RQ} \cong \overline{QS}$ so $\overline{QX} \cong \overline{QR} \cong \overline{QS}$ $\therefore K = S$. By a similar argument $R_{Q,-90°}(P) = Z$ and $Z = T$. $\therefore \triangle PQR \cong \triangle TQS$.

EXAMPLE 2   **Writing a transformational proof**

2   Use transformations to prove that the sum of the angles of a triangle is 180°.

■ **SOLUTION**

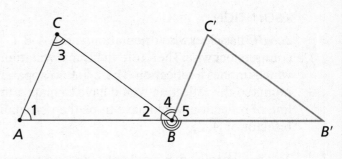

Given $\triangle ABC$, consider the $T_{\overleftrightarrow{AB}}$ where B is the image of A, B' is the image of B, and C' is the image of C under the translation. $\overline{AC} \parallel \overline{BC'}$ because a translation maps a line segment to a parallel line segment and $\angle 3 \cong \angle 4$ by the alternate interior angles theorem. $\angle 1 \cong \angle 5$ because a translation is an isometry and angle measure is preserved. $m\angle 2 + m\angle 4 + m\angle 5 = 180°$ and by substitution $m\angle 2 + m\angle 3 + m\angle 1 = 180°$.

EXAMPLE 3   **Confirming a proof using transformations**

3   **Given:** $\triangle ABC$ and $\triangle DEF$ with $\overline{AB} \cong \overline{DE}$, $\overline{AC} \cong \overline{DF}$, $\overline{BC} \cong \overline{EF}$

Prove: $\triangle ABC \cong \triangle DEF$

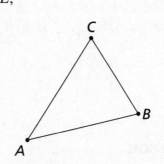
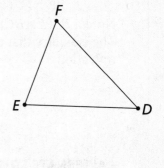

■ **SOLUTION**

1. Since $\overline{AB} \cong \overline{DE}$ there is some isometry m such that $m(\overline{AB}) \rightarrow \overline{DE}$.
2. When $\overline{AB}$ is mapped to $\overline{DE}$ by the isometry m, the point C is mapped to C'. There arc two possible locations for C'. It could be in either half plane of $\overleftrightarrow{DE}$.
3. If C' is in the same half plane of $\overleftrightarrow{DE}$ as F, reflect C' over $\overleftrightarrow{DE}$ so that the case in the accompanying diagram occurs. Thus $m(\triangle ABC) = \triangle DEC'$.
4. Since m is an isometry $\overline{AC} \cong \overline{DF} \cong \overline{A'C'}$ and D lies on the $\perp$ bisector of $\overline{C'F}$. Similarly, $\overline{B'C'} \cong \overline{BC} \cong \overline{EF}$ and E lies on the $\perp$ bisector of $\overline{C'F}$. Therefore, $\overline{DE}$ is the $\perp$ bisector of $\overline{C'F}$. This establishes F as the image of C'; symbolically we write $r_{\overleftrightarrow{DE}}(C') = F$.
5. We now have $r_{\overleftrightarrow{DE}}(\triangle DEC') = \triangle DEF$
6. Since the composition of two isometries is an isometry, $R_{\overleftrightarrow{DE}} \circ m(\triangle ABC) = \triangle DEF$ and therefore $\triangle ABC \cong \triangle DEF$.

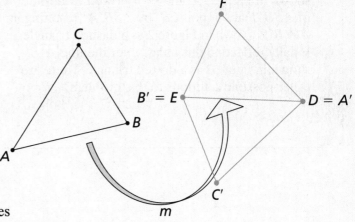

EXAMPLE 4   Identifying a transformation

4) $\triangle ABC \cong \triangle A'B'C'$. Identify the isometry that maps $\triangle ABC$ to $\triangle A'B'C'$.

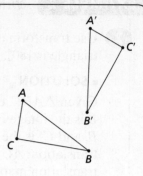

■ **SOLUTION**

$\triangle ABC$ has clockwise orientation and $\triangle A'B'C'$ is counterclockwise. Therefore the transformation is opposite, which implies a reflection. There are no apparent fixed points so the reflection would have to map A to A' and the line of reflection would have to be the perpendicular bisector of $\overline{AA'}$.

The line of reflection would also have to be the perpendicular bisector of $\overline{BB'}$ and $\overline{CC'}$ also. Clearly this is not the case. Therefore the transformation is not a simple reflection, but a composition of two isometries.

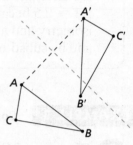

Note a $R_m(\triangle ABC) = \triangle L\,JK$ and $T_{\vec{v}}(\triangle LJK) = \triangle A'B'C'$. The isometry that maps $\triangle ABC$ to $\triangle A'B'C'$ is a glide reflection.

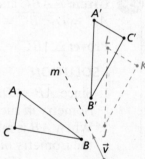

■ **ALTERNATE SOLUTION**

First a translation of $\triangle ABC$ by a vector BB' as shown in Figure 1, could be followed by a rotation of $\triangle SB'T$ about point B' by $\angle SB'A'$ resulting in $\triangle A'B'Z$ shown in Figure 2 as a dashed triangle. Finally reflecting this image over the line $\overline{A'B'}$ shown in figure 2 as a dotted triangle. There are other possible solutions to this problem.

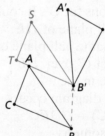
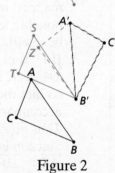

Figure 1   Figure 2

1 Prove that a translation is an isometry.

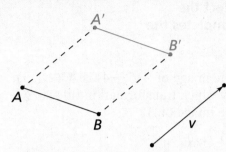

2 Prove the Isosceles Triangle Theorem using transformations.

3 **Given:** $\triangle ABC$ & $\triangle DEF$ with $AB = DE$, $AC = DF$, $\angle A = \angle D$
Prove: $\triangle ABC \cong \triangle DEF$
by showing that $\triangle DEF$ is the image of $\triangle ABC$ under an isometry.

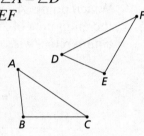

4 **Given:** $\overline{AB} \cong \overline{AD}$
$\overline{AE} \cong \overline{AC}$

Prove: $\triangle ABC \cong \triangle ADE$

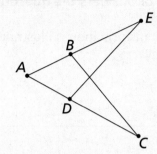

5 **Given:** Rectangle $MATH$ with D the midpoint of $\overline{MA}$

Prove: $\overline{HD} \cong \overline{TD}$

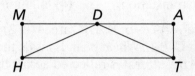

6 Prove a rotation about a point P through an angle θ is an isometry.

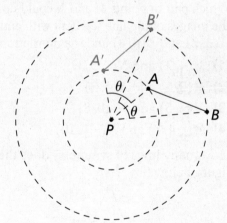

Answer all questions in this part. For each question, select the numeral preceding the word or expression that best completes the statement or answers the question.

1 What transformation is illustrated in this diagram?

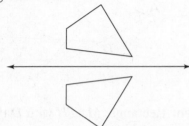

  (1) line reflection   **(3)** rotation

  (2) translation   **(4)** dilation

2 The vertices of $\triangle ABC$ are $A(0, 2)$, $B(0, 5)$, and $C(7, 2)$. Which point is inside the image of $\triangle ABC$ after it is reflected across the y-axis?

  (1) $X(-1, -3)$ **(3)** $X(-1, 3)$

  (2) $X(1, -3)$ **(4)** $X(1, 3)$

3 Which pair of points M and N could not be the images of the line segment with endpoints $A(3, 2)$ and $B(6, 4)$ under a translation?

  (1) $M(4, 3)$ and $N(7, 5)$

  (2) $M(2, 1)$ and $N(5, 3)$

  (3) $M(7, 5)$ and $N(10, 8)$

  (4) $M(-4, 8)$ and $N(-1, 10)$

4 How many lines of symmetry does the figure below have?

  (1) 0   **(2)** 2   **(3)** 4   **(4)** 6

5 A polygon $WXYZ$ has four right angles. Two opposite sides have length 6 feet. The other two opposite sides have length 4 feet. How many lines of symmetry does polygon $WXYZ$ have?

  (1) 0   **(2)** 2   **(3)** 4   **(4)** 6

6 The image of $A(5, -4)$ is $A'(-4, 5)$. By which transformation rule is A' the image of A?

  (1) $r_{x\text{-axis}}$

  (2) $r_{y\text{-axis}}$

  (3) $r_{(0, 0)}$

  (4) $r_{y=x}$

7 Which points A' and B' are the images of the endpoints of $\overline{AB}$ under a 90° counterclockwise rotation about the origin?

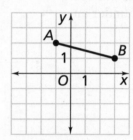

  (1) $A'(-1, -2)$ and $B'(3, -4)$

  (2) $A'(2, 1)$ and $B'(1, 3)$

  (3) $A'(-2, -1)$ and $B'(-1, 3)$

  (4) $A'(-2, 1)$ and $B'(1, -3)$

8 A figure in the plane has point symmetry if it is its own image under which transformation?

  (1) 90° counterclockwise rotation about the origin

  (2) half-turn

  (3) reflection in a line

  (4) some translation

9 $\triangle ABC$ has vertices $A(-3, 5)$, $B(2, 1)$, and $C(5, 3)$. What are the coordinates of vertex B' under $T_{3, -2}$?

  (1) $(0, 3)$ **(3)** $(3, 2)$

  (2) $(5, -1)$ **(4)** $(8, 1)$

10 If quadrilateral *LMNP* is reflected in the *x*-axis, which of the following statements is **not** true?

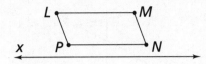

(1) *MM'* is perpendicular to line *x*.

(2) *MN* = *M'N'*

(3) The distance from *P* to line *x* is congruent to the distance from *M* to line *x*.

(4) $m\angle L = m\angle L'$

11 △*ABC* has coordinates of *A*(1, 6), *B*(5, 2), and *C*(2, 1). What are the coordinates of △*A'B'C'* after a 90° counterclockwise rotation about the origin?

(1) *A'*(−1, 6), B'(−5, 2), and *C'*(−2, 1)

(2) *A'*(1, −6), B'(5, −2), and *C'*(2, −1)

(3) *A'*(−6, 1), B'(−2, 5), and *C'*(−1, 2)

(4) *A'*(6, −1), B'(2, −5), and *C'*(1, −2)

12 Which of the following characteristics of translations are true?

(1) A translated line segment is congruent to the original line segment.

(2) A translated angle is congruent to the original angle.

(3) The orientation of the image is the same as that of the original figure.

(4) All of the above.

13 Which figure has rotational symmetry?

(1) right triangle

(2) equilateral triangle

(3) isosceles triangle

(4) none of the above

14 A regular hexagon *DEFGHI* is rotated about its center by an angle *A*. Which value(s) of *A* will carry the hexagon onto itself?

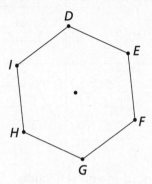

(1) 30° **(2)** 60° **(3)** 72° **(4)** −180°

15 △*ONT* is the image of △*CAT* under which transformation?

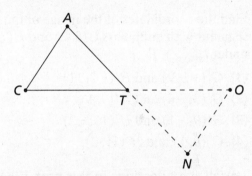

(1) Rotation of +180° about *T*.

(2) Rotation of −180° about *T*.

(3) Reflection in the point *T*.

(4) A half-turn about point *T*.

16 △*JKL* ≅ △*J'K'L'*. Which of the following transformations could possibly map △*JKL* to △*J'K'L'*?

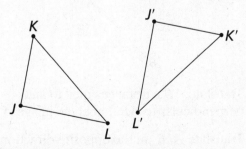

(1) Reflection (*r*)   **(3)** *R* ∘ *T*

(2) *r* ∘ *T*   **(4)** *T* ∘ *r*

17 Which two consecutive transformations does the figure illustrate?

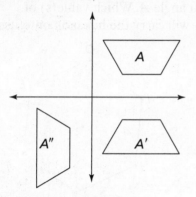

(1) translation and reflection

(2) rotation and translation

(3) reflection and rotation

(4) translation and tessellation

18 Find the coordinates of the image of the line segment with endpoints $G(5, 2)$ and $H(7, 3)$ under $r_{x\text{-axis}} \cdot T_{4,-1}$.

(1) $G'(-1, 9)$ and $H'(-2, 11)$

(2) $G'(3, -6)$ and $H'(9, 1)$

(3) $G'(9, -1)$ and $H'(11, -2)$

(4) $G'(9, 1)$ and $H'(11, 2)$

Answer all the questions in this part. Clearly indicate the necessary steps, including appropriate formula substitutions, diagrams, graphs, charts, etc. For all questions in this part, a correct numerical answer with no work shown will receive only one credit.

19 Draw a line segment $\overline{AB}$ and complete the following translations.

Translate AB a distance equal to and perpendicular to $\overline{AB}$. Label the image $\overline{A'B'}$.

Translate $\overline{A'B'}$ in the opposite direction, a distance equal to twice the length of $\overline{AB}$ and perpendicular to $\overline{AB}$.

20 $\triangle ABC$ lies on the coordinate plane such that $A(-3, 4)$, $B(2, 3)$, and $C(-2, 1)$.

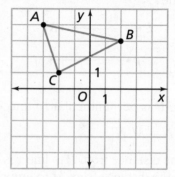

What are the coordinates of $\triangle A'B'C'$ when the figure is rotated 180° about the origin?

What are the coordinates of $\triangle A''B''C''$ of the image of $A'B'C'$ under a reflection about the x-axis?

What transformation is equivalent to $r_{x\text{-axis}} \cdot R_{(0, 0), 180°}$?

21 The library is located at the origin on the coordinate grid. The locations of three houses are given in terms of blocks east or west and north or south of the library: $A(-4, 3)$, $B(1, 4)$, and $C(1, -2)$.

Locate and label the three houses on the coordinate grid.

Locate and label three other houses, A', B', and C', relative to the library if they are each 4 blocks east and 2 blocks north of houses A, B, and C.

Describe the transformation involved in solving this problem and the effect that the transformation has on the relative distance of A', B', and C' from the library.

5 Transformations and Similarity

Fractals and Triangles

The Sierpinski triangle, or Sierpinski gasket, is an example of a fractal formed from an equilateral triangle. Search the Internet to find an example of a Sierpinski triangle and construct one on your own.

G.SRT.4
G.SRT.5

Two triangles are similar if they have the same shape but different size. **Similar triangles** have corresponding angles that are equal in measure and corresponding sides that are proportional.

Corresponding angles in a triangle are congruent, and the **corresponding sides** are opposite congruent angles. In the figure below, $\angle A$ corresponds to $\angle D$, $\angle B$ corresponds to $\angle E$, and $\angle C$ corresponds to $\angle F$. The sides correspond in the following way:

$\overline{AB}$ corresponds to $\overline{DE}$.
$\overline{BC}$ corresponds to $\overline{EF}$.
$\overline{CA}$ corresponds to $\overline{FD}$.

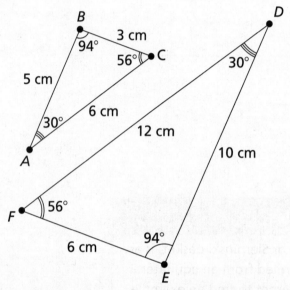

The ratio of the lengths of corresponding sides is called the **similarity ratio,** or the **scale factor.** In the triangles above, the similarity ratio is $\frac{1}{2}$ or 1:2. To show that the triangles are similar, you write $\triangle ABC \sim \triangle DEF$. When naming similar triangles, list the vertices in the order of the corresponding angles.

Note

The symbol to show similarity is $\sim$.

Proving That Triangles Are Similar		
Angle-Angle (AA) Similarity Postulate If two angles of one triangle are congruent to two angles of another triangle, then the triangles are similar.	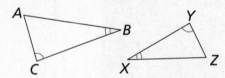	$\triangle ABC \sim \triangle ZXY$ $\angle C \cong \angle Y$ $\angle B \cong \angle X$
Side-Side-Side (SSS) Similarity Theorem If corresponding sides of two triangles are in proportion, then the triangles are similar.		$\frac{AB}{XZ} = \frac{BC}{ZY} = \frac{CA}{YX}$ $\triangle ABC \sim \triangle XZY$
Side-Angle-Side (SAS) Similarity Theorem If an angle of one triangle is congruent to an angle of another triangle, and the lengths of the sides including these angles are in proportion, then the triangles are similar.	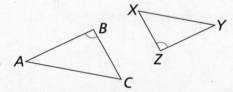	$\frac{AB}{YZ} = \frac{BC}{ZX}$ $\triangle ABC \sim \triangle YZX$ $\angle B \cong \angle Z$

EXAMPLE 1 **Using the AA Postulate**

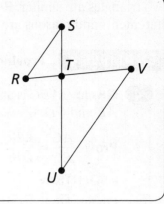

1 In the accompanying figure $\overline{RS} \| \overline{VU}$. Explain whether the triangles are similar.

■ **SOLUTION**

Because $\overline{RS} \| \overline{VU}$, we know $\angle R \cong \angle V$ and $\angle S \cong \angle U$ by the Alternate Interior Angles Theorem. The triangles are similar by AA, and $\triangle RST \sim \triangle VUT$.

When lengths are difficult to measure, similar triangles often can be used to find missing distances. This is referred to as **indirect measurement**.

EXAMPLE 2 **Using indirect measurement**

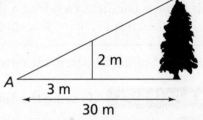

2 A tree casts a shadow 30 m long, and a 2 m stick casts one that is 3 m long. How tall is the tree?

■ **SOLUTION**

These two triangles are similar because they are both right triangles and share $\angle A$. Therefore, their corresponding sides are in the same ratio. This results in the proportion $\frac{2}{h} = \frac{3}{30}$. Solving, we find that $h = 20$ m.

You can use the similarity postulate and theorems to formally prove that two triangles are similar.

EXAMPLE 3 **Proving triangles are similar**

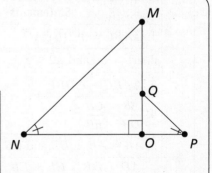

3 **Given:** $\angle N \cong \angle P$ and $\overline{MO} \perp \overline{NP}$
Prove: $\triangle MNO \sim \triangle QPO$

■ **SOLUTION**

Statements	Reasons
1. $\overline{MO} \perp \overline{NP}$	1. Given
2. $\angle MON \cong \angle MOP$	2. Perpendiculars form right angles, and all right angles are congruent.
3. $\angle N \cong \angle P$	3. Given
4. $\triangle MNO \sim \triangle QPO$	4. Angle-Angle Similarity Postulate

In the above example, a two-column proof was used to show that two triangles are similar. Recall that a **paragraph proof** is a proof where the statements and reasons are written as sentences in a paragraph.

EXAMPLE 4   Proving a proportion

 Given: $\triangle ABC$ is an isosceles triangle with $\overline{AB} \cong \overline{AC}$ and altitudes $\overline{AE}$ and $\overline{CD}$.

Prove: $\dfrac{AC}{EC} = \dfrac{CB}{DB}$

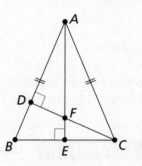

■ **SOLUTION**

Given $\overline{AB} \cong \overline{AC}$ implies $\angle B \cong \angle ACB$ because base angles of an isosceles triangle are congruent. $\overline{CD} \perp \overline{AB}$ and $\overline{AE} \perp \overline{BC}$ by the definition of altitude. Therefore, $\angle AEC \cong \angle CDB$, as perpendicular lines form right angles and all right angles are congruent. This leads to $\triangle AEC \sim \triangle CDB$ by AA. Now, $\dfrac{AC}{CB} = \dfrac{EC}{DB}$ because corresponding sides of similar triangles are proportional, and that proportion can be rewritten as $\dfrac{AC}{EC} = \dfrac{CB}{DB}$.

Side-Splitter Theorem

If a line is parallel to a side of a triangle and intersects the other two sides, then it splits those sides proportionally.

The Side-Splitter Theorem uses overlapping triangles that are similar.

EXAMPLE 5   Proving the Side-Splitter Theorem

 Given: $\triangle ABC$ with $\overline{DE} \parallel \overline{AC}$

Prove: $\dfrac{AD}{DB} = \dfrac{CE}{EB}$

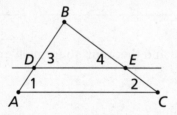

■ **SOLUTION**

Statements	Reasons
1. $\triangle ABC$ with $\overline{DE} \parallel \overline{AC}$	1. Given
2. $\angle 1 \cong \angle 3$ and $\angle 2 \cong \angle 4$	2. Corresponding angles are congruent.
3. $\triangle ABC \sim \triangle DBE$	3. AA
4. $\dfrac{AB}{DB} = \dfrac{CB}{EB}$	4. Corresponding sides of similar triangles are proportional.
5. $AB = AD + DB$ and $CB = CE + EB$	5. Segment Addition Postulate
6. $\dfrac{AD + DB}{DB} = \dfrac{CE + EB}{EB}$	6. Substitution
7. $\dfrac{AD}{DB} + \dfrac{DB}{DB} = \dfrac{CE}{EB} + \dfrac{EB}{EB} \Rightarrow \dfrac{AD}{DB} + 1 = \dfrac{CE}{EB} + 1$	7. Algebra and simplification
8. $\dfrac{AD}{DB} = \dfrac{CE}{EB}$	8. Subtraction Property of Equality

Additional Theorems About Similarity and Proportions

- If three parallel lines intersect two transversals, they divide them proportionally.
- The perimeters of similar triangles are proportional to the measures of the corresponding sides.
- Similarity of triangles is reflexive, symmetric, and transitive.
- If a ray bisects an angle of a triangle, then it divides the opposite side into two segments that are proportional to the other two sides of the triangle.
- If two triangles are similar, the lengths of corresponding altitudes are proportional to the measures of the corresponding sides.

Triangle similarity theorems allow you to solve a wide range of problems involving similar triangles.

EXAMPLES 6 through 8   Using triangle similarity theorems

6 Use a graphing calculator or geometry software to investigate the theorem concerning the angle bisector of a triangle. If $\overline{BD}$ is the angle bisector of $\angle ABC$, then $AD : DC = BA : BC$. Verify this proportion for many cases by dragging the vertices of the triangle and observing the results of the calculated ratios.

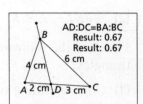

- **SOLUTION**

In the accompanying figure we can see one case where the proportion is true, accurate to two decimal places.

7 In the accompanying figure, M is the midpoint of side $\overline{JK}$ and N is the midpoint of side $\overline{JL}$. Prove that $\triangle JKL \sim \triangle JMN$.

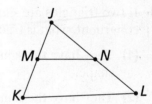

- **SOLUTION**

$\frac{JM}{JK} = \frac{JN}{JL} = \frac{1}{2}$ by the definition of midpoint. $\angle J$ is in both triangles and is included between the proportional sides. Therefore, $\triangle JKL \sim \triangle JMN$ by the SAS Similarity Theorem.

8 Hazelwood Ave., Fernwood Ave., and Pinehurst St. run parallel to each other. The distance along Golden Glow Dr. between Hazelwood and Fernwood is 1,320 ft. Between Fernwood and Pinehurst, the distance is 540 ft. The distance along Alvord Dr. between Pinehurst and Fernwood is 620 ft. What is the distance between Pinehurst and Hazelwood along Alvord Dr.?

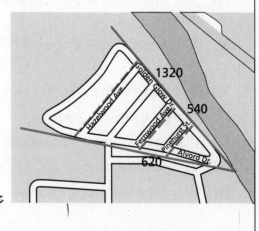

- **SOLUTION**

$$\frac{620}{n} = \frac{540}{1860} \Rightarrow 1{,}153{,}200 = 540\, n \Rightarrow n \approx 2135.56 \text{ ft}$$

Choose the numeral preceding the word or expression that best completes the statement or answers the question.

1 Based upon the accompanying figure, which is the correct expression of the similarity?

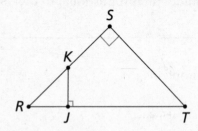

  (1) $\triangle RST \sim \triangle RKJ$ **(3)** $\triangle RST \sim \triangle JKR$

  (2) $\triangle RST \sim \triangle RJK$ **(4)** $\triangle RST \sim \triangle JRK$

2 Which of the following is true for similar triangles?

  (1) Corresponding sides are congruent.

  (2) Corresponding angles are proportional.

  (3) Corresponding sides are proportional.

  (4) All of the above

3 If two triangles are similar but not congruent, what is true about them?

  (1) They have the same size and same shape.

  (2) They have the same size but different shapes.

  (3) They have different sizes and different shapes.

  (4) They have the same shape but different sizes.

4 Which of the following is true?

  (1) All right triangles are similar.

  (2) All isosceles triangles are similar.

  (3) All equilateral triangles are similar.

  (4) All scalene triangles are similar.

In the figure below, $\overline{MN} \parallel \overline{AC}$. Use this figure for Exercises 5–11.

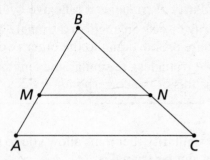

5 Write a similarity statement and justify your answer.

6 If $AM = 4$, $MB = 8$, and $BC = 36$, find BN.

7 If $AB = 9$, $AC = 15$, and $MB = 6$, find MN.

8 If $MB = 7$, $MA = 5$, and $BN = 10$, find NC.

9 If $AM = 4$, $AB = 12$, and the perimeter of $\triangle ABC$ is 32, find the perimeter of $\triangle MBN$.

10 If $MN = 10$, $AC = 15$, and $MB = 4$, find MA.

11 If $MB = 4$, $BN = 5$, and $NC = 10$, find MA.

12 Determine whether the triangles in the accompanying figure are similar. If they are, write a similarity statement and list the six pairs of corresponding parts.

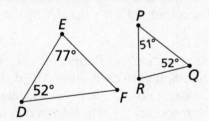

13 A meter stick casts a shadow that is 90 cm long. At the same time a tree has a shadow that is 4.3 m long. Determine the height of the tree.

In Exercises 14–16, write a similarity statement and identify the postulate or theorem that justifies the similarity.

14

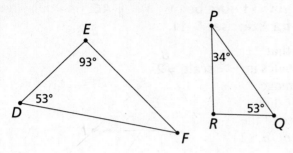

15

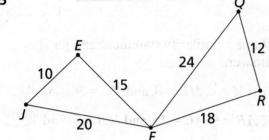

16

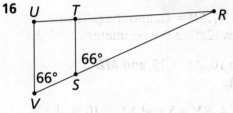

17 In the accompanying figure $\angle 1 \cong \angle 2$. Write a paragraph proof to show $\triangle ACB \sim \triangle DCE$.

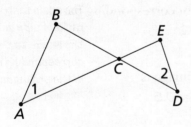

18 Given $\triangle ABC$ with altitudes $\overline{CD}$ and $\overline{AE}$, write a two column proof that $\frac{BC}{AB} = \frac{DC}{AE}$.

19 Complete the following proof of the converse of the Side-Splitter Theorem.

Given: $\dfrac{XR}{RQ} = \dfrac{YS}{SQ}$

Prove: $\overline{RS} \parallel \overline{XY}$

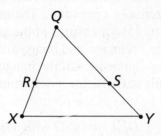

Statements	Reasons
1. $\dfrac{XR}{RQ} = \dfrac{YS}{SQ}$	1.
2. $\dfrac{XR+RQ}{RQ} = \dfrac{YS+SQ}{SQ}$	2.
3. $\dfrac{XQ}{RQ} = \dfrac{YQ}{SQ}$	3.
4. $\angle Q \cong \angle Q$	4.
5. $\triangle XQY \sim \triangle RQS$	5.
6. $\angle QXY \cong \angle QRS$	6.
7. $\overline{RS} \parallel \overline{XY}$	7.

20 The sides of a triangle are 6 cm, 12 cm, and 15 cm long. Determine the lengths, to the nearest tenth, of the segments formed when each angle bisector divides the opposite side.

21 To determine the width of Small Lake, the measurements of two similar right triangles are taken as shown in the accompanying figure. What is the width of Small Lake?

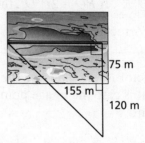

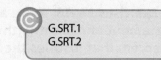
5.2 Dilations

Not all transformations are isometries.

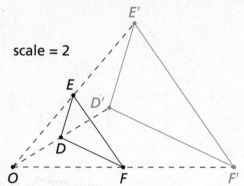

scale = 2

A **dilation** or **size transformation** is a transformation that enlarges or reduces a preimage. The measures of the angles in the image equal the measures of the angles in the preimage. Therefore the preimage and image are similar to each other. However, the dimensions of the image are n times those of the preimage. This **scale factor** n determines an *enlargement* ($n > 1$) or *reduction* ($n < 1$) of the preimage.

A dilation of $\triangle DEF$ about O with a scale factor of two is shown in the accompanying diagram. Note that each preimage point is collinear with the center and its image point. In this diagram, the preimage point is between the center and the image point. Because dilations preserve angle measure $\triangle DEF \sim \triangle D'E'F'$.

Furthermore, $\dfrac{OE'}{OE} = \dfrac{OD'}{OD} = \dfrac{OF'}{OF} = 2$ and $\dfrac{D'E'}{DE} = \dfrac{E'F'}{EF} = \dfrac{D'F'}{DF} = 2.$

Definition of a Dilation

A dilation $D_{O,k}$ with O a fixed point and k a nonzero real number, is a transformation of the plane where $D_{O,k}(O) = O$, $D_{O,k}(P) = P'$ when $P \neq O$, and with O, P, and P' being collinear. O is called the **center** of the dilation and k is the **scale factor** or **constant of proportionality.**

EXAMPLE 1   **Identifying a scale factor for a dilation**

 When $\triangle PQR$ is dilated, its image is $\triangle P'Q'R'$ and $PQ = 2P'Q'$. What is the scale factor?

(1) 2   **(2)** 1   **(3)** 0.5   **(4)** 0.25

■ **SOLUTION**

Under the dilation, the original figure is $\triangle PQR$ and the image is $\triangle P'Q'R'$. If $PQ = 2P'Q'$, then $P'Q' = 0.5(PQ)$. So, $\frac{P'Q'}{PQ} = 0.5$.

The correct choice is **(3)**.

Note

The scale factor is the ratio of side lengths in the image to the corresponding lengths in the preimage.

If the scale factor is less than one the image triangle is smaller than the preimage. In this case the image point is between the center and the preimage point.

scale = 0.5

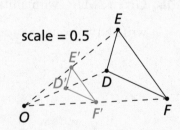

The scale factor of a dilation can be negative.

EXAMPLE 2 **Identifying a negatvie scale factor**

2 What is the image of $\triangle JKL$ under $D_{c,-0.5}$?

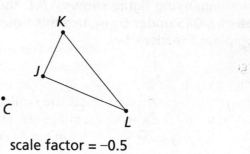

scale factor = −0.5

■ **SOLUTION**

We know the image points must be collinear with the preimage point and the center of the dilation. Therefore J' must lie on the line CJ. Knowing the scale factor is −0.5 indicates that $CJ' = 0.5CJ$ and on the opposite side of C. Once J' is located, K' and L' can be located in similar fashion.

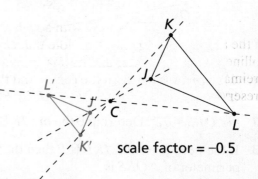

scale factor = −0.5

Properties of a Dilation			
Transformation	Fixed Points	Orientation	Image of segment a parallel segment
Dilation	One	Direct	Yes

EXAMPLE 3 **Determining a scale factor**

 $\triangle DEF$ is the image of $\triangle ABC$ under $D_{O,k}$. Determine the value of k.

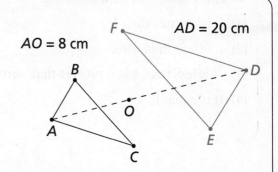

$AO = 8$ cm

$AD = 20$ cm

■ **SOLUTION**

$$r = \frac{12}{8} = \frac{3}{2}$$

The center of the dilation is between the preimage and image. Therefore the scale factor is negative. Using the given values $AD = 20$ and $AO = 8$, we know that $OD = 12$ cm. Therefore

$$k = -r \therefore k = -\frac{3}{2}$$

The accompanying figure shows △*JKL*, the image of △*QRS* under $D_{O,1/3}$. Use this figure to complete Exercises 1–5.

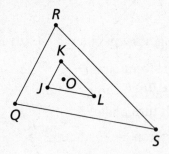

1 $\dfrac{JK}{QR} = ?$

2 $m\angle QRS = 72°$. Determine the $m\angle JKL$.

3 If the perimeter of △*JKL* is *P* then the perimeter of △*QRS* is

    (1) $\dfrac{P}{3}$ **(3)** $\dfrac{3}{P}$

    (2) $3P$ **(4)** $2P$

4 If *KL* = 6 then *RS* = ?

5 What is true about these two triangles?

6 If the center of a dilation is between a preimage point and its image point what do we know about the dilation factor?

    (1) It is greater than 1.

    (2) It is less than zero.

    (3) It is less than 1 and greater than zero.

    (4) It is equal to 1.

7 A 4″ by 6″ photo is enlarged to a width of one foot. What is the length of the enlarged photograph?

8 **Given:** $D_{O,k}$ with $D(A) = A'$ and $D(B) = B'$
    Prove: $\overleftrightarrow{AB} \parallel \overleftrightarrow{A'B'}$

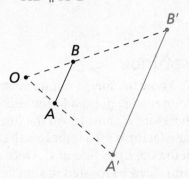

9 △*GHI* is the image of △*WXY* under a dilation. Describe how you can determine the center of this dilation and the scale factor.

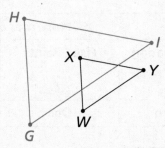

10 True or False? If $m\angle A = 35°$, then the image of $\angle A$ under a size transformation of magnitude 2 has a measure of 70°.

11 *C* is the center of a dilation with a scale factor of 5.5. *M*, *N*, and *P* are collinear. Will the images of *M*, *N*, and *P* be collinear?

12 If a circle whose radius is 12 inches is dilated about its center O by a scale factor of $\frac{1}{2}$, describe the image.

13 In the accompanying figure X, is the midpoint of $\overline{GH}$ and Y is the midpoint of $\overline{GI}$. Describe $\triangle GHI$ as an image of a dilation of $\triangle GXY$.

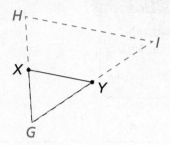

14 Which of the following are true about a dilation?

(1) It is an isometry.

(2) It preserves side measure.

(3) It preserves angle measure.

(4) It preserves collinearity.

(5) Images are parallel to preimages.

15 The transformation $D_{C,-1}$ is the same as which of the following transformations?

(1) Half turn about C

(2) Rotation of 90° about C

(3) Reflection about the line $y = -x$

(4) $D_{C,1}$

Similarly to other transformations, dilations can be performed in the coordinate plane.

Dilations in the Coordinate Plane

The image of $P(x, y)$ under a dilatation in the coordinate plane with the **origin as the center** of dilation and a scale factor of $k \neq 0$ is $P'(kx, ky)$.

NOTE: This rule only applies when the center of the dilation is the origin.

EXAMPLE 1   **Sketching a dilation in the coordinate plane**

 A triangle has vertices $K(1, 2)$, $L(1, 4)$, and $M(4, 1)$. Sketch the image of $\triangle KLM$ under a dilation with center of dilation at the origin and scale factor 2.

■ **SOLUTION**

Sketch $K(1, 2)$, $L(1, 4)$, $M(4, 1)$, and $\triangle KLM$.
Under the dilation with the origin as center and scale factor 2:
$D_2(1, 2) \rightarrow (2, 4)$ $D_2(1, 4) \rightarrow (2, 8)$ $D_2(4, 1) \rightarrow (8, 2)$

Plot $K'(2, 4)$, $L'(2, 8)$, and $M'(8, 2)$ to form $\triangle K'L'M'$.

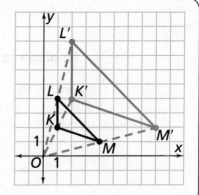

You can use one pair of corresponding points to find the scale for the dilation of an entire figure.

EXAMPLE 2   **Finding unknown coordinates under a dilation**

 Under a dilation with center at the origin, the image of $\triangle ABC$ is $\triangle A'B'C'$. Complete this table of coordinates.

preimage	image	preimage	image	preimage	image
$A(3, 6)$	$A'(4.5, 9)$	$B(-4, 0)$	$B'(\ ,\ )$	$C(\ ,\ )$	$C'(9, -3)$

■ **SOLUTION**

Find the scale. Because $\dfrac{4.5}{3} = \dfrac{9}{6} = 1.5$, the scale factor is 1.5.

coordinates of B': $B'(-4 \times 1.5, 0 \times 1.5) = B'(-6, 0)$ ← Multiply to find the coordinates of the image.

coordinates of C: $C'(9 \div 1.5, -3 \div 1.5) = C(6, -2)$ ← Divide to find the coordinates of the preimage.

If A is the area of the preimage, then what would be the area of the image A' after a dilation of A with a scale factor k? It would be $A' = k^2A$.

EXAMPLE 3   **Relating areas of figures under a dilation** ──────

 A triangle has vertices $P(1, 5)$, $Q(6, 1)$, and $R(1, 1)$. Under a dilation with scale factor 2 and center at the origin, the image of the triangle is $\triangle P'Q'R'$. What is the area of $\triangle P'Q'R'$?

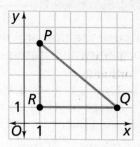

■ **SOLUTION**

Sketch a coordinate diagram and graph $P(1, 5)$, $Q(6, 1)$, and $R(1, 1)$. Find the area of $\triangle PQR$.

$$\text{Area of } \triangle PQR = \frac{1}{2}(RQ)(RP) = \frac{1}{2}(6-1)(5-1) = 10$$

The image $\triangle P'Q'R'$ is similar to $\triangle PQR$ and the similarity ratio is $2 : 1$.

The area of $\triangle P'Q'R'$ is four times the area of $\triangle PQR$.

Therefore, the area of $\triangle P'Q'R'$ is 4(10) square units, or 40 square units.

You can perform two different transformations on the same object, one after the other.

EXAMPLE 4   **Finding a composition of transformations** ──────

 $\triangle RST$ has vertices $R(1, 1)$, $S(0, 4)$, and $T(5, 2)$. Find the coordinates of $\triangle R'S'T'$ under a 90° counterclockwise rotation around the origin followed by a dilation scale factor 2 with the origin as the center.

■ **SOLUTION**

		90° counterclockwise rotation around the origin		Dilation scale factor 2
$P(x, y)$	$\rightarrow$	$P'(-y', x')$	$\rightarrow$	$P''(2(-y'), 2(x'))$
$R(1, 1)$	$\rightarrow$	$R'(-1, 1)$	$\rightarrow$	$R''(2(-1), 2(1)) = R''(-2, 2)$
$S(0, 4)$	$\rightarrow$	$S'(-4, 0)$	$\rightarrow$	$S''(2(-4), 2(0)) = S''(-8, 0)$
$T(5, 2)$	$\rightarrow$	$T'(-2, 5)$	$\rightarrow$	$T''(2(-2), 2(5)) = T''(-4, 10)$

The coordinates of the final image are $R''(-2, 2)$, $S''(-8, 0)$, and $T''(-4, 10)$.

EXAMPLE 5   **Finding a dilation with center other than the origin** ──────

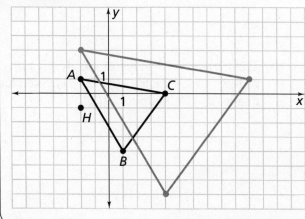 Sketch the image of $\triangle ABC$ under $D_{H, 2}$.

■ **SOLUTION**

Choose the numeral preceding the word or expression that best completes the statement or answers the question.

1 Under a dilation with center at $O(0, 0)$, the image of $A(-4, 2)$ is $A'(-2, 1)$. What is the scale factor for the dilation?

(1) 0.5 **(2)** 1 **(3)** 2 **(4)** -2

2 What is the image of $A(-4, 2)$, under $D_{0.25}$?

(1) $A'(-1, 8)$ **(3)** $A'(-1, 0.25)$

(2) $A'(-1, 0.5)$ **(4)** $A'(-100, 50)$

3 Identify the scale factor for this dilation. The image of $\overline{AB}$ is $\overline{A'B'}$.

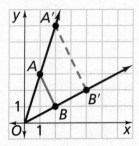

(1) 0.5 **(2)** 1 **(3)** 2 **(4)** 3

4 What are the coordinates of the image of a line segment with the endpoints $R(2, 2)$ and $S(5, 6)$ after a dilation with the origin as the center and a scale factor 2 followed by a dilation with the origin as center and a scale factor of 3?

(1) $R''(7, 7)$; $S''(11, 12)$

(2) $R''(10, 10)$; $S''(25, 30)$

(3) $R''(12, 12)$; $S''(30, 36)$

(4) $R''(6, 6)$; $S''(15, 18)$

5 What are the coordinates of parallelogram $C'D'E'F'$ after $C(-7, 2)$, $D(2, 2)$, $E(0, -2)$, and $F(-9, -2)$ are dilated with the origin as the center with scale factor 0.5?

(1) $C'(-3.5, 1)$, $D'(1, 1)$, $E'(0, -1)$, $F'(-4.5, -1)$

(2) $C'(-3.5, -1)$, $D'(1, 1)$, $E'(0, -1)$, $F'(4.5, 1)$

(3) $C'(-35, -10)$, $D'(10, 10)$, $E'(0, -10)$, $F'(45, 10)$

(4) $C'(-35, 10)$, $D'(10, 10)$, $E'(0, -10)$, $F'(-45, -10)$

6 Under D_4, the image of $\triangle ABC$ is $A'(3, 6)$, $B'(7, 1)$, $C'(6, 6)$. What are the coordinates of A, B, and C?

(1) $A(0.75, 1.5)$, $B(1.75, 0.25)$, $C(1.5, 1.5)$

(2) $A(7, 10)$, $B(11, 5)$, $C(10, 10)$

(3) $A(-1, 2)$, $B(3, -3)$, $C(2, 2)$

(4) $A(12, 24)$, $B(28, 4)$, $C(24, 24)$

7 If the coordinates of $\triangle XYZ$ are $X(-1, 5)$, $Y(3, -1)$, $Z(-2, -3)$, and the coordinates of $\triangle X'Y'Z'$ after a dilation with the origin as the center are $X'(-2.5, 12.5)$, $Y'(7.5, -2.5)$, $Z'(-5, -7.5)$, what is the scale factor?

(1) 1.5 **(2)** 4.5 **(3)** 2.5 **(4)** 4

In Exercises 8–10, sketch the image of each dilation.

8 The center of dilation is X and the scale factor is 0.5.

9 The center of dilation is O and the scale factor is 2.

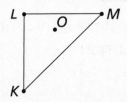

10 The vertices of a polygon are $A(-1, 1)$, $B(1, 2)$, $C(1, -2)$, and $D(-2, -1)$. Sketch the image of $ABCD$ under $D_{1.5}$.

In Exercises 11–12, write the coordinates of the vertices of the image of each polygon under the dilation with the given scale factor and the origin as center of dilation.

11 $\triangle ABC$ with vertices $A(-2, 1)$, $B(3, 1)$, and $C(-2, 5)$; scale factor 1.5

12 the square $WXYZ$ with vertices $W(-3, 3)$, $X(3, 3)$, $Y(3, -3)$, and $Z(-3, -3)$; scale factor 4

In Exercises 13–14, find the coordinates of the vertices of the image of the given figure after each pair of transformations.

13 the line segment with endpoints $X(-3, 1)$ and $Y(3, 4)$ after a translation 4 units right and 2 units down followed by a dilation with the origin as center and scale factor 3

14 the line segment with endpoints $A(0, -2)$ and $T(3, 5)$ after a dilation with the origin as center and scale factor 2 followed by a dilation with the origin as center and scale factor 0.5

5.4 Midsegments of Triangles

A **midsegment of a triangle** is a segment that connects the midpoints of two sides of a triangle.

Triangle Midsegment Theorem

If a segment joins the midpoints of two sides of a triangle, then it is parallel to the third side and equal to one half its length. That is, in $\triangle ABC$ with D the midpoint of $\overline{AB}$ and E the midpoint of $\overline{AC}$, then $\overline{DE} \parallel \overline{BC}$ and $DE = \frac{1}{2} BC$.

EXAMPLE 1   **Proving the Triangle Midsegment Theorem**

1   **Given:** $\triangle ABC$ with D and E midpoints of $\overline{AB}$ and $\overline{AC}$, respectively
Prove: $\overline{DE} \parallel \overline{BC}$ and $DE = \frac{1}{2} BC$

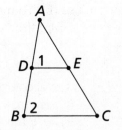

■ **SOLUTION**

Statements	Reasons
1. $\triangle ABC$ with D and E midpoints of $\overline{AB}$ and, $\overline{AC}$, respectively	1. Given
2. $\dfrac{AD}{AB} = \dfrac{AE}{AC} = \dfrac{1}{2}$	2. Definition of midpoint
3. $\angle A \cong \angle A$	3. Reflexive Property
4. $\triangle ABC \sim \triangle ADE$	4. SAS Similarity Theorem
5. $\angle 1 \cong \angle 2$	5. Corresponding $\angle$s of similar $\triangle$s are $\cong$.
6. $\overline{DE} \parallel \overline{BC}$	6. If two lines cut by a transversal such that corresponding $\angle$s are $\cong$, the lines are parallel.
7. $\dfrac{AD}{AB} = \dfrac{DE}{BC}$	7. Corresponding sides of similar $\triangle$s are proportional.
8. $\dfrac{DE}{BC} = \dfrac{1}{2}$	8. Substitution
9. $DE = \frac{1}{2} BC$	9. Multiplication Property of Equality

An **alternate** proof using transformations, specifically dilation, is presented here. M and N are the midpoints of two sides of $\triangle ABC$ as shown. Now perform $D_{A,2}(M)$. The image of M will be on $\overrightarrow{AC}$; call it D. Since $AD = 2(AM) = AC$, D must be at point C. Similarly, the image of N is B. Then $D_{A,2}(\overline{MN}) = \overline{CB}$. Also $\overline{MN} \parallel \overline{CB}$ because under a dilation a segment is parallel to its image. Finally $CB = 2(MN)$ implies $MN = \frac{1}{2} CB$.

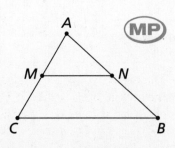

If the midpoints of the sides of a triangle are connected consecutively, another triangle is formed. This triangle is called the **medial triangle**. In the figure to the right, $\triangle DEF$ is the medial triangle of $\triangle ABC$.

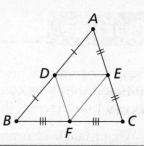

Properties of Medial Triangles

Given: $\triangle DEF$ is the medial triangle of $\triangle CBA$. The following statements are true:

- $\triangle ADE \cong \triangle DBF \cong \triangle EFC \cong \triangle FED$

- $\triangle ABC \sim \triangle ADE \sim \triangle DBF \sim \triangle EFC \sim \triangle FED$

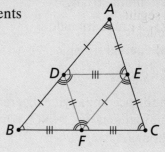

You can use the Triangle Midsegment Theorem and the properties of medial triangles to find the various measurements of triangles.

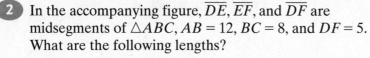

EXAMPLES 2 through 4   **Working with medial triangles**

2 In the accompanying figure, $\overline{DE}, \overline{EF},$ and $\overline{DF}$ are midsegments of $\triangle ABC$, $AB = 12$, $BC = 8$, and $DF = 5$. What are the following lengths?

$DE =$ $EF =$ $AC =$ $AE =$

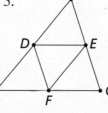

■ SOLUTION

$DE = 4$ $EF = 6$ $AC = 10$ $AE = 5$

3 Determine the ratio of the areas of $\triangle ADE$ to $\triangle ABC$.

■ SOLUTION

Because the four small triangles are all congruent, their areas are equal. Therefore, the area of $\triangle ADE$ is $\frac{1}{4}$ the area of $\triangle ABC$.

4 In the accompanying figure, $\overline{MN}$ and $\overline{PN}$ are midsegments. If $RS = 14$, $NT = 8$, and $PN = 10$, find MN and RT and the perimeter of the medial triangle.

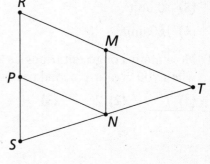

■ SOLUTION

$MN = \frac{1}{2}RS = \frac{1}{2}(14) = 7$

$RT = 2(PN) = 2(10) = 20$

$PM = NT = 8$

Perimeter of $\triangle PMN = PN + NM + MP$

$\qquad\qquad = 10 + 7 + 8 = 25$

The above examples illustrate two properties of medial triangles. If $\triangle DEF$ is the medial triangle of $\triangle ABC$, then the perimeter of $\triangle DEF$ is one-half the perimeter of $\triangle ABC$ and the area of $\triangle DEF$ is one-quarter the area of $\triangle ABC$.

Choose the numeral preceding the word or expression that best completes the statement or answers the question.

1 What triangle is formed by joining the midpoints of the sides of a triangle?

(1) middle triangle

(2) average triangle

(3) medial triangle

(4) center triangle

2 In the accompanying diagram $\overline{JK}$ is a midsegment of $\triangle MNO$. What is true about $\overline{JK}$?

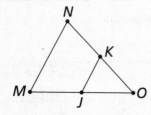

(1) $\overline{JK} \perp \overline{NO}$

(2) $JK = JO$

(3) $JK = 0.5NO$

(4) $\overline{JK} \parallel \overline{MN}$

3 If the area of a triangle $\triangle HIJ$ is 40 unit², what is the area of the medial triangle of $\triangle HIJ$?

(1) 10 unit²

(2) 20 unit²

(3) 80 unit²

(4) 160 unit²

4 How many congruent triangles are formed when you create a medial triangle?

(1) 1   **(2)** 2   **(3)** 4   **(4)** 5

Use the following figure to answer Exercises 5 and 6.

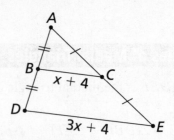

5 What is the value of x?

(1) 2   **(2)** 6   **(3)** 4   **(4)** 8

6 What is the perimeter of $\triangle ADE$ if the perimeter of $\triangle ABC$ is 28?

(1) 14   **(2)** 32   **(3)** 28   **(4)** 56

7 What is the ratio of the area of $\triangle RST$ to $\triangle ABC$ knowing that $\triangle JKL$ and $\triangle RST$ are medial triangles?

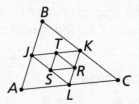

(1) $\dfrac{1}{2}$ **(2)** $\dfrac{1}{3}$ **(3)** $\dfrac{1}{4}$ **(4)** $\dfrac{1}{16}$

8 The top of a 10-ft pole is halfway between you and a tree. How tall is the tree shown in the diagram?

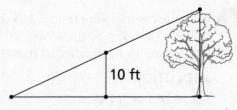

(1) 10 ft   **(2)** 20 ft   **(3)** 30 ft   **(4)** 40 ft

9 In the accompanying diagram, D, E, and F are midpoints of sides $\overline{AC}$, $\overline{AB}$, and $\overline{CB}$, respectively. Name three pairs of parallel segments.

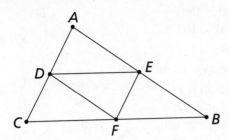

10 In $\triangle HIJ$, M is the midpoint of $\overline{HI}$ and N is the midpoint of $\overline{IJ}$. If $MN = 5x + 3$ and $HJ = 4x + 18$, what is the value of x?

11 In the figure below, each medial triangle was shaded. If the perimeter of the original triangle is 1, what is the perimeter of all the shaded triangles in the figure?

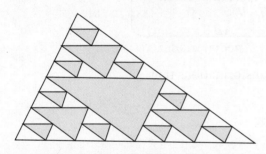

12 A midsegment of a triangle is represented by $3x + 7$. The side of the original triangle parallel to the midsegment is represented by $7x + 6$. Determine the length of this midsegment.

13 **Given:** $\triangle DEF$ is a medial triangle of $\triangle ABC$.
Prove: $\triangle FED \cong \triangle ADE$.

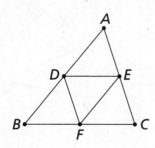

Use the accompanying figure for Exercises 14–16. In the figure, J and K are midpoints.

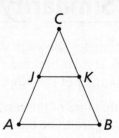

14 **Given:** Isosceles $\triangle ABC$ with $\overline{AC} \cong \overline{BC}$, and midsegment $\overline{JK}$
Prove: $\triangle CJK$ is isosceles.

15 If $\overline{JK}$ is 7 inches long and $AC = BC = 20$ in., what is the perimeter of $\triangle CJK$?

16 If $m\angle AJK = 113°$, what is $m\angle ABC$?

Use the accompanying figure for Exercises 17–21. In the figure S, T, and U are midpoints.

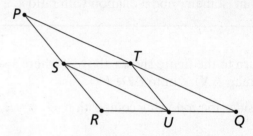

17 If $PR = 10$ and $RQ = 17$, find $TU + ST$.

18 Find the perimeter of $\triangle TSU$ given the following values; $PR = 8$, $RQ = 12$, and $PQ = 18$.

19 If $PS = 3x + 5$ and $TU = 21 + x$, find SR.

20 If $RU = x^2$ and $ST = 6x + 16$, find UQ.

21 If $PR = z^2$ and $TU = 10(z - 5)$, find PR and TU.

22 The segment joining the midpoints of two adjacent sides of a rectangle is 55 in. Determine the length of the diagonal of the rectangle.

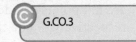
Consider the triangles shown in the accompanying figure. Notice that the triangles are similar because all the angles of one are equal to the corresponding angles of the other.

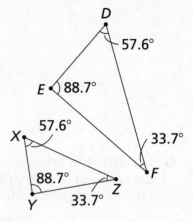

It might seem that one of these triangles is a dilation of the other. However, for a figure to be the image of another under a dilation it is necessary that each pair of corresponding sides for the two figures be either collinear of parallel. When two non-congruent, similar figures are situated such that at least one pair of their corresponding sides are not parallel nor collinear then a dilation will not map one to the other.

What is needed here is a new transformation that is a composition of transformations.

Definition of Similarity S_k

A *similarity* S_k is a transformation of the plane that is the composition of an isometry and a dilation with ratio k.

Return to the figure shown above. Is there a series of transformations that will map $\triangle XYZ$ onto $\triangle DEF$?

Consider the following compostion: $D_{F,\frac{DF}{X'F}} \circ R_{F,\angle X'FD} \circ T_{\overrightarrow{ZF}}$

First	Second	Third
$T_{\overrightarrow{ZF}}(\triangle XYZ) = \triangle X'Y'F$	$R_{F,\angle X'FD}(\triangle X'Y'F) = \triangle X''Y''F$	$D_{F,\frac{DF}{X''F}}(\triangle X''Y''F) = \triangle DEF$

EXAMPLE 1   Determining transformations

1   Given that $\triangle XYZ \sim \triangle PQR$ with $\frac{YZ}{QR} = \frac{1}{4}$ determine a series of transformations that will map $\triangle XYZ$ onto $\triangle PQR$.

■ **SOLUTION**

First, rotate $\triangle XYZ$ about O, 90°. The image is $\triangle PY'Z'$. Second, dilate $\triangle PY'Z'$ about P by a factor of $\frac{1}{4}$.

$\therefore S_{\frac{1}{4}}(\triangle XYZ) = D_{P,\frac{1}{4}} \circ R_{o,90°}$.

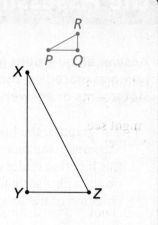

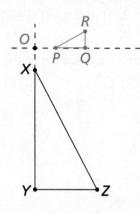

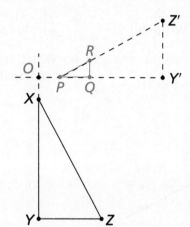

Practice

1   Given $\triangle ABC$, perform the similarity transformation defined as $S_2 = D_{A',2} \circ R_{P,90°}$.

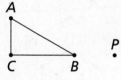

2   Which of the following is not preserved by a similarity transformation?

   (a) Angle measure   **(c)** Betweenness

   (b) Collinearity   **(d)** Side measure

In Exercises 3–5, determine whether the blue figure is the image of the black figure under a similarity.

3   4   5

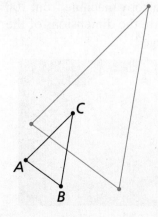

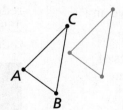

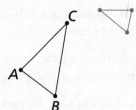

Answer all questions in this part. For each question, select the numeral preceding the word or expression that best completes the statements or answers the questions.

1 The graph of the line is shown in the accompanying figure. Sketch the image of this function under a dilation about the origin with a scale factor of two. Write the equation of the image.

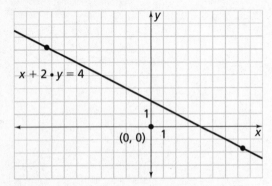

2 The hexagon in the accompanying figure has been dilated by a scale factor of $-\frac{1}{2}$, twice. If the area of the original hexagon was 240 in.^{2} what is the area of the innermost hexagon?

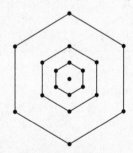

In Exercises 3–6, write true or false and explain your answer.

3 An image under a dilation cannot have any fixed points

4 For dilations, the corresponding angles of the preimage and image are congruent.

5 A dilation is an isometry.

6 A dilation with a scale factor less than one is an enlargement.

7 Write the coordinate of the vertices of the image of $\triangle JKL$ with vertices $J(-2, 1)$, $K(3, 1)$, and $L(-2, 5)$ under a dilation with a scale factor of 1.5.

8 Which transformation is shown in the accompanying figure?

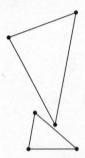

(a) Dilation   **(b)** Translation

(c) Rotation   **(d)** Similarity

9 $\triangle JKL$ is the image of $\triangle JIH$ with $\frac{HJ}{LJ} = \frac{1}{2}$. Describe a sequence of transformations that maps $\triangle JIH$ onto $\triangle JKL$.

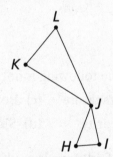

10 An 8.5 in. × 11 in. photo of a rose is to be reduced on a copy machine from 100% to 25%. What are the dimensions of the reduced image?

11 $\triangle ABC$ is the image of $\triangle RST$. What is the center of this dilation and what is the scale factor?

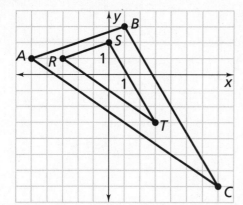

In the following diagram, K is the midpoint of $\overline{JM}$, L is the midpoint of $\overline{JN}$, and $\overline{KL} \parallel \overline{MN}$. Use this information to answer Exercises 12 and 13.

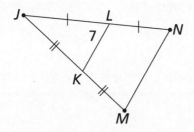

12 What is the length of $\overline{NM}$?

(1) 3.5   **(2)** 7   **(3)** 10.5   **(4)** 14

13 If the perimeter of $\triangle JMN$ is x, which of the following represents the perimeter of $\triangle JKL$?

(1) $\dfrac{x}{2}$ **(2)** x **(3)** $2x$ **(4)** $7x$

14 Using the accompanying figure, determine the value of x.

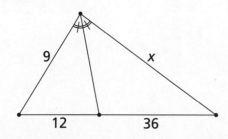

(1) 18   **(2)** 27   **(3)** 45   **(4)** 48

15 What is the value of x?

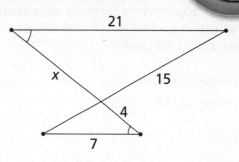

(1) 5   **(2)** 10   **(3)** 12   **(4)** 16

16 What is the value of x?

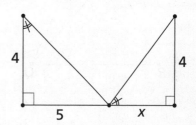

(1) 2   **(2)** $2\frac{1}{2}$ **(3)** $3\frac{1}{5}$ **(4)** 5

17 What is the value of x?

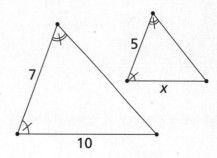

(1) 5   **(2)** 6   **(3)** $7\frac{1}{7}$ **(4)** 9

Answer the following question. Clearly indicate the necessary steps, including appropriate formula substitutions, diagrams, graphs, charts, etc. A correct numerical answer with no work shown will receive only one credit.

18 **Given:** $\angle RSQ \cong \angle RQT$

   Prove: $\triangle QSR \sim \triangle TQR$

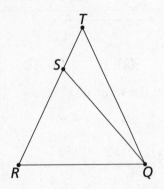

6 Quadrilaterals and Other Polygons

Varignon's Theorem

French mathematician Pierre Varignon received his M.A. from the University in Caen in 1682 where he had also attended the Jesuit College.

The Varignon Theorem, bearing his name, was first published in 1731.

Given any quadrilateral *MATH,* connect the midpoints of each side in successive order forming quadrilateral *QUED.* What type of quadrilateral is formed?

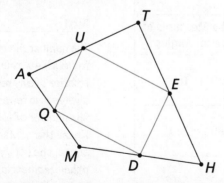

6.1 Polygons

Recall that a **polygon** is a closed plane figure with at least three sides.

All closed plane figures can be classified as either *convex* or *concave*. In a **convex polygon,** no point on any diagonal lies outside the figure. In a **concave polygon,** at least one diagonal will contain points that lie outside the figure.

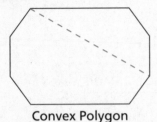

Convex Polygon

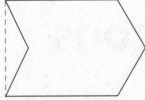

Concave Polygon

Note

A **diagonal** of a polygon is any line segment whose endpoints lie on non-consecutive vertices.

The properties, theorems, and postulates discussed in this lesson will pertain to convex polygons.

You can classify any polygon by its number of sides. The following table lists names for the most common polygons.

| Classifying a Polygon by the Number of Sides ||
Number of Sides	Name
3	triangle
4	quadrilateral
5	pentagon
6	hexagon
8	octagon
9	nonagon
10	decagon
12	dodecagon

Note

If a polygon has *n* sides, you call it an *n-gon*. For example, a 16-sided polygon is called a 16-gon.

The following table shows how you can find the sum of the interior angles of a convex polygon by drawing all the diagonals from one vertex.

| Interior Angles of a Polygon ||||
Polygon	Number of Sides	Number of Triangles Formed	Sum of the Measures of the Interior Angles
	3	$3 - 2 = 1$	$1 \cdot 180° = 180°$
	4	$4 - 2 = 2$	$2 \cdot 180° = 360°$
	5	$5 - 2 = 3$	$3 \cdot 180° = 540°$
	8	$8 - 2 = 6$	$6 \cdot 180° = 1080°$

Note

The number of triangles found this way in the interior of any polygon is always two fewer than the number of sides. Recall that, "Many times, the study of other geometric figures is done by decomposing them into triangles and then using the properties of triangles to investigate the more complex figures."

The relationship between the number of sides and the number of interior triangles of any polygon leads to the following theorem.

Polygon Interior Angle-Sum Theorem

The sum of the measures of the interior angles of a convex polygon with n sides is $(n - 2)180°$.

EXAMPLE 1   **Using the Polygon Interior Angle-Sum Theorem**

 Find the sum of the measures of the interior angles of a dodecagon.

■ **SOLUTION**

A dodecagon is a polygon that has 12 sides. Use the Polygon Interior Angle-Sum Theorem with $n = 12$.

sum of measures of interior angles $= (n - 2)180°$
$$= (12 - 2)180°$$
$$= (10)180° = 1800°$$

Note

An **exterior angle of a convex polygon** is an angle that forms a linear pair with one of its interior angles.

The sum of the exterior angles of a polygon is consistent, regardless of the number of sides of a given figure.

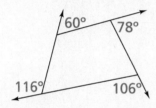

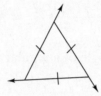

$$116° + 60° + 78° + 106° = 360° \qquad 120° + 120° + 120° = 360°$$

Polygon Exterior Angle-Sum Theorem

The sum of the measures of the exterior angles of a convex polygon, one at each vertex, is 360°.

EXAMPLE 2   **Using the Polygon Exterior Angle-Sum Theorem**

 Find the $m\angle A$.

■ **SOLUTION**

$m\angle A + m\angle B + m\angle C + m\angle D + 87°$ ← Use the Polygon
$\quad = 360°$ Exterior
$m\angle B + 126° = 180°$ ← Linear pair   Angle-Sum
$\qquad m\angle B = 54°$ Theorem.

$m\angle C = 90°$

$m\angle D + 112° = 180°$
$\qquad m\angle D = 68°$

$m\angle A + 54° + 90° + 68° + 87° = 360°$ ← Substitute.
$\qquad\qquad m\angle A + 299° = 360°$ ← Solve.

Therefore, $m\angle A = 61°$.

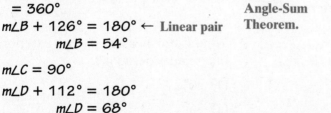

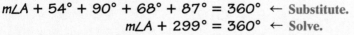

An **equilateral polygon** is a polygon in which all sides are congruent. An **equiangular polygon** is a polygon in which all angles are congruent. A **regular polygon** is both equilateral and equiangular. There is a relationship between the number of sides and the angle measure of regular polygons.

Corollaries for Regular Polygons

The measure of each interior angle of a regular n-gon is $\frac{(n-2)180°}{n}$.

The measure of each exterior angle of a regular n-gon is $\frac{360°}{n}$.

EXAMPLES 3 and 4   **Using the corollaries for regular polygons**

3 Find the measure of each interior angle of the polygon shown at the right.

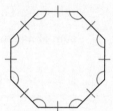

■ **SOLUTION**

All sides are congruent and all angles are congruent, so the figure is a regular polygon. Use the first corollary with $n = 8$.

measure of each interior angle $= \dfrac{(n-2)180°}{n}$

$= \dfrac{(8-2)180°}{8} = \dfrac{(6)180°}{8} = \dfrac{1080°}{8} = 135°$

4 The measure of each exterior angle of a regular polygon is 40°. Find the number of sides.

■ **SOLUTION**

measure of each exterior angle $= \dfrac{360°}{n}$

$40° = \dfrac{360°}{n}$

$n = 9$

The polygon has 9 sides.

Practice

Choose the numeral preceding the word or expression that best completes the statement or answers the question.

1 Four interior angles of a pentagon each measures 110°. What is the measure of the fifth interior angle?

(1) 72°

(2) 100°

(3) 108°

(4) 110°

2 What is the measure of each exterior angle of a regular decagon?

(1) 30°

(2) 36°

(3) 72°

(4) 144°

3 Which expression represents the measure of each interior angle of a regular *n*-gon?

(1) $(180n)°$ **(3)** $(n-2)180°$

(2) $\dfrac{360°}{n}$ **(4)** $\dfrac{(n-2)180°}{n}$

4 The measure of each interior angle of a regular polygon is 144°. How many sides does the polygon have?

(1) 6 **(2)** 7 **(3)** 8 **(4)** 10

5 In the figure below, one side of polygon *RSTU* has been extended as shown. What is $m\angle S$?

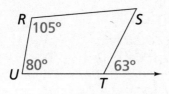

(1) 58° **(3)** 75°

(2) 63° **(4)** 112°

In Exercises 6–9, find the values for each regular polygon.

6

7
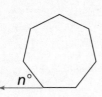

8

9
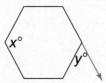

10 The measures of four interior angles of a pentagon are 115°, 92°, 107°, and 83°. Find the measure of the fifth interior angle.

In Exercises 11–13, the sum of the measures of the interior angles of a polygon is given. Find the number of sides.

11 180° **12** 900° **13** 2700°

In Exercises 14–16, the measure of an exterior angle of a regular polygon is given. Find the number of sides.

14 120° **15** 72° **16** 18°

In Exercises 17–19, the measure of an interior angle of a regular polygon is given. Find the number of sides. Then name the figure.

17 120 **18** 108 **19** 135

In Exercises 20–21, classify the polygon by its number of sides. Then find the value of *a*.

20
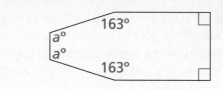

21
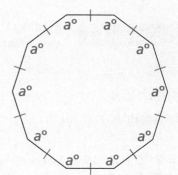

22 Find $m\angle B$.

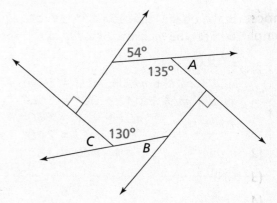

155

A **quadrilateral** is a 4-sided polygon. To name a quadrilateral, start at any vertex and list the other **vertices** consecutively. **Consecutive** vertices are next to each other and determine the consecutive angles of the quadrilateral. You can name these vertices either clockwise or counterclockwise.

Note

Nonconsecutive vertices of a quadrilateral are opposite angles.

EXAMPLES 1 and 2   **Naming quadrilaterals**

Use the diagram at the right for Examples 1 and 2.

1   Name the quadrilateral.

■ SOLUTION

ABCD, BCDA, CDAB, or *DABC* are the clockwise names.

2   Name each angle of the quadrilateral.

■ SOLUTION

∠*A*, ∠*B*, ∠*C*, ∠*D* or ∠*DAB*, ∠*ABC*, ∠*BCD*, ∠*CDA* or ∠*BAD*, ∠*CBA*, ∠*DCB*, ∠*ADC*

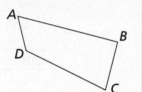

All quadrilaterals have four sides, four angles, and a sum of the angles equal to 360°. Quadrilaterals can be further classified according to specific unique relationships between the sides and the angles of the figure. These unique relationships form a subcategory known as **special quadrilaterals**.

EXAMPLES 3 and 4   **Finding the measure of a missing angle in a quadrilateral**

3   Find the value of *x*.

■ SOLUTION

In a quadrilateral, all the angles add up to 360°.

$x = 360 - (131 + 66 + 112)$
$x = 360 - 309$
$x = 51$

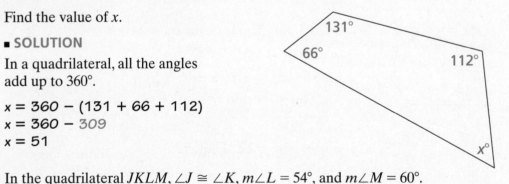

4   In the quadrilateral *JKLM*, ∠*J* ≅ ∠*K*, $m\angle L = 54°$, and $m\angle M = 60°$. What is the measure of ∠*J*?

■ SOLUTION

$m\angle J + m\angle K + m\angle L + m\angle M = 360°$
$m\angle J + m\angle K + 54° + 60° = 360°$
$\qquad\qquad m\angle J + m\angle K = 360° - 114°$
$\qquad\qquad\qquad 2m\angle J = 246°$ ← $m\angle J + m\angle K = 2m\angle J$
$\qquad\qquad\qquad m\angle J = 123°$

The following table lists seven major **special quadrilaterals.**

Special Quadrilaterals	
Definition	**Properties**
A **parallelogram** is a quadrilateral with two pairs of parallel sides.	If a quadrilateral is a parallelogram, then • its opposite sides are congruent; • its opposite angles are congruent; • its consecutive angles are supplementary; and • its diagonals bisect each other.
A **rhombus** is a parallelogram with four congruent sides.	If a quadrilateral is a rhombus, then it has all the properties of a parallelogram, plus • each diagonal bisects a pair of opposite angles; and • its diagonals are perpendicular.
A **rectangle** is a parallelogram with four right angles.	If a quadrilateral is a rectangle, then it has all the properties of a parallelogram, plus • its diagonals are congruent.
A **square** is a parallelogram with four congruent sides and four right angles.	If a quadrilateral is a square, then it has all the properties of a parallelogram, plus • each diagonal bisects a pair of opposite angles; • its diagonals are perpendicular; and • its diagonals are congruent.
A **trapezoid** is a quadrilateral with at least one pair of parallel sides.	The parallel sides of a trapezoid are called its **bases.** Two angles whose vertices are the endpoints of a single base form a pair of **base angles.** The nonparallel sides of a trapezoid are its **legs.** The **midsegment** of a trapezoid is the segment that joins the midpoints of the legs. If a quadrilateral is a trapezoid, then • two consecutive angles whose vertices are endpoints of different bases are supplementary.
An **isosceles trapezoid** is a trapezoid whose base angles are congruent.	If a quadrilateral is an isosceles trapezoid, then it has all the properties of a trapezoid, plus • its diagonals are congruent. • its legs are congruent.
A **kite** is a quadrilateral with two pairs of congruent adjacent sides and no opposite sides congruent.	In a kite, the common endpoint of a pair of congruent sides is called an **endpoint of the kite.** If a quadrilateral is a kite, then • its diagonals are perpendicular; and • one diagonal bisects the angles whose vertices are the endpoints of the kite.

You can use these properties to solve problems involving quadrilaterals. If you know a quadrilateral is of a given type, you can use the properties of the quadrilateral to find the lengths of missing angles and sides.

EXAMPLES 5 through 8   **Using the properties of quadrilaterals**

5 In the figure at the right, *WXYZ* is a parallelogram. Find $m\angle X$.

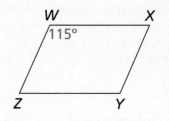

■ SOLUTION

Consecutive angles of a parallelogram are supplementary.
Therefore: $m\angle X = 180° - 115° = 65°$

6 Given that *ABCD* is an isosceles trapezoid, find $m\angle D$.

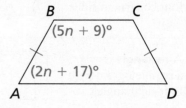

■ SOLUTION

In a trapezoid, two consecutive angles whose vertices are endpoints of different bases are supplementary.
Therefore: $m\angle A$ + $m\angle B = 180°$
$(2n + 17°) + (5n + 9)° = 180°$
$7n + 26 = 180$
$n = 22$

Base angles of an isosceles trapezoid are congruent.
Therefore: $m\angle D = m\angle A = (2n + 17)° \rightarrow m\angle D = (2[22] + 17)° = 61°$

7 In the figure at the right, *EFGH* is a kite with congruent sides and angle measure as marked. Find $m\angle FEH$.

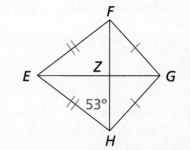

■ SOLUTION

The diagonals of a kite are perpendicular.
Therefore, in $\triangle EZH$: $m\angle EZH = 90°$

The sum of the measures of the angles of a triangle is 180°.
Therefore, in $\triangle EZH$: $m\angle ZEH = 180° - (53° + 90°) = 37°$

In a kite, one diagonal bisects the angles whose vertices are the endpoints of the kite.
Therefore, in kite *EFGH*: $m\angle FEH = 2(m\angle ZEH) = 2(37°) = 74°$

8 In the figure at the right, *PQRS* is a rectangle with diagonals $\overline{PR}$ and $\overline{QS}$. Find *PR* and *QS*.

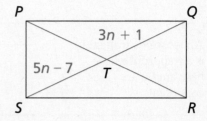

■ SOLUTION

A rectangle is a type of parallelogram.

The diagonals of a parallelogram bisect each other.
Therefore: $5n - 7 = 3n + 1 \rightarrow n = 4$
$QS = (5n - 7) + (3n + 1)$
$= (5[4] - 7) + (3[4] + 1) = 26$

The diagonals of a rectangle are congruent.
Therefore: $PR = QS = 26$

The diagram below shows how the special quadrilaterals are related.

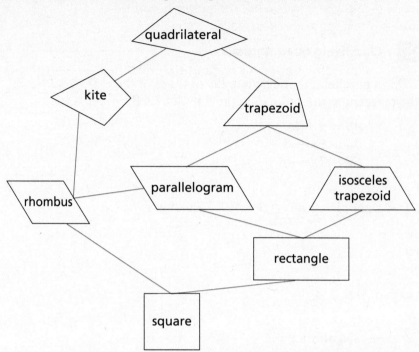

You can see from the diagram why statements such as the following are true.

All squares are rectangles.

All parallelograms are trapezoids.

No trapezoid is a kite.

Some rectangles are trapezoids.

Similarly, you can see why statements like these are false.

All rectangles are squares.

No square is a rhombus.

EXAMPLES 9 and 10   **Classifying quadrilaterals**

9 Is the following statement true or false? Explain your reasoning.

All kites are parallelograms.

■ **SOLUTION**

The statement is false.

For a quadrilateral to be a parallelogram, its opposite sides must be congruent and parallel to each other. Unlike a parallelogram, a kite does not have parallel sides, and consecutive sides are congruent, not opposite sides.

10 Is the following statement true or false? Explain your reasoning.

All squares are parallelograms.

■ **SOLUTION**

The statement is true.

In order for a quadrilateral to be a parallelogram, it must have two pairs of parallel sides. All squares have two pairs of parallel sides. Therefore, a square must also be a parallelogram.

159

You can use the properties of quadrilaterals to help you identify and classify figures.

EXAMPLES 11 and 12   **Classifying quadrilaterals**

11 Quadrilateral $ABCD$ is a parallelogram. The lengths of three of the legs are shown in the diagram to the right. Find the length of AB.

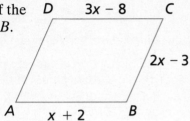

$$AB = x + 2$$
$$BC = 2x - 3$$
$$CD = 3x - 8$$

■ SOLUTION

Step 1 Since $ABCD$ is a parallelogram, $AB = CD$. Solve for x.

$$x + 2 = 3x - 8$$
$$2x = 10$$
$$x = 5$$

Step 2 Find the length of $\overline{AB}$.

$$AB = x + 2$$
$$AB = 5 + 2 \quad \leftarrow \text{ substitute } x = 5$$
$$AB = 7$$

12 Find the length of $\overline{DA}$ in the quadrilateral from Example 11.

■ SOLUTION

Since $ABCD$ is a parallelogram, opposite sides are congruent.

$$DA = BC$$
$$DA = 2x - 3$$
$$DA = 2(5) - 3 \quad \leftarrow \text{ substitute } x = 5$$
$$DA = 7$$

Properties of **special quadrilaterals** can be used to demonstrate algebraically that a quadrilateral is a parallelogram.

EXAMPLE 13   **Showing that a quadrilateral is a parallelogram**

13 Find the values of x and y for which $PQRS$ is a parallelogram.

■ SOLUTION

A quadrilateral is a parallelogram if both pairs of opposite sides are congruent.

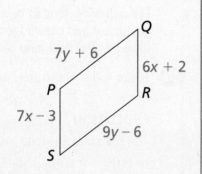

Therefore: $SP = QR$ and $PQ = RS$

$7x - 3 = 6x + 2$	$7y + 6 = 9y - 6$
$x - 3 = 2$	$6 = 2y - 6$
$x = 5$	$12 = 2y$
	$6 = y$

So $PQRS$ is a parallelogram when $x = 5$ and $y = 6$.

To prove that a particular figure is a specific type of quadrilateral, it is not necessary to prove that the figure has all the properties of that type of quadrilateral. It is sufficient to show the minimal properties required to be a specific type of quadrilateral.

Minimal Properties Necessary to Prove...	
A quadrilateral is a parallelogram if...	**A quadrilateral is a rhombus if...**
• both pairs of opposite sides are parallel. • both pairs of opposite sides are congruent. • both pairs of opposite angles are congruent. • consecutive angles are supplementary. • 1 pair of sides are parallel and congruent. • the diagonals bisect each other.	• it is parallelogram with perpendicular diagonals. • all 4 sides are congruent. • it is a parallelogram with 2 consecutive congruent sides.

For example, in order to prove that a quadrilateral is a parallelogram, it is sufficient to show that both pairs of opposite angles are congruent. You do not need to show that the quadrilateral has all the properties of a parallelogram.

Note that definitions are biconditional statements. For example, if both pairs of opposite sides are parallel, then the quadrilateral is a parallelogram. The converse is also true: If a quadrilateral is a parallelogram, then both pairs of opposite sides are parallel.

EXAMPLE 14 **Proving if opposite sides of a quadrilateral are congruent then the quadrilateral is a parallelogram**

14 If both pairs of opposite sides of a quadrilateral are congruent, prove that the quadrilateral is a parallelogram.

■ SOLUTION

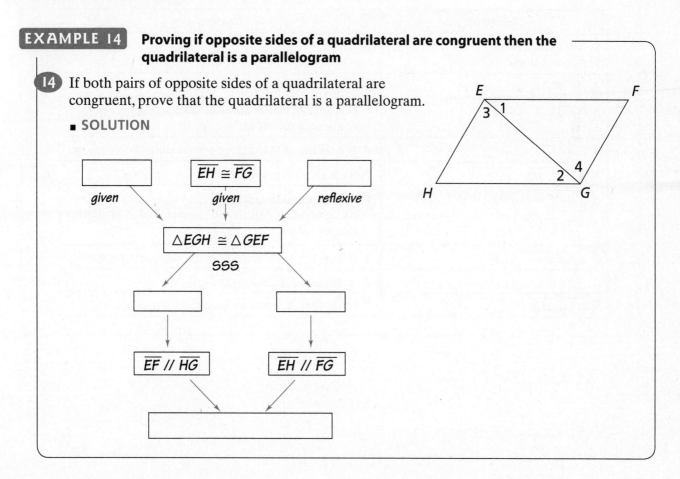

EXAMPLE 15 **Proving a parallelogram has opposite sides congruent**

15 **Given:** Parallelogram *MATH*

Prove: $\overline{MA} \cong \overline{TH}, \overline{MH} \cong \overline{TA}$

■ SOLUTION

Construct the midpoint of diagonal $\overline{AH}$. Rotate $\triangle ATH$ about the midpoint 180°. $\triangle HMA$ is the image of $\triangle ATH$ under this rotation. A rotation is an isometry therefore side measure is preserved. Therefore,

$\overline{MA} \cong \overline{TH}, \overline{MH} \cong \overline{TA}$.

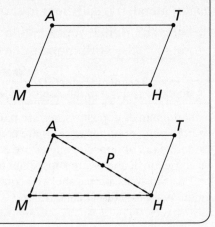

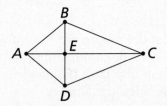

EXAMPLE 16 **Proving that the diagonals of a kite are perpendicular**

16 **Given:** *ABCD* is a kite with $\overline{AB} \cong \overline{AD}$ and $\overline{BC} \cong \overline{DC}$

Prove: $\overline{AC} \perp \overline{BD}$

■ SOLUTION

Statements	Reasons
1. Kite *ABCD* with $\overline{AB} \cong \overline{AD}$ and $\overline{BC} \cong \overline{DC}$	1. Given
2. $\overline{AC} \cong \overline{AC}$	2. Reflexive Property
3. $\triangle ABD \cong \triangle ADC$	3. If 3 sides of one $\triangle$ are $\cong$ to corresponding 3 sides of another the $\triangle$s are $\cong$.
4. $\angle BAC \cong \angle DAC$	4. If 2 $\triangle$s are $\cong$ then their corresponding parts are $\cong$.
5. $\overline{AE} \cong \overline{AE}$	5. Reflexive Property
6. $\triangle ABE \cong \triangle ADE$	6. If 2 sides and the included $\angle$ of one $\triangle$ are $\cong$ to the corresponding 2 sides and the included $\angle$ of another the $\triangle$s are $\cong$.
7. $\angle AEB \cong \angle AED$	7. If 2 $\triangle$s are $\cong$ then their corresponding parts are $\cong$.
8. $\angle AEB$ & $\angle AED$ are right angle.	8. $\cong$ linear pairs form right angle.
9. $\overline{AC} \perp \overline{BD}$	9. Lines that intersect to form right angles are $\perp$.

Choose the numeral preceding the word or expression that best completes the statement or answers the question.

1 In quadrilateral $ABCD$, $\angle A$ is a right angle, $m\angle B = 126°$, and $\angle C \cong \angle D$. What is the measure of $\angle D$?

(1) $36°$ **(3)** $72°$

(2) $54°$ **(4)** $108°$

2 In which type of quadrilateral are the diagonals not necessarily perpendicular?

(1) rectangle   **(3)** kite

(2) square   **(4)** rhombus

3 This figure is a trapezoid with congruent sides as marked. Which statement is false?

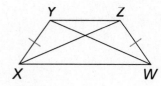

(1) $\overline{YZ} \cong \overline{XW}$

(2) $\overline{XZ} \cong \overline{WY}$

(3) $m\angle XYZ = m\angle WZY$

(4) $m\angle XYZ + m\angle YXW = 180°$

4 In the figure below, $EFGH$ is a parallelogram. What is $m\angle F$?

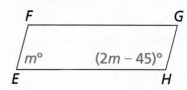

(1) $15°$ **(3)** $105°$

(2) $75°$ **(4)** $255°$

5 Which conditions will not guarantee that quadrilateral $QUAD$ is a parallelogram?

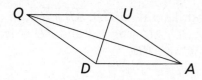

(1) $\overline{QD} \cong \overline{QU}$ and $\overline{AD} \cong \overline{AU}$

(2) $\overline{QD} \cong \overline{AU}$ and $\overline{QU} \cong \overline{AD}$

(3) $\overline{QD} \cong \overline{AU}$ and $\overline{QD} \parallel \overline{AU}$

(4) $\overline{QU} \parallel \overline{AD}$ and $\overline{QD} \parallel \overline{AU}$

6 In quadrilateral $PQRS$, find $m\angle P$, $m\angle Q$, and $m\angle R$.

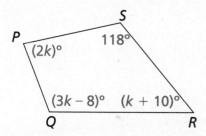

7 Given that $JKLM$ is a parallelogram, find $m\angle K$, $m\angle L$, and $m\angle M$.

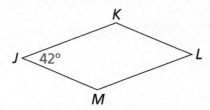

8 Given that $MATH$ is a rhombus, find MA, AT, TH, and HM.

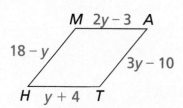

9 In quadrilateral $NOPQ$, $m\angle POQ = 70°$ and $m\angle PQN = 135°$. Find $m\angle ONQ$.

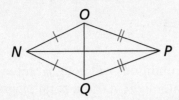

10 In quadrilateral $ABCD$, $\overline{AB} \parallel \overline{DC}$, $\overline{AD} \cong \overline{BC}$, $AC = 5z - 3$, and $BD = 4z$. Find AC and BD.

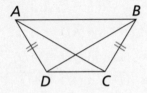

In Exercises 11–16, tell whether each statement is *always true*, *sometimes true*, or *never true*.

11 A rectangle is a square.

12 A trapezoid is a parallelogram.

13 A rhombus is a rectangle.

14 A rhombus is a square.

15 The diagonals of a square bisect each other.

16 The diagonals of a parallelogram are congruent.

17 Quadrilateral $ABCD$ is a parallelogram. Under what conditions will $ABCD$ also be a trapezoid, rhombus, kite, or square?

6.3 More Special Quadrilaterals

 G.CO.11

In the last section, the minimal properties necessary to prove a quadrilateral is a parallelogram or a rhombus were summarized. In the table below the minimal properties for other special quadrilaterals are given.

A quadrilateral is a rectangle if…	A quadrilateral is a trapezoid if…
• it is a parallelogram with congruent diagonals. • it is a parallelogram with right angles.	• at least one pair of opposite sides are parallel.
A quadrilateral is a square if…	**A quadrilateral is an isosceles trapezoid if…**
• it is a rectangle with 2 congruent consecutive sides. • it is rhombus with 1 right angle.	• it is a trapezoid with congruent base angles. • it is a trapezoid with congruent diagonals. • it is a trapezoid with congruent nonparallel sides.

To show that a quadrilateral is a rectangle, you can first show that it is a parallelogram, and then show that it has right angles.

 EXAMPLE 1 **Proving a quadrilateral is a rectangle**

1 Prove that a parallelogram containing one right angle is a rectangle.

Given: Parallelogram $KLMN$ with right $\angle N$
Prove: $KLMN$ is a rectangle.

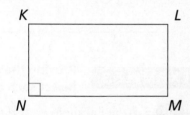

■ **SOLUTION**

Given $KLMN$ is a parallelogram and $\angle N$ is a right angle, then $\angle L$ is also a right angle since opposite angles of a parallelogram are congruent. Since the sum of the four angles equals 360°, the other two angles add up to 180°. Since those angles are congruent, each one is also a right angle.

Therefore, if a parallelogram has one right angle, it is a rectangle.

You can use the definitions of special types of quadrilaterals to prove their properties.

EXAMPLE 2 **Proving properties**

2 Prove that the diagonals of an isosceles trapezoid are congruent.

Given: Isosceles trapezoid $PQRS$, with bases $\overline{QR}$ and $\overline{PS}$
Prove: $\overline{PR} \cong \overline{QS}$

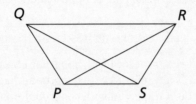

■ **SOLUTION**

Given $PQRS$ is an isosceles trapezoid with bases $\overline{QR}$ and $\overline{PS}$, then $\overline{PQ} \cong \overline{RS}$, and $\angle QPS \cong \angle RSP$. That is, the legs of an isosceles trapezoid are congruent, and the base angles are also congruent. We know $\overline{PS} \cong \overline{PS}$ by the reflexive property, so $\triangle PQS$ and $\triangle SRP$ are congruent by SAS. Therefore, the diagonals $\overline{PR}$ and $\overline{QS}$ are congruent by CPCTC.

EXAMPLE 3 **Proving the diagonals of a parallelogram bisect each other**

3 **Given:** Parallelogram $ABCD$ with diagonals $\overline{AC}$ and $\overline{BD}$ intersecting at P
Prove: $AP = PC$ and $BP = PD$

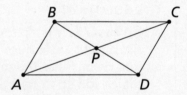

■ **SOLUTION**

Statements	Reasons
1. Parallelogram $ABCD$ with diagonals AC and BD intersecting at P	1. Given
2. $\overline{BC} \cong \overline{DA}$, $\overline{BC} \parallel \overline{DA}$	2. Opposite sides of a parallelogram are congruent and parallel.
3. $\angle BCP \cong \angle DAP \,\&\, \angle CBP \cong \angle ADP$	3. Two parallel lines cut by a transversal alternate interior angles are congruent.
4. $\triangle BPC \cong \triangle DPA$	4. ASA
5. $\overline{BP} \cong \overline{DP} \,\&\, \overline{AP} \cong \overline{CP}$	5. If two $\triangle$s are $\cong$ their corresponding parts are $\cong$.
6. $BP = DP \,\&\, AP = CP$	6. Definition of congruence

EXAMPLE 4   **Proving properties**

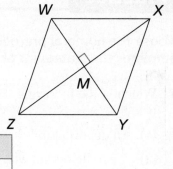

4 Prove that the diagonals of a rhombus are perpendicular to each other.

Given: $WXYZ$ is a rhombus.
Prove: $\overline{WY} \perp \overline{XZ}$

■ SOLUTION

Statements	Reasons
1. $WXYZ$ is a rhombus.	1. Given
2. $\overline{WZ} \cong \overline{ZY}$	2. Consecutive sides of a rhombus are congruent.
3. $\overline{ZM} \cong \overline{MZ}$	3. Reflexive property
4. $\overline{WM} \cong \overline{MY}$	4. Diagonals of a rhombus bisect each other.
5. $\triangle WMZ \cong \triangle YMZ$	5. SSS
6. $\angle WMZ \cong \angle YMZ$	6. CPCTC
7. $\angle WMZ$ is the supplement to $\angle YMZ$.	7. Definition of supplementary
8. $\angle WMZ$ and $\angle YMZ$ are right $\angle$s.	8. If two angles are congruent and supplementary, they are right angles.
9. $\overline{WY} \perp \overline{XZ}$	9. If two angles are right angles, the lines that form them are perpendicular.

EXAMPLE 5   **Proving that a rectangle has congruent diagonals**

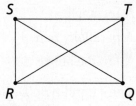

5 **Given:** Rectangle $RSTQ$.
Prove: $\overline{RT} \cong \overline{SQ}$

■ SOLUTION

Statements	Reasons
1. $RSTQ$ is a rectangle with diagonals $\overline{RT}$ and $\overline{SQ}$.	1. Given
2. $\overline{ST} \cong \overline{RQ}, \overline{RS} \cong \overline{QT}$	2. Opposite sides of a rectangle are congruent.
3. $\angle SRQ \cong \angle TQR$	3. A rectangle is a parallelogram with four right angles and all right angles are congruent.
4. $\triangle SRQ \cong \triangle TQR$	4. SAS
5. $\overline{RT} \cong \overline{SQ}$	5. If two $\triangle$s are $\cong$ their corresponding parts are $\cong$.

Choose the numeral preceding the word or expression that best completes the statement or answers the question.

1 Which of the following statements is *not* true?

(1) All quadrilaterals have four sides.

(2) A parallelogram with one right angle is a rectangle.

(3) A rhombus is always a square.

(4) The diagonals of a rhombus are perpendicular to each other.

2 If a parallelogram has four congruent sides, then it must be a

(1) square.   **(3)** parallelogram.

(2) rhombus.   **(4)** kite.

3 If a quadrilateral has both pairs of opposite angles congruent, then the figure is *at least* a

(1) square.   **(3)** trapezoid.

(2) rhombus.   **(4)** parallelogram.

4 If any two angles of a quadrilateral are supplementary and congruent, the quadrilateral can be which of the following?

(1) A square

(2) A rectangle

(3) A parallelogram

(4) All of the above

5 In quadrilateral $ABCD$, $\overline{BC} \cong \overline{AD}$. Which of the following would make $ABCD$ a parallelogram?

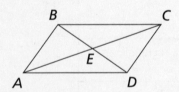

(1) $\overline{AC}$ bisects $\overline{BD}$

(2) $\angle CBD \cong \angle ADB$

(3) $\overline{BD} \cong \overline{AC}$

(4) $\overline{AB} \parallel \overline{DC}$

6 Which pairs of quadrilaterals are congruent?

I. Two squares whose corresponding diagonals are congruent

II. Two rectangles whose corresponding diagonals are congruent

III. Two rhombuses whose corresponding diagonals are congruent

(1) II only

(2) I and II

(3) I and III

(4) I, II, and III

7 Use a two-column proof to prove that given kite $DEFG$, with $\overline{EF} \cong \overline{GF}$, $\overline{DF}$ bisects $\overline{EG}$.

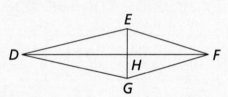

8 Use a flow proof to prove the following:

Given: $ABCD$ is a rhombus.

Prove: $\triangle ACB = \triangle CAD$

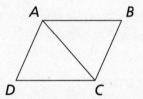

9 Write a paragraph proof showing that the diagonals of a rectangle are congruent.

10 **Given:** Quadrilateral $ABCD$
   $\overline{AB} \parallel \overline{CD}$ and $\overline{AB} \cong \overline{CD}$

Prove: $ABCD$ is a parallelogram.

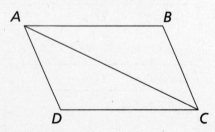

11 Given a parallelogram, prove that its opposite sides are congruent.

Given: Parallelogram $ABCD$
Prove: $\overline{AB} \cong \overline{CD}$, $\overline{AD} \cong \overline{BC}$

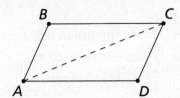

12 Rectangle $HOME$ has diagonals $\overline{HM}$ and $\overline{OE}$ intersecting at D.
If $OD = 3(4x - 1) - x$ and $MD = 4(6 - x) - 12$, determine OD, MD, OE, and MH.

13 The accompanying figure shows isosceles trapezoid $ABCD$ with $\overline{AB} \parallel \overline{CD}$. If $m\angle DAB = 5(x - 2)$ and $m\angle CBA = 3(x + 4)$ determine the measures of $\angle DAB, \angle CBA, \angle ADC,$ and $\angle BCD$.

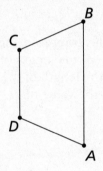

14 **Given:** $ABCD$ is an isosceles trapezoid.
$\overline{AB} \parallel \overline{DC}$, $\overline{AE} \perp \overline{DC}$, $\overline{BF} \perp \overline{DC}$
Prove: $\triangle ADE \cong \triangle BCF$

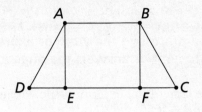

169

Answer all questions in this part. For each question, select the numeral preceding the word or expression that best completes the statement or answers the question.

1 The sum of the exterior angles of any polygon is

(1) 180°.

(2) 360°.

(3) $\dfrac{360°}{n}$.

(4) $(n-2)180°$.

2 The number of triangles found by drawing all the diagonals from one vertex of a polygon is always

(1) the same as the number of sides.

(2) one less than the number of sides.

(3) two less than the number of sides.

(4) three less than the number of sides.

3 What is the measure of each exterior angle of a regular octagon?

(1) 45°

(2) 135°

(3) 360°

(4) 1080°

4 Find the measures of ∠1, ∠2, and ∠3 in the parallelogram drawn below.

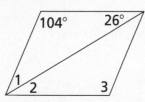

(1) $m\angle 1 = 13°, m\angle 2 = 52°; m\angle 3 = 154°$

(2) $m\angle 1 = 26°, m\angle 2 = 13°; m\angle 3 = 154°$

(3) $m\angle 1 = 26°, m\angle 2 = 50°; m\angle 3 = 104°$

(4) $m\angle 1 = 50°, m\angle 2 = 26°; m\angle 3 = 104°$

5 The figure $ABCD$ below is a rhombus with $m\angle ABC = 120°$, and the length of $\overline{EB}$ is 13. Find the length of $\overline{AB}$.

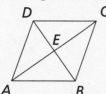

(1) 13　　(2) 26　　(3) 30　　(4) 60

6 The figure below is a rhombus. Find the value of x, y, and z.

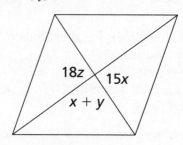

(1) $x = 6, y = 84, z = 5$

(2) $x = 6, y = 89, z = 0$

(3) $x = 12, y = 168, z = 10$

(4) $x = 12, y = 173, z = 5$

7 In an isosceles trapezoid, the length of one base is $10x - 4$, the length of one leg is $6x - 5$, and the length of the other leg is $4x + 7$. Find the value of x.

(1) 1

(2) $\dfrac{11}{6}$

(3) $\dfrac{9}{4}$

(4) 6

8 Determine the values of x and y for which the figure $ABCD$ is a parallelogram.

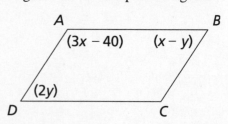

(1) $x = 20, y = 20$

(2) $x = 20, y = 60$

(3) $x = 60, y = 20$

(4) $x = 140, y = 40$

9 In the parallelogram below, if $m\angle 1 = m\angle 3 = 11x$, $m\angle 2 = 3x - 30$, and $m\angle 4 = x$, find the value of x.

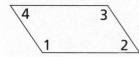

(1) 15   **(2)** 30   **(3)** 45   **(4)** 165

10 Find the value of x in the parallelogram $ABCD$.

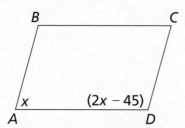

(1) 15   **(2)** 45   **(3)** 75   **(4)** 225

11 The figure below is an isosceles trapezoid with bases $\overline{BI}$ and $\overline{RD}$. Which of the following statements are true?

   I. $m\angle BRD = m\angle DIB$
   II. $m\angle BID = 2m\angle BRD$
   III. $m\angle BID = 180 - m\angle IDR$

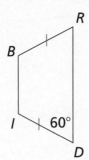

(1) I only   **(3)** I and II

(2) II only   **(4)** II and III

12 Which of the following figures sometimes have diagonals that are not perpendicular?

   I. Isosceles trapezoid
   II. Kite
   III. Rectangle
   IV. Rhombus

(1) I only   **(3)** I and III

(2) II only   **(4)** II and III

13 Which property is sufficient to show that a quadrilateral is always a parallelogram?

(1) Both pairs of opposite sides are parallel and congruent.

(2) One pair of its opposite angles is congruent.

(3) One pair of its opposite sides is parallel.

(4) Three sides are congruent.

14 Which of the following conditions is sufficient to prove that a quadrilateral is a square?

(1) It has opposite sides that are parallel.

(2) It has opposite sides that are parallel and congruent.

(3) It has one pair of opposite angles that are right angles and all sides are congruent.

(4) It has one pair of opposite sides that are parallel and noncongruent.

15 The parallelogram $ABCD$ has diagonals $\overline{AC}$ and $\overline{BD}$. If $AC = 5x + 4$, $AE = 4x - 2y$, and $CE = 3x + 2y$, find the value of x.

(1) 1

(2) 2

(3) 3

(4) 4

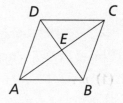

16 What is the sum of the measures of the interior angles of an 18-gon?

(1) 20°

(2) 160°

(3) 360°

(4) 2880°

Answer all questions in this part. Clearly indicate the necessary steps, including appropriate formula substitutions, diagrams, graphs, charts, etc. For all questions in this part, a correct numerical answer with no work shown will receive only one credit.

17 Find the measure of angle x. Show your work.

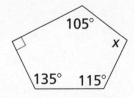

18 Draw a Venn diagram showing the relationship among these quadrilaterals: squares, rectangles, rhombuses, and parallelograms.

19 **Given:** $\triangle PUT \not\cong \triangle NTU$

Prove: *PUNT* is **not** a rectangle.

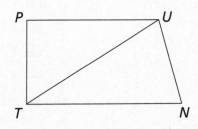

7 Coordinate Geometry

Cartesian Plane

The French philosopher and mathematician René Descartes (1596–1650) is credited with the introduction of the Cartesian coordinate system, which allows reference to a point in space as an ordered pair. This enables algebraic equations to be expressed as geometric objects in a two-dimensional coordinate system. Conversely, it allows for geometric shapes to be described as equations. This marriage between algebra and geometry is referred to as analytical geometry, and is crucial to the discovery of calculus and higher mathematics.

7.1 Slopes of Parallel and Perpendicular Lines

 G.GPE.5

Knowing sufficient information about a line in the coordinate plane, you can write a linear equation in two variables to represent it. This **linear equation** can be written in a number of equivalent forms. Stated below are important forms for an equation of a line.

Slope-Intercept, Point-Slope, and Standard Form

An equation of a line in **slope-intercept form,** $y = mx + b$ has slope m and y-intercept b.

An equation of a line in **point-slope form,** $y - y_1 = m(x - x_1)$ has slope m and passes through (x_1, y_1).

An equation of a line in **standard form,** $Ax + By + C = 0$ has slope of $m = -\frac{A}{B}$ and y-intercept $b = -\frac{C}{B}$.

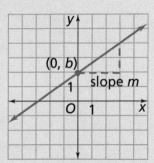

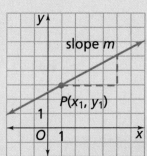

Note

The slope of a line passing through (x_1, y_1) and (x_2, y_2) is $\frac{(y_2 - y_1)}{(x_2 - x_1)}$. The slope of a horizontal line is 0. The slope of a vertical line is undefined.

Any vertical line containing $P(x_1, y_1)$ has equation $x = x_1$. For example, if a vertical line contains the point $(5, 2)$, an equation for that line is $x = 5$.

Any horizontal line containing $P(x_1, y_1)$ has equation $y = y_1$. For example, if a horizontal line contains the point $(4, -8)$, an equation for that line is $y = -8$.

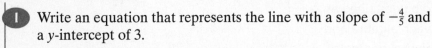

EXAMPLES 1 and 2 **Using slope and y-intercept to identify an equation for a line**

1 Write an equation that represents the line with a slope of $-\frac{4}{5}$ and a y-intercept of 3.

■ **SOLUTION**

Use the slope-intercept form.

$$y = mx + b.$$

$$y = -\frac{4}{5}x + 3 \quad \leftarrow \text{Replace } m \text{ with } -\frac{4}{5} \text{ and } b \text{ with 3.}$$

2 Which equation represents the line at the right?

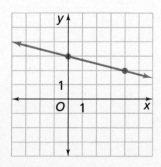

(1) $y = \frac{1}{4}x + 3$ **(3)** $y = \frac{1}{4}x - 3$

(2) $y = -\frac{1}{4}x + 3$ **(4)** $y = -2x + 3$

■ **SOLUTION**

The y-intercept is 3. The slope of the line is $-\frac{1}{4}$. Using the slope-intercept form, the correct choice is **(2)**.

When you are given the slope and a point on a line, you can use the point-slope form to write an equation for that line.

EXAMPLES 3 through 5   **Writing an equation for a line by using slope and a point on the line**

Write an equation in slope-intercept form for each line, if possible.

3 the line with slope $\frac{3}{4}$ and containing $P(2, -3)$

■ SOLUTION

$$y - (-3) = \frac{3}{4}(x - 2)$$

$$y = \frac{3}{4}x - 4.5$$

4 the line with slope 0 and containing $P(2, -3)$

■ SOLUTION

Because the slope is 0, the line is horizontal.

$$y = -3$$

5 the line with no slope and containing $P(2, -3)$

■ SOLUTION

Because there is no slope, the line is vertical.

$$x = 2$$

You can also use the point-slope form to find an equation of a line through two specific points. The point-slope form requires that you first find the slope. Recall that slope $= m = \frac{y_2 - y_1}{x_2 - x_1}$. You can write an equation of a line in slope-intercept or standard form.

EXAMPLES 6 through 9   **Writing an equation for a line given two points**

Write an equation for

6 the line containing $A(-5, -6)$ and $B(3, 8)$.

■ SOLUTION

First determine the slope.

$$m = \frac{y_2 - y_1}{x_2 - x_1} = \frac{-6 - 8}{-5 - 3}$$

$$= \frac{-14}{-8} = \frac{7}{4}$$

Using the point $B(3, 8)$ and the point-slope form results in:

$$y - 8 = \frac{7}{4}(x - 3)$$

$$y - \frac{32}{4} = \frac{7}{4}x - \frac{21}{4}$$

$$y = \frac{7}{4}x + 2.75$$

7 $\overleftrightarrow{DG}$ containing $D(2, 3)$ and $G(8, 11)$ in standard form.

■ SOLUTION

First determine the slope.

$$m = \frac{y_2 - y_1}{x_2 - x_1} = \frac{11 - 3}{8 - 2} = \frac{8}{6} = \frac{4}{3}$$

Using the point $D(2, 3)$ and the point-slope form results in:

$$y - 3 = \frac{4}{3}(x - 2)$$

$$3y - 9 = 4x - 8$$
$$-4x + 3y = 1$$

The standard form for the equation is $-4x + 3y = 1$.

8 the line containing $L(-5, -6)$ and $M(3, -6)$.

■ SOLUTION

The y-coordinates of L and M are equal. The line is horizontal.

$$y = -6$$

9 the line containing $R(4.2, -6)$ and $S(4.2, 9)$.

■ SOLUTION

The x-coordinates of R and S are equal. The line is vertical.

$$x = 4.2$$

Use what you know to solve problems involving points on a line.

10 The point $Z(3, w)$ is on the graph of $y = 2x + 5$. What is the value of w?

    (1) -1 **(2)** $w - 5$ **(3)** 11 **(4)** $2w + 5$

    ■ **SOLUTION**

    If $x = 3$ and $y = w$, then $w = 2(3) + 5$; that is, $w = 11$.
    The correct choice is **(3)**.

11 Which point lies on the line containing $P(-3, -1)$ and $Q(5, 6)$?

    (1) $A(-3, 0)$ **(2)** $B(21, 19)$ **(3)** $C(21, 20)$ **(4)** $D(-3, -2)$

    ■ **SOLUTION**

$$m = \frac{6 - (-1)}{5 - (-3)} = \frac{7}{8} \quad \leftarrow \text{Determine the slope.}$$

$$y = \frac{7}{8}(x - 5) + 6 \quad \leftarrow \text{Write an equation for the line containing } P \text{ and } Q.$$

Because $\frac{7}{8}(21 - 5) + 6 = 20$, the correct choice is **(3)**.

Two lines in a plane either intersect or do not intersect. If the lines never intersect, they are **parallel.** If the lines intersect at a right angle, the lines are **perpendicular.**

$m: y = \dfrac{1}{2}x + 3$ $n: y = \dfrac{1}{2}x - 1$ $p: y = -2x - 6$ $q: y = \dfrac{1}{2}x - 1$

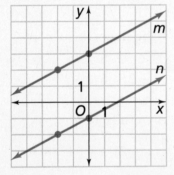   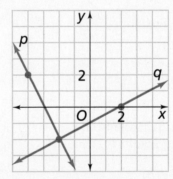

slope of m: $\dfrac{1}{2}$ slope of n: $\dfrac{1}{2}$ slope of p: -2 slope of q: $\dfrac{1}{2}$ Note: $-2 \cdot \dfrac{1}{2} = -1$

The lines are **parallel lines.**   The lines are **perpendicular lines.**
The **slopes** of these lines are **equal.**   The slopes are **negative reciprocals** of each other.

Parallel and Perpendicular Lines

  ■ Two lines with slopes m_1 and m_2 are parallel if and only if $m_1 = m_2$.
    (Also, any two vertical or horizontal lines are parallel.)

  ■ Two lines with slopes m_1 and m_2 are perpendicular if and only if
    $m_1 m_2 = -1$.
    (Also, every vertical line is perpendicular to every horizontal line.)

EXAMPLE 12   **Prove the slopes of parallel lines are equal**

12 Given: $m \parallel n$

Prove: slope of m = slope of n;

that is, $\frac{EC}{AC} = \frac{FD}{BD}$.

■ **SOLUTION**

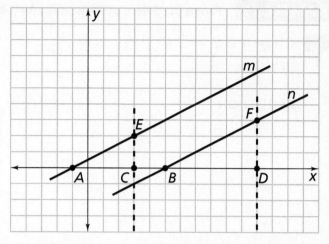

Statements	Reasons
1. $m \parallel n$	1. Given
2. $\angle EAC \cong \angle FBD$	2. If two parallel lines are cut by a transversal corresponding angles are congruent.
3. Construct $\overleftrightarrow{EC}$ & $\overrightarrow{FD} \perp x$-axis	3. By construction
4. $\angle ECA \cong \angle FDB$	4. $\perp$ form right angles and all right angles are congruent.
5. $\triangle ECA \sim \triangle FDB$	5. If two angles of one triangle are congruent to the corresponding two angles of another the triangles are similar.
6. $\dfrac{EC}{FD} = \dfrac{AC}{BD}$	6. If two triangles are similar corresponding sides are proportional.
7. $\dfrac{EC}{AC} = \dfrac{FD}{BD}$	7. Properties of proportions

The following proof is rather lengthy. However, it is not difficult to follow.

EXAMPLE 13   **Prove the Slope of Perpendicular Lines have a product of –1**

13 **Given:** $j \perp k$

Prove: $m_j \cdot m_k = -1$.

■ **SOLUTION**

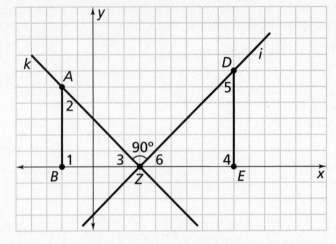

Statements	Reasons
1. $j \perp k$	1. Given
2. $m\angle AZD = 90°$	2. Perpendicular lines form right angles.
3. Construct $\overleftrightarrow{AB}$ & $\overleftrightarrow{DE} \perp x$-axis.	3. By construction
4. $m\angle 1 \cong m\angle 4$	4. $\perp$ form right angles and all right angles are congruent.
5. $\triangle ABZ$ & $\triangle DEZ$ are right triangles.	5. Def. of a right triangle
6. $m\angle 2 + m\angle 3 = 90°$ and $m\angle 5 + m\angle 6 = 90°$	6. The acute angles of a right triangle are complementary. Complementary angles add to 90°.
7. $m\angle BZD + m\angle 6 = 180°$	7. Two adjacent angles whose exterior sides form a straight line are supplementary. Supplementary angles add to 180°.
8. $m\angle BZD = m\angle 3 + 90°$	8. Angle addition axiom
9. $m\angle 3 + 90° + m\angle 6 = 180°$	9. Substitution
10. $m\angle 3 + m\angle 6 = 90°$ $m\angle 2 + m\angle 3 = m\angle 3 + m\angle 6$	10. Subtraction Property of Equality Perpendicular lines form right angles which equal 90°.
11. $m\angle 5 + m\angle 6 = m\angle 3 + m\angle 6$	11. Substitution
12. $m\angle 2 = m\angle 6$ and $m\angle 5 = m\angle 3$	12. Subtraction Property of Equality
13. $\triangle ABZ \sim \triangle ZED$	13. AA
14. $\dfrac{AB}{ZE} = \dfrac{BZ}{ED}$, so $\dfrac{AB}{BZ} = \dfrac{ZE}{DE}$	14. If two triangles are similar corresponding sides are proportional; Properties of proportions.
15. $m_k = -\dfrac{AB}{BZ}$; $m_j = \dfrac{DE}{ZE}$	15. Definition of slope
16. $-m_k = \dfrac{1}{m_j} \Rightarrow m_k m_j = -1$	16. Substitution and by algebra

Practice

Choose the numeral preceding the word or expression that best completes the statement or answers the question.

1 What is the slope of a line parallel to a line with slope -2?

(1) 2   **(2)** -2 **(3)** $\dfrac{1}{2}$ **(4)** $-\dfrac{1}{2}$

2 What is the slope of a line perpendicular to a line with slope -2?

(1) 2   **(2)** -2 **(3)** 0.5   **(4)** -0.5

3 Which describes the relationship between two distinct nonvertical parallel lines?

(1) equal slopes; unequal y-intercepts

(2) unequal slopes; unequal y-intercepts

(3) equal slopes; equal y-intercepts

(4) unequal slopes; equal y-intercepts

4 The slope of a line perpendicular to line p is

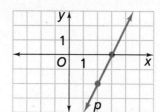

(1) 2.   **(2)** 0.5.   **(3)** -2.   **(4)** -0.5.

5 Which equation represents the line with slope -3 and y-intercept -7?

(1) $y = -3x + 7$ **(3)** $y = -3x - 7$

(2) $y = -7x + 3$ **(4)** $y = 7x - 3$

6 What is the slope of a line parallel to m?

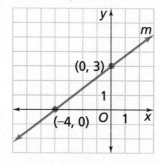

(1) $-\dfrac{4}{3}$

(2) $\dfrac{4}{3}$

(3) $-\dfrac{3}{4}$

(4) $\dfrac{3}{4}$

7 Which equation could not represent a line parallel to the graph of $y = -2.5x + 1$?

(1) $y = -2.5x + 3$ **(3)** $y = -2.5x - 1$

(2) $y = 2.5x + 1$ **(4)** $y = -2.5x$

In Exercises 8–17, write an equation in slope-intercept form for the specified line, where possible.

8 the line containing $A(0, 7)$ and $B(7, 0)$

9 the line containing $C(3, -7)$ and $D(-3, 5)$

10 slope: 2; containing $P(4, 5)$

11 slope: -0.6; containing $Z(-1, 1)$

12 slope: -0.2; y-intercept -3

13 slope: 0; y-intercept 7

14 slope: 0; y-intercept -7

15 no slope; x-intercept -11

16 no slope; containing $S(-1, -3)$

17 slope 0; containing $(0, 0)$

18 Is the suggested relationship between y and x linear? Explain your answer.

x	0	4	8	12
y	2	5	8	11

19 Write an equation in standard form for this graph.

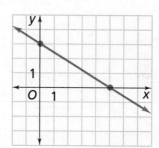

20 A student can work at a job that pays \$4 an hour for 25 hours to earn \$100 or can work at a second job that pays \$5 per hour for 20 hours to earn \$100. If the student spends time at each job, find two other amounts of time at each job needed to earn \$100. Show your work.

21 Is $S(93, 83)$ on the line containing $P(-3, -1)$ and $Q(5, 6)$? Justify your response.

22 Is $C(-102, 142)$ on the line that crosses the x-axis where $x = 17$ and crosses the y-axis where $y = 20$? Explain.

Equations of Parallel and Perpendicular Lines

G.GPE.5

Knowing that parallel lines (l_1 and l_2) have slopes that are equal ($m_1 = m_2$) and different y-intercepts enables you to determine whether lines are parallel to each other.

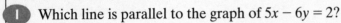

EXAMPLES 1 and 2   **Identifying a line parallel to another line**

1 Which line is parallel to the graph of $5x - 6y = 2$?

(1) the line with slope $-\frac{5}{6}$ and y-intercept $-\frac{1}{3}$ (3) the line with slope $-\frac{6}{5}$ and y-intercept $-\frac{1}{3}$

(2) the line with slope $\frac{5}{6}$ and y-intercept 3   (4) the line with slope $-\frac{6}{5}$ and y-intercept 3

■ **SOLUTION**

Write $5x - 6y = 2$ in slope-intercept form.

$$5x - 6y = 2$$
$$-6y = -5x + 2$$
$$y = \frac{5}{6}x - \frac{1}{3}$$

A line parallel to the graph of $5x - 6y = 2$ must have slope $\frac{5}{6}$. The y-intercept can be any value other than $-\frac{1}{3}$. Therefore, eliminate choices **(1)**, **(3)**, and **(4)**. The correct choice is **(2)**.

Note

To see whether two distinct nonvertical lines are parallel, check to see whether:
- slopes are equal;
- y-intercepts are unequal.

2 Which line is parallel to $3x + 4y = 12$?

(1)
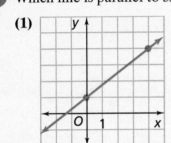

(3)
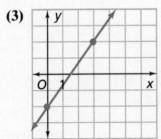

(2)
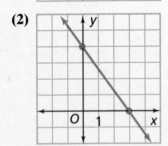

(4)
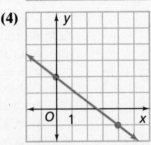

■ **SOLUTION**

Write $3x + 4y = 12$ in slope-intercept form.

$$y = -\frac{3}{4}x + 3$$

A line parallel to $3x + 4y = 12$ must have slope $-\frac{3}{4}$ and any y-intercept except 3. You can eliminate choices **(1)** and **(3)** because the lines have positive slopes. The slope in line **(2)** is $-\frac{4}{3}$ and the slope in line **(4)** is $-\frac{3}{4}$. Therefore, **(4)** is the correct choice.

You can also use the slope to determine whether lines are perpendicular to each other. If two lines are perpendicular, then their slopes are negative reciprocals of each other ($m_1 \times m_2 = -1$).

EXAMPLES 3 and 4 **Identifying a line perpendicular to a given line**

 3 Which equation represents line q perpendicular to line p?

(1) $-x + 4y = -2$ (3) $-x + 4y = -7$

(2) $4x + y = 11$ (4) $4x + y = 2$

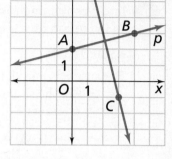

■ **SOLUTION**

Write the equation for each answer choice in slope-intercept form.

(1) $y = \dfrac{1}{4}x - \dfrac{1}{2}$ (3) $y = \dfrac{1}{4}x - \dfrac{7}{4}$

(2) $y = -4x + 11$ (4) $y = -4x + 2$

Because the slope of p is $\frac{1}{4}$, the slope of q is -4. Eliminate choices **(1)** and **(3)**. $C(3, -1)$ does not satisfy the equation in choice **(4)**. The correct choice is **(2)**.

4 Is the line given by the equation $x - 3y = 3$ perpendicular to $y = 3x + 3$? Explain your answer.

■ **SOLUTION**

Write the equation of both lines in slope intercept form:

$$y = \dfrac{1}{3}x - 1$$

$$y = 3x + 3$$

Since their slopes are not negative reciprocals of each other, the lines are not perpendicular.

By comparing the slopes of two lines, you can determine whether they are perpendicular or parallel to each other.

EXAMPLE 5 **Identifying if lines are parallel or perpendicular**

 5 Given points $J(-1, 4)$, $K(2, 3)$, $L(5, 4)$, $M(0, -3)$, are $\overline{JK}$ and $\overline{LM}$ parallel, perpendicular, or neither?

■ **SOLUTION**

Slope of $\overline{JK} = \frac{3 - 4}{2 - (-1)} = -\frac{1}{3}$

Slope of $\overline{LM} = \frac{-3 - 4}{0 - (5)} = \frac{-7}{-5} = \frac{7}{5}$

Since their slopes are not equal, $\overline{JK}$ and $\overline{LM}$ are not parallel.

The product of their slopes is not -1.

$$-\dfrac{1}{3} \times \dfrac{7}{5} = -\dfrac{7}{15}$$

$\overline{JK}$ and $\overline{LM}$ are not perpendicular.

Therefore, they are neither parallel nor perpendicular.

Given a line containing a point, you can find the equation of a line parallel or perpendicular to it by using the slope-intercept form.

EXAMPLES 6 and 7   **Finding equations for parallel or perpendicular lines**

Find an equation in slope-intercept form for the specified line.

 line z containing $P(4, -3)$ and parallel to the graph of $y = \frac{1}{2}x + 3$

■ **SOLUTION**

Because z is parallel to the graph of $y = \frac{1}{2}x + 3$, the slope of z is $\frac{1}{2}$. Also, z contains $P(4, -3)$.

$$y - (-3) = \frac{1}{2}(x - 4)$$

$$y = \frac{1}{2}x - 5$$

 line n containing $Q(-2, 5)$ and perpendicular to the graph of $y = -\frac{1}{2}x + 5$

■ **SOLUTION**

Because n is perpendicular to the graph of $y = -\frac{1}{2}x + 5$, the slope of n is 2. Also, n contains $Q(-2, 5)$.

$$y - 5 = 2(x - (-2))$$
$$y - 5 = 2(x + 2)$$
$$y = 2x + 9$$

Practice

Choose the numeral preceding the word or expression that best completes the statement or answers the question.

1 Which line is perpendicular to the graph of $3y + 2x = 12$?

(1) $y = -2x + 6$ (3) $2x - 3y = 6$

(2) $y = 3x - 2$ (4) $3x - 2y = 12$

2 If two lines have the same slope and the same y-intercept, they are

(1) parallel lines.

(2) the same line.

(3) undefined lines.

(4) perpendicular lines.

3 Which lines below are parallel?

    I. $32y - 16x = 6$

    II. $-16x - 32y = 6$

    III. $-4y = 2x + 6$

(1) I and II

(2) I and III

(3) II and III

(4) None of the above

4 Which equation graphs a line that is *not* perpendicular to the graph of $2x + y = 8$?

(1) $x - 2y = 3$ (3) $y - \dfrac{x}{2} = 6$

(2) $2x - y = 4$ (4) $2y - x = 4$

5 Lines are perpendicular if

(1) one slope is the negative reciprocal of the other slope.

(2) one slope is the opposite sign of the other slope.

(3) one slope is the reciprocal of the other slope.

(4) one slope is identical to the other slope.

6 Which equation is perpendicular to the line given by the equation $3x - 5y = 15$ and passes through $(-2, 2)$?

(1) $3x + 5y = -4$

(2) $3x - 5y = -4$

(3) $5x + 3y = -4$

(4) $5x - 3y = -4$

In Exercises 7–13, write an equation in slope-intercept form for the specified line, where possible.

7 containing $H(2, 2)$ and parallel to the graph of $x - y = 3$

8 containing $A(-2, -2)$ and parallel to the graph of $y = 2x - 1$

9 containing $D(3, -5)$ and parallel to the graph of $y = -3x + 8$

10 containing $L(4, 7)$ and parallel to the graph of $x - 2y = 10$

11 containing $V(4, 0)$ and perpendicular to the graph of $y = -0.5x$

12 containing $B(0, 7)$ and perpendicular to the graph of $y = -0.6x$

13 containing $M(1, 4)$ and perpendicular to the graph of $y = -\frac{2}{3}x + 5$

14 What are the coordinates of the point where the line containing $K(-3, 5)$ and $L(5, -4)$ crosses the y-axis?

In Exercises 15–23, find the slopes of $\overline{JK}$ and $\overline{LM}$, and tell if the lines are parallel, perpendicular, or neither.

15 $J(2, 0)$ $L(0, 4)$
   $K(-1, 3)$ $M(-1, 5)$

16 $J(-4, -5)$ $L(6, 0)$
   $K(5, 1)$ $M(4, 3)$

17 $J(-4, -4)$ $L(1, 3)$
   $K(-1, 5)$ $M(5, 3)$

18 $J(0, 2)$ $L(3, 5)$
   $K(4, 1)$ $M(5, 3)$

19

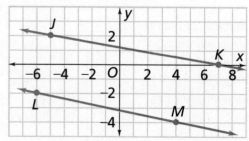

20

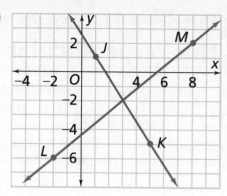

21

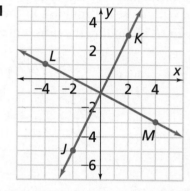

22 $\overline{JK}: y = \frac{1}{5}x + 8$

   $\overline{LM}: y = 5x - \frac{1}{2}$

23 $\overline{JK}: 2y + \frac{1}{2}x = -2$

   $\overline{LM}: 2x + 8y = 8$

24 Write the equation of a line in standard form that is parallel to the line drawn below and goes through the point P.

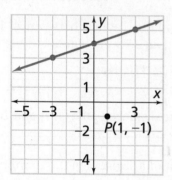

183

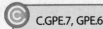
You can use the Pythagorean Theorem to find the distance between any two points in the coordinate plane. If you graph any two points in the coordinate plane such that the line that connects them is not parallel to either axis, you can form a right triangle. The distance between the two points will be the length of the line segment joining those points.

In the figure below, you can see that if the coordinates of P are (x_1, y_1) and the coordinates of Q are (x_2, y_2), then the coordinates of R will be (x_2, y_1). With these coordinates known, you can determine the lengths of $\overline{PR}$ and $\overline{QR}$ by finding the difference in the x or y values.

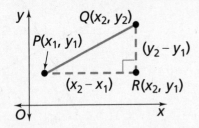

Using the Pythagorean Theorem, you can then find the distance between P and Q using the *Distance Formula*.

The Distance Formula

The distance PQ between $P(x_1, y_1)$ and $Q(x_2, y_2)$ is given by the formula below.

$$PQ = \sqrt{(x_2 - x_1)^2 + (y_2 - y_1)^2}$$

 EXAMPLE 1   **Finding the distance between two points in the coordinate plane**

1. Find the distance between $A(4, -1)$ and $B(-3, 5)$. Give an exact answer and an answer rounded to the nearest hundredth.

■ **SOLUTION**

$AB = \sqrt{(-3-4)^2 + (5-[-1])^2} = \sqrt{(-7)^2 + (6)^2} = \sqrt{85} \approx 9.22$

The distance between A and B is $\sqrt{85}$, or *about 9.22*.

A midpoint of a segment in the coordinate plane is the point halfway between the endpoints of the segment. You can use the coordinates of the endpoints to find the midpoint. In the diagram at the right, the coordinates of P are (x_2, y_2), and the coordinates of Q are (x_1, y_1). The coordinates of the midpoint, M, are found by calculating the average of the x-values $\frac{x_1 + x_2}{2}$ and the average of the y-values $\frac{y_1 + y_2}{2}$.

Therefore, to find the midpoint of a line segment in the coordinate plane, use the *Midpoint Formula*.

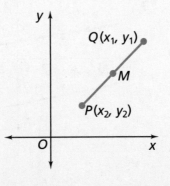

The Midpoint Formula

The coordinates of the midpoint (x_m, y_m) of the segment with endpoints $P(x_1, y_1)$ and $Q(x_2, y_2)$ are given by the following.

$$(x_M, y_M) = \left(\frac{x_1 + x_2}{2}, \frac{y_1 + y_2}{2}\right)$$

EXAMPLES 2 and 3   **Using the Midpoint Formula**

2 Find the coordinates of the midpoint of the segment whose endpoints are $A(-2, -3)$ and $B(5, 4)$.

■ **SOLUTION**

$$(x_M, y_M) = \left(\frac{x_1 + x_2}{2}, \frac{y_1 + y_2}{2}\right)$$

$$(x_M, y_M) = \left(\frac{-2 + 5}{2}, \frac{-3 + 4}{2}\right)$$

$$= \left(\frac{3}{2}, \frac{1}{2}\right)$$

3 The point $Z(3, -5)$ is the midpoint of the segment with endpoints $K(4, 6)$ and $P(x, y)$. Find x and y.

■ **SOLUTION**

$$(x_Z, y_Z) = \left(\frac{x_1 + x_2}{2}, \frac{y_1 + y_2}{2}\right)$$

$$(3, -5) = \left(\frac{4 + x}{2}, \frac{6 + y}{2}\right)$$

$$3 = \frac{4 + x}{2} \text{ and } -5 = \frac{6 + y}{2}$$

$$x = 2 \text{ and } y = -16$$

You can use the midpoint formula to help you find the perpendicular bisector of a given line segment.

EXAMPLE 4   **Identifying the perpendicular bisector of a line segment**

4 Which equation represents the set of all points in the coordinate plane equidistant from $A(4, -2)$ and $B(6, -2)$?

(1) $y = 5$

(2) $x = 5$

(3) $y = -5$

(4) $x = -5$

■ **SOLUTION**

If you look at the graph of the points, you can see $\overline{AB}$ is horizontal. The set of all points equidistant from A and B is the perpendicular bisector, and it will be vertical.

You can eliminate choices (1) and (3) since they are also horizontal. The coordinates of the midpoint of $\overline{AB}$ are $\left(\frac{4 + 6}{2}, \frac{-2 + (-2)}{2}\right) = (5, -2)$. Since the x-value of $(5, -2)$ is 5, the vertical line $x = 5$ is the correct choice. This eliminates choice (4). Therefore, choice (**2**) is the correct answer.

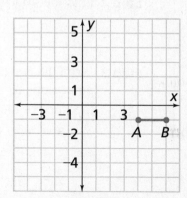

You can find the midpoint of a line segment with the midpoint formula. By using the midpoint of the segment and the slope of a line perpendicular to the given segment, you can write an equation for the perpendicular bisector of any segment using the point-slope form.

Revisiting the Point-Slope Form

A line with slope m that goes through the point (x_1, y_1) can be written using the equation

$$(y - y_1) = m(x - x_1).$$

The steps for writing an equation for the perpendicular bisector of any given line segment are summarized below.

Finding the Perpendicular Bisector of a Line Segment

1 Find the coordinates of the midpoint using the midpoint formula.
2 Find the slope m of the given line segment.
3 Find the equation of the line containing the midpoint, having slope $= -\frac{1}{m}$ using the point-slope method.

The resulting equation is the perpendicular bisector of the given segment.

Note

In the case where the slope of the segment is zero the segment is horizontal. Therefore the $\perp$ bisector would have the equation $x = x$ value of the midpoint.

In the case where the slope of the segment is undefined the segment is vertical. Leading to the equation of the $\perp$ bisector being $y = y$ value of the midpoint.

EXAMPLE 5　**Finding an equation for the perpendicular bisector of a segment**

5 Find an equation that represents the set of all points in the coordinate plane equidistant from $A(3, 8)$ and $B(-1, 2)$.

■ SOLUTION

The set of all points that are equidistant from A and B is the perpendicular bisector of $\overline{AB}$. So, you need to find the perpendicular bisector of $\overline{AB}$.

Step 1 Find the midpoint of $\overline{AB}$ using the midpoint formula.

$$\left(\frac{3+(-1)}{2}, \frac{8+2}{2}\right) \text{ or } (1, 5)$$

Step 2 Find the slope of $\overline{AB}$. The slope of $\overline{AB}$ is $\dfrac{2-8}{-1-3} = \dfrac{-6}{-4} = \dfrac{3}{2}$.

If the slope of $\overline{AB}$ is $\frac{3}{2}$, the slope of the line perpendicular to $\overline{AB}$ is $-\frac{2}{3}$.

Step 3 Write the equation of the perpendicular bisector using the point-slope formula, $(y - y_1) + m(x - x_1)$. Remember to use the slope of the line perpendicular to $\overline{AB}$.

$$y - 5 = -\tfrac{2}{3}(x - 1) \leftarrow \text{substitute } x_1 = 1, y_1 = 5, \text{ and } m = -\tfrac{2}{3}$$
$$y - \tfrac{15}{3} = -\tfrac{2}{3}x + \tfrac{2}{3}$$
$$y = -\tfrac{2}{3}x + \tfrac{17}{3}$$

Therefore, an equation for the perpendicular bisector of $\overline{AB}$ is $y = -\tfrac{2}{3}x + \tfrac{17}{3}$.

Consider the situation where a point C divides a directed line segment AB in such a way that the ratio of $AC:CB = m:n$. How could the coordinates of the point C be determined knowing the coordinates of A and B?

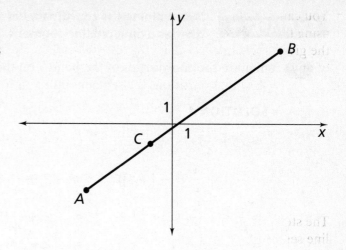

Study the figure in the diagram shown at the right. $\overline{AE} \parallel x$-axis with $\overline{CD} \perp \overline{AE}$ and $\overline{BE} \perp \overline{AE}$. Therefore, $\triangle ACD \sim \triangle ABE$. The similarity ratio is $\frac{m}{m+n}$. Using this ratio the coordinates of C can be determined using the following:

$x_C = x_A + \frac{m}{m+n}(x_B - x_A)$.

Likewise, $y_C = y_A + \frac{m}{m+n}(y_B - y_A)$.

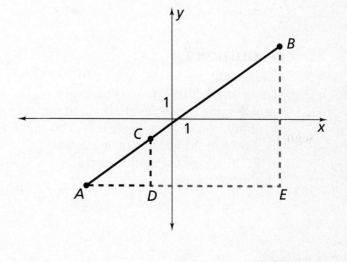

If C divides the directed segment $\overline{AB}$ in a ratio of 3:2 using the formulas above the coordinates of C will be:

$x_C = -2 + \dfrac{3}{5}(8 - [-2])$ $\qquad$ $y_C = -5 + \dfrac{3}{5}(5 - [-5])$

$x_C = -2 + \dfrac{3}{5}(10)$ $\qquad$ $y_C = -5 + \dfrac{3}{5}(10)$

$x_C = -2 + 6 = 4$ $\qquad\qquad$ $y_C = -5 + 6 = 1$

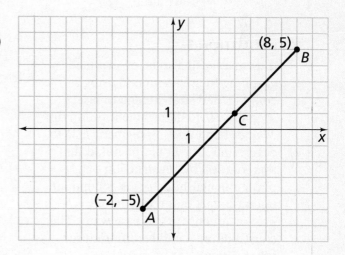

EXAMPLE 6 | **Determining the coordinates of a point that divides a directed line segment**

6 What are the coordinates of the point J on the directed line segment for $H(-4, -2)$ to $I(8, 6)$ that partitions the segment into a ratio of one to three?

■ **SOLUTION 1**

$$x_J = x_H + \frac{1}{4}(x_I - x_H) \qquad y_J = y_H + \frac{1}{4}(y_I - y_H)$$

$$= -4 + \frac{1}{4}(8 - [-4]) \qquad = -2 + \frac{1}{4}(6 - [-2])$$

$$= -4 + \frac{1}{4}(12) \qquad = -2 + \frac{1}{4}(8)$$

$$= -4 + 3 \qquad\qquad = -2 + 2$$

$$= -1 \qquad\qquad\quad = 0$$

■ **SOLUTION 2**

This result can be determined by using interactive geometry software and dilating the segment $\overline{HI}$ about the point H by a scale factor of 0.25. This is shown in the accompanying figure with the image segment shown as dashed and blue.

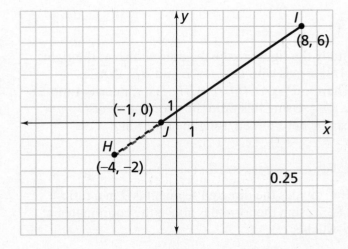

■ **SOLUTION 3**

This result can also be determined by graphing the segment and using a compass and straightedge to bisect segment $\overline{HI}$ to determine its midpoint M and then bisecting segment $\overline{HM}$ to determine J. It should be noted that this solution by construction of perpendicular bisectors is dependent upon the fact that the ratio of proportionality in this case was $\frac{1}{4}$. The construction would be different for other ratios.

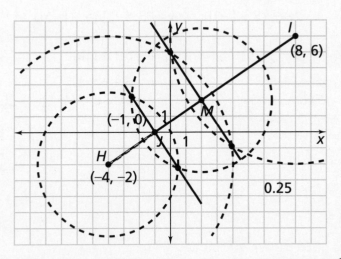

188

Choose the numeral preceding the word or expression that best completes the statement or answers the question.

1 Find the midpoint of a segment with endpoints $(-1, 5)$ and $(6, -3)$.

(1) $\left(3\frac{1}{2}, 4\right)$ **(3)** $\left(-3\frac{1}{2}, -4\right)$

(2) $\left(2\frac{1}{2}, 1\right)$ **(4)** $\left(-2\frac{1}{2}, -1\right)$

2 If the midpoint of a segment is $(2, 8)$, and an endpoint is $(-4, 0)$, the other endpoint is

(1) $(-1, 4)$.   **(3)** $(8, 16)$.

(2) $(4, 8)$.   **(4)** $(3, 4)$.

3 Which pair of points has $(3.5, -9)$ as the midpoint of the segment joining them?

(1) $(6, -2)$ and $(10, 11)$

(2) $(0, -4)$ and $(-7, 5)$

(3) $(-2, -3)$ and $(9, 15)$

(4) $(-1, -7)$ and $(8, -11)$

4 Which represents the midpoint of the segment with endpoints $(4, 8)$ and $(-2, 1)$?

(1) $(3, 3.5)$ **(3)** $(6, -0.5)$

(2) $(3, 4.5)$ **(4)** $(1, 4.5)$

5 Which represents the length of the segment with endpoints $(1, 3)$ and $(4, 5)$?

(1) $\sqrt{13}$ **(2)** 5 **(3)** 13 **(4)** 25

In Exercises 6–9, find the coordinates of the midpoint and the length of the segment whose endpoints are given.

6 $A(3, -2)$ and $B(5, -4)$

7 $X(9, 15)$ and $Y(-6, -2)$

8 $P(1, 2)$ and $Q(4, 6)$

9 $M(3, -4)$ and $N(8, 6)$

In Exercises 10–15, give the distance between each pair of points. Round to the nearest hundredth as necessary.

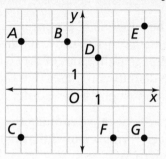

10 A and F

11 E and C

12 C and G

13 E and G

14 B and D

15 D and G

In Exercises 16–20, write an equation of the perpendicular bisector for the given line segment.

16 $\overline{CD}$ when $C = (2, 6)$ and $D = (4, 3)$

17 $\overline{XY}$ when $X = (3, 5)$ and $Y = (-3, -1)$

18 $\overline{AB}$ when $A = (-4, 1)$ and $B = (4, -3)$

19 $\overline{EF}$ when $E = (5, -5)$ and $F = (1, 1)$

20 $\overline{VW}$ when $V = (0, 3)$ and $W = (4, 4)$

21 Find the distance between the parallel lines given by the equations $y = x + 2$ and $y = x - 3$.

22 Find the distance between the line given by the equation $x + y = 2$ and a parallel line that passes through the origin.

23 Point H divides directed line segment $\overline{GO}$ in the ratio of 2:1. Determine the coordinates of point H when G and O have coordinates $(-6, -4)$ and $(6, 5)$ respectively.

24 Point K divides the directed line segment $\overline{JL}$ in the ratio of 3:1. If the coordinates of J are $(-2, -4)$ and the coordinates of K are $(4, 2)$ determine the coordinates of point L.

7.4 Proof in the Coordinate Plane

G.GPE.4, G-CO.10, G-CO.11, G-GPE.5

Coordinate geometry is the study of geometric figures identified by their vertices on the coordinate plane. You can apply the definitions of triangles and quadrilaterals along with calculations of slope, midpoint, and distance to analyze and classify geometric figures in the coordinate plane.

You must show that all of the criteria in the definition of a specific geometric figure are met in order to prove its classification. If the definition of a geometric figure requires that the sides of the figure be parallel or perpendicular, you use slope. If the definition requires that the sides be congruent, you use the distance formula. You must prove these criteria algebraically.

You can use the distance formula to prove that two segments are congruent. If the distance formula shows that the segments have the same length, then they are congruent.

Properties of geometric figures can be **verified** by using specific points. To **prove** properties of geometric figures on the coordinate plane variables must be used to represent the coordinates of the vertices.

> **Note**
>
> Recall that parallel lines have equal slopes and that slopes of perpendicular lines multiply to -1.

Coordinate Proofs Using General Coordinates

1 Begin by placing one of the vertices at a convenient location, often the origin.

2 Place the figure so that the coordinates of as many points as possible are simplified.

3 When possible place one of the sides of the figure on the x-axis.

4 Place the figure in the first quadrant.

> **Note**
>
> This convenient orientation can be achieved for any figure in the plane by applying a sequence of isometry transformations.

EXAMPLE 1   Verifying that S is the midpoint of $\overline{RT}$

1 Show that $RS = ST$ using the distance formula:

$$d = \sqrt{(x_1 - x_2)^2 + (y_1 - y_2)^2}$$

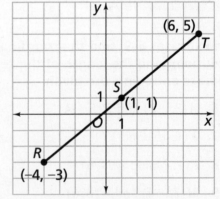

■ **SOLUTION**

$$RS = \sqrt{(-4 - 1)^2 + (-3 - 1)^2} = \sqrt{(-5)^2 + (-4)^2} = \sqrt{41}$$

$$ST = \sqrt{(6 - 1)^2 + (5 - 1)^2} = \sqrt{(5)^2 + (4)^2} = \sqrt{41}$$

Therefore S is the midpoint of segment $\overline{RT}$. It divides the segment into two equal segments.

2 Given *ABCD* is a rectangle, verify that its diagonals are congruent.

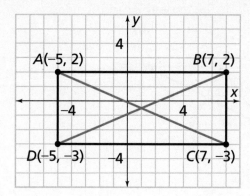

■ **SOLUTION**

Show $\overline{AC} \cong \overline{BD}$.

$AC = \sqrt{(x_2 - x_1)^2 + (y_2 - y_1)^2}$

$= \sqrt{(7 - (-5))^2 + (-3 - 2)^2}$ **Apply the Distance Formula to $\overline{AC}$.**

$= \sqrt{(12)^2 + (5)^2}$

$= \sqrt{169}$

$= 13$

$BD = \sqrt{(x_2 - x_1)^2 + (y_2 - y_1)^2}$

$= \sqrt{((-5 - 7))^2 + (-3 - 2)^2}$ **Apply the Distance Formula to $\overline{BD}$.**

$= \sqrt{(-12)^2 + (-5)^2}$

$= \sqrt{169}$

$= 13$

The length of $\overline{AC}$ equals the length of $\overline{BD}$. Therefore $\overline{AC} \cong \overline{BD}$.

3 Prove the diagonals of a rectangle are congruent.

■ **SOLUTION**

Place rectangle *ABCD* on the coordinate axes as shown in the figure. Since the coordinate axes are perpendicular to each other we know $\angle BAD$ is a right angle. Knowing opposite sides of a rectangle are congruent after locating *B* on the *y* axis and *D* on the *x* axis we can locate point *C* with coordinates (a, b). Using the distance formula leads to

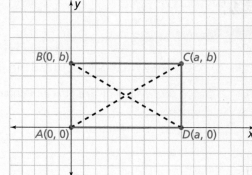

$AC = \sqrt{(a - 0)^2 + (b - 0)^2} = \sqrt{a^2 + b^2}$

$BD = \sqrt{(0 - a)^2 + (b - 0)^2} = \sqrt{(-a)^2 + (b)^2} = \sqrt{a^2 + b^2}$

$\therefore AC = BD \Rightarrow \overline{AC} \cong \overline{BD}$

To show that segments are perpendicular, you need to show that the slope of one segment is the negative reciprocal of the slope of the other segment.

EXAMPLE 4   **Verifying a quadrilateral is a rhombus**

4 Use coordinate geometry to show that *EFGH* is a rhombus.

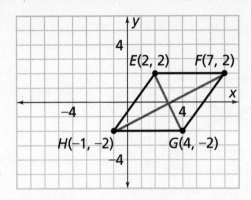

■ **SOLUTION**

To verify that the quadrilateral *EFGH* is a rhombus, you need to show that the diagonals bisect each other and that they are perpendicular to each other.

Step 1 Show that $\overline{EG}$ and $\overline{FH}$ bisect each other by showing they have the same midpoint.

Midpoint of $\overline{EG} = \left(\dfrac{2+4}{2}, \dfrac{2-2}{2}\right) = (3, 0)$

Midpoint of $\overline{FH} = \left(\dfrac{-1+7}{2}, \dfrac{-2+2}{2}\right) = (3, 0)$

Therefore $\overline{EG}$ and $\overline{FH}$ bisect each other.

Step 2 Show that the slopes of $\overline{EG}$ and $\overline{FH}$ are negative reciprocals of each other.

Slope of $\overline{EG} = \dfrac{2-(-2)}{2-4} = \dfrac{4}{-2} = -2$

Slope of $\overline{FH} = \dfrac{2-(-2)}{7-(-1)} = \dfrac{4}{8} = \dfrac{1}{2}$

The slopes are negative reciprocals of each other. Therefore, the diagonals are perpendicular.

Since **the diagonals are perpendicular and bisect each other, EFGH is a rhombus.**

You can also verify or prove other properties of triangles by using the midpoint and distance formulas.

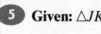

EXAMPLES 5 and 6 — **Verifying and proving the median to the hypotenuse of a right triangle is half the hypotenuse**

5 **Given:** $\triangle JKL$ with $\angle K = 90°$ and median $\overline{KM}$.

Verify: $KM = \dfrac{LJ}{2}$

■ SOLUTION

Step 1 Find the coordinates of the midpoint M.

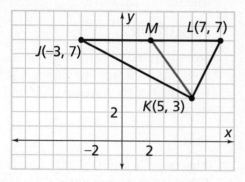

$$M = \left(\frac{7 + (-3)}{2}, \frac{7 + 7}{2}\right)$$
$$M = (2, 7)$$

Step 2 Find the length of $\overline{LJ}$ and $\overline{KM}$.

$$LJ = \sqrt{(7 - (-3)^2 + (7 - 7)^2}$$
$$= \sqrt{10^2} = 10$$

$$KM = \sqrt{(5 - 2)^2 + (3 - 7)^2}$$
$$= \sqrt{3^2 + (-4)^2} = \sqrt{5^2} = 5$$

Therefore, **the length of the median to the hypotenuse of this right triangle is half the length of the hypotenuse.**

6 Prove the median to the hypotenuse of a right triangle is half the hypotenuse.

■ SOLUTION

Knowing that the coordinate axes are perpendicular to each other and placing points D, E, and F as shown right $\triangle DEF$ is formed. For convenience the coordinates of E and F were chosen as shown. By applying the midpoint formula the coordinates of M are determined. Now using the distance formula leads to the following result.

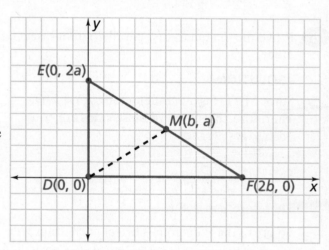

$$FE = \sqrt{(2b - 0)^2 + (0 - 2a)^2} = \sqrt{4b^2 + 4a^2} = \sqrt{4(b^2 + a^2)} = 2\sqrt{b^2 + a^2}$$

$$DM = \sqrt{(b - 0)^2 + (a - 0)^2} = \sqrt{b^2 + a^2}$$

$$\therefore FE = 2DM \Rightarrow DM = \frac{1}{2}FE$$

Proving theorems and postulates using general coordinates

7 Prove the line joining the midpoints of two sides of a triangle is parallel to the third side and equal to one half its measure.

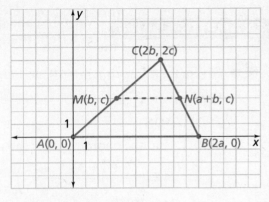

■ **SOLUTION**

Note that by choosing convenient coordinates the computations will be simpler. Using the midpoint formula the coordinates of M and N are determined.

Part 1

The slope of segment $\overline{MN}$ is zero because it is a horizontal segment. Likewise with segment $\overline{AB}$. $\therefore \overline{MN} \parallel \overline{AB}$.

Part 2

$$MN = \sqrt{(a + b - b)^2 + (c - c)^2} = \sqrt{a^2} = a$$
$$AB = \sqrt{(2a - 0)^2 + (0 - 0)^2} = \sqrt{(2a)^2} = \sqrt{4a^2} = 2a$$

$$\therefore MN = \frac{1}{2} AB$$

8 Prove the diagonals of a parallelogram bisect each other.

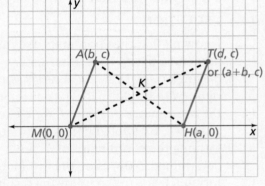

■ **SOLUTION**

Since MATH is a parallelogram, $\overline{AT} \parallel \overline{MH}$. Therefore, the slopes of these sides are equal. Also, $\overline{AM} \parallel \overline{TH}$ so

$$\frac{c - 0}{b - 0} = \frac{c - 0}{d - a} \Rightarrow \frac{c}{b} = \frac{c}{d - a} \Rightarrow b = d - a$$

Therefore, $d = a + b$.

To prove these diagonals bisect each other will require showing that the midpoints of both diagonals coincide. The midpoint of $\overline{MT}$ is $\left(\frac{a + b}{2}, \frac{c}{2}\right)$. The midpoint of $\overline{AH}$ is also $\left(\frac{a + b}{2}, \frac{c}{2}\right)$. Therefore, the diagonals bisect each other.

Practice

Choose the numeral preceding the word or expression that best completes the statement or answers the question.

1 If the diagonals of a quadrilateral are perpendicular, then the quadrilateral could be a

(1) rectangle.   **(3)** square.

(2) parallelogram.   **(4)** trapezoid.

2 If a quadrilateral has four congruent sides and one of the properties listed, it must be a square. Which property?

(1) opposite angles congruent   **(3)** opposite sides parallel

(2) four right angles   **(4)** four acute angles

3 Classify the quadrilateral with vertices $W(-3, 4)$, $X(6, 4)$, $Y(4, -5)$, and $Z(-5, -4)$.

(1) rhombus   **(3)** parallelogram

(2) trapezoid   **(4)** none of the above

In Exercises 4–6, solve each problem and clearly show all necessary work.

4 Show that the coordinates graphed below form a scalene triangle. Assume a unit scale.

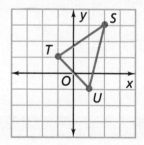

5 Show that the quadrilateral with vertices $A(1, 2)$, $B(3, 3)$, $C(5, 2)$, and $D(3, 1)$ is a rhombus.

6 Show that the quadrilateral below is a trapezoid.

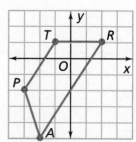

In Exercises 7–8, find the coordinates of the point described, given the points $K(-1, 0)$, $L(0, 3)$ and $M(3, 1)$.

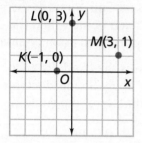

7 Determine point N so that $KLMN$ is a parallelogram.

8 Determine point P so that $KLPM$ is a parallelogram.

In Exercises 9–11, use coordinate geometry and the isosceles trapezoid below to verify each theorem.

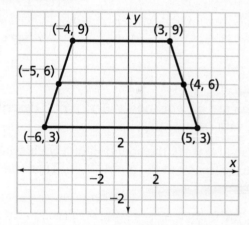

9 The line joining the midpoints is parallel to the base.

10 The line joining the midpoints is one-half the sum of the bases.

11 The diagonals of the isosceles trapezoid are congruent.

12 A quadrilateral has vertices $(a, 0)$, $(-a, 0)$, $(0, a)$ and $(0, -a)$. Show that it is a square.

13 A quadrilateral has vertices $(a, 0)$, $(0, a + 1)$, $(-a, 0)$, and $(0, -a - 1)$. Show that it is a rhombus.

7.5 Equations and Graphs of Circles & Parabolas

Recall that a locus is a set of points that satisfies specified conditions. For example, we can define a circle as a locus of points equidistant from one point. It is the set of all points in the plane at a fixed distance, called the **radius,** from a fixed point, called the **center.** In the coordinate plane this locus can be represented as an equation.

Since the radius is the fixed distance of a set of points in a plane from the center, you can apply the distance formula to find the length of the radius, given the coordinates of the circle center, Q, and a point on the circle, P.

$$PQ = \sqrt{(x_2 - x_1)^2 + (y_2 - y_1)^2}$$

EXAMPLE 1 — Finding the equation of a circle with center at (0, 0)

 Find the equation of a circle with center $O(0, 0)$ and radius r passing through the point (x, y).

- **SOLUTION**

$\sqrt{(x - 0)^2 + (y - 0)^2} = r$ ← **Apply the Distance Formula.**

$\sqrt{x^2 + y^2} = r$

$x^2 + y^2 = r^2$ ← **Square both sides.**

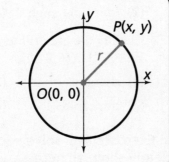

You can use the equation $x^2 + y^2 = r^2$ to describe a circle centered at the origin with radius r.

You can also write the equation of a circle whose center is not at the origin. Let the center be at the point (h, k). Then the formula will be $(x - h)^2 + (y - k)^2 = r^2$.

Equation of a Circle

The set of all points a fixed distance r from a fixed point $P(h, k)$ in the coordinate plane can be represented by the equation below, called the **standard form for an equation of a circle.**

$$(x - h)^2 + (y - k)^2 = r^2$$

If the point $P(h, k)$ is the origin, then the equation becomes what is shown here.

$$x^2 + y^2 = r^2$$

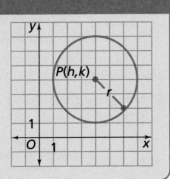

EXAMPLE 2 **Finding the equation of a circle with center (h, k)**

2 Write the equation of the circle passing through the point $P(x, y)$ and three units from the center $C(4, 5)$.

■ SOLUTION

Given: Center $C(4, 5)$, and $r = 3$

$(x - h)^2 + (y - k)^2 = 3^2$
$(x - 4)^2 + (y - 5)^2 = 3^2$ ← Substitute $h = 4$ and $k = 5$.

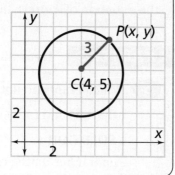

If you are given the equation of the circle, you can find its center and its radius.

EXAMPLE 3 **Finding the center and radius of a circle, given its equation**

3 What is the center and radius of a circle whose equation is $(x - 4)^2 + (y + 5)^2 = 64$?

■ SOLUTION

Write $(x - 4)^2 + (y + 5)^2 = 64$ in the form $(x - h)^2 + (y - k)^2 = r^2$.

$$(x - h)^2 + (y - k)^2 = r^2$$
$$(x - 4)^2 + (y + 5)^2 = 64$$
$$(x - 4)^2 + (y - (-5))^2 = 8^2$$

$h = 4, k = -5$, and $r = 8$

The radius is 8 and the center is $(4, -5)$.

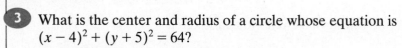

Note

If $-k = +5$, then $k = -5$.

EXAMPLE 4 **Determining the center and radius of a circle from its equation in standard form**

4 Determine the center and radius of the circle whose equation is $x^2 - 6x + y^2 + 4 = 0$.

■ SOLUTION

Rewrite the equation in center-radius form by using completing the square.

$$x^2 - 6x + y^2 + 4y + 4 = 0$$
$$x^2 - 6x + y^2 + 4y = -4$$
$$x^2 - 6x + 9 + y^2 + 4y + 4 = -4 + 9 + 4$$
$$(x - 3)^2 + (y + 2)^2 = 9$$
$$(x - 3)^2 + (y + 2)^2 = 3^2$$

$h = 3, k = -2$, and $r = 3$.

The circle has a center with coordinates $(3, -2)$ and a radius of 3.

You can determine whether a point lies on a circle by looking at the equation of the circle. If the x- and y-coordinates of a point are a solution to the equation of a circle, then that point is a solution to the equation.

EXAMPLE 5   **Determining whether points lie on a circle from its equation**

 Which points do not lie on the circle with equation $x^2 + y^2 = 5^2$?

(1) $(0, 5)$ and $(5, 0)$ **(2)** $(5, 5)$ and $(-5, 5)$ **(3)** $(0, -5)$ and $(-5, 0)$ **(4)** $(3, 4)$ and $(-4, 3)$

▪ **SOLUTION**

A point lies on the circle if the ordered pair is a solution to the equation.

choice **(1)**	$(0, 5)$ and $(5, 0)$ are 5 units from O.	$(0, 5)$ and $(5, 0)$ are on the circle.
choice **(2)**	$(5, 5)$ and $(-5, 5)$ are $5\sqrt{2}$ units from O.	$(5, 5)$ and $(-5, 5)$ are not on the circle.
choice **(3)**	$(0, -5)$ and $(-5, 0)$ are 5 units from O.	$(0, -5)$ and $(-5, 0)$ are on the circle.
choice **(4)**	$3^2 + 4^2 = 5^2$ and $(-4)^2 + 3^2 = 5^2$.	$(3, 4)$ and $(-4, 3)$ are on the circle.

The correct choice is (2).

Once you have determined the center and radius of a circle, you can sketch its graph.

EXAMPLE 6   **Sketching a circle from an equation**

 Graph $x^2 + y^2 = 4$.

▪ **SOLUTION**

The equation represents a circle with radius 2 and center at the origin. Graph the points where the circle intersects each axis.

$$x = 0 \qquad\qquad y = 0$$
$$0^2 + y^2 = 4 \qquad\qquad x^2 + 0^2 = 4$$
$$So, y = -2 \text{ or } 2. \qquad So, x = -2 \text{ or } 2.$$

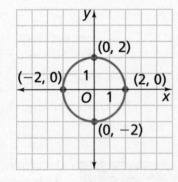

Graph $(0, -2)$, $(0, 2)$, $(2, 0)$, and $(-2, 0)$. Sketch the circle as shown here.

You can also write the equation of a circle, given its graph.

Writing the equation of a circle given its graph

 7 Find the equation of a circle with the endpoints of its diameter at $(-6, 0)$ and $(2, 0)$.

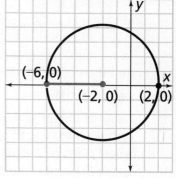

■ **SOLUTION**

Step 1 You can use the midpoint formula to locate the midpoint of the diameter, which is the center of the circle, (h, k).

$$h = \frac{-6 + 2}{2} = \frac{-4}{2} = -2, k = \frac{0 + 0}{2} = 0$$

$$(h, k) = (-2, 0)$$

Step 2 Find the length of the radius, r, which is half the length of the diameter. Looking at the graph, you can see that $r = 4$.

$$(x - h)^2 + (y - k)^2 = r^2$$
$$(x - (-2))^2 + (y - 0)^2 = 4^2$$
$$(x + 2)^2 + y^2 = 16$$

8 Find the equation of the circle to the right.

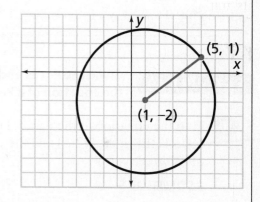

■ **SOLUTION**

Step 1 Use the distance formula to find r.

$$r = \sqrt{(5 - 1)^2 + (1 - (-2)^2}$$

$$r = \sqrt{4^2 + 3^2}$$

$$r = \sqrt{25} = 5$$

Step 2 Substitute the values for h, k, and r.

$$(x - h)^2 + (y - k)^2 = r^2$$
$$(x - 1)^2 + (y - (-2))^2 = 5^2$$
$$(x - 1)^2 + (y + 2)^2 = 25$$

The graph of the locus of points equidistant from a given point and a given line is called a **parabola**.

Equation of a Parabola

The set of points equidistant from a given point F, called the focus, and a given line called the directrix can be represented by the equation below, called the standard form for the equation of a parabola.

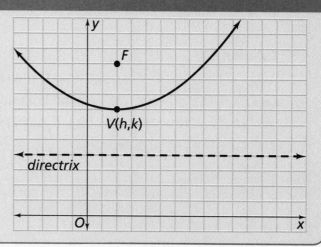

$f(x) = a(x - h)^2 + k$, where $V(h, k)$ is called the vertex. If a is positive the graph opens up, if a is negative the graph opens down. $a \neq 0$.

The expanded form of this equation $f(x) = ax^2 + bx + c$ is called the general form for the equation of a parabola.

EXAMPLE 9   **Determining the equation of a circle**

⑨ A new car design is drawn as shown. The distance between the centers of the two wheels is 11.6 units and the center and radius of the rear wheel are (6, −1) and 1.5 units, respectively. Write an equation for the front wheel in standard form. Assume all wheels on this vehicle are the same size.

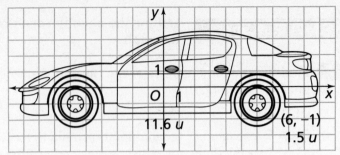

■ **SOLUTION**

First the center of the front wheel must be determined. Given the distance between the two wheels as 11.6 units the center of the front wheel must be (−5.6, −1). The radii of the two wheels are the same. Using the center-radius form for the equation of a circle results in the following.

$$(x - h)^2 + (y - k)^2 = r^2$$
$$(x - (-5.6))^2 + (y - (-1))^2 = (1.5)^2$$
$$x^2 + 11.2x + y^2 + 2y + 32.36 = 2.25$$
$$x^2 + 11.2x + y^2 + 2y + 30.11 = 0$$

EXAMPLE 10   **Given the Focus and Directrix Determine the Equation of a Parabola**

⑩ Find the equation of the parabola whose focus is the point $F(2, 5)$ and the equation of its directrix is $y = 3$.

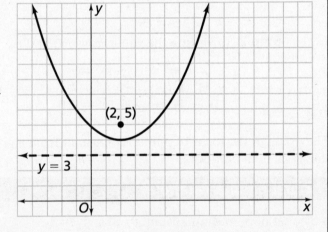

■ **SOLUTIONS**

If the point $P(x, y)$ is on the parabola then its distance from the focus is equal to its distance from the directrix.

Using the distance formula to determine the distance between P and F and the vertical distance from P to the directrix yields the equation:

Solution 1

$\sqrt{(x - 2)^2 + (y - 5)^2} = |y - 3|$, Square both side yields

$(x - 2)^2 + (y - 5)^2 = (y - 3)^2$, expand both sides

$x^2 - 4x + y^2 - 10y + 29 = y^2 - 6y + 9$, simplify

$x^2 - 4x - 4y + 20 = 0$, solve for y

$y = \dfrac{x^2}{4} - x + 5$

Solution 2

Use CAS to solve yields.

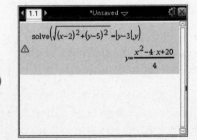

EXAMPLE 11   **Given the Focus and Directrix in General Terms Determine the Equation of a Parabola**

11 Determine the equation of the parabola whose focus is the point with coordinates (h, c) and whose directrix is the line $y = d$.

■ SOLUTIONS

Using the locus definition of a parabola: The locus of points in a plane equidistant from a given point and a given line in the same plane, results in the following solution.

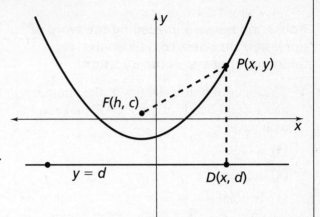

Solution 1

$FP = PD$

$\sqrt{(x - h)^2 + (y - c)^2} = |y - d|$, Square both side yields

$(x - h)^2 + (y - c)^2 = (y - d)^2$, expand both sides in y

$(x - h)^2 + y^2 - 2cy + c^2 = y^2 - 2dy + d^2$, simplify

$(x - h)^2 + c^2 - d^2 = 2(c - d)y$, solve for y

$y = \dfrac{1}{2(c - d)}(x - h)^2 + \dfrac{(c + d)}{2}$

Solution 2

Using CAS to solve yields.

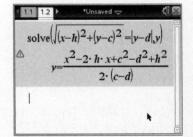

A further use of CAS software allows for the verification of the equality of the expression found in solution 1 and that found in solution 2. Setting the two expressions equal to each other results in a response of *true*. This use of CAS prevents avoidable errors in the symbol manipulation to determine this equality.

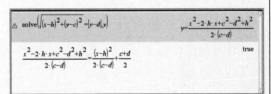

Choose the numeral preceding the word or expression that best completes the statement or answers the question.

1 The locus of points the tips of the minute and second hands of a clock will make in an hour is

   (1) a line.

   (2) a circle.

   (3) two lines.

   (4) two concentric circles.

2 Which equation represents a circle whose center is the origin and whose radius is 9?

   (1) $x^2 - y^2 = 9$

   (2) $x^2 + y^2 = 81$

   (3) $x^2 + y^2 = 9$

   (4) $3x^2 + 3y^2 = 3^2$

3 Which equation represents a circle with radius 3 and center $(2, 3)$?

   (1) $9 = 2x^2 + 3y^2$

   (2) $3^2 = (x - 2) + (y - 3)$

   (3) $3^2 = (x - 2)^2 + (y - 3)^2$

   (4) $9 = (x - 3)^2 + (y - 2)^2$

4 Which equation represents a circle with center $(-2, -2)$ passing through the point $(2, 1)$?

   (1) $(x - 2)^2 + (y - 2)^2 = 25$

   (2) $2x^2 + y^2 = 4$

   (3) $x^2 + y^2 = 25$

   (4) $(x + 2)^2 + (y + 2)^2 = 5^2$

5 Which of the following equations represents a circle with its center at the origin and with a radius of $\sqrt{5}$?

   (1) $x^2 + y^2 = \sqrt{5}$

   (2) $x^2 + y^2 = 5$

   (3) $x^2 + y^2 = 25$

   (4) $x^2 - y^2 = 5$

6 Which points are *not* on the circle given by the equation $x^2 + y^2 = 64$?

   (1) $(8, 0)$ and $(0, 8)$

   (2) $(0, -8)$ and $(8, 0)$

   (3) $(8, -8)$ and $(8, 8)$

   (4) $(0, -8)$ and $(-8, 0)$

In Exercises 7–12, sketch each circle, then name its center, find the radius, and identify any point on the circle.

7 $x^2 + y^2 = 9$

8 $(x - 2)^2 + y^2 = 16$

9 $(x + 2)^2 + (y - 2)^2 = 4$

10 $x^2 + (y + 3)^2 = 16$

11 $(x - 2)^2 + (y - 1)^2 = 25$

12 $(x + 3)^2 + (y - 1)^2 = 1$

In Exercises 13–15, write the equation for each locus.

13 The set of all points that are in the coordinate plane and are 5 units from $P(-5, 2)$

14 The set of all points that are 5 units from the origin

15 The set of points 3 units from the point $(1, -3)$

16 Write the equation of a circle passing through the point $(4, 3)$ and centered at the origin.

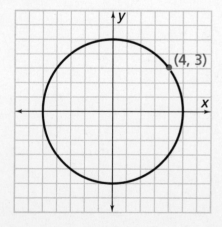

Solutions of Quadratic
7.6 and Linear Systems

 A.REI.7

You can solve a system of a linear and quadratic equations algebraically. You can use the substitution method to find the solution to a system of linear and quadratic equations.

EXAMPLES 1 and 2   **Solving systems of linear-quadratic equations algebraically**

Solve each system of equations algebraically.

 $y = x^2$ and $y = 2x$

■ SOLUTION

$$x^2 = 2x \quad \leftarrow \text{(substitute } 2x \text{ for } y\text{)}$$
$$x^2 - 2x = 0$$
$$x(x - 2) = 0$$
$$x = 0 \text{ or } x = 2$$

If $x = 0$, then $y = 0$. If $x = 2$, then $y = 4$.

Check the solutions in each equation. The solutions are $(0, 0)$ and $(2, 4)$.

2 $y = x$ and $x^2 + y^2 = 50$

■ SOLUTION

$$x^2 + x^2 = 50 \quad \leftarrow \text{(substitute } x \text{ for } y\text{)}$$
$$2x^2 = 50$$
$$x^2 = 25$$
$$x = 5 \text{ or } x = -5$$

If $x = 5$, then $y = 5$. If $x = -5$, then $y = -5$.

Check the solutions in each equation. The solutions are $(5, 5)$ and $(-5, -5)$.

A linear-quadratic system can also be solved graphically. You will find that either there are two solutions, one solution, or no solutions. This is illustrated in the graphs below.

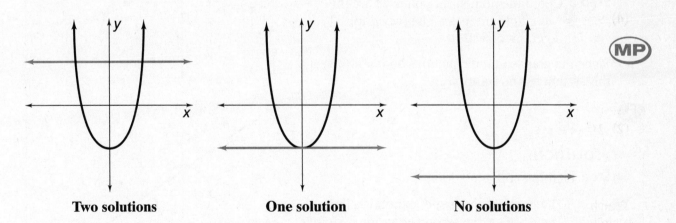

Two solutions   **One solution**   **No solutions**

You can find the number of solutions a system of equations has by looking at the number of points where the graphs of each equation intersect. If the graphs do not intersect, then the system has no solutions.

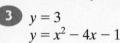 **Finding the number of solutions to a system of equations graphically**

> **Note**
>
> The graph of $y = ax^2 + bx + c$, where $a \neq 0$, has the line $x = -\frac{b}{2a}$ as its **axis of symmetry**.
>
> The vertex has coordinates $\left(-\frac{b}{2a}, f\left(-\frac{b}{2a}\right)\right)$
>
> The equation $x^2 + y^2 = r^2$ describes a circle with its center at $(0, 0)$ and a radius of r.

How many solutions are there to the following systems of equations?

3 $y = 3$
$y = x^2 - 4x - 1$

■ SOLUTION

Step 1 Graph the parabola. The equation for the axis of symmetry is $x = 2$.

x	0	1	2	3	4
y	−1	−4	−5	−4	−1

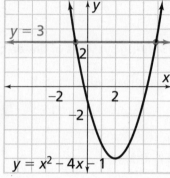

Step 2 Graph the line. The line is a horizontal line passing through the y-axis at the point $(0, 3)$.

Step 3 Count the number of points where the two graphs intersect. The line crosses the parabola at two points.

The graphs intersect at two points, so this system has two solutions.

4 $y = (x - 3)^2$
$2y + x = 2$

■ SOLUTION

Step 1 Graph both equations.

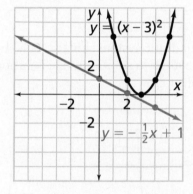

Step 2 Count the number of points where the two graphs intersect. The two graphs do not intersect.

Since the graphs of the equations do not intersect, this system has no solutions.

5 $2x + 3y = 5$
$x^2 + y^2 = 4$

■ SOLUTION

Step 1 Graph both equations.

The graph of the first equation is a line. The graph of the second equation is a circle centered at the origin and with a radius of 2.

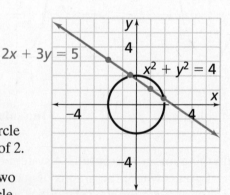

Step 2 Count the number of points where the two graphs intersect. The line crosses the circle at two points.

Because the graphs intersect at two points, this system has two solutions.

The coordinates of the points where the graphs intersect give the solutions to the system of equations.

 EXAMPLES 6 and 7   **Finding solutions to a system of equations**

6 Solve the following system of equations by graphing.

$$y = -x + 1$$
$$y = x^2 + x - 2$$

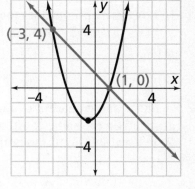

■ **SOLUTION**

Step 1 Graph the equations.

Step 3 Locate the points where the parabola and the line intersect.

The line intersects the parabola at the points $(-3, 4)$ and $(1, 0)$.

There are two solutions: $(-3, 4)$ and $(1, 0)$.

7 Solve the following system of equations by graphing.

$$x^2 + y^2 = 16$$
$$y = 2x - 4$$

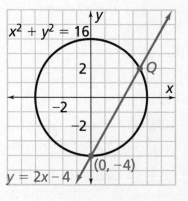

SOLUTION

Step 1 Graph both equations.

Step 2 Identify the points where the graphs intersect.

The graphs intersect at the point $(0, -4)$ and the point labeled Q, which is approximately at $(3, 2)$.

There are two solutions. One solution is $(0, -4)$. The other solution is approximately $(3, 2)$.

When you plot the above example on a coordinate grid, it's easy to find the coordinates of one of the points where the graphs intersect. However, the coordinates of the second point, Q, are not as easy to find just by looking at the graph.

You can use a graphing calculator to find more accurate coordinates of Q. The display below shows the graphs of $x^2 + y^2 = 16$ and $y = 2x - 4$. The calculator shows the coordinates of Q, which are $(3.2, 2.4)$.

To find the points of intersection algebraically, substitute $y = 2x - 4$ into the equation of the circle and solve for x.

$$x^2 + (2x - 4)^2 = 16$$
$$x^2 + 4x^2 - 16x + 16 = 16$$
$$x(5x - 16) = 0$$

Solving for x, you get $x = 0$ or $x = 3.2$. Substituting these values into the equation $y = 2x - 4$, you see that the points of intersection are $(0, -4)$ and $(3.2, 2.4)$.

Note

You can check your answers by substituting the values for x and y into the equations.

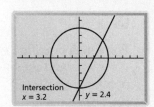

Choose the numeral preceding the word or expression that best completes the statement or answers the question.

1 In how many points does the graph of $y = (x - 3)(x + 5)$ intersect the x-axis?

(1) none **(3)** two

(2) one **(4)** three

2 A linear and a quadratic function are graphed on the same coordinate plane. Which are solution(s) to both equations?

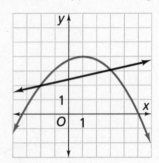

(1) $(-2, 2)$

(2) $(3, 3)$

(3) $(3, 3)$ and $(-2, 2)$

(4) $(-3, 3)$ and $(2, 2)$

3 A circle and a line lie in the same coordinate plane. Which situation is not possible?

(1) The graphs do not intersect.

(2) The graphs can intersect in one point.

(3) The graphs can intersect in two points.

(4) The graphs can intersect in three points.

4 A circle has radius 4 and center at the origin. For which equation will the circle and the line not intersect?

(1) $x = 2$ **(3)** $x = 4$

(2) $y = 2$ **(4)** $x = 5$

5 For which equation will the graph of $y = x^2 + 1$ and the line intersect in two points?

(1) $y = -2x$ **(3)** $y = 2$

(2) $x = 1$ **(4)** $y = 2x$

6 Which system of equations has two solutions?

(1) $x = 0; y = x^2$ **(3)** $y = -1; y = x^2$

(2) $y = 2; y = x^2$ **(4)** $y = 0; y = x^2$

In Exercises 7–13, graph the system of equations and name the intersecting points.

7 $y = 2x + 3$ and $y = x^2$

8 $y = x$ and $2y = x^2$

9 $y = x^2 - 4x + 8$ and $y + x = 1$

10 $x^2 + y^2 = 25$ and $x = y + 7$

11 $y = x^2 - 3x - 10$ and $y = 2x - 4$

12 $y = 5 - 4x - x^2$ and $y = 4x + 21$

13 $x^2 + y^2 = 25$ and $y - 3 = -(x + 4)$

In Exercises 14–15, use graphs to show that the pair of equations has no solution.

14 $x^2 + y^2 = 9$
$x^2 + y^2 = 4$

15 $y = x^2 + 1$
$y = -x^2 - 2$

In Exercises 16–20, determine the number of points of intersection of the specified graphs. Justify your response.

16 A parabola opens up and has vertex $P(-2, 3)$. A line has equation $y = 3$.

17 A parabola opens down and has vertex $P(-2, 3)$. A line has equation $y = 3$.

18 A circle has center at the origin and radius 3. A line has equation $y = 2x$.

19 A circle has equation $x^2 + y^2 = 9$. A line contains the points $(0, 6)$ and $(6, 0)$.

20 A parabola opens up and has vertex $(-\frac{1}{2}, \frac{3}{4})$. A line containing the points $(0, -2)$ and $(2, 0)$.

21 For what value(s) of k does the system of equations have no solution? 1 solution? 2 solutions?
$$x^2 + y^2 = k^2$$
$$x = 4$$

Answer all questions in this part. For each question, select the numeral preceding the word or expression that best completes the statement or answers the question.

1 Which is the slope of a line perpendicular to the graph $y = \frac{5}{4}x + 8$?

(1) 1.25   **(3)** -0.8

(2) 0.8   **(4)** -1.25

2 Which of the following points is on the circle whose equation is $x^2 + y^2 = 25$?

(1) $(0, 0)$ **(3)** $(5, 5)$

(2) $(3, 4)$ **(4)** $(25, 0)$

3 The equation of a circle with center $(-2, 2)$ and radius 4 is

(1) $x^2 + y^2 = 4$.

(2) $(x - 2)^2 + (y + 2)^2 = 4$.

(3) $(x - 2)^2 + (y + 2)^2 = 16$.

(4) $(x + 2)^2 + (y - 2)^2 = 16$.

4 The system pictured in the graph has how many solutions?

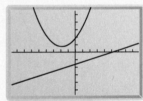

(1) 0   **(3)** 2

(2) 1   **(4)** Cannot determine

5 At how many points does the line $y = 3$ intersect the graph of $x^2 + y^2 = 9$?

(1) 0

(2) 1

(3) 2

(4) Cannot determine

6 The equation of a circle whose center is the origin and whose radius is $\sqrt{5}$ is

(1) $x^2 + y^2 = \sqrt{5}$.   **(3)** $x^2 + y^2 = 5$.

(2) $x^2 - y^2 = 5$.   **(4)** $x^2 + y^2 = 25$.

7 Which equation represents a line perpendicular to the line drawn below?

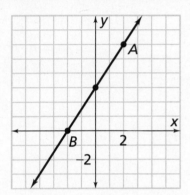

(1) $y = -\frac{3}{2}x + 3$ **(3)** $y = \frac{2}{3}x + 3$

(2) $y = -\frac{2}{3}x + 3$ **(4)** $y = \frac{3}{2}x + 3$

8 What is the slope of the line parallel to the line graphed by the equation $x + 4y = 7$?

(1) 4   **(3)** $-\frac{1}{4}$

(2) $\frac{7}{4}$ **(4)** -4

9 Which of the following points is the midpoint of a segment with the endpoints $(-1, 1)$ and $(4, 5)$?

(1) $\left(\frac{3}{2}, 3\right)$

(2) $\left(\frac{5}{2}, 2\right)$

(3) $\left(3, \frac{3}{2}\right)$

(4) $(5, 4)$

10 What is the length of a segment with endpoints $(-5, 1)$ and $(2, 4)$?

(1) $2\sqrt{6}$

(2) $\sqrt{34}$

(3) $\sqrt{58}$

(4) 58

11 Which of the following graphs represents a system of equations with one real solution?

(1)

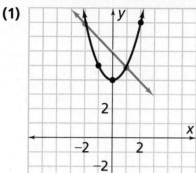

(2)

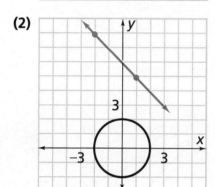

(3)

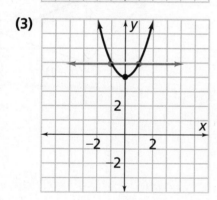

(4)

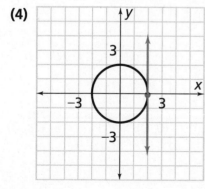

12 Which of the following is the equation to the perpendicular bisector of $\overline{AB}$?

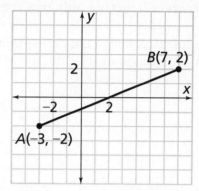

(1) $5x + 2y = 10$ **(3)** $2x + 5y = 24$

(2) $5x + 2y = -2$ **(4)** $2x + 5y = -4$

13 Which equation represents a line perpendicular to the graph below?

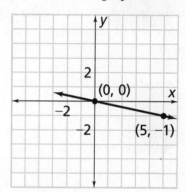

(1) $y = -5x + 3$

(2) $y = -\frac{1}{5}x - 3$

(3) $y = \frac{1}{5}x - 3$

(4) $y = 5x + 3$

14 A diameter of a circle has endpoints on the circle at $(-6, -6)$ and $(12, 8)$. What are the coordinates of the center of the circle?

(1) $(1, 3)$ **(3)** $(9, 1)$

(2) $(3, 1)$ **(4)** $(18, 14)$

209

Answer all questions in this part. Clearly indicate the necessary steps, including appropriate formula substitutions, diagrams, graphs, charts, etc. For all questions in this part, a correct numerical answer with no work shown will receive only one credit.

15 Write the equation of the circle passing through (5, 4) with center (1, 1).

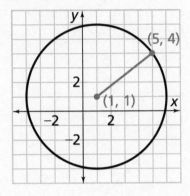

16 Given the triangle to the right, prove that the line joining the midpoints of $\overline{AB}$ and $\overline{AC}$ is parallel to $\overline{BC}$ and one-half its length.

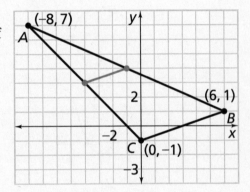

17 Prove that the figure is an isosceles trapezoid.

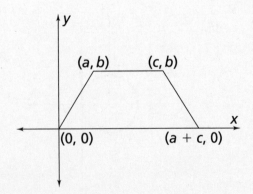

8 Circles

8.1 Circle Similarity

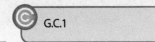

Intuitively, similarity has been defined for polygons as two figures that have the same shape but different sizes. Functionally, similarity is defined as a set of transformations that move a figure exactly to cover the other figure.

All circles are intuitively similar:

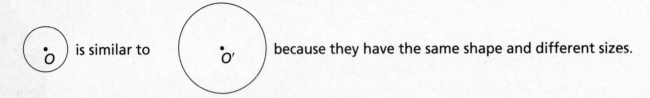

is similar to ... because they have the same shape and different sizes.

What set of transformations would prove $\odot O \sim \odot O'$?

EXAMPLE 1   **Proving circles similar using transformations**

 Given: Circle O with radius $= a$ units.
Circle O' with radius $= b$ units.

Prove: Circle $O \sim$ Circle O'

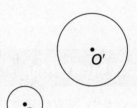

■ **SOLUTION**
Translate $\odot O$ along vector $\overrightarrow{OO'}$ until O and O' coincide.

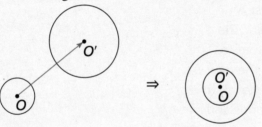

Dilate $\odot O$ by a factor of $\dfrac{b}{a}$ to get ... so $\odot O \sim \odot O'$.

If the circles are given on a coordinate plane, the transformation can be defined using the x and y directed distances of the vector connecting the circles' centers.

EXAMPLE 2   **Demonstrating circle similarity on the coordinate plane**

2 If circle P is centered at the point $(-3, -1)$ with a radius of 4 units and circle P' is centered at the point $(3, 3)$ with radius of 2 units, define a set of transformations that shows $\odot P$ similar to $\odot P'$.

■ **SOLUTION**

Vector $\overrightarrow{PP'}$ has a directed horizontal component of $+6$ units and a directed vertical component of $+4$ units. So, the translation of P to P' is defined by $T_{(x+6,\,y+4)}$.

After the translation, a dilation of factor $\frac{1}{2}$ results in $\odot P \sim \odot P'$.

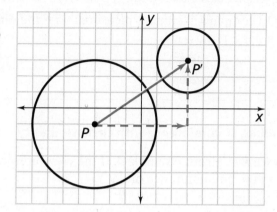

EXAMPLE 3   **Using circle similarity**

3 Circle M is centered at the point $(5, 4)$ with a radius of 2 units. Circle M is similar to circle N under a set of transformations defined by $T_{(x-7,\,y+3)}$ and $D_{\frac{5}{2}}$. What is the center and radius of circle N?

■ **SOLUTION**

The translation defines the center of circle N as the center of M moved 7 units left and then 3 units up. The coordinates of N are $(5 - 7, 4 + 3) = (-2, 7)$. The dilation factor of $\frac{5}{2}$ makes the radius of circle $N = \frac{5}{2} \cdot 2 = 5$.

Circle N is centered at the point $(-2, 7)$ with a radius of 5 units.

When circles are similar, then corresponding linear measures are proportional.

Relations in Similar Circles

If circle O is similar to circle O' with a constant of proportionality of k, then

$$\frac{\text{radius}_O}{\text{radius}_{O'}} = \frac{\text{diameter}_O}{\text{diameter}_{O'}} = \frac{\text{circumference}_O}{\text{circumference}_{O'}} = k$$

EXAMPLE 4   Finding a constant of proportionality with circles

 Circle X has a diameter of 8 and circle Y has a radius of 3. If $\odot X \sim \odot Y$, what is the constant of proportionality for this similarity?

■ **SOLUTION**

It is important to compare like linear measures, so if the diameter of $\odot X$ is 8 then it has a radius of 4.

$$\frac{radius_X}{radius_Y} = \frac{4}{3} = k$$

EXAMPLE 5   Finding circumference with circle similarity

5 $\odot X \sim \odot Y$ with $k = \frac{4}{3}$ from Example 4. If the circumference of $\odot X = 48\pi$, find the circumference of $\odot Y$.

■ **SOLUTION**

Let y represent the circumference of $\odot Y$.

$$k = \frac{4}{3} = \frac{48\pi}{y} \text{ so}$$

$$4y = 3 \cdot 48\pi \text{ and}$$

$$y = 36\pi = \text{circumference of } \odot Y.$$

Practice

For Exercises 1–2: Define the transformations needed to prove $\odot P$ similar to $\odot P'$.

1 $\odot P$ has radius of 1 unit; $\odot P'$ has radius of 3 units.

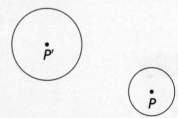

2 $\odot P$ has radius of 3 unit; $\odot P'$ has radius of 8 units.

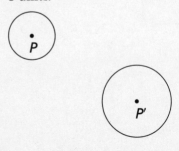

For Exercises 3–8: Define the transformations needed to prove $\odot T$ similar to $\odot T'$.

3 $\odot T$ centered at $(-4, 5)$ with radius of 2 units;
$\odot T'$ centered at $(2, -1)$ with radius of 5 units.

4 $\odot T$ centered at $(1, -3)$ with radius of $\frac{2}{3}$ unit;
$\odot T'$ centered at $(-5, 1)$ with radius of 6 units.

5 $\odot T$ centered at $(-2, -5)$ with radius of $\frac{1}{4}$ unit;
$\odot T'$ centered at $(5, 3)$ with radius of $\frac{3}{8}$ unit.

6 $\odot T$ centered at $(3, -4)$ with radius of 5 units;
$\odot T'$ centered at $(3, 4)$ with radius of 5 units.

7 $\odot\, T$ defined by $(x - 3)^2 + (y + 3)^2 = 9$;
$\odot\, T'$ defined by $(x + 1)^2 + (y + 5)^2 = 25$.

8 $\odot\, T$ defined by $(x + 5)^2 + (y - 7)^2 = 16$;
$\odot\, T'$ defined by $(x - 1)^2 + (y - 1)^2 = 5$.

For Exercises 9–12: $\odot\, X$ similar to $\odot\, Y$.
Find the constant of proportionality for
$\odot\, X$ to $\odot\, Y$.

9 $\odot\, X$ has radius of 5 units;
$\odot\, Y$ has diameter of 20 units.

10 $\odot\, X$ has a circumference of 25π units;
$\odot\, Y$ has diameter of 5 units.

11 $\odot\, X$ has radius of 9 units;
$\odot\, Y$ has circumference of 81π units.

12 $\odot\, X$ has a circumference of 36π units;
$\odot\, Y$ has a circumference of 24π units.

8.2 Area of Circles and Sectors

G-C.5
G-GMD.1

The formula for the area of a circle, $A = \pi r^2$, is probably not new to you, but its derivation or proof may be. While there are many different ways to prove that $A = \pi r^2$, the derivation presented below uses an important idea learned earlier.

Recall that a regular polygon is a polygon that is both equilateral and equiangular. Visualize a regular hexagon inscribed in a circle.

The center O of the inscribed regular polygon is also the center of the circumscribed circle.

$\overline{OP}$ is the apothem and is perpendicular to the side of the regular polygon.

A formula for the area of a regular polygon is

$A = \dfrac{1}{2} \cdot$ apothem $\cdot$ perimeter.

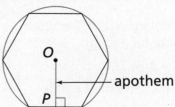

apothem

EXAMPLE I Changing area of regular polygon ⇒ area of a circle

MP

1 Using the formula for the Area of a regular polygon, derive the formula for the area of a circle.

■ SOLUTION

What happens to an inscribed polygon as the number of sides of the polygon increases to infinity?

Regular Polygon as the number of sides increases to infinity becomes a Circle

What happens to the apothem and perimeter as the number of sides of the polygon increases to infinity?

Apothem as the number of sides increases to infinity becomes the Radius
Perimeter as the number of sides increases to infinity becomes the Circumference

What happens to the formula for the area of a regular polygon as the number of sides of the polygon increases to infinity?

$$\textit{Area of a regular polygon} = \frac{1}{2} \cdot \textit{apothem} \cdot \textit{perimeter}$$

$$= \frac{1}{2} \cdot \textit{radius} \cdot \textit{circumference} \quad \textit{as the number of sides increases to infinity}$$

$$\textit{Area of a circle} = \frac{1}{2} \cdot r \cdot 2\pi r = \pi r^2$$

$$\textit{Area of a circle} = \pi r^2$$

Notice that the area formula has a constant, π, and two linear factors, r and r. So in comparing similar circles the product $r \cdot r$ affects the constant of proportionality.

Area in Similar Circles

If circle O is similar to circle O' with a constant of proportionality of **k**, then

$$\frac{\text{Area}_O}{\text{Area}_{O'}} = \left(\frac{\text{radius}_O}{\text{radius}_{O'}}\right)^2 = \left(\frac{\text{diameter}_O}{\text{diameter}_{O'}}\right)^2 = \left(\frac{\text{circumference}_O}{\text{circumference}_{O'}}\right)^2 = k^2$$

EXAMPLES 2 and 3   **Using area and circle similarity**

2   Circle P has a diameter of 8 and circle Q has a diameter of 10. If the area of circle P is 64π, find the area of circle P.

■ **SOLUTION**

Remember that area is not a linear measure: $\dfrac{\text{Area}_P}{\text{Area}_Q} = k^2$.

Using diameter as our linear measure: $\left(\dfrac{\text{diameter}_P}{\text{diameter}_Q}\right)^2 = k^2$

$$\left(\frac{8}{10}\right)^2 = \left(\frac{4}{5}\right)^2 = \frac{16}{25}$$

$$\frac{16}{25} = \frac{64\pi}{A_Q}$$

$$16A_Q = 25 \cdot 64\pi$$

$$A_Q = 100\pi$$

3   Circle L has an area of 63π and circle J has an area of 28π. What is the value of $\dfrac{\text{circumference}_L}{\text{circumference}_J}$?

■ **SOLUTION**

We know that any two circles are similar, so

$$\frac{63\pi}{28\pi} = \frac{9}{4} = k^2, \text{ so } k = \frac{\text{circumference}_L}{\text{circumference}_J} = \frac{3}{2}.$$

The part of a circle that looks like a piece of pizza from a round pizza pie is called a **sector of a circle**. The sector is formed by two radii, a **central angle,** and the **arc** determined by the endpoints of the angle.

$\angle AOB$ is a central angle and its measure is a degree measure between 0° and 360°.

$\overset{\frown}{AB}$ is called the intercepted arc of $\angle AOB$ and can be measured in degrees, also a measure between 0° and 360°. Intuitively, the area of the sector of a circle is a proportional part of the area of the circle. The part can be defined either in terms of the measure of the central angle or the measure of the intercepted arc.

Area of a Sector of a Circle

OR

$$\text{Area}_{\text{sector}} = \frac{\text{measure central angle}}{360} \cdot \text{Area}_{\text{circle}}$$

$$\text{Area}_{\text{sector}} = \frac{\text{measure intercepted arc}}{360} \cdot \text{Area}_{\text{circle}}$$

EXAMPLES 4 and 5   **Using areas of sectors**

4 The radius of a circle is 8. What is the area of a sector having a central angle of 90°?

■ **SOLUTION**

$$Area_{sector} = \frac{measure\ central\ angle}{360°} \cdot Area_{circle}$$

$$Area_{sector} = \frac{90°}{360°} \cdot \pi r^2$$

$$Area_{sector} = \frac{1}{4} \cdot 64\pi = 16\pi$$

5 A circle with radius 3 has a sector with area of 3π. What is the measure of the arc of the sector.

■ **SOLUTION**

$$Area_{sector} = \frac{measure\ intercepted\ arc}{360} \cdot Area_{circle}$$

$$3\pi = \frac{measure\ intercepted\ arc}{360} \cdot 9\pi$$

$$\frac{3\pi}{9\pi} = \frac{measure\ intercepted\ arc}{360} = \frac{1}{3}$$

$$3 \cdot measure\ intercepted\ arc = 360°$$

$$measure\ intercepted\ arc = 120°$$

Choose the numeral preceding the word or expression that best completes the statement or answers the question.

1 Find the area of a circle whose radius is 4.

(1) 4π **(2)** 8π **(3)** 16π **(4)** 64π

2 Find the area of a circle whose circumference is 14π.

(1) 7π **(2)** 14π **(3)** 28π **(4)** 49π

3 Find the diameter of a circle whose area is 100π.

(1) 5   **(2)** 10   **(3)** 20   **(4)** 25

4 Find the area of a regular hexagon whose apothem is $5\sqrt{3}$.

(1) $300\sqrt{3}$ **(3)** 10

(2) $150\sqrt{3}$ **(4)** 60

5 If two circles are similar with $k = \dfrac{2}{5}$, find the ratio of the circles' areas.

(1) $\dfrac{\text{Area}_1}{\text{Area}_2} = \dfrac{2}{5}$ **(3)** $\dfrac{\text{Area}_1}{\text{Area}_2} = \dfrac{4}{10}$

(2) $\dfrac{\text{Area}_1}{\text{Area}_2} = \dfrac{\sqrt{2}}{\sqrt{5}}$ **(4)** $\dfrac{\text{Area}_1}{\text{Area}_2} = \dfrac{4}{25}$

6 If two circles are similar with $\dfrac{\text{Area}_1}{\text{Area}_2} = \dfrac{64}{81}$, find the constant of the circles' similarity.

(1) $\dfrac{2}{3}$ **(2)** $\dfrac{4}{9}$ **(3)** $\dfrac{8}{9}$ **(4)** $\dfrac{16}{27}$

7 $\odot X$ similar to $\odot Y$. Area $\odot X = 25$ m^2 and Area $\odot Y = 100$ m^2. Find the constant of similarity for $\odot X$ to $\odot Y$.

(1) $\dfrac{1}{4}$ **(2)** $\dfrac{1}{2}$ **(3)** $\dfrac{1}{8}$ **(4)** $\dfrac{1}{16}$

8 $\odot X$ similar to $\odot Y$. Circumference $\odot X = 25$ m and Circumference $\odot Y = 100$ m. Find the constant of similarity for $\odot X$ to $\odot Y$.

(1) $\dfrac{1}{4}$ **(2)** $\dfrac{1}{2}$ **(3)** $\dfrac{1}{8}$ **(4)** $\dfrac{1}{16}$

For Exercises 9–12: Find the area of the sector with the given central angle and radius of the circle.

9 measure of central angle = $90°$; $r = 6$

10 measure of central angle = $36°$; $r = 10$

11 measure of central angle = $240°$; $r = 12$

12 measure of central angle = $135°$; $r = 4$

For Exercises 13–14: Find the measure of the sector's central angle.

13 Area of the sector = 8π; $r = 8$

14 Area of the sector = 45π; $r = 15$

For Exercises 15–16: Find the measure of the sector's central angle.

15 Area of the circle = 36π; Area of a sector = 12π

16 Area of the circle = 36π; Area of a sector = 16π

17 An **annulus**, shown below, is a region **MP** bounded by 2 concentric circles. Find the area, in terms of π, of the annulus bounded by the inscribed and circumscribed circles of an equilateral triangle of side 12.

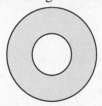

18 A **segment** of a circle, shown below, is a region bounded by an arc of the circle and the chord of that arc. Find, in terms of π, the area of a segment in a circle of radius 10 cm with a central angle of $90°$.

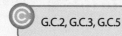
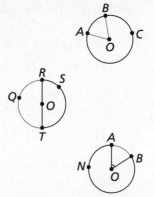

Recall that a **central angle** of a circle is an angle whose vertex is at the center of the circle. $\angle AOB$ is a central angle and $\overarc{AB}$ is part of the circle.

Each arc formed by the endpoints of a diameter is a **semicircle.** In the accompanying figure $\overarc{RST}$ is one semicircle of circle O and $\overarc{RQT}$ is another.

A **minor arc** is smaller than a semicircle. A **major arc** is larger than a semicircle. Two letters are used to designate a minor arc. $\overarc{AB}$ is a minor arc of circle O. Three letters are used to designate a major arc. $\overarc{ANB}$ is a major arc of circle O.

Arc Length and Measures

The **measure of a minor arc** is equal to the measure of its central angle.

$$m\overarc{AB} = m\angle AOB$$

The **measure of a major arc** is 360° minus the measure of its minor arc.

$$m\overarc{BNA} = 360° - m\overarc{AB}$$

The **measure of a semicircle** is 180°.

Note

1. All radii of a given circle are congruent.
2. Congruent circles have congruent radii.
3. Radii of congruent circles are congruent.

EXAMPLE 1   **Finding the measure of an arc**

   In the accompanying figure, $m\angle JKL = 50°$. Find the $m\overarc{JL}$ and $m\overarc{JCL}$

   ■ **SOLUTION**
$m\overarc{JL} = 50°$ and $m\overarc{JCL} = 360° - 50° = 310°$.

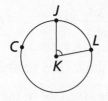

An angle whose vertex is a point on a circle and whose sides intersect the circle is an **inscribed angle** of the circle. In the figure at the right, $\angle ABC$ and $\angle JKL$ are inscribed angles. $\overarc{AC}$ is the intercepted arc of $\angle ABC$ and $\overarc{JL}$ is the intercepted arc of $\angle JKL$.

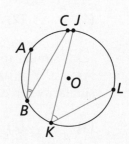

Inscribed Angle Theorem

The **measure of an inscribed angle** is half the measure of its intercepted arc.

$$m\angle BAC = \frac{m\overarc{BC}}{2} = \frac{1}{2}m\overarc{BC}$$

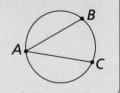

EXAMPLE 2   **Using the Inscribed Angle Theorem**

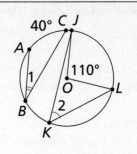

2   Find the measures of $\angle 1$ and $\angle 2$.

■ **SOLUTION**

$$m\angle 1 = \frac{m\,\widehat{AC}}{2}$$

$$\frac{40}{2} = 20° \quad \leftarrow m\widehat{AC} = 40°$$

$$m\angle 2 = \frac{m\,\widehat{JL}}{2}$$

$$\frac{110}{2} = 55° \quad \leftarrow m\widehat{JL} = 110°$$

The Inscribed Angle theorem is the basis for many related relationships in circles. One states that if a quadrilateral is inscribed in a circle, then opposite angles are supplementary. This is easily proved using inscribed angles.

EXAMPLE 3   **Proving a property of angles of an inscribed quadrilateral**

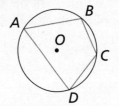

3   **Given:** Quadrilateral $ABCD$ inscribed in circle O

     Prove: $\angle A$ and $\angle C$ are supplementary.

■ **SOLUTION**

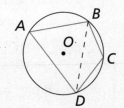

Statements	Reasons
1. Draw $\overline{BD}$.	**1.** Two points determine a line.
2. $m\angle A = \frac{1}{2}m\widehat{BCD}$ and $m\angle C = \frac{1}{2}m\widehat{BAD}$	**2.** Measure of inscribed angle is $\frac{1}{2}$ measure of its arc.
3. $m\angle A + m\angle C = \frac{1}{2}m\widehat{BCD} + \frac{1}{2}m\widehat{BAD}$	**3.** addition prop of =.
4. $m\angle A + m\angle C = \frac{1}{2}(m\widehat{BCD} + m\widehat{BAD})$	**4.** common factor
5. $m\widehat{BCD} + m\widehat{BAD} = 360°$	**5.** The arc of a circle is 360°.
6. $m\angle A + m\angle C = \frac{1}{2}(360°) = 180°$	**6.** substitution
7. $\angle A$ and $\angle C$ are supplementary.	**7.** If the measures of two angles add to 180°, then angles are supplementary.

A similar argument can be written to prove that $\angle B$ and $\angle D$ are supplementary.

More Inscribed Angle Corollaries

1. An angle inscribed in a semicircle is a right angle.
2. If two inscribed angles intercept congruent arcs, the angles are congruent.

A **chord** of a circle is a segment whose endpoints are on the circle.
A **tangent to a circle** is a line, segment, or ray in the same plane of the circle that intersects the circle in exactly one point, called the **point of tangency.**

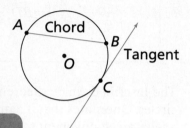

Angle Formed by a Chord and a Tangent Theorem

The measure of an angle formed by a chord and a tangent to an endpoint of the chord is equal to half the measure of the intercepted arc.

$$m\angle ACB = \frac{1}{2}m\widehat{BDC}$$

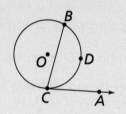

EXAMPLE 4 — Finding the measure of an angle formed by a chord and a tangent

4 $m\widehat{CD} = 60°$ and $\overline{BC}$ is a diameter of circle O. Determine the $m\angle DBA$.

■ SOLUTION

$\overline{BC}$ is a diameter of O, so $m\widehat{CDB} = 180°$.

$m\widehat{BD} = m\widehat{CDB} - m\widehat{CD}$
$\quad\quad = 180° - 60° = 120°$

$m\angle DBA = \frac{1}{2}\widehat{BD}$ ← Apply the Angle Formed by a Chord and a Tangent Theorem.

$m\angle DBA = \frac{1}{2}(120°) = 60°$

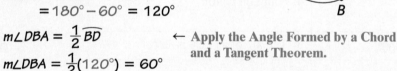

A **secant** is a line or ray that intersects a circle at two points. Determining the measure of the angles formed by intersecting secants depends on where the secants intersect. Secants can intersect inside or outside the circle.

Secants That Intersect Inside a Circle

The measure of an angle formed by two chords or secants that intersect inside a circle is half the sum of the measures of its intercepted arcs.

$$m\angle 1 = \frac{m\widehat{AB} + m\widehat{CD}}{2} = \frac{1}{2}(m\widehat{AB} + m\widehat{CD})$$

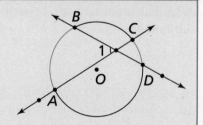

222

You can prove the formula for finding the measure of the angle formed by secants that intersect inside the circle. Draw $\overline{AD}$. The measure of the exterior angle of a triangle equals the sum of the remote interior angles, so $m\angle 1 = m\angle 2 + m\angle 3$. The measure of an inscribed angle is half its intercepted arc. That is, $m\angle 2 = \frac{1}{2}m\widehat{BD}$ and $m\angle 3 = \frac{1}{2}m\widehat{AC}$. By substituting these values for $m\angle 2$ and $m\angle 3$, you get

$m\angle 1 = \frac{m\widehat{BD}\ +\ m\widehat{AC}}{2} = \frac{1}{2}(m\widehat{BD} + m\widehat{AC})$.

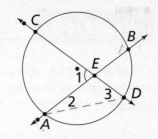

Secants That Intersect Outside a Circle

The measure of an angle formed by two secants that intersect outside a circle is half the difference of the measures of its intercepted arcs.

$$m\angle 2 = \frac{m\widehat{QR} - m\widehat{ST}}{2} = \frac{1}{2}(m\widehat{QR} - m\widehat{ST})$$

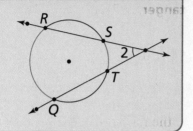

EXAMPLE 5   **Finding the measure of angles formed by secants**

5 In the figure to the right $m\widehat{RQ} = 100°$ and $m\widehat{ST} = 40°$. Find the measures of $\angle 1$ and $\angle 2$.

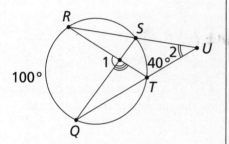

■ **SOLUTION**

$\angle 1$ is formed by the intersection of two secants, $\overline{RT}$ and $\overline{SQ}$, inside the circle.

$$m\angle 1 = \frac{m\widehat{RQ} + m\widehat{ST}}{2} = \frac{100° + 40°}{2} = \frac{140°}{2} = 70°$$

The measure of $\angle 1$ is 70°.

$\angle 2$ is formed by the intersection of two secants, $\overline{UR}$ and $\overline{UQ}$, outside the circle.

$$m\angle 2 = \frac{m\widehat{RQ} - m\widehat{ST}}{2} = \frac{100° - 40°}{2} = \frac{60°}{2} = 30°$$

The measure of $\angle 2$ is 30°.

Choose the numeral preceding the word or expression that best completes the statement or answers the question.

Use the accompanying figure to answer Exercises 1–3.

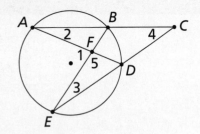

1 The measure of ∠1 is half the _____ of the measures of $\overarc{AE}$ and $\overarc{BD}$.

   (1) sum

   (2) difference

   (3) product

   (4) quotient

2 The measure of ∠4 is half the difference of the measures of which arcs?

   (1) $\overarc{AE}$ and $\overarc{AB}$

   (2) $\overarc{AED}$ and $\overarc{BDE}$

   (3) $\overarc{AB}$ and $\overarc{ED}$

   (4) $\overarc{AE}$ and $\overarc{BD}$

3 If $m\overarc{AE} = 90°$ and $m\overarc{BD} = 40°$, then

   (1) $m\angle1 = 130°$ and $m\angle4 = 50°$.

   (2) $m\angle1 = 25°$ and $m\angle4 = 65°$.

   (3) $m\angle1 = 65°$ and $m\angle4 = 25°$.

   (4) $m\angle1 = 50°$ and $m\angle4 = 130°$.

4 Use the accompanying figure to determine the measures of ∠A, ∠B, and $\overarc{ADC}$.

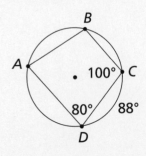

5 In the accompanying figure, $\overline{AB}$, $\overline{BC}$, and $\overline{DE}$ are chords of the circle.

Given: $\overline{BG} \cong \overline{BF}$; $\overarc{DB} \cong \overarc{BE}$
Prove: $\overarc{DA} \cong \overarc{CE}$

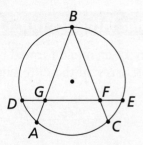

6 Use the accompanying figure to determine the measures of ∠1, ∠2, ∠3, and ∠4.

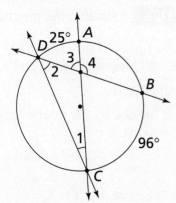

7 **Given:** Circle O with $\overarc{AC} \cong \overarc{BD}$
   Prove: $\overline{AB} \parallel \overline{CD}$ **MP**

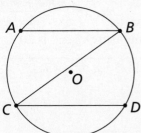

8 Prove the converse of Exercise 7.

9 Prove the theorem for the measure of the angle formed by two secants intersecting outside a circle. HINT: Draw chord $\overline{RT}$.

Angles and Segments Formed by Secants and Tangents

G.C.2
G.C.4

A **secant** is a line, ray, or segment in the plane of the circle that intersects a circle at two points. A **tangent** to a circle is a line, segment, or ray in the plane of the circle that intersects the circle at exactly one point. The point of intersection is called the **point of tangency.**

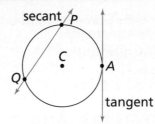

Note

The measure of any angle whose vertex is an exterior point of a circle is calculated by finding 1/2 the difference of their arcs.

Angles Formed by a Tangent and a Secant

The measure of an angle formed by a tangent and secant or by two tangents with a common endpoint is equal to half the difference of the measures of the intercepted arcs.

$$m\angle ACB = \frac{1}{2}(m\widehat{ADB} - m\widehat{AEB})$$

$$m\angle RSU = \frac{1}{2}(m\widehat{RVU} - m\widehat{RWT})$$

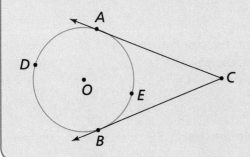

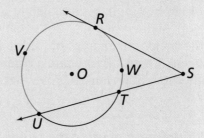

EXAMPLE 1   **Using tangent/secant relationships**

In the accompanying figure, $m\angle RSU = 42°$ and $m\widehat{RT} = 82°$. Find $m\widehat{RU}$.

- **SOLUTION**

$$m\angle RSU = \frac{1}{2}(m\widehat{RU} - m\widehat{RT})$$
$$42° = \frac{1}{2}(m\widehat{RU} - 82°)$$
$$84° = m\widehat{RU} - 82°$$
$$166° = m\widehat{RU}$$

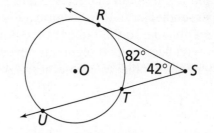

A radius is a segment from the center of the circle to any point on the circle. In a plane through any given point on a segment, one, and only one, line can be drawn perpendicular to that segment at that point. This fact leads to the following relationships.

Radius-Tangent Relationships

If a line is tangent to a circle, then the line is perpendicular to the radius drawn to the point of tangency. That is, $\overleftrightarrow{AB} \perp \overline{OP}$.

The converse is also true. If a line is perpendicular to the radius at its endpoint on the circle, then the line is tangent to the circle.

EXAMPLE 2   **Using radius-tangent relationships**

 In the accompanying figure, is $\overline{KL}$ tangent to circle J?

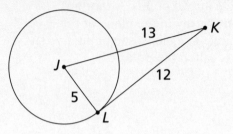

■ **SOLUTION**

You can use the Pythagorean Theorem to show that $\overline{KL} \perp \overline{JL}$.

$$5^2 + 12^2 \stackrel{?}{=} 13^2$$
$$25 + 144 \stackrel{?}{=} 169$$
$$169 = 169$$

Since the last equation is true, $\triangle JKL$ is a right triangle by the converse of the Pythagorean Theorem with $\angle L$ a right angle. So, $\overline{KL} \perp \overline{JL}$.

If a line m is tangent to two or more circles, then m is called a common tangent. If the circles are on the same side of the tangent line, the line is an **external tangent**. If the circles are on opposite sides of the tangent line, the line is an **internal tangent**. If two circles share a common tangent, then you can use the radius-tangent relationship to prove that radii to the points of tangency are parallel.

EXAMPLE 3   **Writing a proof using the radius-tangent relationship**

 Given: $\overleftrightarrow{AB}$ is an external tangent to circle O and circle P at points A and B.
Prove: $\overline{OA} \parallel \overline{PB}$

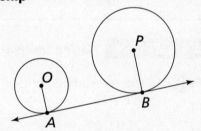

■ **SOLUTION**

$\overline{OA}$ and $\overline{PB}$ are radii of circles O and P, respectively that are perpendicular to $\overleftrightarrow{AB}$ because a line tangent to a circle is perpendicular to the radius at the point of tangency. Therefore, because two segments perpendicular to the same segment are parallel to each other, $\overline{OA} \parallel \overline{PB}$.

The radius-tangent relationships are the basis for the following constructions.

4 Construct the tangent to a circle at a point on the circle.

■ **SOLUTION**

Step 1 Draw and extent $\overrightarrow{OP}$ through point R.

Step 2 Construct a perpendicular to $\overline{OR}$ at P.

Step 3 Draw perpendicular $\overline{XP}$.

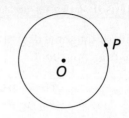

(MP)

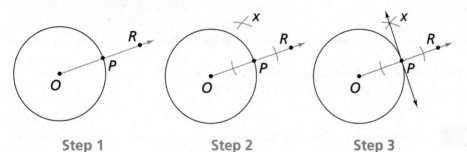

Step 1	Step 2	Step 3

Therefore, $\overline{XP}$ is the tangent to circle O at P.

5 Construct the tangents to a circle from a point outside the circle.

■ **SOLUTION**

Step 1 Draw $\overline{OP}$.

Step 2 Construct a perpendicular bisector of $\overline{OP}$. Label the midpoint M.

Step 3 Construct circle M with radius $\overline{MP}$ intersecting circle O at two points A and B.

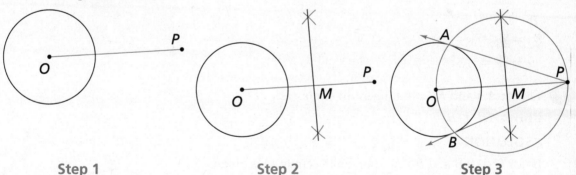

Step 1	Step 2	Step 3

$\overrightarrow{PA}$ and $\overrightarrow{PB}$ are tangents to circle O from point P.

It may not be intuitively obvious as to why this construction works, but if you look more closely at $\angle OAP$ the justification should be clear. $\overline{OA}$ is a radius and by the radius-tangent relationship, $\overline{AP}$ would be a tangent if $\angle OAP$ were a right angle. In circle M, $\angle OAP$ is an inscribed angle whose intercepted arc is formed by diameter $\overline{OMP}$. An angle inscribed in a semi-circle is a right angle. So, $\overline{AP}$ is a tangent.

Two intersecting lines, segments, or rays that are tangent to the same circle have a special relationship that is formalized as the following theorem.

Two-Tangent Theorem

The two segments of tangents drawn to a circle from a point outside the circle are congruent.

$$\overline{AB} \cong \overline{BC}$$

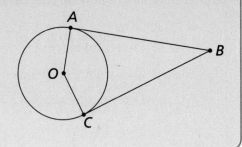

You can use the relationships between the radius of a circle and the tangent, as well as the Two-Tangent Theorem, to solve problems.

EXAMPLES 6 and 7   **Applying properties of tangents**

 $\odot O$ and $\odot Q$ are externally tangent to $\overline{AE}$ and $\overline{BD}$. Find $\overline{CE}$.

■ **SOLUTION**

$\angle QCE \cong \angle ACO$ because they are vertical angles. $\angle A \cong \angle E$ because they are right angles by the Radius-Tangent relationship. Therefore, $\triangle CQE \sim \triangle COA$ by the AA postulate. Because corresponding sides of similar triangles are proportional,

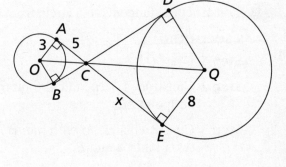

$$\frac{3}{8} = \frac{5}{x}$$

$$3x = 40$$

$$x = \frac{40}{3} = 13\frac{1}{3}$$

 Given: $\overline{AB}$ and $\overline{BC}$ are tangent to circle O.
Prove: $\overline{AB} \cong \overline{BC}$

■ **SOLUTION**

Draw $\overline{OB}$. $\overline{AB}$ and $\overline{BC}$ are tangent to circle O is given. Therefore, $\overline{AB} \perp \overline{AO}$ and $\overline{BC} \perp \overline{OC}$, because a line tangent to a circle is perpendicular to the radius drawn to the point of tangency. By the definition of a right triangle, $\triangle BAO$ and $\triangle BCO$ are right triangles. All radii of a circle are congruent, so $\overline{OA} \cong \overline{OC}$.

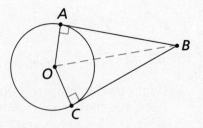

By the Reflexive Property, $\overline{OB} \cong \overline{OB}$. $\triangle BAO \cong \triangle BCO$ by the Hypotenuse-Leg Theorem. Since congruent parts of congruent triangles are congruent, $\overline{AB} \cong \overline{BC}$.

Choose the numeral preceding the word or expression that best completes the statement or answers the question.

1 $\overline{RT}$ and $\overline{ST}$ are tangent to circle O. What is the value of x?

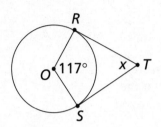

(1) 58°   (2) 63°   (3) 90°   (4) 117°

2 A radius drawn to a tangent at the point of tangency in a circle forms which kind of angle?

(1) acute   (3) right

(2) obtuse   (4) reflex

3 In which of the following figures is $\overline{AB}$ tangent to the circle?

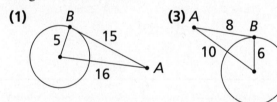

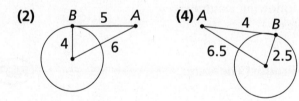

4 In the accompanying diagram, $m\overset{\frown}{RQ} = 166°$ and $m\overset{\frown}{QT} = 92°$. What is the measure of $\angle RSQ$?

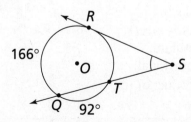

(1) 32°   (2) 51°   (3) 83°   (4) 102°

Use the following figure to answer Exercises 5–10.

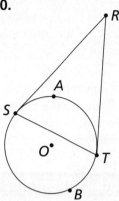

$\overline{SR}$ and $\overline{TR}$ are tangent to circle O.

5 $m\overset{\frown}{SAT} = 100°$. Find $m\angle SRT$.

6 $m\overset{\frown}{SBT} = 204°$. Find $m\angle SRT$.

7 $m\angle SRT = 60°$. Find $m\overset{\frown}{SAT}$.

8 $m\angle SRT = k$. Find $m\overset{\frown}{SAT}$.

9 $m\angle RST = 70°$. Find $m\overset{\frown}{SBT}$.

10 $m\angle SRT = 50°$. Find $m\angle RST$.

11 A belt runs around two circular gears as shown. The large gear has radius 12 cm and the small gear has radius 3 cm. The distance between the gears centers is 18 cm. Find the length, to nearest centimeter the length of the belt. (Hint: Focus on $\triangle BLT$) **MP**

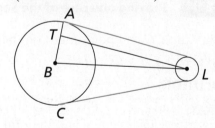

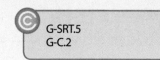
8.5 Segments in a Circle

A **chord** is a segment whose endpoints are on a circle. In the figure to the right, $\overline{AB}$ is a chord and its related arc is $\overset{\frown}{AB}$.

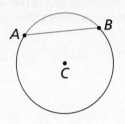

You should note that the diameter of a circle is a chord. In fact, the diameter is the longest chord of a circle, and its arcs are semicircles.

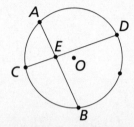

If you use a graphing calculator (or other interactive geometry software) to construct the figure to the right, you may notice that the product of the length of the segments of each chord is constant. This result is summarized by the following theorems.

Segment Product Theorems

For a given circle and point E not on the circle, the product of the lengths of the two segments from E to points on the circle is constant.

$AE \cdot EB = CE \cdot ED$ $EP \cdot EQ = ET \cdot ES$ $EP \cdot EQ = ES \cdot ES$
$EP \cdot EQ = ES^2$

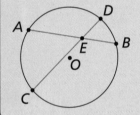   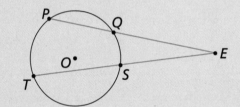   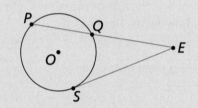

The proofs of the three cases of the Segment Product Theorem are much the same, so only the proof of the first case is given in the following example. Notice the use of auxiliary segments and similar triangles.

EXAMPLE 1   Proving one case of the Segment Product Theorems   (MP)

1   **Given:** Circle O and point E not on the circle.
Prove: $AE \cdot EB = EC \cdot DE$

■ **SOLUTION**

Draw $\overline{AC}$ and $\overline{BD}$. $m\angle C = \frac{1}{2}m\overset{\frown}{AD}$ and $m\angle B = \frac{1}{2}m\overset{\frown}{AD}$ because the inscribed angles equal half their intercepted arc. Similarly, $m\angle A = \frac{1}{2}m\overset{\frown}{BC}$ and $m\angle D = \frac{1}{2}m\overset{\frown}{BC}$. By substitution, $m\angle A = m\angle D$ and $m\angle C = m\angle B$. Now $\triangle AEC \sim \triangle DEB$ by the AA postulate. Because corresponding parts of similar triangles are proportional, $\frac{AE}{EC} = \frac{DE}{EB}$. Since the product of the means is equal to the product of the extremes, we get $AE \cdot EB = EC \cdot DE$.

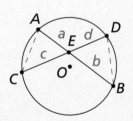

You can use the Segment Product Theorems to find missing lengths of tangents and secants.

EXAMPLES 2 through 4 **Applying the Segment Product Theorems**

Determine the value of x in each of the following figures.

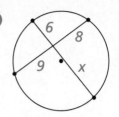

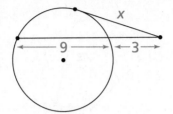

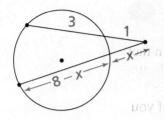

■ SOLUTION

$(6)(x) = (9)(8)$

$6x = 72$

$x = 12$

■ SOLUTION

$(x)(x) = 3(9 + 3)$

$x^2 = 36$

$x = 6$

■ SOLUTION

$x(x + 8 - x) = (1)(4)$

$8x = 4$

$x = \dfrac{1}{2}$

The following table summarizes the remaining theorems about chords of a circle.

Theorems About Chords of a Circle		
In the same circle or in congruent circles, congruent chords have congruent arcs. The converse is also true: In the same circle or in congruent circles, congruent arcs have congruent chords.	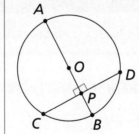	$\overline{AB} \cong \overline{CD} \rightarrow \widehat{AB} \cong \widehat{CD}$ $\widehat{AB} \cong \widehat{CD} \rightarrow \overline{AB} \cong \overline{CD}$
A diameter that is perpendicular to a chord bisects the chord and its two arcs. A diameter that bisects a chord is perpendicular to the chord.	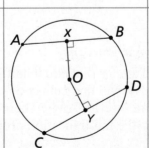	$\overline{AB} \perp \overline{CD} \rightarrow \overline{CP} \cong \overline{DP}$, $\widehat{CB} \cong \widehat{DB}$ $\overline{AB}$ bisects $\overline{CD} \rightarrow \overline{AB} \perp \overline{CD}$
In the same circle or in congruent circles, chords that are equidistant from the center are congruent. The converse is also true: In the same circle or in congruent circles, congruent chords are equidistant from the center of the circle.		$\overline{AB} \perp \overline{OX}, \overline{CD} \perp \overline{OY}$, and $\overline{OX} \cong \overline{OY} \rightarrow \overline{AB} \cong \overline{CD}$ $\overline{AB} \cong \overline{CD}$, and $\overline{OX} \perp \overline{AB}$, $\overline{OY} \perp \overline{CD} \rightarrow \overline{OX} \cong \overline{OY}$

You can use the theorems about chords of a circle to find the missing lengths of segments in a circle.

EXAMPLES 5 through 7 **Applying theorems about chords**

Determine the value of *x* in each of the following.

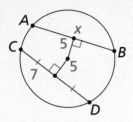

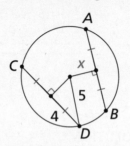

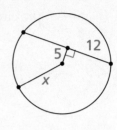

■ SOLUTION

$x = 14$

■ SOLUTION

$$x^2 + 4^2 = 5^2$$
$$x^2 = 9$$
$$x = 3$$

■ SOLUTION

$$12^2 + 5^2 = x^2$$
$$x^2 = 169$$
$$x = 13$$

Since congruent central angles intercept congruent arcs, and congruent arcs intercept congruent chords, you can conclude that congruent central angles also intercept congruent chords. Or, stated in another way, if two chords are congruent, then the central angles they intercept are congruent.

Suppose that a circle is cut by two parallel chords. What can you conclude about the arcs intercepted by them? You know that when two parallel lines are cut by a transversal, their alternate interior angles are congruent. Given two parallel chords, you can create a third chord that is the transversal between them. This fact can be used to prove the following theorem.

Parallel Chords Theorem

In a circle cut by parallel lines, the interior intercepted arcs are congruent.

EXAMPLE 8 **Proving the Parallel Chord Theorem**

8 **Given:** Circle O cut by $\overline{AB}$ and $\overline{CD}$, where $\overline{AB} \parallel \overline{CD}$.
Prove: $\overset{\frown}{AC} \cong \overset{\frown}{BD}$

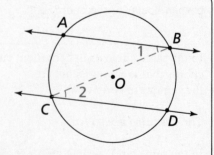

■ SOLUTION

Proof: Draw $\overline{BC}$. $m\angle 1 = \frac{1}{2}\overset{\frown}{AC}$ and $m\angle 2 = \frac{1}{2}\overset{\frown}{BD}$ because $\angle 1$ and $\angle 2$ are inscribed angles that equal half their intercepted arc. $\overline{BC}$ is a transversal that cuts two parallel segments. By the Aternate Interior Angle Theorem, $m\angle 1 = m\angle 2$. By substitution and the multiplication property of equality, we have $\overset{\frown}{AC} \cong \overset{\frown}{BD}$.

Choose the numeral preceding the word or expression that best completes the statement or answers the question.

1 $\overline{ST}$ is tangent to the circle at point T. Determine ST.

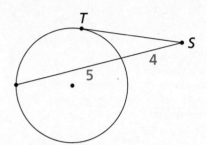

(1) 6   (2) $\sqrt{20}$ (3) 4.5   (4) 20

In Exercises 2 and 3, use the following diagram.

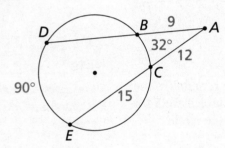

2 Find $m\angle BAC$.

(1) 58°   (2) 32°   (3) 29°   (4) 61°

3 Find BD.

(1) 20   (2) 24   (3) 27   (4) 28

In Exercise 4, determine the value of x.

4 $\overline{AD}$ is tangent to the circle at D and $\overline{AE}$ is tangent to the circle at E.

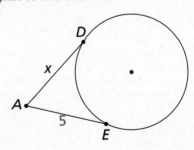

5 **Given:** $\overline{AEB}$ and $\overline{CED}$ are common internal tangents of circles O and Q.

Prove: $\overline{AB} \cong \overline{CD}$

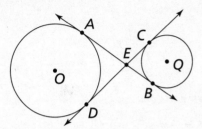

6 Find the value of x and y.

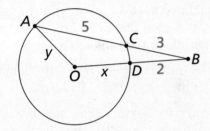

7 Find the value of x.

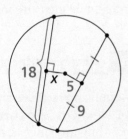

8 Find the value of x and y.

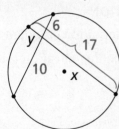

233

G-C.5
G-GMD.1

During this chapter we have measured angles in degrees. We know that the degree measures the amount of rotation from one side of an angle to the other side. For example, a complete revolution around a circle contains 360°. So 1° is $\frac{1}{360}$ th of a revolution around a circle. To see an angle that measures 1° would require you to magnify the figure shown below.

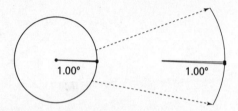

In mathematics, there is a second unit used to measure angles. This unit is called a **radian.** One radian is defined as the measure of the angle formed by two radii that intercept an arc that is **equal in length to the radius.** That is, if

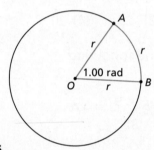

length of the radius = $r = OA = OB$ = length $\overparen{AB}$,
        then $m\angle AOB = 1$ radian.

Unlike degree measures, radian measure is unit-less. Therefore when using radian measure the result of a calculation remains in the units of the problem situation. In the arc length formula, the variables are **S** for arc length, **θ** for an angle measure in radians, and **r** for radius of the circle.

Note

The symbol θ is read Theta and is a Greek letter like π.

EXAMPLE 1 **Using similar circles to derive arc length**

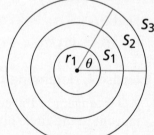

The diagram shows three similar circles all with center O, where $\overline{OA}$, $\overline{OA'}$, and $\overline{OA''}$ are corresponding radii, S_1, S_2, and S_3 are corresponding arc lengths, and **θ** is the common central angle measured in radians. Show that $S = r \cdot \theta$.

■ **SOLUTION**

By the definition of radian $\theta = \dfrac{S_1}{r_1}$. Since all circles are similar and corresponding linear measures are proportional, then

$$\theta = \frac{S_1}{r_1} = \frac{S_2}{r_2} = \frac{S_3}{r_3}$$

$$S = r \cdot \theta.$$

EXAMPLE 2   **Using arc length**

2 Find the radian measure, θ, of an angle that intercepts an arc of 6 cm in a circle whose radius is 2 cm. Draw and label a sketch of θ.

■ SOLUTION

$$S = r \cdot \theta$$
$$6 \text{ cm} = 2 \text{ cm} \cdot \theta$$
$$\frac{6 \text{ cm}}{2 \text{ cm}} = \theta = 3 \text{ radians}$$

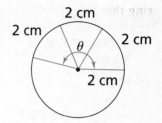

Intuitively, how does 1 radian compare to degree measure? Think of a sector of the circle with a central angle of 1 radian. It would look sort of like an equilateral triangle, so a good "rule of thumb" is that 1 radian is close to 60°. We need to be more exact and have a method of measure conversion.

EXAMPLE 3   **Finding the radian measure of a straight angle**

3 Determine the measure of a straight angle, 180°, in radians.

■ SOLUTION

The length of the intercepted arc is half the circumference of the circle. The circumference of a circle is $2\pi r$, so the length of the intercepted arc is πr.

Using $\theta = \dfrac{S}{r}$, then $m\angle AOB = \dfrac{\pi r}{r} = \pi$ radians. Thus 180° = π radians.

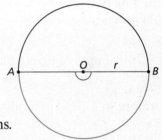

Converting Between Degrees and Radians

Using proportional reasoning and the conversion fact that 180° = π radians:

$$\frac{angle\ radian\ measure}{\pi} = \frac{angle\ degree\ measure}{180°}$$

Solving for radian measure: $angle\ radian\ measure = \dfrac{angle\ degree\ measure}{180°} \cdot \pi$

Solving for degree measure: $angle\ degree\ measure = \dfrac{angle\ radian\ measure}{\pi} \cdot 180°$

Note

When no unit of angle measure is given, radian measure is implied.

EXAMPLES 4 through 11 Converting between degrees and radians

Convert each of the following from degrees to radians or from radians to degrees.

4 50°

■ **SOLUTION**

$$\frac{50°}{180°} \cdot \pi$$

$$= \frac{5\pi}{18} \approx 0.8727$$

5 30°

■ **SOLUTION**

$$\frac{30°}{180°} \cdot \pi$$

$$= \frac{\pi}{6} \approx 0.5236$$

6 18°

■ **SOLUTION**

$$\frac{18°}{180°} \cdot \pi$$

$$= \frac{\pi}{10} \approx 0.3142$$

7 45°

■ **SOLUTION**

$$\frac{45°}{180°} \cdot \pi$$

$$= \frac{\pi}{4} \approx 0.7854$$

8 $\frac{\pi}{5}$

■ **SOLUTION**

$$\frac{\left(\frac{\pi}{5}\right)}{\pi} \cdot 180°$$

$$= \frac{180°}{5} = 36°$$

9 2 radians

■ **SOLUTION**

$$\frac{2}{\pi} \cdot 180°$$

$$= \frac{360°}{\pi} \approx 114.6°$$

10 $\frac{5\pi}{18}$

■ **SOLUTION**

$$\frac{\left(\frac{5\pi}{18}\right)}{\pi} \cdot 180°$$

$$= 5 \cdot 10° = 50°$$

11 3

■ **SOLUTION**

$$\frac{3}{\pi} \cdot 180°$$

$$= \frac{540°}{\pi} \approx 171.9°$$

Recall, the length of an arc along a circle is given by the formula

$$S = \theta r$$

where θ is measured in radians.

EXAMPLE 12 Finding the length of an arc

12 Determine the length of an arc intercepted by an angle of 220° in a circle with a radius of 3 inches.

■ **SOLUTION**

$\frac{220°}{180°} \cdot \pi = \frac{11\pi}{9}$ radians ← **Convert from degrees to radians.**

$S = \theta r$ ← **Apply the formula for arc length.**

$S = \frac{11\pi}{9} \cdot 3$ ← **Substitute.**

$S = \frac{11\pi}{3}$

$S \approx 11.52$ inches

The formula $S = \theta r$ has some interesting real-world applications.

EXAMPLE 13   Determining arc length in a real-world situation

 The boundary between the infield and the outfield of a baseball field is part of a circle. The angle at home plate between first base and third base is 90°, or $\frac{\pi}{2}$ radians. The distance from home plate to the outfield grass is 110 feet. How long is the arc that forms the boundary between the infield and outfield? Round your answer to the nearest tenth of a foot.

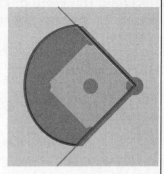

■ SOLUTION

Use the formula $S = \theta r$.

$S = \dfrac{\pi}{2} \cdot 110$

$S = 55\pi$

$S \approx 172.8 \text{ feet}$

You can use the formula $S = \theta r$ to derive the circumference of a circle formula.

EXAMPLE 14   Deriving the circumference formula

14 Use the formula $S = \theta r$ where S is the circle's circumference.

■ SOLUTION

One rotation around the circle measures 360°, or 2π radians.

$S = \theta \cdot r$

$\text{circumference} = 2\pi r$

In Exercises 1–7, choose the numeral preceding the word or expression that best completes the statement or answers the question.

1 How many degrees are in π radians?

   (1) 1°   **(3)** 180°

   (2) 90°   **(4)** 360°

2 Which of the following is equivalent to 135°?

   (1) $\dfrac{4\pi}{3}$ **(3)** $\dfrac{3\pi}{4}$

   (2) $\dfrac{\pi}{180}$ **(4)** 2π

3 Which pair of measurements represent the same angle measure?

   (1) 240°, $\dfrac{7\pi}{6}$ radians

   (2) 135°, $\dfrac{5\pi}{4}$ radians

   (3) 270°, 3π radians

   (4) 150°, $\dfrac{5\pi}{6}$ radians

4 Which of the following is true about an angle of 1 radian?

   (1) For a central angle of 1 radian, the radius of the circle is 1 unit.

   (2) For a central angle of 1 radian, the intercepted arc is 1 unit.

   (3) For a central angle of 1 radian, the intercepted arc is equal to the radius.

   (4) For a central angle of 1 radian, the terminal side is rotated $\frac{1}{360}$ around the circle.

5 An angle that measures $\frac{7\pi}{8}$ radians is the same as which of the following?

   (1) 315°   **(3)** 22.5°

   (2) 157.5°   **(4)** 2.75°

6 Which of the following is true?

   (1) 1° = 1 radian   **(3)** 1° = π

   (2) 1° < 1 radian   **(4)** 1° > 1 radian

7 An arc in a circle with a radius of 10 inches is intercepted by a central angle that measures $\frac{3\pi}{2}$ radians. What is the length of the arc?

   (1) 10 inches   **(3)** $\dfrac{20\pi}{3}$ inches

   (2) 10π inches   **(4)** 15π inches

In Exercises 8–13, the radius and measure of a central angle is given. Find the length of the arc with the given values of θ and r.

8 $\theta = \dfrac{\pi}{6}, r = 3$ 9 $\theta = \dfrac{\pi}{3}, r = 5$

10 $\theta = \dfrac{11\pi}{4}, r = 8$ 11 $\theta = \dfrac{4\pi}{3}, r = 9$

12 $\theta = \dfrac{3\pi}{2}, r = 4$ 13 $\theta = \dfrac{2\pi}{3}, r = 2$

14 The windshield wiper on an automobile is 23 inches long and rotates through an angle of 100°. How far does the tip of the wiper travel as it moves once across the windshield? **(MP)**

15 In the accompanying figure, the arc of the fan is 23.56 inches and the length of the fan is 9 inches. What is the measure of θ? Round your answer to the nearest degree.

23.56

θ

9

16 The radius of a bicycle wheel is 14 inches. If the bicycle is moved forward a distance of 15 feet, through what angle will a point on the tire turn?

17 A wrench is 14 inches long from sprocket to tip. How far does the end of the wrench move if it turns through an angle of 1.5 radians?

18 Using interactive geometry software or string, construct a circle and transfer the length of the radius to the boundary of the circle. How many times can this length be transferred to the boundary of the circle? Explain.

Answer all the questions in this part. For each question, select the numeral preceding the word or expression that best completes the statement or answers the question.

1 Find the area of a circle whose circumference is 16π.

   (1) 4π **(2)** 16π **(3)** 64π **(4)** 256π

2 If two circles are similar with $k = \frac{4}{25}$, find the ratio of the circles' areas.

   (1) $\dfrac{\text{Area}_1}{\text{Area}_2} = \dfrac{2}{5}$ **(3)** $\dfrac{\text{Area}_1}{\text{Area}_2} = \dfrac{4}{25}$

   (2) $\dfrac{\text{Area}_1}{\text{Area}_2} = \dfrac{4}{10}$ **(4)** $\dfrac{\text{Area}_1}{\text{Area}_2} = \dfrac{16}{625}$

3 $\odot X$ similar to $\odot Y$. Area $\odot X = 36$ m^2 and Area $\odot Y = 100$ m^2. Find the constant of similarity for $\odot X$ to $\odot Y$.

   (1) $\dfrac{3}{5}$ **(3)** $\dfrac{81}{225}$

   (2) $\dfrac{\sqrt{3}}{\sqrt{5}}$ **(4)** $\dfrac{9}{25}$

4 Find the area of a sector with measure of central angle $= 150°$ and radius of 6.

   (1) 15π **(2)** 30π **(3)** 60π **(4)** 120π

5 Find the measure of the central angle if the area of the sector $= 8\pi$ and circle's radius is 4.

   (1) $45°$ **(2)** $135°$ **(3)** $180°$ **(4)** $225°$

6 What can you conclude from the diagram of circle O?

   (1) $AD = BC$

   (2) $m\angle A = m\angle D$

   (3) $\overline{AC}$ and $\overline{BD}$ bisect each other.

   (4) all of the above

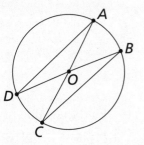

7 Determine the value of x in the accompanying figure.

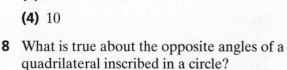

   (1) 7

   (2) 8

   (3) 9

   (4) 10

8 What is true about the opposite angles of a quadrilateral inscribed in a circle?

   (1) They are complementary.

   (2) They are supplementary.

   (3) They are congruent.

   (4) They are right.

9 Which equation could be used to determine the value of the radius in the circle below?

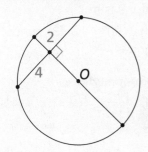

   (1) $2^2 + 4^2 = r^2$

   (2) $r^2 = (r-2)^2 + 4^2$

   (3) $r^2 + (r-2)^2 = 4^2$

   (4) $r^2 = (r+2)^2 + 4^2$

10 Which statement is true about $\angle 1$ and $\angle 2$ in the figure below?

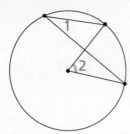

(1) $m\angle 1 = m\angle 2$

(2) $m\angle 1 = 2 \cdot m\angle 2$

(3) $m\angle 1 = \dfrac{1}{2} \cdot m\angle 2$

(4) $m\angle 1 \geq m\angle 2$

11 What is the measure of an angle inscribed in a semicircle?

(1) less than 90°   **(3)** equal to 90°

(2) more than 90°   **(4)** equal to 180°

12 The angle formed by a tangent to a circle and a radius to the point of tangency will have what measure?

(1) less than 90°   **(3)** more than 90°

(2) equal to 90°   **(4)** equal to 45°

13 In the accompanying figure, the $m\angle 2 = 115°$. Find the $m\angle 1$.

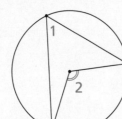

(1) 57.5°

(2) 60°

(3) 90°

(4) 245°

14 Which of the following describes the measure of a major arc?

(1) 360° divided by the measure of a semicircle

(2) 360° minus the measure of its minor arc

(3) 360° plus the measure of its minor arc

(4) It is equal to the measure of its central angle.

15 An inflated tire has a diameter of 30 in. The tire is mounted on a rim with a diameter of 18 in. When the tire goes flat, the flat part is tangent to the rim at the center of the tire. Determine the length of the flat part of the tire.

(1) 6 in.   **(2)** 12 in.   **(3)** 24 in.   **(4)** 48 in.

16 Find the area of a sector whose central angle is $\frac{2}{3}\pi$ radians in a circle of radius 9 units.

For Exercises 17 and 18, define the transformations needed to prove $\odot T$ similar to $\odot T'$.

17 $\odot T$ centered at $(-4, 5)$ with radius of 2 units; $\odot T'$ centered at $(2, -1)$ with radius of 5 units.

18 $\odot T$ defined by $(x - 3)^2 + (y - 4)^2 = 36$; $\odot T'$ defined by $(x)^2 + (y + 1)^2 = 1$.

$\overline{AB}$ and $\overline{CD}$ are chords of the circle shown below. $m\angle 1 = 7x + 11$, $m\overset{\frown}{AC} = 2x$, and $m\overset{\frown}{DB} = x + 88$. Use this information to answer Exercises 19–20.

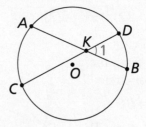

19 Find the value of x.

(1) 5   **(2)** 6   **(3)** 8   **(4)** 12

20 Find length of $\overline{KD}$ if $AK = 6$, $KB = 5$, and $CD = 13$.

(1) 3   **(2)** 5   **(3)** 6   **(4)** 8

21 Which of the following is true about the measure of an inscribed angle?

  (1) The measure of an inscribed angle is double the measure of its intercepted arc.

  (2) The measure of an inscribed angle is one half the measure of its intercepted arc.

  (3) The measure of an inscribed angle is equal to the measure of its intercepted arc.

  (4) The measure of an inscribed angle is the sum of 180° and the measure of its intercepted arc.

Use the following figure for Exercises 22–23.

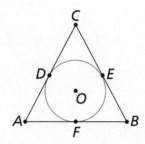

22 The sides of triangle ABC are tangent to circle O at points D, E, and F. $m\widehat{DE} = 100°$, and $AF = FB = 10$. Triangle ABC is an isosceles triangle. Find $m\angle A$.

  (1) 40°   **(2)** 50°   **(3)** 60°   **(4)** 80°

23 Find the length of side AB.

  (1) 10   **(2)** 15   **(3)** 20   **(4)** 30

24 Which of the following is true about secants?

  (1) The measure of an angle formed by two secants that intersect outside a circle is the difference of the measures of its intercepted arcs.

  (2) The measure of an angle formed by two secants that intersect inside a circle is half the sum of the measures of its intercepted arcs.

  (3) The measure of an angle formed by two secants that intersect inside a circle is double the sum of the measures of its intercepted arcs.

  (4) The measure of an angle formed by two secants that intersect outside a circle is double the difference of the measures of its intercepted arcs.

25 Two circles share a common tangent and the centers of the circles lie on the opposite sides of the common tangent. These circles are said to be

  (1) externally tangent.

  (2) internally tangent.

  (3) commonly tangent.

  (4) literally tangent.

26 An angle measures 210°. What is its radian measure?

  (1) $\dfrac{6}{7}\pi$ **(2)** $\dfrac{7}{6}\pi$ **(3)** $\dfrac{7}{12}\pi$ **(4)** $\dfrac{12}{257}\pi$

27 Find the length of an arc if its measure is 45° in a circle of radius 12.

  (1) 1.5π **(2)** 3π **(3)** 6π **(4)** 48π

Answer all the questions in this part. Clearly indicate the necessary steps, including appropriate formula substitutions, diagrams, graphs, charts, etc. For all questions in this part, a correct numerical answer with no work shown will receive only one credit.

28 Complete the following flow proof.

Given: Circle O with $\overline{AB} \cong \overline{CD}$
Prove: $m\overset{\frown}{AB} \cong m\overset{\frown}{CD}$

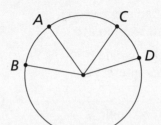

$\overline{AO} \cong \overline{BO} \cong \overline{CO} \cong \overline{DO}$

_____

_____

$\triangle AOB \cong \triangle COD$

_____ CPCTC

$m\overset{\frown}{AB} \cong m\overset{\frown}{CD}$

_____

29 $\overline{PQ}$ and $\overline{PR}$ are chords of circle O. Prove that if O is on the bisector of $\angle QPR$, then $\overline{PQ} \cong \overline{PR}$.

30 $\odot X$ similar to $\odot Y$. $\odot X$ has radius of 10 units and $\odot Y$ has diameter of 50 units. Find the constant of proportionality for $\odot X$ to $\odot Y$.

31 A pendulum swings through an angle of 72° and cuts an arc of 20π inches. Find the length of the pendulum.

32 Assume the radius of Earth is 3,960 mi and that there are no hills or obstructions on its surface. How far can you see from the top of the Eiffel Tower, which is 986 ft tall? How far can you see from the top of the CNN Tower, which is 1,815 ft tall?

9 Solid Geometry and Its Applications

Donald Coxeter

Donald Coxeter was possibly the greatest geometer of the 20th century. The "Platonic solids," figures whose faces are identical regular polygons, were known to the ancient Greeks. Three have (equilateral) triangular faces—the tetrahedron, the octahedron, and the icosahedron. Additionally, there are the cube, and dodecahedron. Coxeter's *Regular Polytopes* (1948) gives a systematic account of these, and their relatives. One of these, involving both hexagons and pentagons, is now well-known for its use on soccer balls.

Although he never used computers in his own mathematics, similar ideas are important to the information age, specifically, in the theory of error-correcting codes.

Source: *www-history.mcs.st-and.ac.uk/Obits/Coxeter.html*

9.1 Points and Lines Perpendicular to the Plane

A line has only one dimension. A line has length (or distance). It has no width or depth.

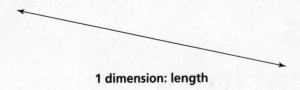

1 dimension: length

A plane exists in two dimensions. A plane has length and width, but no depth or thickness.

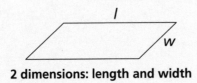

2 dimensions: length and width

Plane geometry deals with flat geometric figures that exist in a plane. You can find perimeters and areas in plane geometry using length and width.

To consider all of the objects of our everyday existence, you have to include depth (or height). In order to understand 3-dimensional geometry, you have to consider points and lines that do not lie in the same plane.

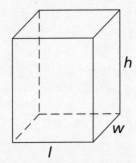

3 dimensions: length, width, and height

The postulates on the next page will help you analyze the characteristics and properties of perpendicular lines and planes. These postulates are essential to understanding 3-dimensional (or *solid*) geometry.

For example, you can see that adjacent walls in your classroom are perpendicular to each other, and that the walls intersect at the corners of the room. These postulates can be applied to large buildings as well as the construction of everyday objects.

Postulates About Perpendicular Lines and Planes

1 Points and lines that lie in the same plane are coplanar. Collinear points are points that lie on the same line. If two lines intersect or are parallel, then they are coplanar.

Lines *l* and *m* are coplanar.

2 Through any 3 noncollinear points, there is exactly one plane.

Plane *M* is determined by the points *A*, *B*, and *C*.

3 If a line intersects a plane, then it can intersect the plane at only one point.

Line *l* intersects plane *M* at point *P*.

4 If a line is perpendicular to each of 2 intersecting lines at their intersection, then it is perpendicular to the plane that contains them.

Line *l* is perpendicular to plane *M* at point *P*.

5 Through a given point not on a plane, there passes one and only one line perpendicular to the plane.

Point *P* can only be on one line that is perpendicular to plane *M*.

6 Through a given point there passes one and only one plane perpendicular to a line containing the point.

Plane *M* is the only plane that will be perpendicular to given line *l* through *P* on *l*.

7 If 2 lines are perpendicular to the same plane, they are parallel to each other and therefore coplanar.

Line *l* and line *n* are both perpendicular to plane *M*. Therefore, they are coplanar and parallel.

8 Two planes are perpendicular to each other if one plane contains a line perpendicular to the second plane.

Line *l* is perpendicular to plane *M*. Therefore, plane *M* is perpendicular to plane *N*.

1 Explain why a 4-legged chair can be wobbly and a 3-legged stool is not.

■ **SOLUTION**

Recall that 3 noncollinear points determine a plane. Therefore, the 3 legs of a stool (*A*, *B*, *C*) form a plane with the floor. If the end of the leg of the chair that ends at *D* is not in the same plane as *A*, *B*, and *C*, then the chair will wobble.

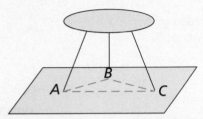   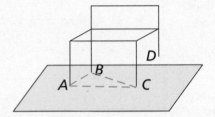

2 Draw a diagram to show why it is not sufficient to say that one and only one plane can pass through 2 points.

■ **SOLUTION**

The diagram shows that several planes include *A* and *B*. Two points will determine one and only one line. Note that the diagram illustrates that a single line lies in an infinite number of planes.

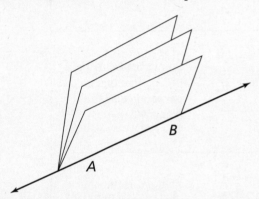

3 Using the rectangular solid to the right, name each of the following:

a. 2 segments perpendicular to *ABCD*
b. 2 planes perpendicular to each other
c. a plane that contains the diagonal *EC*
d. 2 planes that intersect each other, but are not perpendicular
e. the intersection of planes *CHE*, *CHG*, *EHG*

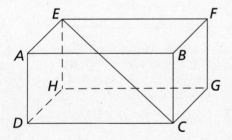

■ **SOLUTION**

a. $\overline{AE}$ and $\overline{BF}$ or $\overline{DH}$ and $\overline{CG}$
b. *CGH* and *GHE* (Answers will vary.)
c. *EHC*
d. *AEH* and *EHC* (Answers will vary.)
e. The 3 planes intersect at point *H*.

Choose the numeral preceding the word or expression that best completes the statement or answers the question.

1 Three noncollinear points determine a
  (1) line.
  (2) cube.
  (3) point.
  (4) plane.

2 The intersection of 2 planes can be a
  (1) line.
  (2) cube.
  (3) point.
  (4) plane.

3 Which is an impossible number of points for a line to intersect a plane?
  (1) 0
  (2) 1
  (3) 2
  (4) infinite

Use the following diagram of a rectangular solid to answer Exercises 4–8.

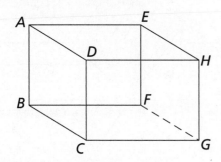

4 Name a set of collinear points.

5 Name a set of coplanar points.

6 Name a plane that contains the diagonal $\overline{AG}$.

7 Name a plane that contains the diagonal $\overline{EC}$.

8 Name each face of the cube.

Use the following diagram of a pyramid to answer Exercises 9–15.

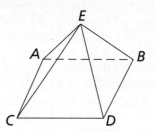

9 Name two intersecting planes.

10 Name a set of points that is not coplanar.

11 Name a set of collinear points.

12 Name a set of noncollinear points.

13 Name a line that is in the same plane as $\overline{AB}$.

14 Name each face of the solid.

15 How many planes in the diagram intersect at E?

In Exercises 16–22, state whether the statement is true or false.

16 If 5 points are coplanar, they are always collinear.

17 If 5 points are collinear, then they are coplanar.

18 Plane P contains the lines m and n, which intersect at point Q. Line l is not in plane P, but it is perpendicular to m and n at Q. Line l is perpendicular to plane P.

19 There is more than one line that can be perpendicular to a plane at the point of intersection.

20 If 2 lines are perpendicular to the same plane, they are coplanar.

21 For a given line and a point not on the line, there is exactly one plane that can contain them.

22 Given any 2 lines, there is only one plane that contains both of them.

If 2 lines are perpendicular to the same plane, then they are coplanar, but are they parallel? If you can show that they are the same distance apart, then you know that the lines are parallel.

Recall that the perpendicular distance is the shortest distance between 2 or more lines, as shown in the diagram to the right.

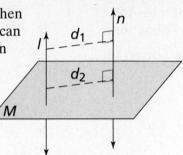

In the corresponding diagram, $d_1 \perp n$ and $d_1 = d_2$, so $l \parallel n$. Therefore, if 2 lines are perpendicular to the same plane, then they are parallel to each other.

 EXAMPLE 1 **Showing that 2 planes perpendicular to the same plane are not always parallel**

1 If 2 planes are perpendicular to the same plane, are they parallel? Look in the corner of your classroom for a solution.

▪ **SOLUTION**

In the figure to the right, you can see that the 2 shaded faces are both perpendicular to the plane B. They are also perpendicular to each other. This counterexample shows 2 planes that are perpendicular to a given plane are not always parallel to each other.

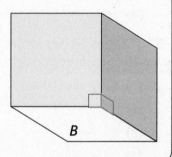

When 2 planes intersect, each plane is divided into a **half plane,** as shown in the figure to the right. W lies in one half plane of A, and Y in the other half plane of A. Similarly, X and Z are relative to plane B.

The angles formed when 2 planes intersect are called **dihedral angles.** Dihedral angles can be acute, obtuse, or right. You can find the measure of a dihedral angle by measuring the plane angle formed by the rays in each half plane. For example, $\angle XPY$ is a plane angle.

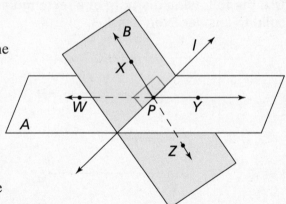

When 2 planes intersect, their vertical dihedral angles are congruent. If the 2 planes intersect so that their dihedral angles form right plane angles, then the planes are perpendicular.

 EXAMPLE 2 **Identifying vertical dihedral angles**

2 Identify a dihedral angle in the figure above that is congruent to $\angle XPY$.

▪ **SOLUTION**

$\angle WPZ$ and $\angle XPY$ are vertical dihedral angles. Since vertical dihedral angles are congruent, $\angle XPY \cong \angle WPZ$.

This leads to the following postulates about perpendicular and parallel lines and planes.

Postulates About Lines Perpendicular to Planes		
1 If a line is perpendicular to a plane, then any line perpendicular to the given line at its point of intersection with the given plane is in the given plane.		If $l \perp$ plane M at P and if lines a, b, and c are perpendicular to l at P, then a, b, and c all lie in plane M.
2 If a line is perpendicular to a plane, then every plane containing the line is perpendicular to the given plane.		If $l \perp$ plane M at P, then all the planes containing l are perpendicular to plane M.

You can use these postulates to describe the faces and properties of geometric solids.

EXAMPLES 3 and 4   **Identifying perpendicular lines and planes**

Use the rectangular prism to the right for Examples 3 and 4.

3 Name all the edges perpendicular to $\overline{AB}$.

■ **SOLUTION**
$\overline{AD}, \overline{AE}, \overline{BC}, \overline{BH}$

4 Name all the planes perpendicular to $\overline{AB}$.

■ **SOLUTION**
To find the planes perpendicular to $\overline{AB}$, name the planes that contain the lines perpendicular to $\overline{AB}$ from Example 3, but do not contain $\overline{AB}$ itself.

ADGE and *BCFH*

When you look at geometric solids, you may see that many of their faces are parallel and lie in different planes. Lines that have no points in common are parallel or skew. Planes that have no points in common are parallel. Two planes are never skew; they either intersect or are parallel.

Parallel planes are planes that do not intersect. If two planes are parallel, then none of the lines contained in one plane will intersect with any of the lines contained in the other plane. If a line and a plane do not intersect, then they are also parallel.

In fact, many postulates about parallel and perpendicular lines can be extended to parallel and perpendicular planes.

<table>
<tr><td colspan="2">Postulates About Perpendicular and Parallel Planes</td></tr>
<tr>
<td>

1 The distance between 2 parallel planes is the perpendicular distance and will be the length of the segment that is perpendicular to both planes.

2 If 2 planes are perpendicular to the same line, then the planes are parallel.
</td>
<td>

$\overline{AB} \perp$ plane X and plane Y. The distance between plane X and plane Y is the length of segment $\overline{AB}$. Therefore plane $X \parallel$ plane Y.
</td>
</tr>
<tr>
<td>

3 If a plane intersects 2 parallel planes, then the intersection is 2 parallel lines.
</td>
<td>

Plane $X \parallel$ plane Y. If plane Z intersects plane X and plane Y, then $r \parallel s$.
</td>
</tr>
</table>

If a plane intersects a 3-dimensional figure so that one half of the figure is identical to the other half, then the plane is called a **symmetry plane**.

Note

Suppose an intersecting plane is parallel to a base of a cube or cylinder. The intersection of the plane with the cube is a square and the intersection of the plane with the cylinder is a circle.

EXAMPLE 5   **Exploring symmetry planes**

5 Draw a symmetry plane parallel to the bases of the solids below.

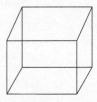

Cube

Cylinder

■ SOLUTION

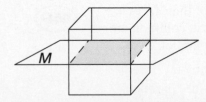

■ SOLUTION

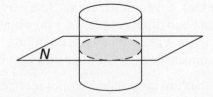

Plane M is a symmetry plane parallel to the base of the cube, and it divides the cube into equal halves.

Plane N is a symmetry plane parallel to the base of the cylinder, and it divides the cylinder into equal halves.

250

6 How many symmetry planes does the cube in Example 5 have?

■ **SOLUTION**

If the bases are the top and bottom, there is one plane parallel to those bases and two planes through opposite vertices of the top and bottom. If the bases are the front and back there are also three symmetry planes, and if the bases are the left and right faces there are three symmetry planes.

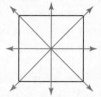

9 symmetry lines altogether

7 How many symmetry planes does the cylinder in Example 4 have?

■ **SOLUTION**

The cylinder has one symmetry plane parallel to its bases, as shown in the solution to Example 4. In the figure to the right, each of the lines passing through the diameter of the cylinder is in a unique symmetry plane. Therefore, there are an infinite number of symmetry planes perpendicular to the cylinder's base.

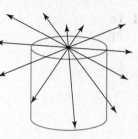

Practice

Choose the numeral preceding the word or expression that best completes the statement or answers the question.

1 Two planes that are not parallel intersect at a

  (1) line.

  (2) plane.

  (3) segment

  (4) point.

2 How many symmetry planes are there in a rectangular solid that is not a cube?

  (1) 4

  (2) 3

  (3) 2

  (4) infinite

3 The corner of many classrooms represents the intersection of

  (1) 4 lines.

  (2) 2 planes.

  (3) 3 planes.

  (4) 2 planes and a line.

In Exercises 4–11, state the postulate or definition that the statement represents.

4 a 4 legged table that is wobbly

5 a revolving door in a building

6 the goal posts on a football field

7 the floor and ceiling of a room

8 slicing an orange exactly in half

9 two adjacent faces of a cube

10 two opposite faces of a cube

11 measuring the intersection of 2 walls of a room to determine the height of the room

12 How many symmetry planes does the figure below have?

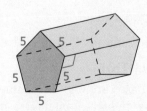

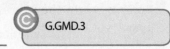
A **polyhedron** is a three-dimensional figure formed by flat surfaces that are bounded by polygons joined along their sides. Each of the flat surfaces is called a **face** of the polyhedron. A segment that is the intersection of two faces is called an **edge.** A point that is the intersection of three or more edges is a **vertex.**

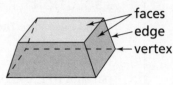

polyhedron

If all of the faces of a polyhedron are regular polygons that are congruent to each other, the figure is a **regular polyhedron.** In a regular polyhedron, the same number of faces meets at each vertex.

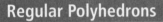

Regular Polyhedrons

- **Tetrahedron:** a polyhedron with 4 congruent faces that are triangles.
- **Hexahedron:** a polyhedron with 6 congruent faces that are squares. (A hexahedron is also called a **cube.**)
- **Octahedron:** a polyhedron with 8 congruent faces that are triangles.
- **Dodecahedron:** a polyhedron with 12 congruent faces that are pentagons.
- **Icosahedron:** a polyhedron with 20 congruent faces that are triangles.

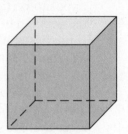

hexahedron

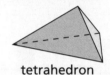

tetrahedron

A **prism** is a polyhedron with two parallel **bases** that are congruent polygons and with **lateral faces** that are parallelograms that connect corresponding sides of the bases. The **height** h of a prism is the length of any perpendicular segment drawn from a point on one base to the plane containing the other base.

A prism is a **right prism** if the segments that join corresponding vertices of the bases are perpendicular to the bases. Otherwise, the prism is called *oblique.* You can further classify a prism by the shape of its bases: triangular, square, rectangular, and so on.

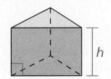

right triangular prism

oblique triangular prism

EXAMPLE 1   **Classifying a prism**

1   Which best describes the prism at the right? The measure of each interior angle of a base is 108°.

(1) dodecahedron

(2) regular pentagonal prism

(3) right pentagonal prism

(4) oblique regular pentagonal prism

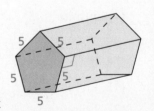

■ **SOLUTION**

The bases are regular pentagons. The right-angle symbol indicates that the segments joining corresponding vertices are perpendicular to the planes containing the bases. The correct choice is **(3).**

The **lateral area of a prism** is the sum of the areas of its lateral faces. If you look at a *net* for the lateral area of a rectangular prism you will see that it is made up of four rectangles laid side by side, all with the same height.

Note

The perimeter of the base of a rectangular prism is $2l + 2w$.

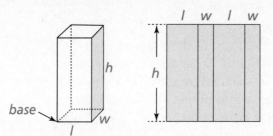

You can calculate the lateral area of a prism if you multiply the height of the figure by the perimeter of its base. The formula for lateral area is ph, where p is the perimeter of the base and h is the height of the figure.

$$\text{L.A.} = ph \text{ or } h(2l + 2w) \text{ or } 2(lh + hw)$$

To find the total **surface area of a prism** you add the lateral area and the areas of the two congruent bases. The formula is **Surface Area = L.A. + 2B**, where **B** is the area of the base.

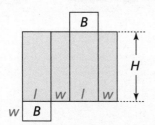

$$\text{S.A.} = \text{L.A.} + 2B$$

Note

The base of a prism is not always the bottom of the drawing.

Since the L.A. $= 2(lh + hw)$ is added to the area of the two bases, $2B = 2lw$, another formula for the surface area of a rectangular prism can be **S.A. $= 2(lh + hw + lw)$.**

EXAMPLES 2 and 3	**Finding lateral and total surface area of a right prism**

 2 Find the lateral and surface area of the right triangular prism below.

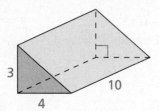

■ **SOLUTION**

The bases are right triangles. The length of the hypotenuse is 5 by the Pythagorean Theorem.

L.A. $= 5 \times 10 + 3 \times 10 + 4 \times 10$
$= 120$ square units

S.A. $= 120 + 2\left(\dfrac{1}{2} \times 3 \times 4\right)$
$= 132$ square units

3 Find the lateral and surface area of the right rectangular prism below.

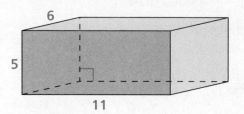

■ **SOLUTION**

Consider the top and the bottom as the bases of the prism.

L.A. $= 2(5 \times 11) + 2(6 \times 5)$
$= 170$ square units

S.A. $= 170 + 2(6 \times 11)$
$= 302$ square units

253

A **pyramid** is a polyhedron with one base that is a polygon, a point outside the plane of the base called the **vertex**, and lateral faces that are triangles connecting the vertex to each side of the base. The **height** h of a pyramid is the length of the perpendicular segment drawn from the vertex to the plane containing the base. Like a prism, a pyramid can be classified by the shape of its base.

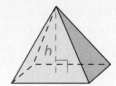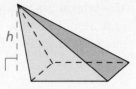

rectangular pyramids

A pyramid is a **regular pyramid** if its base is bounded by a regular polygon and the segment joining the center of this polygon to the vertex is perpendicular to the plane of the base. Its lateral faces are congruent isosceles triangles. The height of one of these triangles is called the **slant height** ℓ of the pyramid.

regular square pyramid regular pentagonal pyramid

The **lateral area** of a pyramid is the sum of the areas of its lateral faces. The surface area of a pyramid is the sum of the area of the base and the lateral area.

Area Formulas for a Regular Pyramid

If the base of a regular pyramid has n sides each having length s and slant height ℓ, then the lateral area L.A. is given by this formula.

$$\text{L.A.} = n\left[\frac{1}{2}s\ell\right] = \frac{1}{2}ns\ell$$

The surface area S.A. is given by the following formula.

$\text{S.A.} = \text{L.A.} + B = \frac{1}{2}ns\ell + B$, where B is the area of the base

MP

EXAMPLE 4 **Finding areas of a regular pyramid given height and slant height**

4 Find the lateral and surface area of a regular square pyramid with a height of 4 in. and a slant height of 5 in.

 ■ **SOLUTION**

 Step 1 To find lateral area and surface area, you need to find the length of a side of the square base. The length of a side of the base is $2x$, where x represents the length shown in the second sketch at the right.

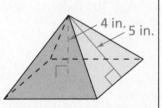

$$4^2 + x^2 = 5^2 \leftarrow \textbf{Use the Pythagorean Theorem.}$$
$$x = 3$$

   The length of a side of the base is 2(3) in., or 6 in.

 Step 2 Apply the formulas for lateral area and surface area.

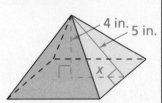

$$\text{L.A.} = 4\left[\frac{1}{2}(6 \times 5)\right] = 60 \rightarrow 60\text{ in.}^2$$
$$\text{S.A.} = 60 + 6^2 = 96 \rightarrow 96\text{ in.}^2$$

254

You may need to find the slant height of a pyramid before finding the areas.

EXAMPLE 5 **Finding areas of a regular pyramid given height and length of one side of the base**

5 Find the lateral and surface area of a regular square pyramid with a height of 6 in. and base with side length 8 in.

■ **SOLUTION**

Step 1 To find lateral area and surface area, you need to find the slant height of the pyramid. This is represented by y in the second sketch at the right.

$$4^2 + 6^2 = y^2 \leftarrow \text{Use the Pythagorean Theorem.}$$
$$y = \sqrt{52} = 2\sqrt{13}$$

The slant height is $2\sqrt{13}$ in.

Step 2 Apply the formulas for lateral area and surface area.

$$\text{L.A.} = 4\left[\frac{1}{2}(8 \times 2\sqrt{13})\right] = 32\sqrt{13} \rightarrow 32\sqrt{13} \text{ in.}^2, \text{ or about } 115.38 \text{ in.}^2$$

$$\text{S.A.} = 32\sqrt{13} + 8^2 = 64 + 32\sqrt{13} \rightarrow (64 + 32\sqrt{13}) \text{ in.}^2, \text{ or about } 179.38 \text{ in.}^2$$

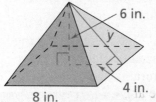

Practice

Choose the numeral preceding the word or expression that best completes the statement or answers the question.

1 What is the surface area of a rectangular prism with length 20 m, width 6 m, and height 7 m?

(1) 604 m^2 **(3)** 564 m^2

(2) 456 m^2 **(4)** 744 m^2

2 Which is the lateral area of a regular square pyramid with base length 6 units and height 4 units?

(1) 12 units^2 **(3)** 84 units^2

(2) 60 units^2 **(4)** 96 units^2

In Exercises 3–4, find the surface area of each right prism. Round answers to the nearest tenth if necessary.

3
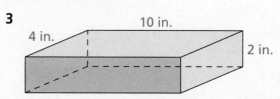

4
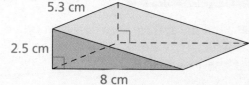

In Exercises 5–7, solve the problem. Clearly show all necessary work.

5 Find the lateral area of a regular pyramid whose base is a square, whose slant height is 5 m, and whose height is 3 m.

6 Find the lateral and surface area of the right rectangular prism whose length is 7.0 cm, width is 5.0 cm, and height is 1.5 cm.

7 Find the lateral and surface area of the regular square pyramid. Give exact answers.

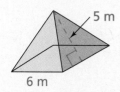

A **cylinder** is a three-dimensional figure with two parallel **bases** that are congruent circles and a curved **lateral surface** that connects the circles. The **height** h of a cylinder is the length of any perpendicular segment drawn from a point on one base to the plane containing the other base. A cylinder is a **right cylinder** if the segment joining the centers of the bases is perpendicular to the planes of the bases. Otherwise, the cylinder is *oblique*.

right cylinder   oblique cylinder

To derive area formulas for a right cylinder, imagine its net as shown at the right. Notice that the length of the lateral surface is equal to the circumference of a base.

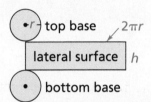

Area Formulas for Cylinders

If a right cylinder has a height h and base with radius r, then the lateral area L.A. is given by this formula.

$$\text{L.A.} = 2\pi rh$$

The surface area S.A. is given by the following formula.

$$\text{S.A.} = \text{L.A.} + 2\pi r^2$$

Note

A cylinder can be generated by rotating a rectangle about one of its sides.

EXAMPLES 1 and 2   **Finding the surface area of a right cylinder**

1. Find the surface area of a right cylinder with a radius of 4.5 ft and height 5 ft. Use $\pi = 3.14$.

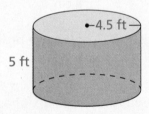

■ SOLUTION

$$\text{S.A.} = 2\pi(4.5)(5) + 2\pi(4.5)^2$$
$$= 85.5\pi$$
$$\approx 268.47$$

The surface area is **268.47 ft²**.

2. Find the surface area of a right cylinder with a diameter of 11 m and height 6 m. Use $\pi = 3.14$.

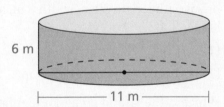

■ SOLUTION

$$\text{S.A.} = 2\pi(5.5)(6) + 2\pi(5.5)^2 \leftarrow r = \frac{11}{2}$$
$$= 126.5\pi$$
$$\approx 397.21$$

The surface area is **397.21 m²**.

You can also use the formulas to solve problems that involve lateral and surface areas of a cylinder.

EXAMPLE 3   **Finding the lateral and surface area of a cylinder**

3 The can shown at the right is shaped like a right cylinder with no top base. It has a radius of 5 inches and a height of 7 inches. Estimate the lateral and total surface area of the outside of the can.

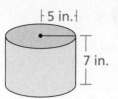

■ **SOLUTION**

Step 1 Estimate the lateral area of the can.

$$7(2 \times \pi \times 5) \approx 7(30) \approx 210$$

Step 2 Estimate the surface area of the can. Add the area of the bottom of the can.

$$210 + \pi \times 5^2 = 210 + 75$$
$$= 285$$

The lateral area ≈ 210 in.^{2} and the surface area ≈ 285 in.^{2}

Many solids can be generated by revolving a plane region about a line. If the rectangle in the accompanying figure is rotated about its right side, a cylinder will result.

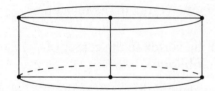
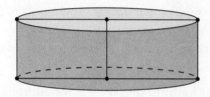

A popular use of generating three dimensional objects from two dimensional figures occurs in the creation of tissue paper decorations. These two-dimensional objects are opened by rotating on an axis, and the three-dimensional figure results. Examples are shown in the accompanying figures.

The two-dimensional shapes when unfolded form varied three-dimensional objects.

You can compare the properties of two different cylinders by evaluating their respective areas.

EXAMPLE 4   **Comparing lateral areas**

4   If the radius and height of a cylinder are doubled, then its lateral area

   (1)   stays the same.

   (2)   doubles.

   (3)   triples.

   (4)   quadruples.

  ■ **SOLUTION**

The lateral area of a cylinder is $2\pi rl$.

$$\text{L.A.} = 2\pi rh$$

If you double the radius and height of the cylinder, you get

$$\text{L.A.} = 2\pi(2r)(2h)$$
$$= 8\pi rh$$

Notice that the lateral area is increased by a factor of 4. The lateral area is quadrupled, so the correct answer is **(4)**.

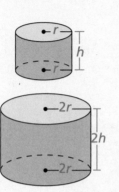

A **cone** is a 3-dimensional figure with a circle as its base and a point outside the plane of the base called the **vertex**. The **lateral surface** is the curved surface that connects the vertex to each point on the boundary of the base. The **height** h of the cone is the perpendicular segment drawn from the vertex to the plane that contains the base of the cone.

A **right cone** is a cone whose height goes from the vertex to the center of the base. If a cone is not a right cone, it is called **oblique**.

The **slant height** l of a cone is the shortest line segment drawn from the vertex of the cone to any point on the circumference of the base.

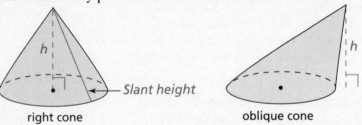

right cone   oblique cone

One way a cone can be generated is by rotating a right triangle in the plane around one of its legs. In the accompanying figure, a right triangle is shown in the coordinate plane. This particular triangle is formed by the regions bounded by the function $f(x) = x$, the line $x = 5$, and the x-axis. If the triangle is rotated about the x-axis, a cone is generated.

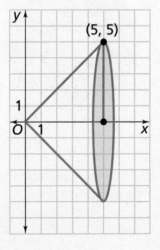

Notice that as the point whose coordinates are $(5, 5)$ rotates about the x-axis it traces a circle. Therefore the base of this cone is a circle. The radius of the base would be 5, the height of this cone is 5 and the slant height would be the length of the hypotenuse of the right triangle, $5\sqrt{2}$.

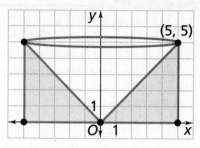

EXAMPLE 5 **Determining the solid generated when a plane figure is rotated**

5 If the triangle shown above is rotated about the y-axis, describe the solid that would be generated.

■ **SOLUTION**

When rotated about the y-axis the triangle would generate a cylinder with a hollow cone shape removed.

Lateral Area and Surface Area of a Right Cone

The lateral area L.A. of a right cone is half the product of the slant height (l) and the circumference of the base.

$$\text{L.A.} = \frac{1}{2}(2\pi r)l$$
$$= \pi r l$$

The surface area S.A. is therefore L.A. $+ B$ where $B = \pi r^2$.
$$\text{S.A.} = \pi r l + \pi r^2$$
$$= \pi r(l + r)$$

EXAMPLE 6 **Finding lateral area and surface area of right cones**

6 Find the lateral and surface area of the cone to the right. (Answer may be left in terms of π.)

■ **SOLUTION**

Notice that the radius of the base, the height, and the slant height are a Pythagorean triple. Therefore, the slant height $l = 5$.

$$\text{L.A.} = \pi r l$$
$$= \pi(4)(5)$$
$$= 20\,\pi \text{ sq. units}$$
$$\text{S.A.} = \pi r l + \pi r^2$$
$$= (4)(5)\,\pi + 4^2\,\pi$$
$$= 20\,\pi + 16\,\pi$$
$$= 36\,\pi \text{ sq. units}$$

Note

Solutions will vary with the approximation of π being used. Solutions shown will be based on using the π key on a calculator.

Choose the numeral preceding the word or expression that best completes the statement or answers the question.

1 Find the lateral area of the cylinder below.

(1) 4π sq. in.　　**(3)** 8π sq. in.

(2) 6π sq. in.　　**(4)** 16π sq. in.

2 A cone-shaped funnel has a height of 8 cm and a rim with a diameter of 12 cm. What is the lateral area of the funnel?

(1) 48π cm^2　　**(3)** 96π cm^2

(2) 60π cm^2　　**(4)** 120π cm^2

3 What is the lateral area of a cylinder with a height of 20 m and a radius of 7 m?

(1) 14π m^2　　**(3)** 280π m^2

(2) 140π m^2　　**(4)** 308π m^2

4 If the radius of a cylinder is doubled and the height remains constant, the lateral area is

(1) quadrupled.

(2) squared.

(3) doubled.

(4) tripled.

In Exercises 5–6, find the surface area of each right cylinder. Round your answer to the nearest tenth.

5

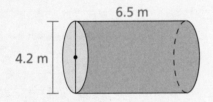

6

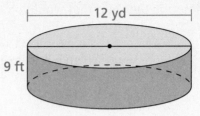

7 Find the lateral area of the cone below to the nearest tenth.

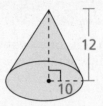

In Exercises 8–9, find the lateral or surface area as specified. Give exact answers.

8 the lateral area of a right cylinder with equal radius and height of 10 in.

9 the surface area of a right cylinder with radius 2.8 cm and height 6 cm.

10 One paint roller has length 11 in. and diameter 2 in. A second roller has length 7 in. and diameter 3 in. Which roller can spread more paint in one revolution?

11 One gallon of paint covers 250 ft^2. How many gallons of paint are needed to paint the top and lateral face of a right cylinder with radius 4.4 ft and height 9 ft? Give your answer to the nearest quarter of a gallon.

12 How does the lateral area of a cone with radius 6 and slant height of 12 compare to the lateral area of a cylinder with a height of 12 and a radius of 6?

13 A right cone has a base with radius of 6 cm and height of 8 cm. What are the dimensions of a cylinder that has the same surface area?

14 A right triangle with height of 5 cm and base of 3 cm is rotated about its height. What is the lateral area of the resulting figure, to the nearest square cm?

9.5 Volume of Selected Geometric Figures

G.MG.1
G.GMD.1
G.GMD.3

Consider the formula for the area of a rectangle, $A = lw$, and try to visualize the rectangle as the base of a 3-dimensional rectangle, with identical rectangles stacked on top to give it its *height*. This is known as a rectangular prism. It is easy to deduce that since the area of a rectangle is lw, the volume of a rectangular prism is $V = lwh$.

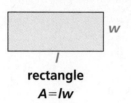

rectangle
$A = lw$

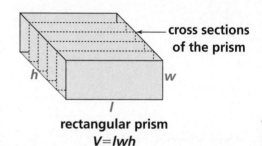

cross sections of the prism

rectangular prism
$V = lwh$

The **volume** of a three-dimensional figure is the amount of space it encloses.

Volume of a Prism

The volume V of a prism is the product of the area B of a base and the height h of the prism.

$$V = Bh$$

In the special case of a right rectangular prism with length l, width w, and height h, you can show that a formula for volume V is $V = (lw)h$, or simply $V = lwh$.

A **cube** is a prism whose faces are six congruent squares, hence the edges of a cube are all congruent to each other. For a cube with edges of length e, you can further refine the formula for volume as $V = (e^2)e$, or $V = e^3$.

> **Note**
>
> Area is two-dimensional and is measured in square units. Since volume involves all three dimensions, it is measured in cubic units.

> **Note**
>
> A **prism** is a polyhedron with two congruent and parallel faces, called *bases*. The lateral faces of a prism are parallelograms.

EXAMPLES 1 and 2   Finding the volume of a prism

1 Find the volume of the right triangular prism below.

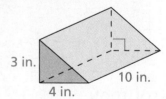

3 in.
4 in.
10 in.

■ **SOLUTION**

$V = (\frac{1}{2} \times 4 \times 3) \times 10 = 60 \leftarrow V = Bh$

The volume is **60 in.³**.

2 Find the volume of the right rectangular prism below.

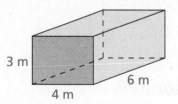

3 m
4 m
6 m

■ **SOLUTION**

$V = 3 \times 4 \times 6 = 72 \leftarrow V = lwh$

The volume is **72 m³**.

261

You can calculate the volume of prisms by multiplying the area of a base by the height. That is, $V = Bh$. If 2 or more prisms have bases of equal area and equal heights, then their volumes will be equal.

EXAMPLE 3   **Comparing volumes of prisms**

3 Find the volume of the prisms below.

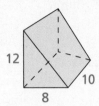

triangular prism

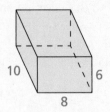

rectangular prism

■ **SOLUTION**

$$V_{triangular\ prism} = (\frac{1}{2} \times 12 \times 8)(10) \leftarrow V = Bh$$
$$= 480\ cu.\ units$$

■ **SOLUTION**

$$V_{rectangular\ prism} = (8 \times 6)(10) \leftarrow V = Bh$$
$$= 480\ cu.\ units$$

The volume of a cylinder is calculated by multiplying the area of the base of the cylinder by the height of the cylinder. The formula for the volume of a cylinder is similar to the formula for the volume of a prism.

Volume of a Cylinder   (MP)

The volume V of a cylinder with base of radius r is the product of the area B of a base and the height h of the cylinder.
$$V = Bh, \text{ or } V = \pi r^2 h$$

You can find the volume of a cylinder by using its radius or diameter.

EXAMPLES 4 and 5   **Finding the volume of a cylinder**

Find the volume of each cylinder. Round your answer to the nearest tenth.

4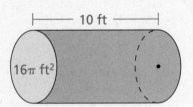

5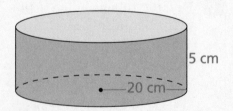

■ **SOLUTION**

$$V = (16\pi)(10) \leftarrow V = Bh$$
$$= 160\pi$$
$$\approx 502.74$$

The volume is $502.74\ ft^3$.

■ **SOLUTION**

$$V = \pi(20)^2(5) \leftarrow V = \pi r^2 h$$
$$= 2000\pi$$
$$\approx 6283.2$$

The volume is $6283.2\ cm^3$.

If you compare a cone to a cylinder with the same base and height, you find that the cylinder is exactly three times the volume of the cone, or the cone is $\frac{1}{3}$ the volume of the cylinder.

right cone

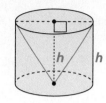

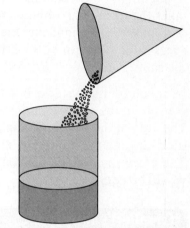

This formula can be verified by using a cone with a base and height equal to the base and height of a cylinder. Fill the cone with water and pour it into the cylinder. How many cones of water are required to fill the cylinder? Three.

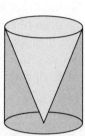

Volume of a Cone

The volume V of a right cone with radius of the base r and height h is given by $V = \frac{1}{3}\pi r^2 h$.

EXAMPLE 6 — **Finding the volume of a right cone given radius of the base and slant height**

6 Find the volume of a right cone whose base has radius 6 cm and whose slant height is 10 cm. Round your answer to the nearest hundredth.

■ SOLUTION

To find the volume of a right cone, find its height h.

$$h^2 + 6^2 = 10^2 \leftarrow h^2 + r^2 = \ell^2$$
$$h = 8$$

Apply the formula for volume.

$$V = \frac{1}{3}\pi(6)^2(8) = 96\pi = 301.59$$

The volume is $301.59\ cm^3$.

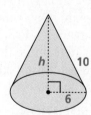

Cavalieri's Principle

What if the volume of an oblique prism, cylinder, or cone is to be determined? For example, imagine a prism formed by a stack of 8.5 in. by 11 in. paper that is 6 in. high. Each slice of this prism is a congruent piece of paper. The stack can now be shifted until it takes the form of an oblique prism. The area of the base, the height, and the number of slices is the same for both of these prisms. Therefore their volumes should be the same, namely $V = Bh$, with B = the area of the base.

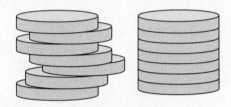

Now consider two stacks of coins. What would be true about the volume of these two stacks of coins? The area of the base and heights of each stack are the same and the number of slices is the same. Therefore, once again, the volume of each stack would be equal.

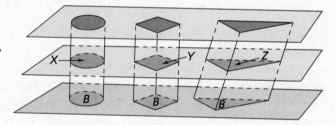

Cavalieri's Principle

If two space figures have the same height and the same cross-sectional area at every level, then they have the same volume.

In the accompanying figure, the three planes are parallel and the areas of each base (B) are equal. Since the cross sections are translations of the base, each also has an area of B. Therefore the volumes of these three solids are equal.

EXAMPLE 7   Using Cavalieri's Principle

7 The objects shown in the accompanying figure have the same height. Determine whether Cavalieri's Principle applies, and, if so, determine the height of each object if the volume of the rectangular prism is 54 cm².

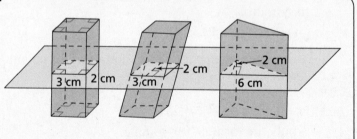

■ SOLUTION

The areas of the three bases are all equal to 6 cm². Since the prisms have the same height, their volumes must be the same by Cavalieri's Principle.

$V = Bh$
$54 = 6h$
$9 = h$

The height of each prism is 9 cm.

264

Volume of a Pyramid

The volume of a pyramid is $\frac{1}{3}$ the volume of a prism with the same base and height. Therefore, $V_{\text{pyramid}} = \frac{1}{3}Bh$, where B is the area of the base.

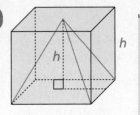

Note

This formula can be verified in a similar way to the formula for volume of a cone shown previously.

If you examine the two right rectangular prisms below, you will see that the length, width, and height of figure B are all 1.5 times the corresponding dimensions of figure A. That is, the prisms are similar, with similarity ratio 1.5.

If you compare the volumes of the two figures, you will see a special relationship between them.

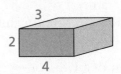

Figure A

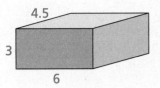

Figure B

Volume of Figure $A = 2 \times 3 \times 4 = 24$ cubic units

Volume of Figure $B = 2(1.5) \times 3(1.5) \times 4(1.5)$
$= 24 \times 1.5^3$ cubic units

Similarity and Volume

If figure B is similar to figure A, and the linear dimensions of figure B are s times the linear dimensions of figure A, then:

volume of figure $B = s^3 \times$ volume of figure A

Practice

Choose the numeral preceding the word or expression that best completes the statement or answers the question.

1 If the volume of a triangular prism is 256 in.³ and its height is 8 in., what is the area of the base of a rectangular prism of equal volume and height?

(1) 32 in.²   (3) 64 in.²

(2) 32 in.³   (4) 64 in.³

2 Find the volume of the figure at the right.

(1) $\dfrac{640\pi}{3}$ cm³

(2) 1920π cm³

(3) $\dfrac{6400\pi}{3}$ cm³

(4) 2560π cm³

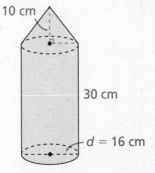

3 What is the volume of the figure at the right?

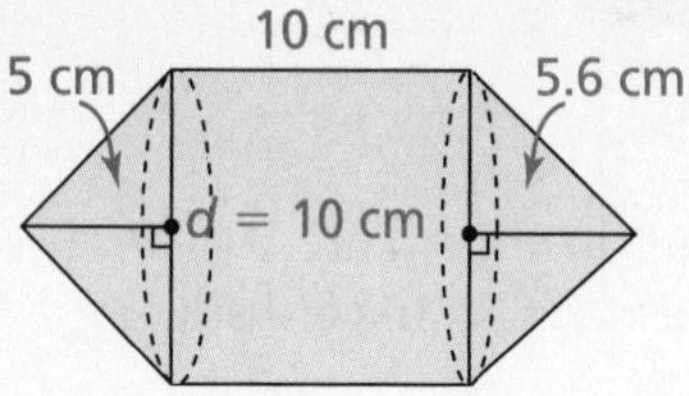

10 cm
5 cm
5.6 cm
d = 10 cm

(1) 1062.3 cm^3

(2) 979.2 cm^3

(3) 538.9 cm^3

(4) 1931.2 cm^3

4 The volume of a right rectangular prism is 20 in.^{3} The linear dimensions of a larger prism are 2 times those of the original prism. Which is the volume of the larger prism?

(1) 40 in.^{3}

(2) 80 in.^{3}

(3) 160 in.^{3}

(4) 8000 in.^{3}

In Exercises 5–7, solve the problem. Clearly show all necessary work.

5 A small can of soup is shaped like a right cylinder with diameter 7 cm and height 12 cm. A family-size can of the soup has diameter 10 cm and height 15 cm. Which contains more soup, two small cans or one family-size can?

6 What is the volume of a right rectangular prism with length 12 ft, width 15 ft, and height 3 ft?

7 Find the weight of the contents of a right rectangular prism with length 13 ft, width 6 ft, and height 2.5 ft if the contents weigh 0.02 pound per cubic inch.

8 A log can be approximated by a cylinder. If 1 ft^3 = 12 board feet, determine the number of board feet (to the nearest board foot) in a log 30 feet long with a diameter of 18 in.

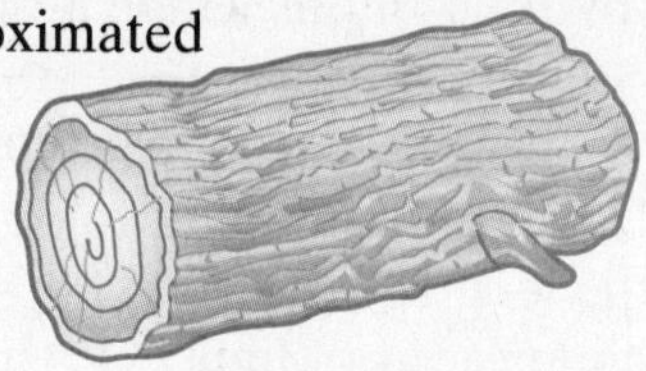

9 What is the maximum amount of waste that can be held in a sewer pipe 200 feet long with a base diameter of 2 feet? Round your answer to the nearest tenth and label it appropriately.

10 The diameter of a US minted quarter is 0.955 inch and its thickness is 0.069 inch. What is the volume of the stack of 8 coins shown in the accompanying figure?

11 The volume of an oblique prism or cylinder is the same as the volume of a prism or cylinder with the same _____ and the same _____.

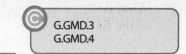

G.GMD.3
G.GMD.4

If you rotated a circle around its center, you would produce a sphere. A **sphere** is the set of all points in 3-dimensional space that are a fixed distance r, the **radius,** from a given point, O, the **center.**

If a plane intersects a sphere at only one point, the plane is **tangent** to the sphere. A tangent plane is perpendicular to the radius of the sphere at the point of intersection.

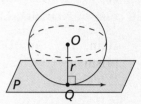

Plane P is tangent to the sphere at Q.

A plane that intersects a sphere at more than one point will intersect it at an infinite number of points; the intersection will form a circle.

If the plane intersects a sphere and passes through the center of the sphere, the intersection is called the **great circle.** The great circle is the largest circle that can be drawn in a sphere.

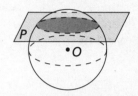

The circumference of a sphere is the circumference of any great circle of the sphere. A great circle divides a sphere into 2 **hemispheres.**

In the figure below, plane X and plane Y are parallel planes that intersect a sphere at 2 circles. If plane X and plane Y are also equidistant from the center of the sphere, then their intersections with the sphere result in 2 congruent circles.

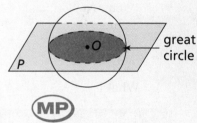

great circle

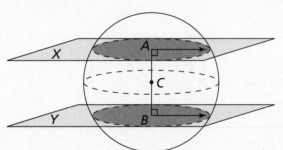

plane $X \parallel$ plane Y
$\overline{AC} \cong \overline{CB}$
circle $A \cong$ circle B

EXAMPLE 1   **Applying the properties of spheres**

1   If the circumference of a great circle of a sphere is 350 cm, find its radius to the nearest tenth.

■ SOLUTION

$C = 2\pi r$

$350 = 2\pi r \leftarrow$ Substitute $C = 350$

$\dfrac{350}{2\pi} = r$

$r = 55.7\ cm$

You can use the formula on the next page to find the volume of a sphere. You can find the volume of a sphere if you are given indirect information about the radius, such as the diameter or the circumference of the sphere.

Volume of a Sphere

The volume V of a sphere with radius r is given by $V = \frac{4}{3}\pi r^3$.

Advanced mathematics is needed to derive the formula for volume of a sphere. However, long before calculus was developed Archimedes developed a formula for volume of a sphere based upon his proof that the volume of a sphere of radius r is equal to the difference in the volume of a cylinder and cone with circular base with a radius of r and a height of $2r$. That is:

sphere $=$ cylinder $-$ cone

Using $h = 2r$, this results in the following:
$$V_{sphere} = \pi r^2(2r) - \frac{1}{3}\pi r^2(2r)$$
$$V_{sphere} = 2\pi r^3 - \frac{2}{3}\pi r^3$$
$$V_{sphere} = \frac{6}{3}\pi r^3 - \frac{2}{3}\pi r^3$$
$$V_{sphere} = \frac{4}{3}\pi r^3$$

EXAMPLES 2 through 4   Finding the volume of a sphere

2 Find the volume of a sphere with a radius of 12 ft. Round your answer to the nearest hundredth.

■ SOLUTION
$$V = \frac{4}{3}\pi r^3 \rightarrow \frac{4}{3}\pi(12)^3 = 2304\pi \approx 7238.23$$
The volume is $7238.23\,\text{ft}^3$.

3 Find the volume of a sphere with a diameter of 15 cm. Round your answer to the nearest hundredth.

■ SOLUTION
The diameter is twice the radius, therefore $r = \frac{15}{2} = 7.5$.
$$V = \frac{4}{3}\pi r^3 \rightarrow \frac{4}{3}\pi(7.5)^3 = 562.5\pi \approx 1767.15\,\text{cm}^3$$

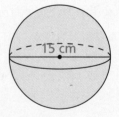

4 Find the volume of a sphere with a circumference of 6π m. Round your answer to the nearest hundredth.

■ SOLUTION
The circumference is $6\pi = 2\pi r$, therefore $r = \frac{6\pi}{2\pi} = 3$.
$$V = \frac{4}{3}\pi r^3 \rightarrow \frac{4}{3}\pi(3)^3 = 36\pi \approx 113.04\,\text{m}^3$$

You can calculate the surface area of a sphere using the following formula.

Surface Area of a Sphere

The surface area S.A. of a sphere with radius r is given by S.A. $= 4\pi r^2$.

Notice that the surface area of a sphere is 4 times the area of its great circle.

EXAMPLE 5 **Finding the surface area of a sphere**

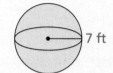

5 Find the surface area of a sphere with a radius of 7 ft. Round your answer to the nearest hundredth.

■ **SOLUTION**

$$\text{S.A.} = 4\pi r^2$$
$$= 4\pi(7^2) \quad \leftarrow \text{Substitute } r = 7$$
$$= 4\pi(49)$$
$$= 615.75 \, \text{ft}^2$$

The volume of a sphere is completely determined by its radius. Suppose that sphere *A* has radius *r* and sphere *B* has radius 2*r*. Then you can compare the volume V_B of sphere *B* to the volume V_A of sphere *A* as follows.

$$\frac{V_B}{V_A} = \frac{\frac{4}{3}\pi(2r)^3}{\frac{4}{3}\pi(r)^3} = \frac{(2r)^3}{r^3} = \frac{2^3 r^3}{r^3} = 2^3$$

So, if the radius is doubled, then the volume is multiplied by 2^3.

Similarity and Volume of a Sphere

If two spheres have radii of r_1 and r_2, then the ratio of their volumes is $\left(\dfrac{r_1}{r_2}\right)^3$.

Practice

Choose the numeral preceding the word or expression that best completes the statement or answers the question.

1 At how many points will a plane 5 units from the center of a sphere with radius 5 intersect the sphere?

(1) 0   **(3)** 2

(2) 1   **(4)** 3

2 If the intersection of 2 parallel planes with a sphere results in 2 congruent circles, then

(1) one plane is tangent to the sphere.

(2) both planes are tangent to the sphere.

(3) both planes contain the center of the sphere.

(4) the planes are equidistant from the center of the sphere.

3 The surface area of a sphere can be found by finding the area of a great circle and multiplying it by

(1) 1.   **(3)** 3.

(2) 2.   **(4)** 4.

4 What is the surface area of a sphere with $r = 2$ m?

(1) 12.6 m^2

(2) 33.5 m^2

(3) 50.2 m^2

(4) 100.5 m^2

5 Find the volume of the sphere shown below.

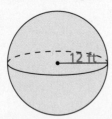

(1) 7238.23 ft^3 **(3)** 3619.11 ft^3

(2) 2412.74 ft^3 **(4)** 1809.56 ft^3

6 Which has the same volume as a sphere with radius 6?

(1) a cylinder with radius 4 and height 16

(2) a cone with radius 6 and height 24

(3) a cube whose edges are 6

(4) a pyramid with base area 36 units^2 and height 6

In Exercises 7–8, find the exact surface area and volume of each sphere.

7 a sphere whose diameter is 10 in.

8 a sphere with a circumference of 144π cm

In Exercises 9–12, solve the following problems. Clearly show all necessary work.

9 Find the volume of the sphere shown here. The circle contains the center of the sphere and its radius is the same as the radius of the sphere. Give an exact answer and an answer rounded to the nearest tenth.

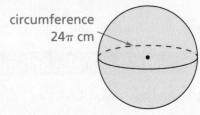

circumference
24π cm

10 The sphere in the diagram below is tangent to the bases and lateral side of the cylinder. Find the volume of the space inside the cylinder but outside the sphere.

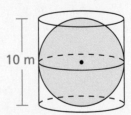

10 m

11 A sphere has a volume of 85.3π cm^3. What is the volume of a sphere with a radius that is 3 times longer?

12 The volume of a sphere is 8π ft^3. What is the radius of the sphere?

In the figure below, plane *X* intersects the sphere at circle *P*. Use this information to answer Exercises 13–15.

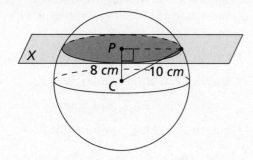

13 What is the circumference of the circle formed by the intersection of plane *X* with the sphere?

14 What is the circumference of the great circle of the sphere?

15 Plane *Y* is parallel to and distinct from plane *X*. The area of the circle formed by the intersection of plane *Y* with the sphere is 36π cm^2. How far is plane *Y* from plane *X*?

16 A great circle of a sphere has an area of 25π in.^{2} What is the surface area of the sphere?

17 Find the area of the great circle of a sphere that has a volume of 36π cm^3.

18 A great circle of a sphere has a circumference of 18π. The circle formed by the intersection of a plane and the sphere has $\frac{1}{3}$ the circumference of the great circle. How far is this plane from the center of the sphere?

19 Lisa has a hoop whose inner diameter is 9 inches. What is the volume of the largest ball that can fit through her hoop?

20 The volume of a spherical balloon is 36π ft^3. If the balloon expands so that the radius is doubled, what is the change in the balloon's surface area?

Answer all the questions in this part. For each question, select the numeral preceding the word or expression that best completes the statement or answers the question.

1 If the radius and height of a cylinder are doubled then its lateral area

(1) stays the same.   (3) triples.

(2) doubles.   (4) quadruples.

2 Find the number of 3 ft × 2 ft × 1 ft boxes that can be packed in the prism below.

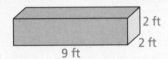
9 ft, 2 ft, 2 ft

(1) 6   (3) 2

(2) 3   (4) 4

3 The volume of a right cylinder is 245 cm³. If the radius of the cylinder is 5.5 cm, find its height to the nearest tenth.

(1) 2.1 cm   (3) 2.4 cm

(2) 2.6 cm   (4) 3.6 cm

4 If a plane intersects 2 parallel planes, the intersection is

(1) a line.

(2) a plane.

(3) 3 points.

(4) 2 parallel lines.

5 Find the surface area of the cone below.

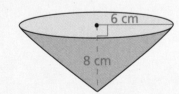
6 cm, 8 cm

(1) 96π cm³   (3) 60π cm³

(2) 72π cm³   (4) 36π cm³

6 Which could be the dimensions of a right rectangular prism that has the same volume as a right rectangular prism with volume 132 cubic units?

(1) length 11, width 2, and height 5

(2) length 12, width 6, and height 2

(3) length 11, width 2, and height 6

(4) length 11, width 2, and height 12

7 Find the volume of the cylinder to the nearest tenth.

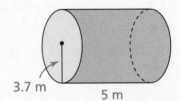
3.7 m, 5 m

(1) 54.95 m³   (3) 192.3 m³

(2) 61.3 m³   (4) 215.0 m³

8 Find the weight of the contents of a right rectangular prism with length 15 ft, width 3 ft, and height 3.5 ft if the contents weigh 0.25 pound per cubic ft.

(1) 39.375 pounds

(2) 630 pounds

(3) 33.75 pounds

(4) 540 pounds

9 The cone-shaped paper cup has a height 9 cm and a rim with circumference 12π cm. What is the approximate volume of the cup?

9 cm

(1) 169.56 cm³   (3) 508.68 cm³

(2) 339.29 cm³   (4) 1017.36 cm³

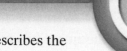

10 Two lines perpendicular to the same plane must be

(1) skew.

(2) coplanar.

(3) intersecting.

(4) perpendicular.

11 A rectangular fish tank has dimensions 2.5 ft × 2 ft × 1.5 ft. It is packed in a 3 ft × 4 ft × 3 ft box. How much filler is needed to securely package the aquarium for shipping?

(1) 2.5 ft³ **(3)** 42 ft³

(2) 4 ft³ **(4)** 28.5 ft³

12 A can has a diameter of 3 inches and a height of 4.5 inches. Approximately how much paper will it take to create the label for the can?

(1) 84.78 in.²

(2) 42.41 in.²

(3) 31.79 in.²

(4) 127.17 in.²

13 The length of each side of the square base of the Pyramid of Cheops originally measured 482 ft and its slant height was 611 ft. Find the lateral area of the pyramid when it was built.

(1) 926,100 ft²

(2) 923,832 ft²

(3) 927,315 ft²

(4) 730,296 ft²

14 If the lateral area of a right cylinder with a 1 ft radius is 9π ft², what is its height?

(1) 6 ft

(2) 2.9 ft

(3) 4.5 ft

(4) 0.9 ft

15 Which best describes the prism below?

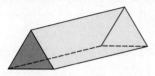

(1) triangular prism

(2) rectangular prism

(3) triangular pyramid

(4) rectangular pyramid

16 A net for a cylinder represents the two bases and the lateral face. What is the shape of the face?

(1) circle

(2) square

(3) rectangle

(4) triangle

17 A right triangular prism has how many lateral faces?

(1) 1 **(3)** 3

(2) 2 **(4)** 4

18 Which solid is constructed from the net below?

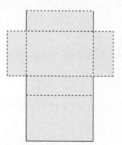

(1) rectangular prism

(2) triangular prism

(3) cylinder

(4) square pyramid

Answer all the questions in this part. Clearly indicate the necessary steps, including appropriate formula substitutions, diagrams, graphs, charts, etc. For all questions in this part, a correct numerical answer with no work shown will receive only one credit.

19 Find the volume of the entire figure below.

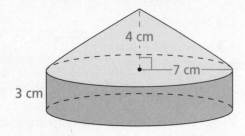

20 A rubber ball has a circumference of 22 in.

Find the radius of the rubber ball.

Find the surface area of the rubber ball.

Find the volume of the rubber ball.

Round your answers to the nearest tenth.

What are the dimensions of the cylinder that will hold exactly 3 rubber balls stacked on top of each other like a tennis ball can?

21 A cylindrical water tank has a diameter of 8 ft and stands 5.5 ft high.

Find the lateral area of the water tank. (Round your answer to the nearest tenth.)

If a company charges $11 per square foot of surface area to install the water tank, how much will the installation cost?

If the pool is to be filled only to 75% of its maximum capacity, how much water can it hold?

10 Probability

The Study of Probability

The study of probability has been developed from the mid 1600's. The popularity of games of chance indicates that there has been an interest in computing the concepts of probability for a long time, while exact mathematical descriptions came about much later. Christiaan Huygens, a Dutch mathematician and scientist, is credited with publishing the first book on probability. The Italian mathematician, physician, and astrologer Gerolamo Cardano demonstrated the usefulness of defining odds as the ratio of favorable to unfavorable outcomes, which implies that the probability of an event is given by the ratio of favorable outcomes to the total number of possible outcomes.

10.1 Experimental and Theoretical Probability

Probability is a measure of the likelihood that an event will occur. You can represent a probability using a ratio or a percent. Some events will never occur, others will always occur, and the likelihood of many events is uncertain.

There are two types of probability: a priori, or theoretical probability, and experimental probability.

The probability of flipping heads with a fair coin as the ratio 1 out of 2, or $\frac{1}{2}$. This is called the **a priori,** or **theoretical probability,** of flipping heads.

Theoretical probability is a calculation of the ratio of the number of favorable outcomes to the total number of outcomes. You can express probability as a fraction, percent, or decimal.

Experimental probability is determined by collecting data from an *experiment*. The sum of the probabilities of all of the events of an experiment is always equal to 1. Suppose you flip a coin and record the occurrence of heads.

Number of flips	10	10	10	10	10
Number of heads	4	5	5	6	5
ratio	4 of 10	5 of 10	5 of 10	6 of 10	5 of 10

In each experiment, heads occurs about 5 times in every 10 flips. You can say that the experimental or **empirical probability** of heads occurring is about 1 out of 2 for this coin.

Theoretical Probability of an Event

If an event E contains m favorable outcomes in a sample space containing n outcomes, the **theoretical probability** of E, denoted $P(E)$, is found as follows.

$$P(E) = \frac{\text{number } m \text{ of favorable outcomes}}{\text{total number } n \text{ of outcomes}} = \frac{m}{n}$$

Note

"At random" means that the selection is made without any preference or bias for one outcome over another.

EXAMPLE 1   **Calculating theoretical probabilities**

 In a local district, there are 1300 Democratic, 1100 Republican, and 400 Independent registered voters. If a voter is to be selected at random, what is the probability, to the nearest whole percent, that the voter selected is Republican?

■ SOLUTION

Calculate the total number of voters in the district. $1300 + 1100 + 400 = 2800$

$$P(\text{Republican}) = \frac{\text{number of Republicans}}{\text{total number of registered voters}} = \frac{1100}{2800} \approx 0.39$$

The probability of selecting a Republican is about 39%.

Sample space is the set of all possible outcomes in a given situation. An **event** is any set of outcomes in the sample space. You can use a two-way table or a tree diagram to identify a sample space.

EXAMPLE 2   Using a table or tree diagram to identify a sample space

2 What is the sample space when two coins are flipped consecutively?

■ **SOLUTION**

Determine all of the possible outcomes of flipping two coins consecutively.

coin 1 \ coin 2	H	T
H	H H	H T
T	T H	T T

coin 1	coin 2	outcome
H	H	H and H
	T	H and T
T	H	T and H
	T	T and T

The sample space is HH, HT, TH, TT.

Note
There are four outcomes. H and T is different from T and H.

The table below shows all possible ordered pairs (cube X, cube Y) in the sample space for rolling two number cubes. Notice that there are 36 outcomes in all.

MP

cube X/cube Y	1	2	3	4	5	6
1	(1, 1)	(1, 2)	(1, 3)	(1, 4)	(1, 5)	(1, 6)
2	(2, 1)	(2, 2)	(2, 3)	(2, 4)	(2, 5)	(2, 6)
3	(3, 1)	(3, 2)	(3, 3)	(3, 4)	(3, 5)	(3, 6)
4	(4, 1)	(4, 2)	(4, 3)	(4, 4)	(4, 5)	(4, 6)
5	(5, 1)	(5, 2)	(5, 3)	(5, 4)	(5, 5)	(5, 6)
6	(6, 1)	(6, 2)	(6, 3)	(6, 4)	(6, 5)	(6, 6)

If one cube shows 1, there are 6 possibilities for the second cube.

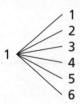

EXAMPLES 3 through 5   Using probability facts with ordered pairs

Find each of the following probabilities using the sample space for rolling a pair of number cubes. Write the probabilities as fractions in lowest terms.

3 P(sum equals 3)

■ **SOLUTION**

The only ordered pairs whose numbers total 3 are (1, 2) and (2, 1). There are two favorable outcomes.

P(sum equals 3)

$$= \frac{2}{36}, or \frac{1}{18}$$

4 P(same number on each)

■ **SOLUTION**

The six ordered pairs (1, 1), (2, 2), (3, 3), (4, 4), (5, 5), and (6, 6) are the only outcomes with identical numbers.

P(same number on each)

$$= \frac{6}{36}, or \frac{1}{6}$$

5 P(sum not equal to 12)

■ **SOLUTION**

There is exactly one ordered pair whose numbers total 12. It is (6, 6).

P(sum not equal to 12)
$$= 1 - P(\text{sum equal to 12})$$

$$= 1 - \frac{1}{36} = \frac{35}{36}$$

You can say the outcomes from rolling a single number cube are **equally likely.**

$$P(1) = \frac{1}{6} \quad P(2) = \frac{1}{6} \quad P(3) = \frac{1}{6} \quad P(4) = \frac{1}{6} \quad P(5) = \frac{1}{6} \quad P(6) = \frac{1}{6}$$

If you roll a pair of number cubes, the probability of rolling one sum is not necessarily equal to the probability of rolling another sum. You can say that the outcomes from rolling a pair of number cubes are *not equally likely.*

$$P(\text{sum } 2) = \frac{1}{36} \text{ but } P(\text{sum } 3) = \frac{2}{36}$$

The possible sums from rolling a pair of number cubes are 2, 3, 4, 5, 6, 7, 8, 9, 10, 11, and 12. If x represents these numbers, you can say that x is a **random variable** and assign to it the probability of each sum. A **probability distribution** represents the values of the variable and corresponding probabilities.

Note

Notice that not all probabilities are equal, but that the sum of the probabilities equals 1.

x	2	3	4	5	6	7	8	9	10	11	12
$P(x)$	$\frac{1}{36}$	$\frac{2}{36}$	$\frac{3}{36}$	$\frac{4}{36}$	$\frac{5}{36}$	$\frac{6}{36}$	$\frac{5}{36}$	$\frac{4}{36}$	$\frac{3}{36}$	$\frac{2}{36}$	$\frac{1}{36}$

EXAMPLE 6   **Making a probability distribution**

 A bag contains marbles identical in every way but color. The bag contains 1 red, 2 blue, 3 green, and 4 orange marbles. Make a probability distribution that represents the probabilities of choosing each color of marble from the bag. Write the probabilities as fractions and as decimals.

■ **SOLUTION**

Find the total number of outcomes. $1 + 2 + 3 + 4 = 10$
Make a table of ratios as shown.

color	red	blue	green	orange
probability	$\frac{1}{10} = 0.1$	$\frac{2}{10} = 0.2$	$\frac{3}{10} = 0.3$	$\frac{4}{10} = 0.4$

The **complement** of an event E is the set of outcomes in the sample space *not* in E. You can find the probability of the complement by subtracting the $P(E)$ from 1. For example, there is a 25% chance that a person's birth month is January, February, or March, so the probability of the complement, that the birth month is *not* in January, February, or March, is $1 - 0.25 = 0.75$ or 75%.

Characteristics of Probabilities

If E is impossible, $P(E) = 0$.	The number of favorable outcomes equals 0.
If E is certain, $P(E) = 1$.	The number of favorable outcomes equals the total number of outcomes.
Otherwise, $0 < P(E) < 1$.	The number of favorable outcomes is less than the total number of outcomes.
$P(\text{not } E) = 1 - P(E)$	The number of outcomes in the complement is the total number of outcomes minus the number of favorable outcomes.
$\sum P(E) = 1$	The sum of the probabilities of all of the events of a sample space is equal to 1.

Practice

Choose the numeral preceding the word or expression that best completes the statement or answers the question.

1 If the probability of an event is 0, then

(1) it is certain.

(2) it is impossible.

(3) it is probable but not certain.

(4) it is probable but not impossible.

2 Which completes this probability distribution?

B	4	2	6	8
P(B)	0.2	0.1	0.3	

(1) 0.2   **(2)** 0.05   **(3)** 0.4   **(4)** 0.6

3 The probability that the sun will set in the west is

(1) 0.   **(2)** 1.   **(3)** −1.   **(4)** $\frac{1}{2}$.

4 A box contains five cutouts of the same triangle differing only in color. If one cutout is drawn at random, what is the probability of choosing a specific color?

(1) $\frac{1}{5}$ **(2)** $\frac{5}{5}$ **(3)** $\frac{2}{5}$ **(4)** $\frac{3}{5}$

5 In a local district, there are 2,000 Democratic, 1,700 Republican, and 300 Independent voters registered. If a voter is to be selected at random, which is the probability that the voter selected is not an Independent?

(1) $1 - \frac{3}{40}$ **(3)** $\frac{17}{40}$

(2) $1 - \frac{37}{40}$ **(4)** $1 - \frac{17}{40}$

6 A bag contains 7 red, 6 green, and 7 white marbles, all identical but for color. The probability of randomly choosing a red marble is

(1) $\frac{7}{20}$.   **(2)** $\frac{13}{20}$.   **(3)** $\frac{3}{10}$ **(4)** $1 - \frac{7}{20}$.

In Exercises 7–10, solve the problem.

7 Which is more likely, an event with probability 0.36 or an event with probability 0.6?

8 In an algebra class, 5 students wear contact lenses, 4 students wear glasses, and 13 students wear neither contact lenses nor glasses. If a student is chosen at random, what is the probability that the student wears contact lenses?

9 A weather forecaster predicts that there is a 45% probability of snow today. What is the probability that it will not snow?

10 For the pair of spinners below, make a tree diagram showing all of the outcomes spinning the two spinners. Calculate the probability of having the pointer land on light gray in spinner 1 and on light blue in spinner 2.

spinner 1   spinner 2

In Exercises 11–14, refer to the table of outcomes for rolling a pair of number cubes. Find each probability as a fraction in lowest terms.

11 *P*(sum equals 8)   **12** *P*(numbers unequal)

13 *P*(sum equals 11)   **14** *P*(sum equals 13)

In Exercises 15–16, use the given data to make a probability distribution for the selection of one object or person at random.

15 A bag contains 8 blue slips of paper, 9 brown slips of paper, and 8 green slips of paper, all identical but for color. The values of a random variable are 1 for blue, 2 for brown, and 3 for green.

16 The science club consists of 13 first-year students, 12 second-year students, 13 third-year students, and 10 fourth-year students. The values of the random variable are 1, 2, 3, and 4 for the class year.

10.2 Using Probability Formulas

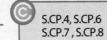
There are situations when two events cannot occur at the same time. For example, the following statements about integers cannot both be true at the same time.

An integer is even.   The same integer is odd.

You can say that these outcomes are *mutually exclusive*. Two events are **mutually exclusive** if there are no outcomes common to both events.

 EXAMPLE 1   **Identifying mutually exclusive events**

1 Which events are mutually exclusive?

   (1) selecting a baseball card showing a Yankee and also a pitcher
   (2) scoring above 80 on a test and scoring above 90 on the same test
   (3) rolling a prime number that is also an even number
   (4) rolling a multiple of 2 that is also a 17

   ■ **SOLUTION**

Seventeen is not a multiple of 2, so the outcomes in choice (4) are mutually exclusive. The correct choice is **(4)**.

To find the probability of two mutually exclusive events, you add the probabilities of each event. Consider the following problem.

What is the probability of drawing a 7 or a queen when drawing a card from a standard deck of playing cards? There are 52 possible outcomes; four of them are 7s and four of them are queens. Since there is no card that is both a 7 and a queen, these events are mutually exclusive. Therefore,

$$P(7 \text{ or } Q) = P(7) + P(Q) = \frac{4}{52} + \frac{4}{52} = \frac{8}{52} = \frac{2}{13}.$$

> **Note**
>
> A standard deck of 52 playing cards consists of 13 red hearts, 13 black clubs, 13 red diamonds, and 13 black spades. Each suit has an ace, a king, a queen, a jack, and the numbers 2 through 10.

Probability Involving Mutually Exclusive Events

If A and B are mutually exclusive events, then $P(A \text{ or } B) = P(A) + P(B)$.

 EXAMPLE 2   **Using the formula for the probability of mutually exclusive events**

2 Suppose you roll a pair of number cubes. Find the probability that the numbers showing are the same or that their sum is 11.

   ■ **SOLUTION**

The events are mutually exclusive since a sum of 11 cannot occur at the same time two number cubes are showing the same number.

Count the outcomes in which the numbers showing are equal.   *There are six.*
Count the outcomes in which the sum of the numbers showing is 11.   *There are two.*

$P(\text{numbers equal or sum is } 11) = P(\text{numbers equal}) + P(\text{sum is } 11)$

$$= \frac{6}{36} + \frac{2}{36} = \frac{8}{36}, or \frac{2}{9}$$

There are also situations when two events can occur at the same time. These events are not mutually exclusive. Consider the following problem.

What is the probability of drawing a red card or a card showing a queen from a standard deck of 52 playing cards?

The diagram at the right shows that these events are not mutually exclusive because there are two cards that show queen and are also red.

26 red cards	26 black cards
2 red queens	2 black queens

You can calculate the probability P(red card or queen) as follows.

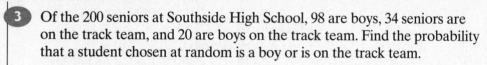

$$P(\text{red card or queen}) = \frac{26 + 2}{52} = \frac{28}{52} \qquad \frac{28}{52} = \overset{\substack{\text{number of}\\\text{red cards}}}{\frac{26}{52}} + \overset{\substack{\text{number of}\\\text{queens}}}{\frac{4}{52}} - \overset{\substack{\text{number of}\\\text{red queens}}}{\frac{2}{52}}$$

To determine the probability of events that are *not* mutually exclusive, you add the probabilities of each event and then subtract the probability of both occurring at the same time.

> **Note**
>
> If A and B are mutually *exclusive*, $P(A \text{ and } B) = 0$.

Probability of Events Involving Or

If A and B are events in a sample space,
$P(A \text{ or } B) = P(A) + P(B) - P(A \text{ and } B)$.

EXAMPLES 3 and 4   **Finding probability of events that are not mutually exclusive**

3 Of the 200 seniors at Southside High School, 98 are boys, 34 seniors are on the track team, and 20 are boys on the track team. Find the probability that a student chosen at random is a boy or is on the track team.

■ **SOLUTION**

Sketch a Venn diagram that shows the sets and relationships.

$P(\text{boy or track}) = P(\text{boy}) + P(\text{track}) - P(\text{boy and track})$

$$= \frac{98}{200} + \frac{34}{200} - \frac{20}{200}$$

$$= \frac{98 + 34 - 20}{200}$$

$$= \frac{112}{200}$$

$$= 0.56$$

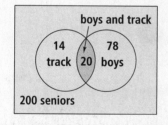

The probability that a student chosen is a boy or is on the track team is 0.56, or 56%.

4 What is the probability that either of two number cubes tossed simultaneously shows a 3?

(MP)

■ **SOLUTION**

$P(3 \text{ or } 3) = P(3) + P(3) - P(\text{both cubes show 3})$

$$= \frac{6}{36} + \frac{6}{36} - \frac{1}{36}$$

$$= \frac{11}{36}$$

The probability that either of the two cubes shows a 3 is $\frac{11}{36}$.

You can use given information to solve many probability problems.

In Examples 5 through 16, use the information about the Sun City Council. Each council member is identified by gender and party. Parties are indicated by D for Democrat, R for Republican, I for Independent, and C for Conservative. Find each probability that a council member fits the criteria specified.

Name	Gender	Party	Name	Gender	Party
B. Green	M	D	M. Adams	M	I
B. White	F	D	R. Jones	M	C
C. Washington	F	D	T. Black	M	D
S. Brown	F	R	D. Jackson	M	I
L. Smith	M	R	N. Goodman	F	R
R. Jackson	M	R			

5 $P(D)$

■ SOLUTION

$P(D) = \dfrac{4}{11}$ ← **four Democrats**

6 $P(\text{not } I)$

■ SOLUTION

$P(\text{not } I) = 1 - \dfrac{2}{11}$ ← **two Independents**

$= \dfrac{9}{11}$

7 $P(F \text{ or } R)$

■ SOLUTION

$P(F \text{ or } R) = \dfrac{4}{11} + \dfrac{4}{11} - \dfrac{2}{11}$ ← **two female Republicans**

$= \dfrac{6}{11}$

8 $P(D \text{ or } C)$

■ SOLUTION

$P(D \text{ or } C) = \dfrac{4}{11} + \dfrac{1}{11}$ ← **4 Democrats 1 Conservative**

$= \dfrac{5}{11}$

9 $P(R \text{ and } D)$

■ SOLUTION

$P(R \text{ and } D) = 0$ ← **impossible event**

10 $P(M \text{ or } D)$

■ SOLUTION

$P(M \text{ or } D) = \dfrac{7}{11} + \dfrac{4}{11} - \dfrac{2}{11}$

$= \dfrac{9}{11}$

11 $P(M \text{ or } I)$

■ SOLUTION

$P(M \text{ or } I) = \dfrac{7}{11} + \dfrac{2}{11} - \dfrac{2}{11}$

$= \dfrac{7}{11}$

12 $P(F \text{ or } C)$

■ SOLUTION

$P(F \text{ or } C) = \dfrac{4}{11} + \dfrac{1}{11} - \dfrac{0}{11}$

$= \dfrac{5}{11}$

13 $P(F \text{ and } C)$

■ SOLUTION

$P(F \text{ and } C) = 0$

14 $P(M \text{ and } D)$

■ SOLUTION

$P(M \text{ and } D) = \dfrac{2}{11}$

15 $P(I \text{ and } F)$

■ SOLUTION

$P(I \text{ and } F) = 0$

16 $P(I \text{ or } F)$

■ SOLUTION

$P(I \text{ or } F) = \dfrac{2}{11} + \dfrac{4}{11} - \dfrac{0}{11}$

$= \dfrac{6}{11}$

Practice

Choose the numeral preceding the word or expression that best completes the statement or answers the question.

1 Two events, A and B, each having at least one outcome, are mutually exclusive. Which of these statements is true?

(1) $P(A \text{ or } B) = 0$

(2) $P(A) = 0$

(3) $P(B) = 0$

(4) $P(A \text{ and } B) = 0$

2 Which events are mutually exclusive?

(1) Bill and Elizabeth both won when they played racquetball against one another.

(2) Bill lost and Elizabeth won when they played racquetball against one another.

(3) The national average age of high school seniors is 17 and for sophomores it is 16.

(4) In one year, the Yankees won the World Series and the Mets won the National League Pennant.

3 A box contains cards, each having exactly one different number from 1 to 19 inclusive on it. Which gives the probability of drawing a card with an odd number on it or a multiple of 3 on it?

(1) $P(\text{odd}) \times P(\text{multiple of 3})$

(2) $P(\text{odd}) + P(\text{multiple of 3})$

(3) $P(\text{odd}) + P(\text{multiple of 3})$
    $- P(\text{odd multiple of 3})$

(4) $P(\text{odd}) \times P(\text{multiple of 3})$
    $- P(\text{odd multiple of 3})$

4 Mikki has 7 different shirts, 8 different pairs of pants, and 8 different pairs of shoes. How many outfits can she make?

(1) $7 + 8 + 8$ **(3)** $7 \times 8 \times 8$

(2) $7^3 + 8^3 + 8^3$ **(4)** $3(7 + 8 + 8)$

In Exercises 5–8, suppose you select a card at random from a standard deck of cards. Find each probability as a fraction in lowest terms.

5 $P(\text{queen or diamond})$

6 $P(\text{king or black card})$

7 $P(\text{heart or 5 of clubs})$

8 $P(\text{even number or clubs})$

In Exercises 9–12, suppose you roll a pair of number cubes. Find each probability as a fraction in lowest terms.

9 P(equal numbers or sum of 7)

10 P(equal numbers or even sum)

11 P(equal numbers or odd sum)

12 P(sum less than 4)

In Exercises 13–15, each card in a bag has exactly one of the numbers 3, $\frac{2}{3}$, −4, $\sqrt{25}$, π, $\sqrt{6}$, 15, 17, or 64 written on it. Find each probability as a fraction in lowest terms.

13 P(perfect square or even number)

14 P(irrational number or negative)

15 P(divisible by 3 or by 5)

16 In a certain area, 104 houses are for sale. Fifty-two houses have garages but not swimming pools, 13 houses have swimming pools but not garages, and 8 houses have both garages and swimming pools. Find the probability that a house for sale has a garage or swimming pool, but not both.

10.3 Independent and Dependent Events

S.CP.1, S.CP.2
S.CP.3, S.CP.6

Sometimes you need to determine the size of a rather large sample space. Suppose that Maggie has 5 pairs of jeans and 6 T-shirts. How many outfits consisting of one pair of jeans and one T-shirt does she have available to her? You could make a tree diagram to count the different outfits; however, there is a simpler way to find the answer.

Since Maggie has 5 choices for jeans and 6 T-shirt choices, she has 5×6, or 30 choices, altogether. You can generalize this discussion to state the *Fundamental Counting Principle*.

Fundamental Counting Principle

If there are m ways to make a selection and n ways to make a second selection, then there are mn ways to make the pair of selections.

If there are m ways to make a selection, n ways to make a second selection, and p ways to make a third selection, then there are mnp ways to make the three selections.

EXAMPLES 1 and 2 **Applying the Fundamental Counting Principle**

1 Ignoring the area code, how many seven-digit telephone numbers are possible if the first three digits are 268 in that order, the fourth digit is not 0, and the seventh digit is not 9?

■ **SOLUTION**

Sketch a diagram showing how many digits are possible for each slot.

$$268 - \underset{\substack{\uparrow \\ \text{9 digits}}}{\text{not 0}} \quad \underset{\substack{\uparrow \\ \text{10 digits}}}{\text{any digit}} \quad \underset{\substack{\uparrow \\ \text{10 digits}}}{\text{any digit}} \quad \underset{\substack{\uparrow \\ \text{9 digits}}}{\text{not 9}}$$

In all, there are $9 \times 10 \times 10 \times 9$, or **8,100**, possible telephone numbers.

2 Bag A contains 5 red marbles, 6 green marbles, and 7 purple marbles. Bag B contains 12 black marbles, 18 blue marbles, and 10 orange marbles. A marble is chosen at random from each bag. Find the probability of selecting a red marble from Bag A and a black marble from Bag B.

■ **SOLUTION**

There are 18×40, or 720, pairs of choices (Bag A, Bag B).

There are 5×12, or 60, pairs of choices (red, black).

$$P(red, then black) = \frac{60}{720}, or \frac{1}{12}$$

Two events are **independent** if the occurrence of one event does not affect the occurrence of the other event.

EXAMPLES 3 and 4   Identifying and finding probabilities of independent events

3 For which is the occurrence of one event dependent on that of the other event?

(1) flipping heads on a coin toss and rolling 6 on a number cube
(2) drawing a jack from a standard deck of cards and rolling a 6 on a number cube
(3) drawing a jack and, without replacing the card, drawing a second jack
(4) drawing a jack and, after replacing the card, drawing a second jack

■ **SOLUTION**

In choice (3), the card is not replaced. So, the sample space for the second draw has only 51 members. The second event is dependent on the first. The correct choice is **(3)**.

4 A card is drawn from a standard deck of playing cards, replaced, and a second card is drawn. What is the probability that the second card drawn is a spade?

■ **SOLUTION**

In this situation the probability of drawing the second spade is $\frac{13}{52}$ since after replacement there are still 13 spades out of 52 cards.

The counting principle for independent events says that if $P(A)$ is the probability of event A and $P(B)$ is the probability of event B, then you can find the probability of both A and B occurring by multiplying $P(A) \cdot P(B)$.

EXAMPLES 5 through 7   Solving problems involving two independent events

Suppose that you flip a coin and spin a spinner with a 50% red region, 25% blue region, and 25% green region. Find each probability.

5 P(heads and green)

■ **SOLUTION**

P(heads and green) = P(heads) × P(green)
                     = 0.5 × 0.25 = 0.125

6 P(heads and not green)

■ **SOLUTION**

P(heads and not green) = P(heads) × P(not green)
                         = P(heads) × (1 − P(green))
                         = 0.5 × (1 − 0.25) = 0.375

7 P(tails and red)

■ **SOLUTION**

P(tails and red) = P(tails) × P(red)
                   = 0.5 × 0.5 = 0.25

Consider this next example.

- A card is drawn from a standard deck of playing cards. It is a spade, and without replacement, a second card is drawn. What is the probability that the second card drawn is a spade?

In this situation the probability of drawing the second spade is $\frac{12}{51}$ since there are now 12 spades out of the remaining 51 cards.

The events of this situation are **dependent** because the occurrence of one event affects the probability of the other.

EXAMPLES 8 and 9   Finding probabilities of dependent events

A bag contains 3 red marbles and 5 blue marbles. Samuel draws a marble from the bag without looking, puts it into his pocket, and then draws a second marble without looking.

8 Find the probability that both marbles Samuel drew from the bag are red.

■ SOLUTION

Make a tree diagram showing the selections. Label the probabilities.

8 marbles in the bag	7 marbles in the bag		
red marble drawn $\frac{3}{8}$	red marble drawn	$\frac{2}{7}$	Only 2 red marbles remain.
	blue marble drawn	$\frac{5}{7}$	All 5 blue marbles remain.
blue marble drawn $\frac{5}{8}$	red marble drawn	$\frac{3}{7}$	All 3 red marbles remain.
	blue marble drawn	$\frac{4}{7}$	Only 4 blue marbles remain.

$P(\text{red, then red}) \; \frac{3}{8} \cdot \frac{2}{7} = \frac{3}{28}$

9 Find the probability that both marbles that Samuel drew at random are the same color.

■ SOLUTION

Refer to the tree diagram in the solution to Example 8.

$P(\text{both marbles the same color}) = P(\text{red, then red}) \text{ or } P(\text{blue, then blue})$

$$= \frac{3}{8} \cdot \frac{2}{7} + \frac{5}{8} \cdot \frac{4}{7}$$

$P(\text{both marbles the same color}) = \frac{26}{56} = \frac{13}{28}$

Independent and Dependent Events

If events A and B are independent, then $P(A, \text{then } B) = P(A) \cdot P(B)$.

If events A and B are dependent, then $P(A, \text{then } B) = P(A) \cdot P(B \text{ given } A)$.

Solving problems: independent and dependent events

Find each probability.

10 A spade is randomly drawn from a standard deck of playing cards on two successive draws, given that the card is replaced.

■ SOLUTION

Number of (spade, spade) cards → 13 × 13
Total number of cards   → 52 × 52

$$P(\text{spade, then spade}) = \frac{13 \times 13}{52 \times 52}$$

$$= \frac{1}{4} \times \frac{1}{4} = \frac{1}{16}$$

11 A spade is randomly drawn from a standard deck of playing cards on two successive draws, given that the card is not replaced.

■ SOLUTION

Number of (spade, spade) cards → 13 × 12
Total number of cards   → 52 × 51

$$P(\text{spade, then spade}) = \frac{13 \times 12}{52 \times 51}$$

$$= \frac{1}{17}$$

The probability of an event occurring given that some other event has already occurred is called **conditional probability.** The conditional probability that an event A occurs, given that event B occurs, can be denoted as $P(A \mid B)$.

EXAMPLE 12   **Finding conditional probability**

12 High school students were asked to identify their most likely after-school activity. The data are shown below.

Class	Sports Activity	Club Meetings	Homework	Watch TV	Total
Freshman	68	55	22	30	175
Sophomore	56	48	29	27	160
Junior	72	50	20	20	162
Senior	60	45	25	25	155
Total	256	198	96	102	652

Given that a student is a junior, what is the probability that the student's most likely after-school activity is a sports activity?

■ SOLUTION 1

Use the formula.

$P(\text{sports} \mid \text{junior})$

$$= \frac{P(\text{junior and chose sports})}{P(\text{junior})}$$

$$= \frac{\dfrac{72}{652}}{\dfrac{162}{652}} = \frac{72}{162} = 0.44$$

■ SOLUTION 2

Intuitively, the condition is that you are a junior, so our total sample space is now made up of just juniors (162). The probability that sports are a junior student's most likely after-school activity is

$$\frac{72}{162} = 0.44.$$

Conditional Probability

The conditional probability of event A, given event B, is

$$P(A|B) = \frac{P(A \text{ and } B)}{P(B)}, P(B) \neq 0.$$

A coin is *fair* if the probability of heads is the same as the probability of tails. A coin is *unfair* if one of these probabilities does not equal the other. You can apply this to the coin problem in Example 13.

EXAMPLE 13 — **Finding probabilities involving successive independent events**

 A fair coin is tossed three times. Find P(heads, then heads, then heads).

■ **SOLUTION**

$$P(\text{heads, heads, heads}) = \frac{1}{2} \cdot \frac{1}{2} \cdot \frac{1}{2} = \left(\frac{1}{2}\right)^3 = \frac{1}{8} \leftarrow \text{three independent events with } P(\text{heads}) = \frac{1}{2}$$

Just as one event can be dependent on a second event, a third event can be dependent on the two events preceding it.

EXAMPLE 14 — **Finding probabilities involving successive dependent events**

 A student council sends 4 boys and 6 girls to the local school board meeting. Three of the students will be interviewed. Find the probability that all three students interviewed are girls.

■ **SOLUTION**

Sketch a diagram showing the three successive selections.

first selection   second selection   third selection

6 girls of 10 students   5 girls of 9 students   4 girls of 8 students

       ↖ one student   ↖ two students
       already selected   already selected

↑   ↑
one girl already selected   two girls already selected

$$P(\text{girl, girl, girl}) = \frac{\overset{3}{\cancel{6}}}{\underset{5}{\cancel{10}}} \times \frac{5}{9} \times \frac{\overset{1}{\cancel{4}}}{\underset{2}{\cancel{8}}} = \frac{\overset{1}{\cancel{3}}}{\underset{1}{\cancel{5}}} \times \frac{\overset{1}{\cancel{5}}}{\underset{3}{\cancel{9}}} \times \frac{1}{2} = \frac{1}{6}$$

Practice

Choose the numeral preceding the word or expression that best completes the statement or answers the question.

1 A fair coin is flipped four times. If the coin lands heads up on the first three tosses, what is the probability that it will land heads up on the fourth toss?

(1) $\dfrac{1}{2}$ (2) $\left(\dfrac{1}{2}\right)^4$ (3) $4 \cdot \dfrac{1}{2}$ (4) $\dfrac{1}{4 \cdot 2}$

2 Which is the probability of a coin landing heads up each time on three tosses of a fair coin?

(1) $\dfrac{1}{2}$ (2) $\left(\dfrac{1}{2}\right)^3$ (3) $3 \cdot \dfrac{1}{2}$ (4) $\dfrac{1}{3 \cdot 2}$

3 A marble is randomly selected from among 5 red and 4 blue marbles, kept, and then a second marble is drawn at random. What is the probability that both marbles drawn will be red?

(1) $\dfrac{5}{9} \cdot \dfrac{4}{9}$ (2) $\dfrac{5}{9} + \dfrac{4}{9}$ (3) $\dfrac{5}{9} \cdot \dfrac{4}{8}$ (4) $\dfrac{5}{9} + \dfrac{3}{8}$

4 A marble is randomly selected from among 5 red and 4 blue marbles, replaced, and then a second marble is drawn at random. What is the probability of selecting red both times?

(1) $\dfrac{5}{9} \cdot \dfrac{5}{9}$ (2) $\dfrac{5}{9} + \dfrac{4}{9}$ (3) $\dfrac{5}{9} \cdot \dfrac{3}{8}$ (4) $\dfrac{5}{9} + \dfrac{3}{8}$

5 A coin is tossed and the arrow on the spinner shown here is spun. What is the probability of heads showing and the arrow landing in the light gray region?

(1) $\dfrac{1}{2} \cdot \dfrac{1}{4}$ (3) $\dfrac{1}{2} \cdot \dfrac{1}{2}$

(2) $\dfrac{1}{2} + \dfrac{1}{4}$ (4) $\dfrac{1}{2} \cdot \left(1 - \dfrac{1}{4}\right)$

In Exercises 6–11, a bag contains 3 red, 4 blue, and 5 green marbles, identical but for color. Find each probability given the specified condition.

6 P(red, then red); with replacement

7 P(green, then blue); with replacement

8 P(red, then green); without replacement

9 P(blue, then blue); without replacement

10 P(neither is green); with replacement

11 P(neither is green); without replacement

In Exercises 12–15, find the probability that a family having three children has the indicated number of boys or girls. Use this tree diagram.

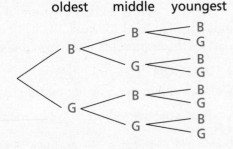

12 All three children are boys.

13 The family has one boy and two girls.

14 The family has at least one girl.

15 The youngest is a boy given that the oldest is a girl.

In Exercises 16–19, use the spinners below to find the probability of the situation described. Assume the spinners are fair.

spinner 1   spinner 2   spinner 3

16 The arrows land in region I, in the red region, and in region A.

17 The arrows land in region I or II, in the tan region, and in region B.

18 The arrows land in region III, in the tan or red region, and in region E.

19 The arrows land in region II, in the blue region, and in regions A, B, or C.

In Exercises 20–23, teachers send 7 boys and 8 girls to the local science fair. The first three students leaving the fair at lunch time are interviewed. Find each probability.

20 All students interviewed are boys.

21 Exactly two girls are interviewed.

22 A girl is interviewed, then a boy is interviewed, and then a girl is interviewed.

23 Another boy is interviewed, given that a boy is interviewed first.

In Exercise 24, solve the problem. Clearly show all necessary work.

24 Among Jan's 5 sweaters is a red one and a blue one. Among her 5 blouses is a white one and a yellow one. Among her 5 skirts is a green one and a black one. What is the probability that she chooses a red or blue sweater, a white or yellow blouse, and a green or black skirt?

Using Counting Methods with Probability

S.CP.9

In how many different ways can the letters in the word **MATH** be arranged?

4 letters for
first choice
_____

M A T or H
For example: M

3 letters for
second choice
_____

M̶ A T or H
For example: A

2 letters for
third choice
_____

M̶ A̶ T or H
For example: T

1 letter for
fourth choice
_____

M̶ A̶ T̶ or H
For example: H

Using the Fundamental Counting Principle, there are $4 \times 3 \times 2 \times 1$, or 24, different arrangements. Each of these arrangements is called a *permutation* of the letters in **MATH**. A **permutation** of the members in a set of objects is any arrangement of those objects in a specific order.

MATH and **AMTH** are different permutations.

EXAMPLE 1 — Counting simple arrangements

1. How many different arrangements of the letters in **EIGHT** are there if all the letters are used exactly once?

   (1) 1   (2) 5   (3) 20   (4) 120

   ■ SOLUTION

   There are 5 choices for the first letter, 4 choices for the second, and so on.
   There are $5 \times 4 \times 3 \times 2 \times 1$, or 120 arrangements. The correct choice is **(4)**.

Each of the products below can be abbreviated using **factorial notation**.

$$4 \times 3 \times 2 \times 1 = 4! \qquad 5 \times 4 \times 3 \times 2 \times 1 = 5!$$

In general, $n \times (n-1) \times (n-2) \times \cdots \times 2 \times 1 = n!$. By definition, $0! = 1$.

EXAMPLES 2 and 3 — Evaluating expressions involving $n!$

Evaluate each expression.

 $\dfrac{5!}{3!}$

 $\dfrac{7!}{3!2!}$

■ SOLUTION

$$\frac{5!}{3!} = \frac{5 \times 4 \times 3 \times 2 \times 1}{3 \times 2 \times 1}$$

$$= \frac{5 \times 4 \times \cancel{3} \times \cancel{2} \times \cancel{1}}{\cancel{3} \times \cancel{2} \times \cancel{1}} = 20$$

■ SOLUTION

$$\frac{7!}{3!2!} = \frac{7 \times 6 \times 5 \times 4 \times 3 \times 2 \times 1}{3 \times 2 \times 1 \times 2 \times 1}$$

$$= \frac{7 \times 6 \times 5 \times 4 \times \cancel{3} \times \cancel{2} \times \cancel{1}}{\cancel{3} \times \cancel{2} \times \cancel{1} \times 2 \times 1} = 420$$

There is a formula that you can use to count the permutations of n objects taken n at a time.

Permutations of n Objects Taken n at a Time

The number of permutations of n objects taken n at a time, denoted $_nP_n$, is given by $_nP_n = n!$.

How many four-letter arrangements can be made from the letters in **HERMIT**? The diagram below suggests that there are $6 \times 5 \times 4 \times 3$ arrangements.

6 letters for first choice	**5** letters for second choice	**4** letters for third choice	**3** letters for fourth choice
H E R M I T	~~H~~ E R M I T	~~H~~ ~~E~~ R M I T	~~H~~ ~~E~~ ~~R~~ M I T
For example: H	For example: E	For example: R	For example: M

Notice that $6 \times 5 \times 4 \times 3 = \frac{6 \times 5 \times 4 \times 3 \times 2 \times 1}{2 \times 1} = \frac{6!}{(6-4)!}$. In general, you can state and use the following formula for counting permutations of n objects taken r at a time.

Permutations of n Objects Taken r at a Time

Let n and r be natural numbers with $r \leq n$.

The number of permutations of n objects taken r at a time is $_nP_r = \dfrac{n!}{(n-r)!}$

EXAMPLE 4 **Counting permutations of n objects taken r at a time**

4 A student may select a four-digit sequence with no repetition of digits for a lock on his or her locker. How many such sequences are possible?

■ **SOLUTION**

Calculate $_{10}P_4$. In $_{10}P_4$, $n = 10$ and $r = 4$.

$$_{10}P_4 = \frac{10!}{(10-4)!} = \frac{10!}{6!}$$

$$= \frac{10 \times 9 \times 8 \times 7 \times \cancel{6!}}{\cancel{6!}}$$

$$= 5040$$

The student may choose from **5040** four-digit sequences.

If you list and count the permutations of the letters in **SEE**, you will find 6 permutations. This happens because **E** and **E** are considered distinguishable. If you consider color to be unimportant, permutations 1 and 4, 2 and 5, and 3 and 6 become the same. Then there are only 3 distinguishable permutations.

1	2	3
SEE	ESE	EES

4	5	6
SEE	ESE	EES

Evaluate $\frac{3!}{2!}$ to get the number of distinguishable permutations of **S, E, E**. In general, you can use the following formula.

Permutations of n Objects With Repetition

The number of permutations of n objects with r of them the same is given by $\frac{n!}{r!}$. If r of the n objects are the same and s of the n objects are the same, the number of distinguishable permutations is given by $\frac{n!}{r!s!}$.

In the word **BANANA**, **N** occurs twice and **A** occurs 3 times. The total number of distinguishable permutations of all the letters is given by $\frac{6!}{2!3!}$, or 60.

The permutations of the letters in the word **MATH** taken two letters at a time are shown in the table below. Notice there are 12 such permutations.

MA	MT	MH	AM	AT	AH
TM	TA	TH	HM	HA	HT

Notice that **MA** and **AM** are different permutations that contain the same letters.

Counting permutations plays an important role in solving many probability problems.

EXAMPLES 5 and 6   **Solving probability problems using permutations**

5 The student council at Bradville High School consists of the following students. Three members are to be chosen at random as leader, assistant, and record keeper. Find the probability that R. Jones is the leader.

R. Jones	M. White	J. Green	L. Smith	W. Jackson
B. Brown	E. Schwartz	S. Washington	J. Aaron	C. Pike

■ **SOLUTION**

Step 1 Since order is important, the groups below are different.

R. Jones (leader)   M. White (assistant)   J. Green (record keeper)
M. White (leader)   R. Jones (assistant)   J. Green (record keeper)

Therefore, this problem involves permutations.

Step 2 Count favorable outcomes and total outcomes.
Find how many three-member groups there are with R. Jones as leader.

R. Jones (leader) × 9 for assistant × 8 for record keeper   → **72 groups favorable**

Find how many groups there are with leader, assistant, and record keeper.
In all, there are $_{10}P_3$ groups of three students in the specified order.

Step 3 Calculate $\dfrac{72}{_{10}P_3}$.

$$\frac{72}{_{10}P_3} = \frac{72}{\dfrac{10!}{(10-3)!}} = 72 \times \frac{(10-3)!}{10!} = \frac{72}{10 \times 9 \times 8} = \frac{1}{10}$$

6 A mathematics teacher places an algebra book, a geometry book, and an algebra II book on a shelf. What is the probability that the geometry book is placed first?

■ **SOLUTION**

Step 1 Calculate how many ways the books can be arranged if the Geometry book is placed first.
$$1 \cdot 2 \cdot 1 = 2$$

Step 2 Calculate the total number of ways the books can be arranged on the shelf.
$$_3P_3 = 3! = 3 \cdot 2 \cdot 1 = 6$$

Step 3 Calculate the probability.
$$\frac{2}{6} = \frac{1}{3}$$

Some calculators enable you to calculate a permutation by using functions built into the calculator. This display shows the calculation of $_{10}P_4$. To get the results shown here, enter 10, then choose $_nP_r$, and then enter 4.

```
10 nPr 4
                    5040
```

Practice

Choose the numeral preceding the word or expression that best completes the statement or answers the question.

1 The number of distinct arrangements in a specific order using the letters in **APPLE** is given by

(1) $5!$ (3) $\dfrac{5!}{2!}$

(2) $_5P_5$ (4) $\dfrac{5!}{3!}$

2 In how many ways can 100 people sit in 100 seats on an airplane?

(1) $100!$ (3) $\dfrac{100!}{100!}$

(2) $_{100}P_{10}$ (4) 100

3 A social security number has the form below.

three digits - two digits - four digits

If the first digit in each block is 1, and the other digits are taken from 0, 1, 2, 3, 4, 5, 6, 7, 8, and 9, how many such social security numbers are possible?

(1) $10!$ (3) 9^{10}

(2) $9!$ (4) $10^2 \times 10^1 \times 10^3$

4 How many distinguishable permutations are possible using all the letters in **LETTER**?

(1) $6!$ (3) $6! \times 2! \times 3!$

(2) $\dfrac{6!}{2! \times 2!}$ (4) $\dfrac{6!}{2 \times 3}$

5 A drawer contains twelve T-shirts. A second drawer contains six pairs of slacks. If two T-shirts are white and two pairs of slacks are black, which is the probability of choosing a white T-shirt and a black pair of slacks?

(1) $\dfrac{2+2}{12+6}$ (3) $\dfrac{2}{12} \cdot \dfrac{2}{6}$

(2) $\dfrac{12!}{2!} \cdot \dfrac{6!}{2!}$ (4) $\dfrac{2!}{12!} \cdot \dfrac{2!}{6!}$

In Exercises 6–11, evaluate each expression.

6 $\dfrac{6!}{4!}$ **7** $\dfrac{6!}{(6-3)!}$

8 $\dfrac{8!}{3!(8-3)!}$ **9** $\dfrac{7!}{3!2!}$

10 $\dfrac{11!}{2!(11-2)!}$ **11** $_4P_2 \times {}_5P_3$

In Exercises 12–18, find the number of specified permutations.

12 How many different seven-digit phone numbers are available if the first three digits are 7, 3, and 4 in that order?

13 permutations of all the letters in **SQUARE**

14 permutations of the letters in **SQUARE** using all letters with the first letter a vowel

15 permutations of the letters in **SQUARE** using all letters with the last letter being **R**

16 permutations of the letters in **SQUARE** using all letters and given that the first letter is **Q** and the last letter is **U**

17 Ten points are scattered around a circle. How many triangles can be formed?

18 A four-digit number consists only of even digits, each used exactly once.

In Exercises 19–22, a bag contains 5 red, 6 blue, and 9 green marbles. Three marbles are drawn at random in one scoop. Find the probability of each outcome as a decimal to the nearest hundredth.

19 All 3 marbles are red.

20 All 3 marbles are blue.

21 Two marbles are red and 1 is blue.

22 Two marbles are blue and 1 is green.

Choose the numeral preceding the word or expression that best completes the statement or answers the question.

1 Which represents the probability of randomly drawing a card showing 7 or a card showing 5 from a standard deck of 52 cards?

(1) $\dfrac{4}{52} + \dfrac{4}{52}$ (3) $\dfrac{4}{52} \cdot \dfrac{4}{52}$

(2) $1 - \left(\dfrac{4}{52} + \dfrac{4}{52}\right)$ (4) $\dfrac{5}{52} + \dfrac{7}{52}$

2 Which event is impossible?

(1) choosing a number between 20 and 30 that is also a prime number

(2) rolling a 6 on a number cube and flipping heads on a coin

(3) choosing a rational number between 2.1 and 3.9 that is an even number

(4) getting a perfect score on a mathematics test and passing that test

3 In how many ways can 5 books be placed on a shelf in any order?

(1) 5   (2) 25   (3) 15   (4) 120

4 A bag contains 7 red, 7 blue, and 7 green marbles. Which represents the probability that a red marble will be randomly drawn from the bag and then a green marble will be randomly drawn from the bag given that the first marble drawn is not replaced?

(1) $\dfrac{7}{21} \cdot \dfrac{6}{20}$ (3) $\dfrac{7}{21} \cdot \dfrac{7}{20}$

(2) $\dfrac{7}{21} \cdot \dfrac{7}{21}$ (4) $\dfrac{7}{21} \cdot \dfrac{6}{21}$

5 On a bookshelf, there are 5 red books, 7 green books, and 10 brown books. If a book is picked at random, to the nearest whole percent, what is the probability that it is green?

(1) 7%   (2) 23%   (3) 32%   (4) 45%

6 A weather forecaster predicts that there is a 25% probability of rain today. What is the probability that it will not rain?

(1) 65%   (3) 75%

(2) 5%   (4) 45%

7 A container holds 6 red balls and 3 green balls. One green ball is drawn randomly and set aside. What is the probability the second ball drawn is green?

(1) $\dfrac{1}{4}$ (3) $\dfrac{1}{3}$

(2) $\dfrac{2}{3}$ (4) $\dfrac{3}{4}$

8 How many four-digit numbers can be made using only the even digits 0, 2, 4, 6, and 8, if 0 is never the first digit?

(1) 500   (3) 625

(2) 120   (4) 20

In Exercises 9–12, refer to a table of outcomes for rolling a pair of number cubes. Find each probability to the nearest whole percent.

9 P(you roll two 5s)

(1) 3%   (2) 17%   (3) 33%   (4) 6%

10 P(sum equals 1)

(1) 31%   (2) 0%   (3) 3%   (4) 17%

11 P(sum is not 4)

(1) 16%   (2) 8%   (3) 3%   (4) 92%

12 P(sum is even)

(1) 25%   (3) 10%

(2) 50%   (4) 75%

In Exercises 13–14, the Big Dipper Ice Cream Shop has 8 flavors of ice cream, 4 flavors of syrup, and 3 different toppings.

13 How many different ice cream dishes can be made with one flavor of ice cream, one syrup, and one topping?

(1) 15 **(2)** 3 **(3)** 36 **(4)** 96

14 If vanilla and chocolate are two of the available flavors of ice cream, what is the probability that vanilla or chocolate ice cream will be chosen at random?

(1) $\frac{2}{15}$ **(2)** $\frac{1}{3}$ **(3)** $\frac{1}{8}$ **(4)** $\frac{1}{4}$

15 Bag A contains 10 marbles and Bag B contains 24 marbles. If Bag A contains 2 red marbles and Bag B contains 2 red marbles, what is the probability of randomly drawing a red marble from each bag?

(1) $\frac{17}{60}$ **(2)** $\frac{1}{60}$ **(3)** $\frac{1}{55}$ **(4)** $\frac{1}{120}$

16 There are 3 up escalators and one elevator to take shoppers from the first floor to the second floor. There are 3 down escalators and the same elevator to take shoppers from the second floor to the first floor. In how many ways can a shopper go from the first floor to the second floor and back?

(1) 4 **(2)** 9 **(3)** 16 **(4)** 6

17 For which is the occurrence of one event not dependent on that of the other event?

(1) Drawing a 6 out of a deck of cards, and then drawing an 8 without replacing the 6.

(2) Flipping tails on one coin, and then flipping heads on a second coin.

(3) Drawing a king out of a deck of cards, leaving the king out, and then drawing another king.

(4) Randomly choosing a penny and then a nickel out of a bag of coins without replacing the first coin.

18 Find the probability of choosing two aces from a deck of cards on successive draws, given that the card is replaced.

(1) $\frac{1}{169}$ **(2)** $\frac{1}{26}$ **(3)** $\frac{2}{13}$ **(4)** $\frac{4}{13}$

In Exercises 19–21, a bag contains 4 white, 3 silver, and 9 red paper clips identical in size. Find the probability of each event given the specified condition.

19 P(white, then silver); with replacement

(1) $\frac{7}{16}$ **(2)** $\frac{1}{12}$ **(3)** $\frac{3}{64}$ **(4)** $\frac{7}{12}$

20 P(red, then red); without replacement

(1) $\frac{3}{10}$ **(2)** $\frac{81}{256}$ **(3)** $\frac{2}{9}$ **(4)** $\frac{1}{72}$

21 P(neither is silver); without replacement

(1) $\frac{2}{13}$ **(2)** $\frac{169}{256}$ **(3)** $\frac{1}{156}$ **(4)** $\frac{13}{20}$

22 How many different arrangements of the letters in the word **GOAL** are there if all the letters are used exactly once?

(1) 16 **(2)** 24 **(3)** 1 **(4)** 10

23 Evaluate the expression $\frac{6!}{4!2!}$.

(1) 1 **(2)** 15 **(3)** $\frac{21}{13}$ **(4)** $\frac{1}{8}$

24 In how many ways can 50 students sit in 50 seats on a school bus?

(1) $_{50}P_5$ **(2)** $\frac{50!}{50!}$ **(3)** 50! **(4)** 50

25 A fair spinner has 8 sections numbered 1–8. If the spinner is spun once, what is the probability that it lands on 2?

(1) $\frac{1}{8}$ **(2)** $\frac{1}{2}$ **(3)** $\frac{1}{4}$ **(4)** $\frac{7}{8}$

In Exercises 26–29, use the following information.

In a local district, there are 9,800 Democratic, 11,000 Republican, and 1,200 Independent registered voters. If a voter is to be selected at random, find the probability of each event.

26 P(any of the three parties)

27 P(Democratic)

28 P(Republican)

29 P(not Republican)

In Exercises 30–32, a card is drawn from a standard deck of 52 cards and a number cube is rolled. Find the probability of each event.

30 A spade is drawn then a 1 is rolled.

31 A king or queen is drawn and a 6 is rolled.

32 A red card is drawn and a number at least 3 is rolled.

In Exercises 33–35, a bag contains 5 red, 9 blue, and 6 green marbles. Give probabilities to the nearest hundredth.

33 P(green, then green, then green) given that the marble is not replaced after it is drawn

34 P(green, then green, then green) given that the marble is replaced after it is drawn

35 P(same color each of three selections) given that the marble selected is replaced

In Exercises 36–47, solve each problem. Clearly show all necessary work.

36 How many permutations are there of the letters in the word **COMPUTER** using 2 letters at a time?

37 Which has a greater probability of occurring: rolling a sum of 7 when rolling a pair of number cubes or drawing an ace or a two from a standard deck of 52 cards? Explain.

38 Bag I contains 6 cards labeled 1, 2, 3, 4, 5, and 6. Bag II contains 5 cards labeled *A*, *B*, *C*, *D*, and *E*. Represent the outcomes for drawing a card from Bag I and a card from Bag II in a table.

39 A coin is flipped three times. Represent the possible outcomes for the three successive events in a tree diagram.

40 In how many different ways can you order 4 books selected from a reading list containing 12 books?

41 How many arrangements are there for the letters in the word **MULTIPLY**?

42 If a six-sided number cube is tossed, what is the probability that it shows an odd number given that it shows a number less than 5?

43 How many different license plates can be made if each plate contains four letters from A to J inclusive followed by three digits?

44 The first 3 finishers out of 10 runners in a race will each win a different ribbon. In how many ways can the ribbons be awarded?

45 What is the probability an arrow will land inside one of the blue squares? One of the white squares?

46 A king of hearts is drawn at random from a standard deck of 52 playing cards and set aside. What is the probability that a second card drawn at random is a red king?

47 The Green Hornet football team has found that the probability of winning each game is 60%. Find the probability that they will win 4 games in a row.

Common Core Standards in the New York Geometry Brief Review

This chart includes all standards touched upon in each lesson at both an instructional level and as demonstrated by practice problems.
*indicates modeling standards

ALGEBRA		WHERE TO FIND
Reasoning with Equations and Inequalities		
Solve systems of equations		
A.REI.7	Solve a simple system consisting of a linear equation and a quadratic equation in two variables algebraically and graphically. For example, find the points of intersection between the line $y = -3x$ and the circle $x^2 + y^2 = 3$.	7.6

GEOMETRY		WHERE TO FIND
Congruence		
Experiment with transformations in the plane		
G.CO.1	Know precise definitions of angle, circle, perpendicular line, parallel line, and line segment, based on the undefined notions of point, line, distance along a line, and distance around a circular arc.	1.1, 1.2
G.CO.2	Represent transformations in the plane using, e.g., transparencies and geometry software; describe transformations as functions that take points in the plane as inputs and give other points as outputs. Compare transformations that preserve distance and angle to those that do not (e.g., translation versus horizontal stretch).	4.1, 4.2, 4.3, 4.4
G.CO.3	Given a rectangle, parallelogram, trapezoid, or regular polygon, describe the rotations and reflections that carry it onto itself.	4.2, 5.5
G.CO.4	Develop definitions of rotations, reflections, and translations in terms of angles, circles, perpendicular lines, parallel lines, and line segments.	4.1, 4.2, 4.3
G.CO.5	Given a geometric figure and a rotation, reflection, or translation, draw the transformed figure using, e.g., graph paper, tracing paper, or geometry software. Specify a sequence of transformations that will carry a given figure onto another.	4.1, 4.2, 4.3

(+) Additional mathematics that students should learn in order to take advanced courses such as calculus, advanced statistics, or discrete mathematics is indicated by (+).

* Making mathematical models is a Standard for Mathematical Practice, and specific modeling standards appear throughout the high school standards indicated by a star symbol (*).

Understand congruence in terms of rigid motions

G.CO.6	Use geometric descriptions of rigid motions to transform figures and to predict the effect of a given rigid motion on a given figure; given two figures, use the definition of congruence in terms of rigid motions to decide if they are congruent.	4.5
G.CO.7	Use the definition of congruence in terms of rigid motions to show that two triangles are congruent if and only if corresponding pairs of sides and corresponding pairs of angles are congruent.	4.5
G.CO.8	Explain how the criteria for triangle congruence (ASA, SAS, and SSS) follow from the definition of congruence in terms of rigid motions.	4.5

Prove geometric theorems

G.CO.9	Prove theorems about lines and angles. *Theorems include: vertical angles are congruent; when a transversal crosses parallel lines, alternate interior angles are congruent and corresponding angles are congruent; points on a perpendicular bisector of a line segment are exactly those equidistant from the segment's endpoints.*	1.3
G.CO.10	Prove theorems about triangles. *Theorems include: measures of interior angles of a triangle sum to 180°; base angles of isosceles triangles are congruent; the segment joining midpoints of two sides of a triangle is parallel to the third side and half the length; the medians of a triangle meet at a point.*	2.1, 2.3, 5.4
G.CO.11	Prove theorems about parallelograms. *Theorems include: opposite sides are congruent, opposite angles are congruent, the diagonals of a parallelogram bisect each other, and conversely, rectangles are parallelograms with congruent diagonals.*	6.2

Make geometric constructions

G.CO.12	Make formal geometric constructions with a variety of tools and methods (compass and straightedge, string, reflective devices, paper folding, dynamic geometric software, etc.). *Copying a segment; copying an angle; bisecting a segment; bisecting an angle; constructing perpendicular lines, including the perpendicular bisector of a line segment; and constructing a line parallel to a given line through a point not on the line.*	1.4, 1.5
G.CO.13	Construct an equilateral triangle, a square, and a regular hexagon inscribed in a circle.	1.4

Similarity, Right Triangles, and Trigonometry

Understand similarity in terms of similarity transformations

G.SRT.1	Verify experimentally the properties of dilations given by a center and a scale factor.	5.2, 5.3
G.SRT.2	Given two figures, use the definition of similarity in terms of similarity transformations to decide if they are similar; explain using similarity transformations the meaning of similarity for triangles as the equality of all corresponding pairs of angles and the proportionality of all corresponding pairs of sides.	5.2

Prove theorems involving similarity

G.SRT.4	Prove theorems about triangles. *Theorems include: a line parallel to one side of a triangle divides the other two proportionally, and conversely; the Pythagorean Theorem proved using triangle similarity.*	2.5, 3.5, 5.1
G.SRT.5	Use congruence and similarity criteria for triangles to solve problems and to prove relationships in geometric figures.	3.4, 3.5, 5.1, 8.5

Define trigonometric ratios and solve problems involving right triangles

G.SRT.6	Understand that by similarity, side ratios in right triangles are properties of the angles in the triangle, leading to definitions of trigonometric ratios for acute angles.	2.4
G.SRT.8	Use trigonometric ratios and the Pythagorean Theorem to solve right triangles in applied problems.*	2.5

Circles

Understand and apply theorems about circles

G.C.1	Prove that all circles are similar.	8.1
G.C.2	Identify and describe relationships among inscribed angles, radii, and chords. *Include the relationship between central, inscribed, and circumscribed angles; inscribed angles on a diameter are right angles; the radius of a circle is perpendicular to the tangent where the radius intersects the circle.*	8.3, 8.4, 8.5
G.C.3	Construct the inscribed and circumscribed circles of a triangle, and prove properties of angles for a quadrilateral inscribed in a circle.	8.3
G.C.4	(+) Construct a tangent line from a point outside a given circle to the circle.	8.4

Find arc lengths and areas of sectors of circles

G.C.5	Derive using similarity the fact that the length of the arc intercepted by an angle is proportional to the radius, and define the radian measure of the angle as the constant of proportionality; derive the formula for the area of a sector.	8.2, 8.3, 8.6

Expressing Geometric Properties with Equations

Translate between the geometric description and the equation for a conic section

G.GPE.1	Derive the equation of a circle of given center and radius using the Pythagorean Theorem; complete the square to find the center and radius of a circle given by an equation.	7.5

Use coordinates to prove simple geometric theorems algebraically

G.GPE.4	Use coordinates to prove simple geometric theorems algebraically. *For example, prove or disprove that a figure defined by four given points in the coordinate plane is a rectangle; prove or disprove that the point $(1, \sqrt{3})$ lies on the circle centered at the origin and containing the point $(0, 2)$.*	7.4
G.GPE.5	Prove the slope criteria for parallel and perpendicular lines and use them to solve geometric problems (e.g., find the equation of a line parallel or perpendicular to a given line that passes through a given point).	7.1, 7.2
G.GPE.7	Use coordinates to compute perimeters of polygons and areas of triangles and rectangles, e.g., using the distance formula.*	7.3

Geometric Measurement and Dimension

Explain volume formulas and use them to solve problems

G.GMD.1	Give an informal argument for the formulas for the circumference of a circle, area of a circle, volume of a cylinder, pyramid, and cone. *Use dissection arguments, Cavalieri's principle, and informal limit arguments.*	8.2, 8.6
G.GMD.3	Use volume formulas for cylinders, pyramids, cones, and spheres to solve problems.*	9.3, 9.4, 9.5, 9.6

Visualize relationships between two-dimensional and three dimensional objects

G.GMD.4	Identify the shapes of two-dimensional cross-sections of three-dimensional objects, and identify three-dimensional objects generated by rotations of two-dimensional objects.	9.2, 9.6

| STATISTICS AND PROBABILITY | WHERE TO FIND |

Conditional Probability & the Rules of Probability

Understand independence and conditional probability and use them to interpret data

S.CP.1	Describe events as subsets of a sample space (the set of outcomes) using characteristics (or categories) of the outcomes, or as unions, intersections, or complements of other events ("or," "and," "not").	10.1, 10.3
S.CP.2	Understand that two events A and B are independent if the probability of A and B occurring together is the product of their probabilities, and use this characterization to determine if they are independent.	10.3

S.CP.3	Understand the conditional probability of A given B as $P(A \text{ and } B)/P(B)$, and interpret independence of A and B as saying that the conditional probability of A given B is the same as the probability of A, and the conditional probability of B given A is the same as the probability of B.	10.3
S.CP.4	Construct and interpret two-way frequency tables of data when two categories are associated with each object being classified. Use the two-way table as a sample space to decide if events are independent and to approximate conditional probabilities. *For example, collect data from a random sample of students in your school on their favorite subject among math, science, and English. Estimate the probability that a randomly selected student from your school will favor science given that the student is in tenth grade. Do the same for other subjects and compare the results.*	10.1, 10.2

Use the rules of probability to compute probabilities of compound events.

S.CP.6	Find the conditional probability of A given B as the fraction of B's outcomes that also belong to A, and interpret the answer in terms of the model.	10.2, 10.3
S.CP.7	Apply the Addition Rule, $P(A \text{ or } B) = P(A) + P(B) - P(A \text{ and } B)$, and interpret the answer in terms of the model.	10.2
S.CP.8	(+) Apply the general Multiplication Rule in a uniform probability model, $P(A \text{ and } B) = P(A)P(B/A) = P(B)P(A/B)$, and interpret the answer in terms of the model.	10.2
S.CP.9	(+) Use permutations and combinations to compute probabilities of compound events and solve problems.	10.4

Using Probability to Make Decisions

Calculate expected values and use them to solve problems

S.MD.3	(+) Develop a probability distribution for a random variable defined for a sample space in which theoretical probabilities can be calculated; find the expected value. *For example, find the theoretical probability distribution for the number of correct answers obtained by guessing on all five questions of a multiple-choice test where each question has four choices, and find the expected grade under various grading schemes.*	10.1
S.MD.4	(+) Develop a probability distribution for a random variable defined for a sample space in which probabilities are assigned empirically; find the expected value. *For example, find a current data distribution on the number of TV sets per household in the United States, and calculate the expected number of sets per household. How many TV sets would you expect to find in 100 randomly selected households?*	10.1

STANDARDS FOR MATHEMATICAL PRACTICE		WHERE TO FIND
MP1	Make sense of problems and persevere in solving them.	2.1, 2.4, 2.6, 2PA, 3.5, 4.5, 4PA, 5.5, 7.6, 8.3, 8.4, 8.6, 10.2, 10.3
MP2	Reason abstractly and quantitatively.	2.1, 2.2, 2.3, 2.4, 2.6, 3.1, 3.3, 3.5, 4.1, 4.2, 4.4, 4.5, 5.5, 8.2, 8.3, 8.5, 8.6, 10.2, 10.3, 10.4
MP3	Construct viable arguments and critique the reasoning of others.	2.1, 2.3, 2.4, 2.5, 3.1, 3.2, 3.3, 3.4, 4.1, 4.2, 4.3, 4.5, 4PA, 5.5, 6.3, 6PA, 7.3, 8.3, 8.5
MP4	Model with mathematics.	1.1, 1.4, 1.5, 1PA, 2.1, 2.2, 2.3, 2.4, 2.5, 2PA, 3.4, 5.1, 8.2, 8.4, 8.6, 9.5, 9.6, 10.1, 10.2, 10.3, 10.4
MP5	Use appropriate tools strategically.	1.4, 2.1, 2.4, 4.2, 7.3, 8.2, 8.4
MP6	Attend to precision.	2.5, 2.6, 2PA, 5.2, 5.3, 5.4, 6.1, 6.2, 7.1, 7.2, 7.5, 7.6, 8.4, 8.6, 9.2, 9.3, 9.5, 9.6
MP7	Look for and make use of structure.	1.3, 2.2, 2.5, 3.1, 3.2, 3.3, 3.4, 4.3, 5.2, 5.4, 6.2, 7.4, 7.5, 7.6, 8.2, 8.6, 10.1, 10.3
MP8	Look for and express regularity in repeated reasoning.	1.3, 2.2, 2.4, 2.6, 3.4, 4.4, 7.1, 7.2, 8.2, 8.6, 10.4

PA = Preparing for the Assessment

Designing a Container

Complete this performance task using as many response sheets as you need. Fully answer all parts of the performance task with detailed responses. You should provide sound mathematical reasoning to support your work.

Three teams of students are designing containers that will hold 1000 mL of liquid. The containers must be 10 cm high and be open at the top. The shapes that the teams plan to use for their containers are listed below.

Team 1: rectangular prism with a square base

Team 2: cylinder

Team 3: cone

Task Description

Which team needs the least amount of material to make its container? Which team needs the most material? (Recall that 1 mL = 1 cm^3. Round your answers to the nearest hundredth.)

a. What are the dimensions of Team 1's container? Considering the outside of the container only, what is the surface area?

b. What are the dimensions and surface area of Team 2's container?

c. What are the dimensions and surface area of Team 3's container?

d. Which team needs the least amount of material to make its container? Which team needs the most?

e. Suppose Team 2's cylindrical container does NOT have to be 10 cm high. Can you change the container's dimensions to use less material but still hold 1000 mL of liquid? Show your work.

Urban Planning

Complete this performance task using as many response sheets as you need. Fully answer all parts of the performance task with detailed responses. You should provide sound mathematical reasoning to support your work.

Students are designing a new town as part of a social studies project on urban planning. They want to place the town's high school at point *A* and the middle school at point *B*. They also plan to build roads that run directly from point *A* to the mall and from point *B* to the mall. The average cost to build a road in this area is $550,000 per mile.

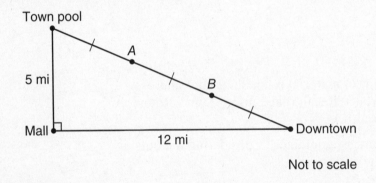

Not to scale

Task Description

What is the difference in the cost of the roads built to the Mall from the two schools?

Show your work and explain the rationale for your technique.

Analyzing an Excavation Site

Complete this performance task using as many response sheets as you need. Fully answer all parts of the performance task with detailed responses. You should provide sound mathematical reasoning to support your work.

Archaeologists find evidence of three houses at a dig site. They believe the houses were arranged in a circle and want to excavate at the center of the settlement. The map shows the locations of the three houses, at points A, B, and C.

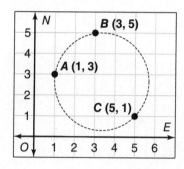

1 unit = 10 m

Task Description

Find the coordinates of the center of the settlement, and how far each house was from the center.

a. Find the center of the circle.

b. Find the midpoints of $\overline{AB}$ and $\overline{BC}$.

c. Find the slopes of $\overline{AB}$ and $\overline{BC}$.

d. Use the midpoints and slopes of $\overline{AB}$ and $\overline{BC}$ to write equations for the perpendicular bisectors of these segments.

e. What are the coordinates of the settlement's center? Explain.

f. How far was each house from the center of the settlement?

g. Give possible coordinates of another house in the settlement.

PERFORMANCE TASKS

Applying Geometric Probability

Complete this performance task using as many response sheets as you need. Fully answer all parts of the performance task with detailed responses. You should provide sound mathematical reasoning to support your work.

Students are competing in a class event, throwing darts at a square dartboard like the one shown below. The points for hitting each region are as shown. All triangles on the dartboard are equilateral triangles, and triangles with the same number of points are the same size.

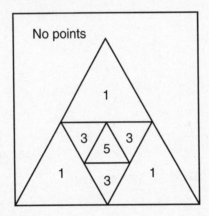

Task Description

You and your friend are playing a game of darts. You have 43 points and your friend has 48 points, but you have 2 darts left to throw and your friend has none. If each dart lands in a random location on the board, what is the probability that you can take the lead and win the game with your last 2 darts?

a. What is the probability that a dart hitting the board lands anywhere within the largest triangle?

b. What is the probability that a dart hitting the board does NOT land in any triangle?

c. What is the probability that a dart lands in a 1-point region? In a 3-point region? In the 5-point region?

d. List each sequence of two dart throws that gives at least 6 points, and therefore wins the game. What is the probability of getting each winning sequence?

e. What is the probability that you get *any* of the sequences from part (d) and win the game?

Glossary

GLOSSARY

Absolute value The distance that a number is from zero on a number line. The symbol for the absolute value of a number *n* is |*n*|.

Acute angle An angle whose measure is greater than 0° and less than 90°.

Acute triangle A triangle that has three acute angles.

Adjacent angles Two coplanar angles that share a common side and a common vertex, but have no interior points in common.

Alternate exterior angles A pair of nonadjacent exterior angles on opposite sides of a transversal.

Alternate Exterior Angles Theorem If two parallel lines are cut by a transversal, then alternate exterior angles are congruent.

Alternate interior angles A pair of nonadjacent interior angles on opposite sides of a transversal.

Alternate Interior Angles Theorem If two parallel lines are cut by a transversal, then alternate interior angles are congruent.

Altitude of a triangle A perpendicular segment from a vertex to the line containing the opposite side.

Angle The figure formed by two rays with a common endpoint.

Angle Addition Postulate If point *B* is in the interior of $\angle AOC$, then $m\angle AOB + m\angle BOC = m\angle AOC$.

Angle-Angle-Side (AAS) Congruence Theorem If two angles and the nonincluded side of one triangle are congruent to two angles and the corresponding nonincluded side of another triangle, then the triangles are congruent.

Angle-Angle (AA) Similarity Postulate If two angles of one triangle are congruent to two angles of another triangle, then the triangles are similar.

Angle bisector The ray that divides a given angle into two congruent angles.

Angle of a convex polygon See *interior angle of a convex polygon*.

Angle of depression An angle whose vertex and horizontal side are level with an observer's eye and whose other side slopes downward from an observer's eye level to an object below.

Angle of elevation An angle whose vertex and horizontal side are level with an observer's eye and whose other side slopes upward from an observer's eye level to an object above.

Angle-Side-Angle (ASA) Congruence Postulate If two angles and the included side of one triangle are congruent to two angles and the included side of another triangle, then the triangles are congruent.

Angle-Sum Theorem The sum of the measures of the angles of a triangle is 180°.

Antecedent See *hypothesis*.

Apothem In a regular polygon, the segment, or the length of the segment, drawn from the center to the midpoint of a side.

Arc An unbroken part of a circle.

Arc length The linear measure of an arc of a circle.

Area of a plane figure The number of nonoverlapping square units contained in its interior.

Axiom See *postulate*.

Base angles See *isosceles triangle*, *trapezoid*.

Base of a plane figure See *parallelogram*, *triangle*, *trapezoid*

Base of a three-dimensional figure See *cone*, *cylinder*, *prism*, *pyramid*.

Base of an isosceles triangle See *isosceles triangle*.

Between On a number line, point *C* is between point *A* and point *B* if the coordinate of point *C* is between the coordinates of points *A* and *B*.

Betweenness See *segment addition postulate*.

Biconditional statement The conjunction of a conditional statement and its converse. The biconditional *If p, then q and If q, then p* is written in abbreviated form as *p if, and only if, q*.

Boundary of a half-plane See *open half-plane*.

Cavalieri's Principle If two space figures have the same height and the same cross-sectional area at every level, then they have the same volume.

Center of a circle See *circle*.

Center of a regular polygon The point that is equidistant from all the vertices of the polygon.

Center of a sphere See *sphere*.

Center of Gravity See *centroid*.

Center of rotation See *rotation*.

Center of symmetry See *rotational symmetry*.

Central angle of a circle An angle whose vertex is the center of the circle.

Centroid Point of concurrency of the medians of a triangle.

Chord of a circle Any line segment that has endpoints on the circle.

Circle The set of all points in a plane that are a fixed distance from a fixed point in the plane. The fixed point is called the *center of the circle*. The fixed distance is called the *radius of the circle*.

Circumcenter Point of concurrency of the perpendicular bisectors of the sides of a triangle.

Circumference of a circle The distance around the circle.

Circumscribed circle The circle that passes through the three vertices of a triangle. Center is the point of concurrency of the triangle's perpendicular bisectors and radius is the distance from that center to any vertex of the triangle.

Closed half-plane The union of an open half-plane and its boundary.

Closed statement A statement that is either true or false.

Collinear points Points that lie on the same line. Points that do not lie on the same line are called *noncollinear points*.

Common external tangent A tangent that does not intersect the segment joining the centers of two circles.

Common internal tangent A tangent that intersects the segment joining the centers of two circles.

Compass A geometric tool used to draw circles and parts of circles, called *arcs*.

Complement of an event The difference between the set of possible outcomes and the set of favorable outcomes of an event.

Complementary angles Two angles whose measures have a sum of 90°. Each angle is the *complement* of the other.

Composition When multiple transformations are applied to a figure.

Compound statement A statement formed by linking two or more simple statements.

Concave polygon A polygon in which at least one diagonal contains a point in the exterior of the polygon.

Conclusion In a conditional statement, the part that follows *then*. Also called *consequent*.

Concurrent lines Three or more lines that intersect at a unique point.

Conditional probability The probability of an event occurring given that some other event has already occurred.

Conditional statement A statement formed by connecting two statements with the words *if* and *then*.

Cone A three-dimensional figure that consists of a face bounded by a circle, called its *base*; a point called the *vertex* that is outside the plane of the base; and a *lateral surface* that connects the vertex to each point on the boundary of the base. The *height* of a cone is the length of a perpendicular segment drawn from the vertex to the plane of the base.

Congruent angles Angles that are equal in measure.

Congruent figures Figures that have the same shape and the same size.

Congruent polygons Polygons whose sides and angles can be placed in a correspondence so that corresponding sides are congruent and corresponding angles are congruent.

Congruent segments Segments that are equal in length.

Conjecture A conclusion based on inductive reasoning.

Conjunction A compound statement that is formed by linking simple statements with the word *and*.

Consecutive angles of a polygon Two angles whose vertices are consecutive vertices of the polygon.

Consecutive sides of a polygon Two sides that have a common endpoint.

Consecutive vertices of a polygon Two vertices that are endpoints of the same side.

Consequent See *conclusion*.

Contrapositive of a conditional statement The statement that results when the hypothesis and conclusion are interchanged, then both negated.

Converse of a conditional statement The statement that results when the hypothesis and conclusion are interchanged.

Conversion factor A ratio of two measurements that is equal to one.

Convex polygon A polygon in which no diagonal contains a point in the exterior of the polygon.

Coordinate plane A number plane determined by a horizontal number line and a vertical number line that intersect at their origins.

Coordinate(s) of a point The real number or numbers that correspond to the point. On a number line, the coordinate of each point is a single number. On a coordinate plane, each point has an ordered pair (x, y) of coordinates. The first number of the ordered pair is called the *x-coordinate* of the point, and the second is called the *y-coordinate*. See also *Ruler Postulate*.

Coplanar figures Figures that lie on the same plane. Figures that do not lie on the same plane are called *noncoplanar figures*.

Corollary A theorem that follows directly from a previously proved theorem.

Corresponding angles A pair of nonadjacent angles, one interior and one exterior, that are on the same side of a transversal.

Corresponding Angles Postulate If two parallel lines are cut by a transversal, then corresponding angles are congruent.

G-3

...s of Congruent Triangles Are ...ate (CPCTCP) If two triangles are ... the corresponding sides and angles of the ... must also be congruent.

...o The cosine of an acute angle of a right ... the ratio of the length of the leg adjacent to the ... the length of the hypotenuse. The symbol for the ...e of an angle *A* is cos *A*.

...ounterexample A particular instance that shows a general statement is not true for all values in the replacement set.

Counting principle If there are *m* ways that a first event can occur and *n* ways that a second event can occur, then there are *m•n* ways that both can occur.

Cube A prism whose faces are bounded by six congruent squares.

Cylinder A three-dimensional figure that consists of two parallel *bases* bounded by congruent circles and a *lateral surface* that connects the circles. The *height* of a cylinder is the length of any perpendicular segment drawn from a point on one base to the plane containing the other base.

Decagon A polygon that has exactly ten sides.

Deductive reasoning The process of reasoning logically from given facts to a conclusion.

Definition The statement of the meaning of a word or phrase. Every definition can be written as a bi-conditional statement.

Degree measure of an angle A unique real number from 0 to 180 that is paired with the angle.

Dependent events Two events are dependent if the occurrence of one affects the occurrence of the other.

Diagonal of a polygon A segment whose endpoints are nonconsecutive vertices of the polygon.

Diameter of a circle A segment, or the length of the segment, whose endpoints are points of the circle and that contains the center of the circle.

Dihedral angle The angle formed by two intersecting planes. Each plane is divided into two *half planes*.

Dilation A dilation with center *O* and *scale factor n*, where $n \neq 0$, is a transformation in which the image of a point *A* is a point *A'* such that point *A'* is on $\overrightarrow{OA}$ and $OA' = n \cdot OA$. The image of point *O* is point *O*. If $n > 1$, the dilation is an *enlargement*. If $0 < n < 1$, it is a *reduction*. A dilation is also called a *similarity transformation*. A dilation with scale factor *n* is denoted $D_n(x, y) \rightarrow (nx, ny)$.

Dimensional analysis A method for converting a measurement from one unit of measure to another by multiplying by a ratio representing the relationship between the units. The ratio is called a *conversion factor*.

Direct measurement See *indirect measurement*.

Direct variation A relationship described by an equation of the form $y = kx$, where *k* is a constant nonzero real number. The number *k* is called the *constant of variation*.

Disjunction A compound statement that is formed by linking simple statements with the word *or*.

Distance between a line and a point not on the line The length of the perpendicular segment from the line to the point.

Distance between two parallel lines The distance between one line and a point on the other line.

Distance between two points (number line) The absolute value of the difference of the coordinates of the points. See also *Ruler Postulate*.

Distance formula (coordinate plane) The distance *PQ* between $P(x_1, y_1)$ and $Q(x_2, y_2)$ is given by the formula $PQ = \sqrt{(x_2 - x_1)^2 + (y_2 - y_1)^2}$.

Dodecagon A polygon with exactly twelve sides.

Dodecahedron A regular polyhedron with 12 congruent faces that are pentagons.

Edge A line segment that joins two vertices.

Edge of a polyhedron A segment that is the intersection of two faces.

Empirical probability A probability determined by collecting data from an experiment. Also called *experimental probability*.

Endpoint See *ray* and *segment*.

Endpoint of a kite The common endpoint of a pair of congruent sides.

Enlargement See *dilation*.

Equiangular polygon A polygon whose angles are all congruent.

Equiangular triangle A triangle that has three congruent angles.

Equilateral polygon A polygon whose sides are all congruent.

Equilateral triangle A triangle that has three congruent sides.

Euler line The line passing through the orthocenter, the centroid, and the circumcenter of a triangle.

Event In probability, any set of outcomes that are in the sample space.

Exterior Angle Corollary The measure of an exterior angle of a triangle is greater than the measure of each of its remote interior angles.

Exterior angle of a convex polygon An angle that forms a linear pair with one of the polygon's interior angles.

External tangent A line, segment, or ray in the plane of the circle that intersects the circle at exactly one point.

Externally tangent Two circles are externally tangent if their centers lie on opposite sides of a common tangent.

Face of a polyhedron One of its flat surfaces.

Factorial notation The notation $n!$, which is read as "n factorial" and which represents the product $n \times (n - 1) \times (n - 2) \times \ldots \times 2 \times 1$. The value of $0!$ is defined to be 1.

Figure In geometry, any set of points.

Fixed point A point that is its own image under a transformation.

Formula A literal equation in which each variable represents a quantity.

Foundation or base drawing A drawing which shows the base of a structure and the height of each part.

Function A mapping of from one set to another.

Geometric construction A drawing that is made using only an unmarked *straightedge* and a *compass*. The straightedge is used to draw segments, rays, and lines. The compass is used to draw arcs and circles.

Geometric mean The number x such that $\frac{a}{x} = \frac{x}{b}$, where a, b, and x are positive numbers.

Given See *hypothesis*.

Graph of a number The point that corresponds to the number on a number line.

Graph of an inequality (number line) The set of the graphs of all solutions to the inequality.

Graph of an ordered pair The point that corresponds to the ordered pair on a coordinate plane.

Great circle The circle that is the cross section of a sphere and a plane that contains the center of the sphere. A great circle divides the sphere into 2 hemispheres.

Half plane See *dihedral angle*.

Half-turn A rotation of exactly 180°.

Height of a plane figure See *parallelogram, trapezoid, triangle*.

Height of a three-dimensional figure See *cone, cylinder, prism, pyramid*.

Hemisphere See *great circle*.

Hexagon A polygon that has exactly six sides.

Hexahedron A polyhedron with 6 congruent faces that are squares. See *cube*.

Hypotenuse The side of a right triangle that is opposite the right angle.

Hypotenuse-Leg (HL) Congruence Theorem If the hypotenuse and one leg of a right triangle are congruent to the hypotenuse and one leg of another right triangle, then the triangles are congruent.

Hypothesis In a conditional statement, the part that follows *if*. Also called the *antecedent*.

Icosahedron A polyhedron with 20 congruent faces that are triangles.

Image See *transformation*.

Implication Conditional statement written using the → symbol.

Incenter Point of concurrency of the angle bisectors of a triangle.

Independent events Two events are independent if the occurrence of one does not affect the occurrence of the other.

Indirect measurement Determining an unknown measurement by using mathematical relationships among known measurements rather than using a *direct measurement* tool such as a ruler or protractor.

Indirect reasoning A type of reasoning in which all possibilities are considered and then the unwanted ones are proved false. The remaining possibility must be true.

Inductive reasoning A type of reasoning that draws conclusions based on a pattern of specific examples or observations.

Inscribed angle An angle inside a circle that is determined by three points that lie on the circle.

Inscribed circle The circle that is tangent to the three sides of a triangle. Center is the point of concurrency of the triangle's angle bisectors and radius is the perpendicular distance from that center to any side of the triangle.

Inscribed quadrilateral A quadrilateral with all four vertices contained on the circle.

Intercepted arc The section of a circle that is between the endpoints of an inscribed angle.

GLOSSARY

Interior angle of a convex polygon An angle determined by two consecutive sides of the polygon. Also called an *angle of the polygon.*

Internally tangent Two circles are internally tangent if their centers lie on the same side of a common tangent.

Intersection of figures The set of all points common to two or more figures. The figures are said to *intersect* at these points.

Intersection of sets The set of all points common to two given sets. Symbol for intersection is ∩.

Invariant property A property that does not change as a result of a transformation.

Inverse of a conditional statement The statement that results when the hypothesis and conclusion are both negated.

Isometry A transformation in which a figure and its image are congruent.

Isosceles trapezoid A trapezoid with congruent base angles.

Isosceles triangle A triangle that has at least two congruent sides, called the *legs.* The third side is the *base.* The angles opposite the congruent sides are called the *base angles.* The third angle is the *vertex angle.*

Isosceles Triangle Bisectors Theorem The bisector of the vertex angle of an isosceles triangle is the perpendicular bisector of the base.

Isosceles Triangle Theorem If two sides of a triangle are congruent, then the angles opposite those sides are congruent. Also stated as: *Base angles of an isosceles triangle are congruent.*

Kite A convex quadrilateral in which two distinct pairs of consecutive sides are congruent.

Lateral area of a prism or pyramid The sum of the areas of the lateral faces.

Lateral face See *pyramid, prism.*

Lateral surface See *cone, cylinder.*

Law of Cosines Used in an oblique triangle if SAS or SSS is given, then $a^2 = b^2 + c^2 - 2bc \cos A$.

Law of Sines Used in an oblique triangle if AAS or SSA is given, then $\frac{\sin A}{a} = \frac{\sin B}{B} = \frac{\sin C}{c}$.

Legs of a right triangle The sides opposite the acute angles.

Legs of a trapezoid The nonparallel sides.

Length of a segment The distance between the endpoints of the segment.

Legs of an isosceles triangle See *isosceles triangle.*

Line A set of points that extends in two opposite directions without end. This is one of the basic *undefined terms* of geometry.

Line Intersection Postulate If two lines intersect, then they intersect in exactly one point.

Line segment See *segment.*

Line symmetry A plane figure that has line symmetry is its own image after reflection across some line in the plane. The line is called a *line of symmetry* for the figure.

Linear pair Adjacent angles whose noncommon sides are opposite rays.

Linear Pair Postulate If two angles form a linear pair, then they are supplementary.

Locus The set of all points that satisfy specified conditions. The plural of *locus* is *loci.*

Logically equivalent statements Statements that have the same truth value.

Major arc A major arc of a circle is an arc that is larger than a semicircle.

Medial triangle The triangle formed by connecting the midpoints of each side of a given triangle.

Median measure theorem The centroid of a triangle is located a distance $\frac{2}{3}$ the length of any medians measured from the vertex of the triangle.

Median of a triangle A segment whose endpoints are a vertex of the triangle and the midpoint of the opposite side.

Midpoint formula The coordinates of the midpoint of the segment with endpoints $P(x_1, y_1)$ and $Q(x_2, y_2)$ are $\left(\dfrac{x_1 + x_2}{2}, \dfrac{y_1 + y_2}{2}\right)$.

Midpoint of a segment The point that divides the segment into two congruent segments.

Midsegment of a triangle A segment that connects the midpoints of two sides of a triangle.

Minor arc A minor arc of a circle is an arc that is smaller than a semicircle.

Mutually exclusive events Two events that have no outcomes in common.

Negation of a statement The statement formed when the word *not* is inserted into or removed from a statement. The negation of a true statement is always false. The negation of a false statement is always true.

Net A 2-dimensional model of a 3-dimensional figure.

Network See *Vertex-edge graph*.

***n*-gon** A polygon that has exactly *n* sides.

Nonagon A polygon that has exactly nine sides.

Noncollinear points Points that do not lie on the same line.

Number line A line whose points have been placed in one-to-one correspondence with the set of real numbers.

Oblique cylinder or prism A cylinder or prism where the segment joining the centers of the bases is not perpendicular to the planes containing the bases.

Oblique triangle A triangle that doesn't contain a right angle.

Obtuse angle An angle whose measure is greater than 90° and less than 180°.

Obtuse triangle A triangle that has one obtuse angle.

Octagon A polygon that has exactly eight sides.

Octahedron A polyhedron with 8 congruent faces that are triangles.

Open half-plane Either of two regions into which a line separates a coordinate plane. The line is called the *boundary* of each half-plane.

Open statement A statement that contains one or more variables.

Opposite angles of a quadrilateral Two angles that are not consecutive.

Opposite rays On a line, if point *B* is between points *A* and *C*, then $\overrightarrow{BA}$ and $\overrightarrow{BC}$ are opposite rays.

Opposite sides of a quadrilateral Two sides that are not consecutive.

Ordered pair In a coordinate plane, the pair of real numbers (x, y) that corresponds to a point.

Origin of a coordinate plane The point where the axes intersect.

Origin of a number line The point that corresponds to the number zero.

Orthocenter Point of concurrency of the altitudes of a triangle.

Orthographic drawing A drawing that shows a top view, a front view, and a right view.

Overlapping figures Figures that have interior points in common.

Parabola The U-shaped curve that is the graph of a quadratic function.

Parallel lines Coplanar lines that do not intersect. The symbol for *parallel* is ∥.

Parallel Postulate Through a point not on a line, there is exactly one line parallel to the given line.

Parallelogram A quadrilateral that has two pairs of parallel sides. To calculate area, any of the sides may be considered the *base*, and the length of that side is also called the base. The *height* is then the length of any perpendicular segment drawn from a point on the side opposite the base to the line containing the base.

Path The sequence of connections between vertices.

Pentagon A polygon that has exactly five sides.

Perimeter of a plane figure The distance around the figure. The perimeter of a polygon is the sum of the lengths of its sides.

Permutation An arrangement of some or all objects from a set in a specific order.

Perpendicular bisector of a segment Any line, ray, or segment that is perpendicular to the segment at its midpoint.

Perpendicular lines Lines that intersect to form right angles. The symbol for perpendicular is ⊥.

Perpendicular Transversal Theorem If a transversal is perpendicular to one of two parallel lines, then it is perpendicular to the other.

Plane A set of points that extends along a flat surface in every direction without end. This is one of the basic *undefined terms* of geometry.

Plane figure A figure whose points all lie in the same plane.

Plane Intersection Postulate If two planes intersect, then they intersect in a line.

Point A location. This is one of the basic *undefined terms* of geometry.

Point of concurrency The unique point where concurrent lines intersect.

Point of tangency The point on a circle where a tangent intersects the circle.

Point-slope form of an equation of a line For an equation in the variables x and y, the point-slope form is $y - y_1 = m(x - x_1)$, where $P(x_1, y_1)$ is a point on the line and m is the slope of the line.

Point symmetry A plane figure that has point symmetry is its own image after a half-turn in the plane.

Polygon A plane figure formed by three or more segments such that each segment intersects exactly two others, one at each endpoint, and no two segments with a common endpoint are collinear. Each segment is a *side* of the polygon. The common endpoint of two sides is a *vertex* of the polygon. A polygon completely encloses a region of the plane, called its *interior*.

GLOSSARY

Polygon Exterior Angle-Sum Theorem The sum of the measures of the exterior angles of a convex polygon, one at each vertex, is 360°.

Polygon Interior Angle-Sum Theorem The sum of the measures of the interior angles of a convex polygon that has n sides is $(n - 2)180°$.

Polyhedron A three-dimensional figure formed by flat surfaces that are bounded by polygons joined in pairs along their sides.

Polynomial A monomial or a sum of monomials.

Population In a statistical study, the set of all individuals or objects being studied.

Postulate A statement whose truth is accepted without proof.

Preimage See *transformation*.

Prism A polyhedron with two parallel faces, called its *bases*, that are bounded by congruent polygons; and with *lateral faces* that are bounded by parallelograms connecting corresponding sides of the bases. The *height* of a prism is the length of any perpendicular segment drawn from a point on one base to the plane containing the other base.

Probability A number from 0 to 1, inclusive, that represents the likelihood an event will occur. If an event is *impossible*, the probability is 0. If the event is *certain*, its probability is 1. Events that are *possible but not certain* are assigned probabilities between 0 and 1.

Probability distribution For a given sample space, a table that pairs each value of the random variable with its probability.

Proof A convincing argument that uses deductive reasoning. In a *two-column proof*, the statements and reasons are aligned in columns. In a *paragraph proof*, the statements and reasons are connected in sentences. In a *flow proof*, arrows show the logical connections between the statements. In a *coordinate proof*, a figure is drawn on a coordinate plane and the formulas for slope, midpoint, and distance are used to prove properties of the figure. An *indirect proof* involves the use of indirect reasoning. In a *transformational proof* the properties of isometries are used to show congruence.

Proportion A statement that two ratios are equal. The proportion that equates the ratios "a to b" and "c to d" can be written in three ways:

$$a \text{ is to } b \text{ as } c \text{ is to } d \quad a:b = c:d \quad \frac{a}{b} = \frac{c}{d}$$

Protractor Postulate Let $\overrightarrow{OA}$ and $\overrightarrow{OB}$ be opposite rays. Consider $\overrightarrow{OA}$, $\overrightarrow{OB}$, and all the rays with endpoint O that can be drawn in a plane on one side of $\overleftrightarrow{AB}$. These rays can be paired with the real numbers from 0 to 180, one-to-one, in such a way that:

• $\overrightarrow{OA}$ is paired with 0 and $\overrightarrow{OB}$ is paired with 180.

• If $\overrightarrow{OP}$ is paired with x and $\overrightarrow{OQ}$ is paired with y, then the number paired with $\angle POQ$ is $|x - y|$. This is called the *measure*, or the *degree measure*, of $\angle POQ$.

Pyramid A polyhedron that consists of a face bounded by a polygon, called its *base*; a point called the *vertex* that is outside the plane of the base; and triangular *lateral faces* that connect the vertex to each side of the base. The *height* of a pyramid is the length of the perpendicular segment drawn from the vertex to the plane of the base.

Pythagorean trigonometric identity In a right triangle with a hypotenuse of length one $\sin^2 A + \cos^2 A = 1$.

Pythagorean Theorem If a triangle is a right triangle with legs of lengths a and b and hypotenuse of length c, then $a^2 + b^2 = c^2$.

Pythagorean triple Any set of three positive integers that satisfy the relationship $a^2 + b^2 = c^2$.

Q

Quadrant One of the four regions into which a coordinate plane is divided by the x- and y-axes.

Quadrilateral A polygon that has exactly four sides.

Quadrilateral Angle-Sum Theorem The sum of the measures of the interior angles of a quadrilateral is 360°.

R

Radian A measure of a central angle of a circle. One radian is the measure of the angle that intercepts an arc of a circle equal in length to a radius of the circle.

Radius of a circle A segment, or the length of the segment, whose endpoints are the center of the circle and a point of the circle. See also *circle*.

Radius of a sphere See *sphere*.

Random variable In probability, a variable that represents the outcomes in a sample space.

Ratio A comparison of two numbers by division. *The ratio of a to b* can be written in three ways:

$$a \text{ to } b \quad a:b \quad \frac{a}{b}$$

Ray Part of a line that begins at one point and extends without end in one direction. The point is called the *endpoint of the ray*.

Reason Theorem, postulate, or property that justifies a statement in a two-column proof.

Reciprocal Two numbers are reciprocals if their product is 1. See also *inverse property of multiplication*.

Rectangle A quadrilateral that has four right angles.

Reflection in a line A reflection across line m is a transformation such that, if point A is on line m, then the image of point A is point A; and if point B is not on line m, then its image B' is the point such that line m is the perpendicular bisector of $\overline{BB'}$. Line m is called the *line of reflection*. The reflection of point P across line m is denoted by $r_m P \rightarrow P'$.

Reflection in a point A reflection about point P is a transformation such that the image of point P is point P; and the image of any other point Q is the point Q' such that point P is the midpoint of $\overline{QQ'}$. Point P is called the *point of reflection*. The reflection of point Q about point P is denoted by $r_p Q \rightarrow Q'$.

Regular polygon A polygon that is both equilateral and equiangular.

Regular polyhedron All of the faces of a polyhedron are regular polygons that are congruent to each other.

Regular pyramid A pyramid whose base is bounded by a regular polygon and in which the segment joining the center of the base to the vertex is perpendicular to the plane of the base. The lateral faces of a regular pyramid are congruent isosceles triangles.

Remote interior angles For each exterior angle of a triangle, the two nonadjacent interior angles are called remote interior angles.

Rhombus A quadrilateral that has four congruent sides.

Right angle An angle whose measure is 90°.

Right cone A cone in which the segment joining the center of the base to the vertex is perpendicular to the plane of the base. If a cone is not a right cone, then it is called *oblique*.

Right cylinder A cylinder in which the segment joining the centers of the bases is perpendicular to the planes of the bases. If a cylinder is not a right cylinder, then it is called *oblique*.

Right prism A prism in which the segments that connect corresponding vertices of the bases are perpendicular to the planes of the bases. The lateral faces of a right prism are bounded by rectangles. If a prism is not a right prism, then it is called *oblique*.

Right triangle A triangle with one right angle.

Rigid Motion See *isometry*.

Right triangle 30° -60° -90° The length of the hypotenuse is twice the length of the leg opposite the 30° angle. The length of the side opposite the 60° angle is the product of $\sqrt{3}$ and the length if a leg opposite the 30° angle.

Right triangle 45° -45° -90° The length of the hypotenuse is the product of $\sqrt{2}$ and the length of a leg, Also known as an isosceles right triangle.

Rotation A rotation of $x°$ about point O is a transformation such that the image of point O is point O; and for any other point P, its image is the point P' such that $\overline{OP} = \overline{OP'}$ and $m\angle POP' = x°$. Point O is called the *center of rotation*. The direction of rotation is specified as *clockwise* or *counterclockwise*. The rotation of $x°$ about point O is denoted $R_{o,x°} P \rightarrow P'$.

Rotational symmetry A plane figure that has rotational symmetry is its own image after a rotation of 180° or less around some point in the plane. The point is called the *center of symmetry* for the figure.

Ruler Postulate The points of a line can be paired with the real numbers, one-to-one, so that any point corresponds to 0 and any other point corresponds to 1. The real number that corresponds to a point is the *coordinate* of that point. The *distance* between two points is equal to the absolute value of the difference of their coordinates.

Same-Side Interior Angles Theorem If two parallel lines are cut by a transversal, then interior angles on the same side of the transversal are supplementary.

Sample space The set of all possible outcomes in a given situation.

Scale drawing A two-dimensional drawing that is similar to the object it represents. The ratio of the size of the drawing to the actual size of the object is the *scale* of the drawing.

Scale factor See *dilation ratio, similarity*.

Scalene triangle A triangle that has no congruent sides.

Secant A line, ray, or segment that intersects a circle at 2 points.

Sector of a circle The part of the interior of a circle formed by two radii and the arc they intercept.

Segment Part of a line that begins at one point and ends at another. The points are called the *endpoints of the segment*. Also called *line segment*.

Segment Addition Postulate If point C is between point A and point B, then $AC + CB = AB$.

Segment bisector Any line, ray, or segment that intersects a given segment at its midpoint.

Semicircle Half of a circle.

Side of a polygon See *polygon*.

Side of an angle One of the two rays that form the angle.

Side-Angle-Side (SAS) Congruence Postulate If two sides and the included angle of one triangle are congruent to two sides and the included angle of another triangle, then the triangles are congruent.

GLOSSARY

Side-Angle-Side (SAS) Similarity Theorem If an angle of one triangle is congruent to an angle of another triangle, and the lengths of the sides including these angles are in proportion, then the triangles are similar.

Side-Side-Side (SSS) Congruence Postulate If three sides of one triangle are congruent to three sides of another triangle, then the triangles are congruent.

Side-Side-Side (SSS) Similarity Theorem If corresponding sides of two triangles are in proportion, then the triangles are similar.

Side-Splitter Theorem If a line is parallel to one side of a triangle and intersects the other two sides at distinct points, then it divides those two sides proportionally.

Similar figures Figures that have the same shape, but not necessarily the same size.

Similar polygons Polygons whose sides and angles can be placed in a correspondence so that corresponding angles are congruent and corresponding sides are in proportion.

Similarity A composite transformation made up of a dilation and an isometry.

Similarity ratio The ratio of the lengths of corresponding sides of similar polygons. Also called the *scale factor*.

Similarity transformation See *dilation*.

Sine ratio The sine of an acute angle of a right triangle is the ratio of the length of the leg opposite the angle to the length of the hypotenuse. The symbol for the sine of an angle is sin A.

Skew lines Lines that are noncoplanar.

Slant height of a regular pyramid The height of a lateral face.

Slant height of a right cone The distance between the vertex of the cone and any point on the boundary of the base.

Slope On a coordinate plane, the steepness of a nonvertical line, described informally as $\frac{\text{rise}}{\text{run}}$. Formally, if $P(x_1, y_1)$ and $Q(x_2, y_2)$ lie on $\overleftrightarrow{PQ}$, and $x_1 \neq x_2$, then the slope m of $\overleftrightarrow{PQ}$ is defined by $m = \frac{y_2 - y_1}{x_2 - x_1}$.

Slope-intercept form of an equation of a line For an equation in the variables x and y, $y = mx + b$, where m is the slope of the graph and b is the y-intercept.

Solution set of an open statement The set of all solutions to the open statement.

Solution to a system of equations or inequalities in two variables For a system in the variables x and y, any ordered pair (x, y) that is a solution to each equation or inequality in the system.

Solution to an equation or inequality in two variables For an equation or inequality in the variables x and y, any ordered pair of numbers (x, y) that together make the equation or inequality a true statement.

Solution to an open statement Any value of the variable(s) that makes the statement true.

Space In geometry, the set of all points.

Space figure A figure whose points extend beyond a single plane into space. Also called a *three-dimensional figure*.

Sphere The set of all points in space that are a fixed distance from a fixed point. The fixed point is called the *center of the sphere*. The fixed distance is called the *radius of the sphere*.

Square A quadrilateral that has four congruent sides and four right angles.

Standard form of an equation of a circle For a circle with center $P(h, k)$ and radius r, the equation is $(x - h)^2 + (y - k^2) = r^2$. If P is the origin, the equation becomes $x^2 + y^2 = r^2$.

Statement Any mathematical sentence.

Straight angle An angle whose measure is 180°.

Straightedge A straightedge is a ruler with no markings on it.

Supplementary angles Two angles whose measures have a sum of 180°. Each angle is the *supplement* of the other.

Surface area The total area of all surfaces of a three-dimensional figure.

Syllogism The statement-reason pattern used in two-column proof.

Tangent A line, ray, or segment in the plane of the circle that intersects the circle at exactly one point.

Tangent of an angle The tangent of an acute angle of a right triangle is the ratio of the length of the leg opposite the angle to the length of the leg adjacent to it. The symbol for the tangent of an angle A is tan A.

Tetrahedron A polyhedron with 4 congruent faces that are triangles.

Theorem A statement that can be proved true.

Theoretical probability If an event E contains m favorable outcomes in a sample space that consists of n outcomes where all outcomes are equally likely, then the theoretical probability if E, denoted $P(E)$, is given by the formula $P(E) = \frac{m}{n}$.

Three-dimensional figure See *space figure*.

Transformation A correspondence between one figure, called a *preimage*, and a second figure, called its *image*, such that each point of the image is paired with exactly one point of the preimage, and each point of the preimage is paired with exactly one point of the image.

Transitivity of Parallelism Theorem If two lines are parallel to a third line, then the lines are parallel to each other.

Translation A transformation in which the image is the figure that would result if each point of the preimage were moved the same distance and in the same direction. The translation of a point (x, y) in the coordinate plane a units horizontally and b units vertically is given by $T_{a,b}(x, y) \rightarrow (x + a, y + b)$.

Transversal A line that intersects two or more coplanar lines at different points.

Trapezoid A quadrilateral with at least one pair of parallel sides. The parallel sides, and the lengths of the parallel sides, are called the *bases*. Two angles of the trapezoid whose vertices are the endpoints of a single base are a pair of *base angles*. The *height* is the length of any perpendicular segment drawn from a point on one base to the line containing the other base.

Triangle A polygon that has exactly three sides. To calculate area, any of the sides may be considered the *base*, and the length of that side is also called the base. The *height* is then the length of the altitude drawn to the base from the opposite vertex.

Triangle Angle-Sum Theorem The sum of the measures of the angles of a triangle is 180°.

Triangle Exterior-Angle Theorem The measure of each exterior angle of a triangle is equal to the sum of the measures of the remote interior angles.

Triangle Inequality Theorem The sum of the lengths of any two sides of a triangle is greater than the length of the third side.

Truth value A closed statement is either *true* or *false*. These are its possible truth values.

Two Perpendiculars Theorem If two coplanar lines are perpendicular to a third line, then the lines are parallel.

Two-point form of an equation of a line For an equation in the variables x and y, $y - y_1 = \frac{y_2 - y_1}{x_2 - x_1}(x - x_1)$ where $P(x_1, y_1)$ and $Q(x_2, y_2)$ lie on a nonvertical line.

Undefined term A term that is used without a specific mathematical definition. In geometry, the three undefined terms are *point*, *line*, and *plane*.

Unequal Angles Theorem If two angles of a triangle are not congruent, then the side opposite the larger of the two angles is longer than the side opposite the smaller angle.

Unequal Sides Theorem If two sides of a triangle are not congruent, then the angle opposite the longer of the two sides is larger than the angle opposite the shorter side.

Union of sets The set of all elements in either of the two given sets. The symbol for intersection is $\cup$.

Unique Line Postulate Through any two points there is exactly one line. Also stated as: *Two points determine a line.*

Unique Plane Postulate Through any three noncollinear points there is exactly one plane. Also stated as: *Three noncollinear points determine a plane.*

Vector A quantity having direction as well as magnitude.

Venn diagram A diagram in which a rectangle represents all members of a set, with circles within it showing selected subsets and relationships among them.

Vertex angle of an isosceles triangle The angle opposite the base of an isosceles triangle. See *isosceles triangle*.

Vertex of a polygon See *polygon*.

Vertex of a polyhedron A point that is the intersection of three or more edges.

Vertex of a pyramid See *pyramid*.

Vertex of an angle The common endpoint of the sides.

Vertex of a cone See *cone*.

Vertex-edge graph A graph in which the vertices are connected by edges to form a path.

Vertical angles Two angles whose sides form two pairs of opposite rays.

Vertical Angles Theorem If two angles are vertical angles, then they are congruent.

Volume of a three-dimensional figure The amount of space the figure encloses, measured by the number of nonoverlapping cubic units in its interior.

***x*-axis** The horizontal number line in a coordinate plane.

***x*-coordinate** See *coordinate(s) of a point*.

***x*-intercept of a graph** The x-coordinate of any point where the graph intersects the x-axis.

***y*-axis** The vertical number line in a coordinate plane.

***y*-coordinate** See *coordinate(s) of a point*.

***y*-intercept of a graph** The y-coordinate of any point where the graph intersects the y-axis.

PARCC

Partnership for Assessment of
Readiness for College and Careers

High School Assessment Reference Sheet

1 inch = 2.54 centimeters
1 meter = 39.37 inches
1 mile = 5,280 feet
1 mile = 1,760 yards
1 mile = 1.609 kilometers

1 kilometer = 0.62 mile
1 pound = 16 ounces
1 pound = 0.454 kilograms
1 kilogram = 2.2 pounds
1 ton = 2,000 pounds

1 cup = 8 fluid ounces
1 pint = 2 cups
1 quart = 2 pints
1 gallon = 4 quarts
1 gallon = 3.785 liters
1 liter = 0.264 gallons
1 liter = 1000 cubic centimeters

Triangle	$A = \dfrac{1}{2}bh$	Pythagorean Theorem	$a^2 + b^2 = c^2$
Parallelogram	$A = bh$	Quadratic Formula	$x = \dfrac{-b \pm \sqrt{b^2 - 4ac}}{2a}$
Circle	$A = \pi r^2$	Arithmetic Sequence	$a_n = a_1 + (n-1)d$
Circle	$C = \pi d \text{ or } C = 2\pi r$	Geometric Sequence	$a_n = a_1 r^{n-1}$
General Prisms	$V = Bh$	Geometric Series	$S_n = \dfrac{a_1 - a_1 r^n}{1 - r} \text{ where } r \neq 1$
Cylinder	$V = \pi r^2 h$	Radians	$1\,radian = \dfrac{180}{\pi}\,degrees$
Sphere	$V = \dfrac{4}{3}\pi r^3$	Degrees	$1\,degree = \dfrac{\pi}{180}\,radians$
Cone	$V = \dfrac{1}{3}\pi r^2 h$	Exponential Growth/Decay	$A = A_0\,e^{k(t-t_0)} + B_0$
Pyramid	$V = \dfrac{1}{3}Bh$		

SELECTED ANSWERS

SELECTED ANSWERS

Diagnostic Test

Chapter 1

1 (2) **3** (4) **5** (1), (3) and (4) **7** (3)
9 $AC = 5$

Chapter 2

1 (4) **3** (4) **5** (3) **7** (2) **9** $40\sqrt{2}$ sq. cm

Chapter 3

1 (4) **3** (2) **5** (4) **7** (4) **9** $\overline{BC}$

Chapter 4

1 (3) **3** (2) **5** (3) **7** (4) **9** This is a composite transformation of two reflections over parallel lines which is the same as a translation. In a translation an image is parallel to its pre-image. This only appears to be true for triangle #4.

Chapter 5

1 (4) **3** (1) **5** (3) **7** (2) **9** $\frac{7}{24} \approx 0.291667$

Chapter 6

1 (2) **3** (1) **5** (1&4) **7** (4)
9 $x = 3$ & $y = 11$

Chapter 7

1 (3) **3** (2) **5** (4) **7** (4) **9** $x^2 + y^2 = 100$

Chapter 8

1 (3) **3** (1) **5** (3) **7** (1) **9** 10π sq. cm.

Chapter 9

1 (3) **3** (3) **5** (4) **7** (1) **9** $\frac{6}{\pi}$

Chapter 10

1 (1) **3** (3) **5** (1) **7** (4) **9** A and B are mutually exclusive. A = toss die; B = toss coin

Chapter 1

Lesson 1.1

1 (1) **3** (2) **5** (2) **7** Yes **9** Yes
11 Yes **13** No **15** point B **17** point J, point L, and point H **19** $\overleftrightarrow{GH}, \overleftrightarrow{GK}, \overleftrightarrow{KH}$

21 point H **23** 4 **25** 10 **27** U **29** V
31 $JM = 18; JK = 36$
33

35 $B = -2$ **37** $B = 21$

Lesson 1.2

1 (4) **3** (3) **5** (3) **7** (3) **9** (2) **11** $34°$
13 $(90 - x)°$ **15** $138.5°$ **17** $68°$ **19** $29°$
21 True only if a ray in the interior of a right angle forms both angles. **23** R can be any point on any ray $\overleftrightarrow{PQ}$. **25** The measure of each angle is $45°$. **27** $120°$

Lesson 1.3

1 (1) **3** (4) **5** $147°$ **7** $105°$ **9** $75°$ **11** $75°$
13 $49°$ **15** $90°$ **17** $131°$ **19** $96°$ **21** $96°$
23 $128°$ **25** Converse of the Same-Side Interior Angles Theorem

Lesson 1.4

1 (2) **3** (4)
5

7

9

11

13
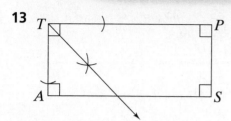

15 Check students' sketches.

17
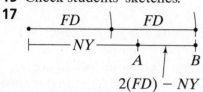

Lesson 1.5

1 (3) **3** (4)
5 perpendicular bisector of $\overline{MN}$.
7
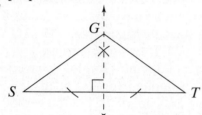

9
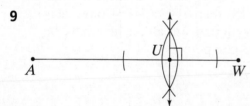

11
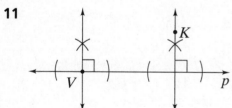

13
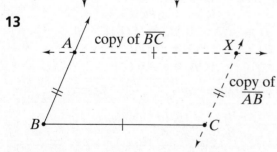

Chapter 1 Preparing for the Assessment

1 (1) **3** (3) **5** (3) **7** (1) **9** (2) **11** (2)
13 (2) **15** (3)

17 Draw any two transversals. Construct the midpoint of both transversals. Draw a line connecting the midpoints to form the locus of points equidistant from the given lines.

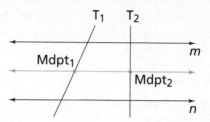

19 Draw line m. Mark points C and R on m. At C draw a transversal and construct $\overline{CD}$ on the transversal. At D construct a copy of $\angle DCR$ to draw line n parallel to m. At R construct a copy of $\angle DCR$ so it intersects n at P. $CDPR$ is an isosceles trapezoid.

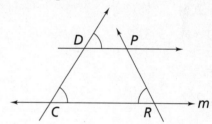

Chapter 2

Lesson 2.1

1 (3) **3** (4) **5** (3) **7** Obtuse, scalene
9 Conditional: If two angles are right angles, then they are congruent. True
Converse: If two angles are congruent, then they are right angles. False
11 Conditional: If a point is a midpoint, then it forms two congruent segments. True
Converse: If two segments are congruent, then there is a midpoint. False **13** They are vertical angles. **15** $\angle 6$ and $\angle 5$ **17** 124° **19** 45, 60, 75
21 $a = 115°$, $b = 30°$ **23** $x = 22$ **25** The congruent angles have the same measure, represented as $x°$. Since the angles are supplementary then $x + x = 180°$ or $2x = 180°$, so $x = 90°$. The angles are both right angles.

Lesson 2.2

1 (4) **3** (2) **5** 6, 7, 8, 9, 10, 11, or 12
7 No. $\overline{AC}$ must be longer than $\overline{AB}$ because $m\angle B > m\angle C$.

SELECTED ANSWERS

Lesson 2.3

1 (4) **3** (4) **5** (1) **7** (1) **9** (1)
11 Construct any two angle bisectors. Label their point of intersection I. Construct a perpendicular from I to side $\overline{AC}$. Label their point of intersection J. Draw the inscribed circle with center I and radius IJ.

Lesson 2.4

1 (1) **3** (2) **5** (3) **7** $y = 4\sqrt{3}, x = 8\sqrt{3}$
9 $y = 4\sqrt{70}, x = 4\sqrt{30}$

Lesson 2.5

1 (2) **3** (3) **5** (4) **7** (1) **9** (2) **11** 8 ft
13 29.4 ft **15** $\frac{2\sqrt{3}}{3}$ meters **17** $4\sqrt{3}$ **19** $16\sqrt{2}$
21 $\sqrt{2}:1 = \frac{\sqrt{2}}{1}$ **23** $6\sqrt{3}$ **25** 2

Lesson 2.6

1 (4) **3** (4) **5** 33.7 **7** $a \approx 24.6; b \approx 17.3$
9 1710 ft
11 $m\angle P \approx 22°; m\angle R \approx 68°; m\angle Q \approx 90°$

Lesson 2.7

1 (3) **3** (4) **5** (1) **7** (1) **9** $\frac{1}{7}$

11 39.39 feet **13** 85.0 unit^2

Chapter 2 Preparing for the Assessment

1 (3) **3** (4) **5** (2) **7** (2) **9** (4) **11** (1)
13 (2) **15** (3) **17** (1) **19** (2) **21** (2)
23 The area of the square built upon the hypotenuse is equal to the sum of the areas built upon the two legs. This relationship holds for any similar figures built upon the sides of the right triangle. For example, the area of the semicircle built upon the hypotenuse is equal to the sum of the areas of the semicircles built upon the legs. **25** (3) **27** 116°

Chapter 3

Lesson 3.1

1 (3) **3** T; *Perpendicular lines do not form right angles.*; F **5** T; *There exists zero or more than one bisector of an angle.*; F **7** T; *The*

complement of an acute angle is not an acute angle.; F **9** Skew lines
11

Number line with points M, A, B. Segment MA = 3 cm, segment AB = 6 cm.

13 50° and 40° **15** $a = 1, b = 2$, and $c = 3; 1^2 + 2^2 \neq 3^2$

Lesson 3.2

1 (1) **3** (2) **5** T and T is T **7** T and T is T
9 The biconditional in Example 15 is false because many people like music and do not watch music videos. **11** If two lines in the same plane are not parallel, then the two lines intersect. True. **13** If two circles have the same radius, then they have the same area. If two circles have the same area, then they have the same radius. Two circles have the same radius if and only if they have the same area. **15** $\overline{AC}$
17 $\overrightarrow{CD}$ **19** B **21** If two segments are congruent, then a midpoint is formed. Converse is false. Counterexample: Two sides of an isosceles triangle are congruent, but the vertex point is not a midpoint. **23** If the triangle is a right triangle, then $a^2 + b^2 = c^2$. Converse is true.
25 <u>Intersection</u> means all the lines have in common is one point.

Lesson 3.3

1 1. D, 2. C, 3. F, 4. A, 5. B, 6. E

Lesson 3.4

1 (3) **3** $\triangle WRT \cong \triangle PQZ$; SAS
5 Not possible **7** Check students' work.
9 $\overline{AB} \cong \overline{CD}, \angle BAC \cong \angle DCA$
$\overline{BC} \cong \overline{DA}, \angle ABC \cong \angle CDA$
$\overline{CA} \cong \overline{AC}, \angle BCA \cong \angle DAC$
11 $\overline{AB} \cong \overline{AD}, \angle BAC \cong \angle DAC$
$\overline{CB} \cong \overline{CD}, \angle ABC \cong \angle ADC$
$\overline{AC} \cong \overline{AC}, \angle ACB \cong \angle ACD$
13

Statements	Reasons
1. $\angle ABC \cong \angle DCB$, $\angle DBC \cong \angle ACB$	1. Given
2. $\overline{BC} \cong \overline{BC}$	2. Reflexive Property
3. $\triangle ABC \cong \triangle DCB$	3. ASA

15

Statements	Reasons
1. $\overline{AB} \cong \overline{DC}$	1. Given
2. $\overline{BC} \cong \overline{BC}$	2. Reflexive Property
3. $AB + BC = DC + BC$	3. Addition Property of Equality
4. $AB + BC = AC$ $BC + CD = BD$	4. Segment Addition Postulate
5. $\overline{AC} \cong \overline{BD}$	5. Substitution
6. $\angle G \cong \angle E$, $\angle 2 \cong \angle 3$	6. Given
7. $\triangle GAC \cong \triangle EDB$	7. AAS

17 No, see the following counterexample:

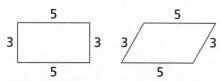

No, think square and a rhombus.

Lesson 3.5

1 (3) **3** (3) **5** Given
7 $m\angle BAC = m\angle 1 + m\angle 2$ **9** Definition of a right angle

11

Statements	Reasons
1. $\overline{AD} \cong \overline{CE}$, $\angle DAC \cong \angle ECA$	1. Given
2. $\overline{AC} \cong \overline{AC}$	2. Reflexive Property
3. $\triangle ACD \cong \triangle CAE$	3. SAS
4. $\overline{AE} \cong \overline{CD}$	4. CPCTC
5. $\overline{ED} \cong \overline{ED}$	5. Reflexive Property
6. $\triangle CED \cong \triangle ADE$	6. SSS

13 1. By construction
2. Definition of angle bisector
3. Given
4. Reflexive Property
5. AAS
6. CPCTC

15

Statements	Reasons
1. $\overline{AD} \cong \overline{BE}$, $\angle DAB \cong \angle EBA$	1. Given
2. $\overline{AB} \cong \overline{AB}$	2. Reflexive Property
3. $\triangle DAB \cong \triangle EBA$	3. SAS
4. $\overline{BD} \cong \overline{AE}$	4. CPCTC

17

Statements	Reasons
1. $\angle 4 \cong \angle 5$	1. Given
2. $\overline{BD} \cong \overline{BD}$	2. Reflexive Property
3. $\angle 2 \cong \angle 3$	3. Given
4. $\angle 3 \cong \angle 1$	4. Intersecting lines form congruent vertical angles.
5. $\angle 1 \cong \angle 2$	5. Substitution
6. $\triangle DAB \cong \triangle DCB$	6. ASA
7. $BA = BC$	7. CPCTC

19 Given: $\overrightarrow{CD}$ is the $\perp$ bisector of $\overline{AB}$.
Prove: $\overline{CA} \cong \overline{CB}$

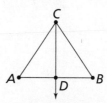

Statements	Reasons
1. Draw $\overline{AC}$ and $\overline{BC}$.	1. Two points determine a line segment.
2. $\overline{AD} \cong \overline{BD}$	2. Definition of perpendicular bisector
3. $\angle ADC \cong \angle BDC$	3. Perpendicular lines form right angles and all right angles are congruent.
4. $\overline{CD} \cong \overline{CD}$	4. Reflexive Property
5. $\triangle ADC \cong \triangle BDC$	5. SAS
6. $\overline{AC} \cong \overline{BC}$	6. CPCTC

Chapter 3 Preparing for the Assessment

1 (1) **3** (2) **5** (3) **7** (1) **9** (2) **11** (1)
13 $\overleftrightarrow{AD}$ **15** $\overline{AC}$

17

Statements	Reasons
1. $\overline{AE} \cong \overline{CD}$, $\angle AED \cong \angle CDE$	1. Given
2. $\overline{ED} \cong \overline{ED}$	2. Reflexive Property
3. $\triangle EAD \cong \triangle DCE$	3. SAS
4. $\angle A \cong \angle C$	4. CPCTC
5. $\overline{AB} \cong \overline{CB}$	5. Given
6. $\triangle ABE \cong \triangle CBD$	6. SAS

19 $\triangle PQR \cong \triangle SRQ$ by ASA using base angles $\angle TQR \cong \angle TRQ$, reflexive side $\overline{QR} \cong \overline{QR}$; Using addition for $\angle PQR \cong \angle SRQ$;, then $\overline{PR} \cong \overline{SQ}$ by CPCTC.

Chapter 4

Lesson 4.1

1 (1) **3** $\overline{d}$ **5** Move 2 units right and 3 units down. **7** S, Q **9** $R, \overline{TU}$ **11** (2)
13 (2) **15** $D'(-1, 0)$

Lesson 4.2

1 image **3** (3) & (4) **5** Yes. It is a transformation that preserves distance. **7** (1)
9 $R'(1, -1), S'(5, -1),$ and $T'(5, -3)$
11 $E'(1, 5), U'(-1, 5), D'(3, 9), P'(5, 9)$
13 $B(-3, 2), C(3, -2),$ and $D(3, 2)$
15

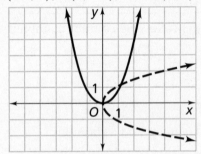

Lesson 4.3

1 (1) **3** (2) **5** $B'(-4, 3)$
7

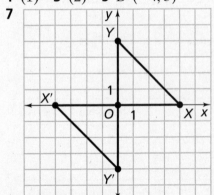

9 $M, 100°$

Lesson 4.4

1 (4) **3** (3) **5** (3) **7** $B''(6, -6)$

Lesson 4.5

1 Suppose A and B are any two different points in the plane. Now let $T_{\vec{v}}$ be a translation that maps A to A' and B to B'. We need to show that $AB = A'B'$. It is known from the definition of a translation that $\vec{v}$, $\overline{AA'}$, and $\overline{BB'}$ are parallel to each other and further $\vec{v} \cong \overline{AA'} \cong \overline{BB'}$. Therefore quadrilateral $AA'B'B$ is a parallelogram because one pair of sides are parallel and congruent. Therefore $\overline{AB} \cong \overline{A'B'}$ so $AB = A'B'$.

3 Triangle ABC and DEF have the same orientation so the transformation is direct. This would imply a translation or a rotation. However, corresponding side are not parallel therefore it is not a translation. Neither does there appear to be a center of rotation. The isometry we seek appears to be a composition. First, translate $\triangle ABC$ by vector $\overline{AD}$ as shown in Figure 1. Since the translation preserves distance and angle measure, $AB = DB'$, $m\angle A = m\angle B'DC'$, and $AC = DC'$. So $\triangle ABC \cong \triangle DB'C'$. Now rotate $\triangle DB'C'$ about D by $\angle C'DF$ as shown in Figure 2. The rotation preserves distance and angle measure so $\triangle DB'C' \cong \triangle DEF$. Therefore $\triangle ABC \cong \triangle DEF$.

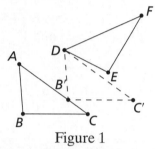

Figure 1

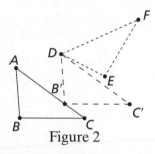

Figure 2

5 To prove $\overline{HD} \cong \overline{TD}$ we will prove $\triangle MDH \cong \triangle ADT$. $\triangle MDH$ is oriented clockwise and $\triangle ADT$ is opposite point D appears to be a fixed point. This would suggest a rotation or a reflection. Consider a $R_{D,180°}$. By definition $R_{D,180°}(D) = D$. Now $R_{D,180°}(A) = X$ with $X \in \overline{MA}$. Given D the midpoint of $\overline{MA}$ results $\overline{AX} \cong \overline{AD} \cong \overline{MD}$. $R_{D,180°}(A) = M$. $R_{D,180°}(T) = T'$ by definition of rotation $\overline{AT} \cong \overline{MT'}$ and since quadrilateral MATH is a rectangle $\overline{MH} \cong \overline{AT} \cong \overline{MT'}$.

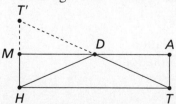

Since angle measure is preserved in a rotation $\angle TAD \cong \angle T'MD$. Therefore $\triangle MT'D \cong \triangle ATD$. Now consider $R_{\overline{MD}}$. Knowing $\overline{MH} \cong \overline{MT'}$ results in $R_{\overline{MD}}(T') = H$ and $\angle T'MD \cong \angle HMD$. We now have $\triangle MDH \cong \triangle ADT$ by the properties of the composite transformation $R_{\overline{MD}} \circ R_{D,180°}$. It should be noted that in this case the composition could be performed it either order.

An alternative transformation to accomplish this could be to construct a line through D perpendicular to HT and reflect $\triangle ADT$ over this line.

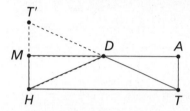

Chapter 4 Preparing for the Assessment

1 (1) **3** (3) **5** (2) **7** (3) **9** (2)
11 (3) **13** (2) **15** (1, 2, 3, 4) **17** (3)
19

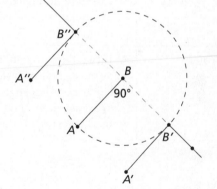

21 The transformation is a translation 4 to the right and up 2. The distances are shown in the figure.

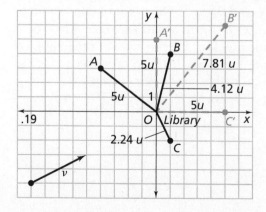

Chapter 5

Lesson 5.1

1 (2) **3** (4) **5** $\triangle ABC \sim \triangle MBN$, AA Similarity Postulate **7** 10 **9** $21\frac{1}{3}$
11 8 **13** $4\frac{7}{9}$ meters **15** $\triangle JEF \sim \triangle QRF$; SSS Similarity **17** $\angle 1 \cong \angle 2$ is given. $\angle ACB \cong \angle DCE$ because intersecting lines form congruent vertical angles. Therefore, $\triangle ACB \sim \triangle DCE$ by AA Similarity.
19

Statements	Reasons
1. $\dfrac{XR}{RQ} = \dfrac{YS}{SQ}$	1. Given
2. $\dfrac{XR+RQ}{RQ} = \dfrac{YS+SQ}{SQ}$	2. Property of Proportions
3. $\dfrac{XQ}{RQ} = \dfrac{YQ}{SQ}$	3. Segment Addition Postulate
4. $\angle Q \cong \angle Q$	4. Reflexive Property
5. $\triangle XQY \sim \triangle RQS$	5. SAS Similarity
6. $\angle QXY \cong \angle QRS$	6. Corresponding angles of similar triangles are congruent.
7. $\overline{RS} \parallel \overline{XY}$	7. If two lines are cut by a transversal such that corresponding angles are congruent, then the lines are parallel.

21 251.875 m

Lesson 5.2

1 $\frac{1}{3}$ **3** (2) **5** Triangles are similar.
7 $18'' = 1.5'$ **9** Draw a line through G and W, H and X, and I and Y. The point of concurrency is the center of the dilation. The scale factor is determined by forming the ratio of the length of the side of the image triangle over the corresponding preimage. For example, $\frac{HG}{XW}$.
11 Yes **13** $D_{G,2}(\triangle GXY) = \triangle GHI$ **15** (a)

Lesson 5.3

1 (1) **3** (3) **5** (1) **7** (3)
9

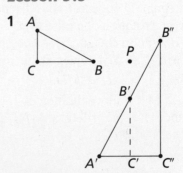

11 $A'(-3, 1.5)$, $B'(4.5, 1.5)$, and $C'(-3, 7.5)$
13 $X''(3, -3)$ and $Y''(21, 6)$

Lesson 5.4

1 (3) **3** (1) **5** (3) **7** (4)
9 $\overline{EF} \parallel \overline{AC}$; $\overline{DE} \parallel \overline{CB}$, $\overline{DF} \parallel \overline{AB}$ **11** $2\frac{3}{8}$
13

Statements	Reasons
1. $\triangle DEF$ is medial triangle of $\triangle ABC$.	1. Given
2. $DE = \frac{1}{2} BC$, $EF = \frac{1}{2} AB$, $DF = \frac{1}{2} AC$	2. Triangle Midsegment Theorem
3. $AD = \frac{1}{2} AB$; $AE = \frac{1}{2} AC$	3. Definition of midpoint
4. $DE = DE$	4. Reflexive
5. $\triangle ADE \cong \triangle FED$	5. SSS Postulate

15 27 in. **17** 13.5 **19** 29
21 $PR = 100$, $TU = 50$

Lesson 5.5

1

3 Appears to be a dilation
5 Similarity Transformation

CHAPTER 7

Lesson 7.1

1 (2) **3** (1) **5** (3) **7** (2) **9** $y = -2x - 1$
11 $y = -\frac{3}{5}x + \frac{2}{5}$ **13** $y = 7$ **15** $x = -11$
17 $y = 0$, or the x-axis **19** $3x + 5y = 15$
21 Yes; An equation for the line containing P
and Q is $y = \frac{7}{8}(x + 3) - 1$. $\frac{7}{8}(93 + 3) - 1 =$
$7(12) - 1 = 83$. So, $(93, 83)$ is on the line.

Lesson 7.2

1 (4) **3** (3) **5** (1) **7** $y = x$ **9** $y = -3x + 4$
11 $y = 2x - 8$ **13** $y = \frac{3}{2}x + \frac{5}{2}$ **15** slope of
$\overline{JK} = -1$, slope of $\overline{LM} = -1$, parallel **17** slope
of $\overline{JK} = 3$, slope of $\overline{LM} = 0$, neither **19** slope
of $\overline{JK} = -\frac{1}{6}$, slope of $\overline{LM} = -\frac{1}{5}$, neither **21** slope
of $\overline{JK} = 2$, slope of $\overline{LM} = -\frac{1}{2}$, perpendicular
23 slope of $\overline{JK} = -\frac{1}{4}$, slope of $\overline{LM} = -\frac{1}{4}$, parallel

Lesson 7.3

1 (2) **3** (4) **5** (1) **7** midpoint:
9 midpoint: $(5.5, 1)$; length: $5\sqrt{5}$
11 $\sqrt{113} \approx 10.63$ **13** 7 **15** $\sqrt{34} \approx 5.83$
17 midpoint: $(0, 2)$; $y = -x + 2$ **19** midpoint:
$(3, -2)$ $y = \frac{2}{3}x - 4$ **21** $\frac{5\sqrt{2}}{2}$ **23** $(2, 2)$

Lesson 7.4

1 (3) **3** (4) **5** $AB = AD = BD = CD = \sqrt{5}$.
The quadrilateral is a rhombus because it has
four congruent sides. **7** $(2, -2)$ **9** The line
joining the midpoints has slope $m = 0$. The base
has slope 0. Therefore, the line joining the
midpoint and the base are parallel. **11** Length
of the segment connecting $(3, 9)$ and
$(-6, 3)$: $\sqrt{9^2 + 6^2} = \sqrt{81 + 36} = \sqrt{117}$.
Length of the segment connecting $(-4, 9)$ and
$(5, 3)$ is also $\sqrt{9^2 + 6^2} = \sqrt{81 + 36} = \sqrt{117}$.
Therefore the diagonals are congruent.
13 The length of each side is $\sqrt{2a^2 + 2a + 1}$.
Therefore, the quadrilateral is a rhombus, since
a quadrilateral with 4 congruent sides is a
rhombus.

Lesson 7.5

1 (4) **3** (3) **5** (2)
7 Center $(0, 0)$; $r = 3$; $(0, 3)$

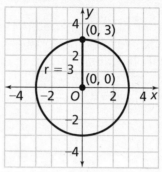

9 Center $(-2, 2)$, $r = 2$; $(-4, 2)$

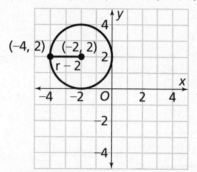

11 Center $(2, 1)$; $r = 5$; $(7, 1)$

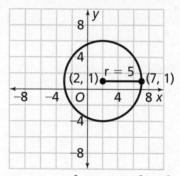

13 $(x + 5)^2 + (y - 2)^2 = 5^2$
15 $(x - 1)^2 + (y + 3)^2 = 3^2$

Lesson 7.6

1 (3) **3** (4) **5** (3) **7** $(-1, 1)$ and $(3, 9)$
9 no solution **11** $(-1, -6)$ and $(6, 8)$
13 $(-4, 3)$ and $(3, -4)$
15 One parabola has vertex $(0, 1)$ and opens up. The other parabola has vertex $(0, -2)$ and opens down. These parabolas cannot intersect.

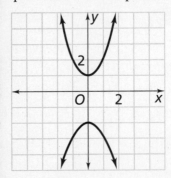

17 one point of intersection

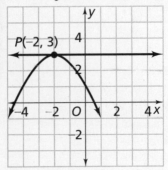

19 no points of intersection

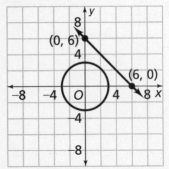

21 The system has no solution when $k < 4$, the system has 1 solution when $k = 4$, and the system has 2 solutions when $k > 4$.

Chapter 7 Preparing for the Assessment

1 (3) **3** (4) **5** (2) **7** (2) **9** (1) **11** (4)
13 (4) **15** $(x - 1)^2 + (y - 1)^2 = 25$
17 The slopes of both bases are 0, therefore they are parallel. The lengths of the nonparallel sides are
$$\sqrt{(a - 0)^2 + (c - 0)^2} = \sqrt{a^2 + c^2} \text{ and}$$
$$\sqrt{(a - (a + b))^2 + (c - 0)^2} = \sqrt{a^2 + c^2}.$$
Since the nonparallel sides are equal length, and the bases are parallel, the figure is an isosceles trapezoid.

Chapter 8

Lesson 8.1

1 Translate $\odot P$ to $\odot P'$ along vector $\overrightarrow{PP'}$. A dilation of factor $\frac{1}{3}$ results in $\odot P \sim \odot P'$.
3 $T_{(x+6, y-6)}$ and $D_{\frac{5}{2}}$ **5** $T_{(x+7, y+8)}$ and $D_{\frac{3}{2}}$
7 $T_{(x-4, y-2)}$ and $D_{\frac{5}{3}}$ **9** $k = \frac{1}{2}$ **11** $k = \frac{2}{9}$

Lesson 8.2

1 (3) **3** (3) **5** (4) **7** (2) **9** 9π **11** 96π
13 $45°$ **15** $120°$ **17** 36π

Lesson 8.3

1 (1) **3** (3)
5

Statements	Reasons
1. $\overline{BG} \cong \overline{BF}$; $\overline{DB} \cong \overline{BE}$	1. Given
2. $\angle BGF \cong \angle BFG$	2. If two sides of a triangle are $\cong$, the angles opposite those sides are $\cong$.
3. $m\angle BGF = \frac{1}{2}m(\widehat{BE} + \widehat{DA})$ $m\angle BFG = \frac{1}{2}m(\widehat{DB} + \widehat{EC})$	3. A measure of an angle formed by intersecting chords is half the sum of the intercepted arcs.
4. $\frac{1}{2}m(\widehat{BE} + \widehat{DA}) = \frac{1}{2}m(\widehat{DB} + \widehat{EC})$	4. Substitution
5. $m\widehat{DA} \cong m\widehat{CE}$	5. Multiplication and Subtraction Property of Equality

7

Statements	Reasons
1. $\widehat{AC} \cong \widehat{BD}$	1. Given
2. $m\angle B = \frac{1}{2}m\widehat{AC}$ $m\angle C = \frac{1}{2}m\widehat{BD}$	2. The measure of an inscribed angle is half its intercepted arc.
3. $m\angle B = m\angle C$	3. Substitution
4. $\overline{AB} \parallel \overline{CD}$	4. If two lines cut by a transversal such that alternate interior angles are congruent, then the lines are parallel.

9

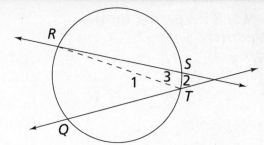

$m\angle 1 = m\angle 2 + m\angle 3$ Exterior angle thm, so $m\angle 2 = m\angle 1 - m\angle 3$ by Subtraction. Since both $\angle 1$ and $\angle 3$ are inscribed angles then $m\angle 1 = \frac{1}{2}m\,\widehat{QR}$ and $m\angle 3 = \frac{1}{2}m\,\widehat{ST}$. Using substitution and factoring:
$m\angle 2 = \frac{1}{2}m\,\widehat{QR} - \frac{1}{2}m\,\widehat{ST} = \frac{1}{2}(m\,\widehat{QR} - m(ST))$.

Lesson 8.4

1 (2) **3** (3) **5** $80°$ **7** $120°$ **9** $220°$
11 $18\sqrt{3} + 18\pi$ which is about 87.7 cm

Lesson 8.5

1 (1) **3** (3)
5

Statements	Reasons
1. $\overline{EC} \cong \overline{EB}$; $\overline{AE} \cong \overline{DE}$	1. Tangent segments drawn to a circle from an exterior pt. are congruent.
2. $EC = EB$; $AE = DE$	2. Definition of congruence
3. $AE + EB = DE + EC$	3. Addition Property of Equality
4. $AB = AE + EB$; $DC = DE + EC$	4. Segment Addition Axiom
5. $AB = DC$	5. Substitution
6. $\overline{AB} \cong \overline{DC}$	6. Segments of equal length are congruent.

7 $x = 5$

Lesson 8.6

1 (3) **3** (4) **5** (2) **7** (4) **9** $\frac{5\pi}{3}$ **11** 12π
13 $\frac{4\pi}{3}$ **15** $150°$ **17** 21 inches

SELECTED ANSWERS

Chapter 8 Preparing for the Assessment

1 (3) **3** (1) **5** (3) **7** (4) **9** (2) **11** (3)
13 (1) **15** (3) **17** $T_{(x+6,\,y-6)}$ and $D_{\frac{5}{2}}$ **19** (2)
21 (2) **23** (3) **25** (1) **27** (2)
29

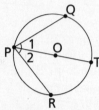

Statements	Reasons
1. $\overline{PQ}$ & $\overline{PR}$ are chords of circle O, $\overline{PT}$ bisects $\angle P$	1. Given
2. $m\angle 1 = m\angle 2$	2. Definition of angle bisector.
3. $\overset{\frown}{QT} \cong \overset{\frown}{TR}$	3. $\cong$ inscribed angles have $\cong$ arcs.
4. $m\overset{\frown}{PQ} = 180° - \overset{\frown}{QT}$ $m\overset{\frown}{PR} = 180° - m\overset{\frown}{RT}$	4. Measure of a semicircle is 180°. Properties of algebra
5. $m\overset{\frown}{PR} = 180° - m\overset{\frown}{QT}$	5. Substitution
6. $\overset{\frown}{PQ} \cong \overset{\frown}{PR}$	6. Substitution
7. $\overline{PQ} \cong \overline{PR}$	7. $\cong$ arcs have $\cong$ chords.

31 50 inches

CHAPTER 9

Lesson 9.1

1 (4) **3** (3) **5** Answers may vary. Sample answer: A, D, and E **7** Answers may vary. Sample answer: plane EFC **9** Answers may vary. Sample answer: plane AEC and plane CDE **11** Answers may vary. Sample answer: $\overleftrightarrow{CE}$ **13** Answers may vary. Sample answer: $\overleftrightarrow{CD}$ **15** 4 **17** T **19** F **21** T

Lesson 9.2

1 (1) **3** (3) **5** The intersection of 2 planes is a line. **7** Definition of two parallel planes **9** By definition, 2 adjacent faces of a cube are perpendicular. **11** The shortest distance between 2 planes is the perpendicular distance between them.

Lesson 9.3

1 (1) **3** 136 in.^{2} **5** 80 m^2
7 L.A. = 60 m^2; S.A. = 96 m^2

Lesson 9.4

1 (3) **3** (3) **5** 113.5 m^2 **7** 490.7 sq. units
9 49.28π cm^2 **11** 1.25 gallons
13 Answers will vary. Sample answer: A cylinder with height = 2 and radius 6

Lesson 9.5

1 (1) **3** (1) **5** one family-sized can
7 6739.2 lb **9** 628.3 ft^3 **11** Cross-sectional area height

Lesson 9.6

1 (2) **3** (4) **5** (1)

7 S.A. = 100π in.^{2}; $V = \dfrac{500}{3}\pi$ in.^{3}

9 V: $2{,}304\pi$ cm^3 **11** $2{,}303.1\pi$ cm^3 **13** 12π cm
15 16 cm **17** 9π cm^2 **19** 121.5π in.^{3}

Chapter 9 Preparing for the Assessment

1 (4) **3** (2) **5** (1) **7** (4) **9** (2) **11** (4)
13 (2) **15** (1) **17** (3) **19** 667.73 cm^3
21 138.2 ft^2 $2,625.70; 207.3 ft^3

CHAPTER 10

Lesson 10.1

1 (2) **3** (2) **5** (1) **7** The event with probability 0.6. **9** 55% **11** $\frac{5}{36}$ **13** $\frac{1}{18}$

15

1	2	3
$\frac{8}{25}$	$\frac{9}{25}$	$\frac{8}{25}$

Lesson 10.2

1 (4) **3** (3) **5** $\frac{4}{13}$ **7** $\frac{7}{26}$ **9** $\frac{1}{3}$ **11** $\frac{2}{3}$

13 $\frac{2}{9}$ **15** $\frac{1}{3}$

Lesson 10.3

1 (1) **3** (3) **5** (1) **7** $\frac{5}{36}$ **9** $\frac{1}{11}$ **11** $\frac{7}{22}$

13 $\frac{3}{8}$ **15** $\frac{1}{2}$ **17** $\frac{1}{30}$ **19** $\frac{1}{20}$ **21** $\frac{28}{65}$ **23** $\frac{21}{65}$

Lesson 10.4

1 (3) **3** (4) **5** (3) **7** 120 **9** 420 **11** 720
13 720 **15** 120 **17** 120 **19** 0.01 **21** 0.05

Chapter 10 Preparing for the Assessment

1 (1) **3** (4) **5** (3) **7** (1) **9** (1) **11** (4)
13 (4) **15** (2) **17** (2) **19** (3) **21** (4)
23 (2) **25** (1) **27** $\frac{49}{110}$ **29** $\frac{1}{2}$ **31** $\frac{1}{39}$

33 0.02 **35** 0.13

37 a roll showing 7; Explanations may vary. Sample explanation: P(a roll showing 7) $= \frac{6}{36}$ and P(ace or 2) $= \frac{8}{52}$ and $\frac{6}{36} > \frac{8}{52}$.

39

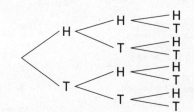

41 40,320 **43** 10^7 **45** $\frac{1}{3}, \frac{1}{2}$

47 $\frac{81}{625}$

INDEX

INDEX

lateral and surface area of pyramids, 254
lateral and surface areas of a cylinder, 256
Midpoint Formula, 184–185
probability, 276, 280–283, 287
surface area of a sphere, 269
volume of a cone, 263
volume of a cylinder, 262
volume of an oblique prism, 264
volume of a sphere, 268
volume of pyramids, 265
volume of rectangular prism, 261
Fractals, 127
Functions, domain and range of, 98
Fundamental Counting Principle, 285–289

Generation of solids
cones, 258
cylinders, 256, 257
determining figure generated, 259
Geometric constructions, 17. *See also*
Constructions
Geometric intersection, 75
Geometric mean, 46–47
Geometric shapes described as equations, 173
Geometric union, 75
Given conditions, 84
Glide reflection, 118
Graphing calculator
construction of circles and chords, 230
investigation of similarity theorems, 131
systems of equations, 203–205
truth values, 74
use of in geometry, xix
Graphs
axis of symmetry, 204
of circles, 196–199
of linear-quadratic equations, 203–205
of systems of equations, 203–205
Great circle, 267

Half-plane, 248
Half-turn, 114–115
Height
of cones, 258
of cylinders, 256
of prisms, 252
of pyramids, 254
Hemispheres, 267
Hexahedrons, 252
Horizontal lines, slope of, 174, 186
Huygens, Christiaan, 275
Hypotenuse, 46–47, 55
Hypotenuse-Leg Theorem (HL), 86, 87
Hypothesis, 34, 75

Icosahedrons, 252
If...then statements, 34, 35, 75
Images, 98–122, 134
Implication, 76
Incenter of triangle, 42, 43
Included angles, 84
Included sides, 84
Independent events
probability of, 286, 287–288
probability of two independent events, 286
successive, 289
Indirect measurement, 57, 129
Indirect proofs, 91
Inductive reasoning, xx, 32
Inequalities in triangles, 39–40

Inscribed Angle Corollaries, 222
Inscribed angles, 220–222
Inscribed Angle Theorem, 220–221
Inscribed circle, 42
Interactive geometry tools
angle measurement, 99
confirming angle measure of reflections, 104
construction and verification of
transformations, 99
construction of circles and chords, 230
construction of triangles, 44
dilation of a segment, 188
function of, xix–xxi
investigating minimum distance problems, 31
investigation of similarity theorems, 131
investigation of triangles, 43
measuring angles, 99
sample activities, xxii–xxiv
verifying line of reflection as perpendicular
bisector of segments joining pre-image
to image, 103
Intercepted arc, 218
Intercepts, slope-intercept form, 174–175
Interior angles, 13–15, 33, 152–153
Angle-Sum Theorem for Triangles, 32–34
finding sum of, 152
Internal tangent, 226
Intersecting lines, 11–12
Intersecting planes, 249. *See also* Perpendicular
planes
Intersection, 74–75
Isometry, 99
reflections as, 105
rotations as, 112
similarity transformation (Sk), 146–147
translations as, 99
Isosceles trapezoids, 157, 158–159, 165, 166
Isosceles triangles, 35, 43
Isosceles Triangle Theorem, 35–36

Kites, 157, 158–159, 162

Larger Side Theorem, 39–40
Lateral area
of cones, 259
of cylinders, 256–258
of a prisms, 253
of pyramids, 254–255
Lateral faces
of prisms, 252, 253
of pyramids, 254
Lateral surface
of cones, 258
of cylinders, 256
Law of Cosines, 59, 60–61, 63, 64
Law of Sines, 59–60, 63
Leg adjacent, 55
Leg opposite, 55
Leg(s)
of right triangles, 49–52, 55
of trapezoids, 157
of triangles, 46, 55
Length
of arcs, 234–237
of line segments, 4
of triangle sides, 40, 44, 46–47, 49–52, 55, 60
of vectors, 98, 101
Lincoln, Abraham, 1
Linear equations
defined, 174
for parallel and perpendicular lines, 182
of perpendicular bisector of a segment, 186
point-slope form, 174–177, 186

slope-intercept form, 174–177
solving, 203–205
standard form, 174–177
Linear pairs of angles, 8
Linear-quadratic equations, solving, 203–205
Line of reflection, 103–104
Lines, 244
concurrent, 42
congruent, 42
coplanar, 2, 248
defined, 2
equations of, 174–177, 186
horizontal, 174, 186
intersecting, 2, 11–12
Parallel Postulate, 12
Perpendicular to Parallels Theorem, 14
reflections over, 104
skew, 2
slope of, 174–177, 180, 181, 186
of symmetry, 109–110
transversals, 13–15, 24
vertical, 186
See also Parallel lines; Perpendicular lines
Line segments, 4–5
addition of, 17
congruent, 4, 190
constructing, 17
copying, 17
endpoints of, 4–5
finding proportional point of, 5
length of, 4
midpoints of, 4, 5, 184–185
perpendicular bisector of, 23–24, 185–186
proportional point of, 5
Segment Addition Postulate, 4
of a triangle, 42
Triangle Midsegment Theorem, 142
Line symmetry, 109
Line y = x, reflections over, 107, 108
Locus (Loci), 17, 196
bisectors, 23
circle as, 17, 196
constructing an angle bisector, 20
describing a figure with, 20, 23
parabola as, 199

Magnitude of vectors, 98
Major arcs, 220
Mathematics and Plausible Reasoning
(Pólya), xix
Mean, geometric, 46–47
Mean proportional, 46–47
Measurement
direct and indirect, 57
of exterior angles of triangles, 34
of interior angles of triangles, 33
Measurement, indirect, 129
Medial triangles, 143
Median Measure Theorem, 44
Median of a triangle, 42
Midpoint Formula, 184–185
Midpoints
finding, 184–185
of segments, 4, 5
Midsegments
of trapezoids, 157
in triangles, 42–43, 142–143
minimum distance problem, 31
Minor arcs, 220
MIRAs™, 17
Mirror, 103–110
Mutually exclusive outcomes, 280

INDEX

INDEX